The Sex of Knowing

The Sex of Knowing

Michèle Le Doeuff

Translated from the French by **Kathryn Hamer and Lorraine Code**

ROUTLEDGE
NEW YORK AND LONDON

Published in 2003 by
Routledge
29 West 35th Street
New York, NY 10001
www.routledge-ny.com

Published in Great Britain by
Routledge
11 New Fetter Lane
London EC4P 4EE
www.routledge.co.uk

Routledge is an imprint of the Taylor & Francis Group.

Originally published as *Le Sexe du savoir* (Paris: Aubier, 1998).

Copyright 1998 by Aubier, Paris.

This translation copyright 2003 by Taylor & Francis Books, Inc.

Printed in the United States of America on acid free paper.

Cataloging-in-Publication Data is available from the Library of Congress.

ISBN 0-415-92859-1 (hb)
ISBN 0-415-92860-5 (pb)

CONTENTS

Acknowledgments

We are grateful to Michèle Le Doeuff for her interest in this translation project at every stage, for her warm hospitality in Oxford, and especially for her critical reading of the first draft of the translation; and to her assistants, Suzanne Dow and Valerie Fehlbaum.

Our thanks to Tony Bruce and Penelope Deutscher for their initial interest in the project; to Damon Zucca, Damian Treffs, and Henry Bashwiner at Routledge, New York, and to Paul State for their work in seeing it through the editorial and production processes, and to Ron Curtis for preparing the index. Thanks also to Samantha Mills for checking quotations, to Judith Le Goff for extensive bibliographical assistance, to Hakam Al-Shawi for proofreading, and especially to Ilya Parkins, our research assistant, who located quotations, footnotes, references, standard translations, and other cited material.

We also thank Bruce Robertson of the Department of Classics at Mount Allison University for assistance with quotations in Latin, and for advice on the translation of Greek terms. Where the text indicates no standard translation of quoted material, translations are our own or were drafted by Ilya Parkins, with the exception of the material from Gabrielle Suchon, which is translated by Kathryn Hamer.

For two internal SSHRC Small Grants to assist with the project (2000 and 2002) Lorraine Code thanks the Office of Research Administration at York University. Kathryn Hamer thanks the Mount Allison University Committee on Research and Creative Activity for funds provided to assist with completion of the project (2002).

Introduction

"Why waste time on Christine de Pisan? She may have been a good daughter, good wife, and good mother; but she was also one of the most dyed-in-the-wool bluestockings our literature has ever known, the first of an insufferable procession of women writers who can effortlessly produce any book on any subject, and who, during their entire God-given lifetime have nothing better to do than to accumulate evidence of their inexhaustible superficiality, equal only to their relentless mediocrity. We must grant that, although she was Italian, she deserves our respect for having had a French heart and having devoted herself to the kings and country whose hospitality had sustained her for so long: such gratitude is uncommon. Moreover, it served her well, for of her entire output, only five or six stanzas or pages in which she effusively thanks kings and country, deserve to survive"... *but should all the rest be consigned to oblivion?*

Being both Italian and a woman, Christine de Pisan was an immigrant twice over. It is her French heart that earns her the minimal recognition she receives in Lanson's *Histoire de la littérature française,*[*] which otherwise dismisses her outright. He is willing to preserve a few stanzas, "especially in the *Dittié de Jeanne d'Arc.*" Joan of Arc is mentioned three times in the brief summary of Christine's work: one might conclude Christine had redeemed herself through service to the saint so dear to the hearts of French men. A brief biographical note indicates that her father, the king's astrologer, had her brought to France in 1368; that she married a native of Picardy; that she refused to present herself at the courts of both England and the duke of Milan ... so much was required of this good daughter, good wife, and good mother, who left Venice at the tender age of four, only to be insulted in the pages of that book—a bluestocking, and insufferable! And even after reading Lanson, you will still not know that she wrote a *Book of the City of Ladies,* which was a success all over Europe. Speaking to the women *of France and of all countries,* of all walks of life—living, dead, or yet unborn—women who love wisdom, have loved it, or will love it, she tells us to rejoice and reclaim the self-esteem that malevolent male writers have undermined. This insufferable bluestocking, whose work cost her so little effort, is the very one who works so heroically to bring joy to our lives! More recent works restore Christine to

---

[*] Gustave Lanson, author of the frequently reprinted *Histoire de la littérature française,* widely used as a standard manual of French literary history until the mid-twentieth century. Lanson applied the historical methods of his time to the study of literary history, and had a significant influence on the definition of a French literary canon.

her rightful place. They often cite Lanson's damning half-paragraph, which may be the sole passage still preserved from his bulky *Histoire* that was annually reedited at the turn of the twentieth century. Preserved and quoted to be ridiculed or to be consulted as a valuable document for analyzing the construction of knowledge? No, as a means of reducing her to silence.

"Equality? You already have it. Women's access to education has been a fait accompli for a long time. Women writers, scientists, and thinkers ostracized? Come on! That doesn't happen any more, and probably never did." Like other stubborn denials of the evidence, this one rejects every counterargument. It is as impervious to debate as the age-old discourse we have inherited from Saint Paul and Joseph de Maistre,* that denies or circumscribes a woman's right to know. We are not even close to equality. In the *lycées*,† young women are often relegated to shorter, less valued courses of study. Families, teachers, and school counsellors are often blamed, as are girls' own fears about the difficulties of professional life or the weight of family responsibilities. It is as if everything conspired against young women and responsibility could be spread around or diluted. Meanwhile, no one bothers to ask about the substance of what is commonly called knowledge or about the cultural milieu in which individuals and "knowing" meet; this milieu extends well beyond the school. Myths regulate our relationship with various modes of knowledge, or with knowledge in general: if they are sexually specific, as the figure of the bluestocking clearly is, then they should be challenged. Conversely, anything that has the status of knowledge can turn out to be riddled with mere beliefs, myths, or shocking misrepresentations. Therefore, to aim at sexual equality in (sometimes pseudo-) knowledge-acquisition is apparently to aim at generating equal credulity in the face of absurdities that defy description. Would it not be wiser and more efficient to prefer a critical epistemology capable of establishing that some things are not worth learning in what generally passes for knowledge?

This book is the product of my own perplexity at what I have read and seen of the small incidents of ordinary life at the end of the twentieth century, as well as my astonishment at the unusual resilience of what to me is a false problem, insoluble precisely because it is false. Renaissance debates, controversies, and underhanded attempts to regulate women's access to knowledge are one issue; we will have more to say about them. It is bad enough that the quarrel persists into the seventeenth century. Fénelon, to cite just one example, writes that for women, science, by which he means knowledge in general, has to be governed by a sense of modesty "almost as delicate as that which inspires a horror of licentiousness."[1] Yet at almost the same time, in

*Joseph de Maistre (1753–1821): monarchist politician, writer, and philosopher, opponent of the French Revolution, and supporter of the papacy. Defended faith as opposed to reason.

† French secondary schools.

1641, Anna Maria van Schurman publishes a work about women's intellect, in Latin, soon to be translated and known throughout Europe, and to be followed by her *Question célèbre: s'il est nécessaire ou non que les filles soient savantes,* clearly a much-needed text at that time.[2] But the very fact that Enlightenment thinkers continue to pursue the question, sometimes with exquisitely refined arguments such as Kant's ("a woman who has a head full of Greek... or carries on fundamental controversies about mechanics... might as well even have a beard...."[3]), and that nineteenth-century thought continues to rationalize women's exclusion from intellectual work, shows just how monotonous this question is. History is exceedingly long when debates never change and the same questions constantly recur! In their preface to the modern French edition of *La Cité des dames,* Thérèse Moreau and Eric Hicks underscore the ongoing relevance of Christine's point of view, but instead of emphasizing how far she is ahead of her time, they dwell on the persistent stupidity of her adversaries with their tenacious reliance on worn-out arguments.[4] We must agree with them, and acknowledge that it is time to react.

In an educational system based on carefully structured discrimination, the snail's pace of reform is obvious in the fact that it has taken more than a century to undo the work of such nineteenth-century pedagogues as Camille Sée, creator of a secondary "education for women" in which there was little science, no Latin or Greek, and no philosophy, although there was instruction in sewing and household science.[5] But History exceeds the limits of acceptability when we realize that, even at the end of the twentieth century, the question could still be raised. Claims that a real woman cannot be an intellectual still appear in print, and under the guise of attacking feminism—about which they know nothing—conscientious spokesmen make antediluvian pronouncements about the sexualization of the intellect. Here, for instance, is how Jacques Derrida says it in a book called *Spurs:* "Feminism is nothing but the operation of a woman who aspires to be like a man. And in order to resemble the masculine dogmatic philosopher this woman lays claim—just as much claim as he—to truth, science and objectivity in all their castrated delusions of virility. Feminism too seeks to castrate. It wants a castrated woman."[6]

If you look beneath the psychoanalytic surface of the sentence, without being distracted by the allusions to castration, which, apparently, would not be only "woman's" castration, you will see that the real target is women's access to what he calls *truth, science,* and *objectivity,* which for him represent intellectual labour in general. These are crude notions that refer, perhaps, to what might more accurately be called methods of verification, definitions of necessarily multiple fields of scientific inquiry, or processes of objectification. Note, by the way, that "feminism," the ostensible target of Derrida's attack, is, in this instance, a complete figment of his imagination. The feminism of the 1970s, prevalent when he wrote this diatribe, was not about emulating men (perish the thought!), still less about constructing philosophical dogma (?!), and even less about the educational issues that concerned earlier feminisms; this was a feminism focused above all on freedom. Engaged in a struggle for reproductive rights, this movement, which was by no means exclusively intellectual, stood for the value of each woman's control of her own fertility and sexual pleasure. Confronting the decrees of prelates and politicians that maternity alone justifies sexuality, we affirmed our taste for pleasure and our interest in a sexuality liberated from all reproductive constraint. This struggle is what our colleague, making no effort to inform himself, describes as a castration *of women too,* by which he really means castration of men. And what kind of nonsense makes "man" a synonym for "dogmatic philosopher"? If the point is that, because of his delusions of virility, any biped of the male sex who dares to venture into the realm of philosophy is doomed to dogmatism, the suggestion is distinctly unkind to our male colleagues, and moreover quite meaningless, since all philosophers criticize dogmatism and all philosophers are prone to it. If this means that a boy who fails his primary school certificate is thereby emasculated—a logical consequence of equating masculinity with philosophy, science, and so on—we come to the bizarre conclusion, plausible only to a narcissist, that men with diplomas are sexually superior to those without. But worse still is the fact that this foolish notion is repeatedly and deferentially cited by one minor writer after another. I found it in a piece published in *Le Temps de la réflexion,* cited in support of quite progressive ideas, themselves ornamented with well-turned phrases such as: "Women, especially the unlettered, that is, those who lay no claim to masculine culture.... " Thanks to Gallimard's good offices, this uncultured comment about culture proclaims that even opening the doors of literacy to women is too great a concession.[7] A few years later, on December 6, 1989, a young man gunned down fourteen female engineering students at Montreal's École Polytechnique, calling them feminists trying to usurp men's rightful place. The shooting enacted something that finds its expression in sexist comments or pseudophilosophical ideas; in a single act of hatred, it exposed the banal resentment many men direct toward women who find satisfaction in an intellectual life.

In the academic world (by which I mean universities, research laboratories, learned journals, union meetings, and so on), this banality circulates casually, as a rumor that women have a problematic relationship with the sciences, and even with knowledge as such. The rumor is repeated so often that it becomes common knowledge and received wisdom in groups who would otherwise have no reason to agree with each other. Thus, the directors of scientific institutions may be heard insisting that science is *men's* affair, in the specific sense, while paradoxically the school of thought called feminist epistemology espouses the same point of view, contending that women who enter the world of science (such as it is) will at least lose their identity if not their soul, unless they develop a specifically feminine mode of knowledge, which this school of thought claims they do in any case. We are assured that "women's ways of knowing" require an affectionate, attentive rapport with the object of knowledge or an involvement typical of the closest emotional relationships, a kind of empathy whose effect would be either to classify Marie and Irène Curie as honorary great men or to erase them entirely from the discussion.[8] Moreover, the system that represents the work of a woman scientist as a gentle rapport with the object of knowledge reveals itself as pure mystification when we recall that scientific work involves more than establishing rapport with an object in a test tube. Scientists have to read what has been published in their discipline: the work of others is also an object to be known and evaluated. If we suppose that a woman necessarily develops a tender emotional connection with anything that enters her intellectual awareness, must we also imagine that she will substitute empathy for critical acumen when she reads a scientific article? A scientific essay may be inaccurate or inadequate; we need not recall such great misadventures as N rays, the memory of water, or cold temperature fusion to remind ourselves that a scientist must be constantly on the alert in evaluating her or his own, or someone else's, work.[9] Even if that work is error free, its scientific value still has to be assessed, and this is never a simple task. It is entirely possible that men of science want their feminine colleagues' critical sense to be anaesthetized to the point where they would admire everything men do. None of this implies that women need to respond with meek and acquiescent behavior. And what about the numerous social scientific objects that provoke an outburst of polemical debate or an openly caustic cognitive response? We know about Claude Lévi-Strauss's famous gaffe while he was staying with the Bororos: "The whole village left the next morning in about thirty canoes, leaving us alone with the women and children in their abandoned houses."[10] So, when the adult men have gone, no one is left ... ? If the methodology exposed in this blunder in turn becomes a focus of women's critical attention, must we still approach it with empathy?

Many recent books, articles, and chapters have gone on about this cognitive difference that, quite inexplicably, has so preoccupied the last quarter-century. But everyone will at least allow, even without having read a single work, that they know the literature on the subject is abundant: a review here, a radio or television program there, will rekindle the rumor, without anyone bothering to examine the arguments or intellectual strategies on which it depends. In today's world, generally speaking and allowing for national variations, 30 percent of so-called "men" of science are in fact women. Yet the massive entry of women into the universe of test tubes and numerical simulations seems to have been received with an extraordinary and fanciful denial by the ideology that, within our own cultural context, seeks so persistently to maintain the old spectre of an incompatibility between women and knowledge. My learned women friends are often irritated to the point of anger, as if this form of feminism undermined their morale at least as much as—if not more than—the ambient misogyny in which they work. I have seen the effects on my female philosophy students of statements such as Luce Irigaray's claim that "if a woman engages with theory she will lose her capacity for pleasure," and I know the legitimate aggravation and even revolt that a foolish comment—a mere throw-away remark duly recorded in the course of an interview—can provoke. But this type of quasi-parental threat, predicting certain punishment of near-mythical proportions, is hardly new. Such a pronouncement, which refuses to recognize that, for a long time, women have in fact engaged in theoretical work and managed to retain all of their joie de vivre, surreptitiously reactivates the whole scenario of original sin. I am bothered by this complicity between tradition and current fashion: the old texts that can be read only under a librarian's strict supervision seem either to anticipate, reinforce, or occasionally dissipate the questions of my friends whose daughters are of school age; what obstacles will stand in the way of my Cléobulina on the road that leads to the heights of intellectual achievement, but (and here uncertainty lurks), is this really the right road for her? There are days when parents simply do not know what to want.

It would be good to put this rumor to rest once and for all, to purge ourselves of the cultural givens produced by centuries of debate, and to erase their last remaining residues, if they really are the last residues. Unfortunately, there is no such thing as "once and for all" where these issues are concerned. Nor is it just a simple rumor—the idea hovers over a whole tissue of practices, attitudes, and decisions whose effect is to punctuate the life of a woman scholar with countless unpleasant incidents. Pierrette wants to submit a thesis topic on some grammarian of late antiquity: "oh," groans the intended supervisor, "that's not a very feminine topic," but he accepts the young woman after having insisted that the topic is a good one, but not for her. Pauline is studying a woman physicist who has made an important contribution to quantum mechanics; her supervisor recommends her admission to a research team working on the history of science. "She wouldn't be a feminist by any chance?" (Good heavens! A woman interested in a woman!). "Is she at least attractive?" After a few such questions, her candidacy will be rejected, and an entire career undermined. This doesn't happen only to other people. Let me give you an example: my own annotated and duly prefaced edition of a work of Bacon is published, I am congratulated ("a formidable piece of work, and not the least bit feminine!"); you would think it astonishing that a woman could have done such a thing. Then I apply again for promotion; once more my application is rejected, and the chair of the ad hoc committee informs me that the committee has reservations about "feminine" scholarship. The quotation marks around "feminine" in the original letter might conceivably cause some pain. The writer of this letter is herself a woman; referring to herself in the masculine form, she declares that, as chairman, she has no choice but to yield to the committee's decision.

Even if the question of inequality still lingering in intellectual institutions is clearly a problem and must be addressed as such, how did it happen that at the end of the twentieth century, institutions of learning had yet to attain even a minimal level of egalitarianism? I cannot help being even more troubled by evidence from society at large. A woman phones a domestic violence hotline: "I'm calling because... my husband, no, no, he isn't violent, but I'm worried.... I'm wondering whether he might become violent. Last night, I didn't feel like having sex, and I said so. Then he got a knife from the kitchen, held it to my throat, and forced me to have sex like that. I think he might become violent." It is quite usual for feminist centers to receive calls like this one, which both attest to the outrages inflicted on women and signal a kind of cognitive blockage. This woman was incapable of recognizing violence for what it was, even when she was experiencing it. Women are forbidden to judge men and be critical of them; they are forbidden to know the wrong a man is doing to them. This woman could describe only as a vague eventuality an action that to an outside observer was an indisputable fact already taking place. Such cognitive paralysis is proof positive of the vicious circle of violence—as though an inhibition had been created by repeated intimidation, to the point where the woman loses confidence in her own judgment and violent acts themselves become invisible.

My real concern is with today and tomorrow, even though I seem to be leading you on an archaeological mission into the dim and distant past, to exhume the long-buried origins of reflexes that are nonetheless still with us, and whose scope remains to be established. Is there a link between the cognitive blockages inculcated in every woman's perception of social relationships, the subtle or blatant ways in which intellectual institutions attempt to perpetuate as much masculine domination as possible, and the way different types of knowledge are produced and constituted before being handed down through the school system? For you will find cognitive issues everywhere, in the everyday world as well as in the sociopolitical sphere that shapes the everyday. Uncovering some aspects of a framework common to certain forms of institutionalized knowledge and everyday life requires forays into the past: it helps to decipher the present hidden beneath optimistic verbiage and demands scrutiny of the myths or images that regulate the relationships between intellect and sex, between the sexes and the order of knowledges. Myths broadly diffused ensure the persistence of the sex question in the collective epistemic imaginary. They also show the link between social beliefs and beliefs current in institutions of learning. By approaching the question from this angle, we are also attempting to address our readers' subjectivity, in the hope that they will be able to distance themselves from the mythification of knowledge.

I believe there is no intellectual activity that is not grounded in an imaginary. We will be able to judge the validity of this idea once we have seen the countless sexist inanities uttered by the erudite, and we will wonder what new imaginary is required to ensure cordial relationships between men and women in the realms of thought and everyday life. Faced with this question, may the gentle women and generous men who read me accept joint responsibility for bringing about some solutions. Of course I am writing for your daughter: may she grow up happier because you have read me! It is for your nephew that I am making such an effort: it is time to prepare boys to live in a world where each woman will be able to establish that she is not a doormat, and where, as a result, every man will have to develop his humanity to the fullest. Such a world already exists in fragmentary form, but it will come to fruition only if the old one is exorcised, and if all men and women commit themselves to achieving it.

CHAPTER 1

Cast-offs

Blue stockings: these were blue worsted stockings, knitted in thick warm wool and worn in England by men even where it was not appropriate—hence, the negative connotation of the term ever since its origin. You may be quite indifferent to all of this, but as I have just learned something about it, allow me to tell you the story of a word. In the seventeenth century, perhaps from one day to the next, these blue stockings, hitherto worn at home for warmth, evolved into a metonymy to refer to the Parliament of 1653. For the members of this *Blue-Stocking Parliament*, Cromwell's chosen few, had little interest in fashionable clothing; velvet and lace had no place in their political program, and they probably thought nothing of appearing in the House dressed in the kind of stockings they wore at home, instead of the black silk stockings deemed essential for such ceremonial occasions, even if they were not so comfortable, especially in winter. So, "Blue Stockings, Blue Stockings" grumbled those who certainly had other grudges against this Parliament. The *Oxford English Dictionary*, which I am meticulously plundering, does not specify whether these members of Parliament actually wore blue worsted stockings or were merely judged capable of something so inappropriate. Let us say these parliamentarians thought—or were reputed to be inclined to think—that any one, without standing on courtly ceremony, could offer an opinion on questions put to him. Perhaps no one ever came in blue stockings, but they were capable of doing such a thing—hence, the epithet—and who knows whether in fact they did not earn it? A century later, still in London, some people began to meet informally for literary conversations, at Montagu House, rather than playing cards like everyone else. "Rather than playing cards" figures in the dictionary definition; you can see what kind of subtle sociohistorical knowledge is required to determine the meaning of a word. One of the pillars of this cardless society, Benjamin Stillingfleet, is reported to have been there and really to have worn such stockings. In a private house, and his hosts tolerated it! A certain Admiral Boscawen, noting the consequences of turning up one's nose at whist, nicknamed the group "the bluestocking society," underscoring the threat some people pose to the best society.

Since then, a lot of water has flowed under Tower Bridge and several other bridges. No one makes much fuss when a man delivers his lectures at the Sorbonne or at Galloway College sporting his most threadbare clothes; in any case, little fuss is made in the university world, which, after all, has always had its traditions of careless dress or ostentatious indifference to the body. How it might be in high-society salons, I have no idea, but no matter: no one expects a gentleman to play cards to prove his unimpeachable morality. So there was no longer any reason to keep the metaphor alive in the repertoire of insults, rude names, common taunts, and invective. The word has nonetheless survived in French and English, thanks to a later meaning, derived from its second metonymic usage: a bluestocking is a woman interested in intellectual pursuits, who, had she frequented Montagu House, might have worn ugly knit stockings beneath her long skirts. For this third use of the word entered both languages at a time when no woman showed her legs: obviously, unprovable charges have the greatest effect and the longest life. Thus, a reproach levelled by gentlemen against austere Puritans has become a term by which even today it is possible to ridicule women who like to read or think, and do not hide the fact. It is a strange story: without a dictionary, no one would know that all of this apparently originated in a clothing choice that may or may not have been made by men who scorned a certain political style. Besides, blue stockings, very blue stockings, could be quite an attractive fashion, now that we show our legs. Alas, the reference to fashion has no effect, and, although its original use has been forgotten, the expression has kept its connotation of austerity, like an unacceptable rejection of all kinds of pleasure in favor of things deemed more essential.

"My grandmother was an odd woman. Her name was Flora Tristan. Proudhon said she was a genius. Since I don't know anything about it, I'll take his word for it. . . . She probably didn't know how to cook. A socialist, anarchist bluestocking," Gauguin wrote about Flora Tristan, whom he had never met.[1] They both had exceptional and terrible destinies. The outcast painter's insensitivity toward the woman who called herself a "pariah" is all the more harsh: his tragedy reduces hers to the level of trivia. Whether or not Flora Tristan knew how to cook (and in any case what does that mean?), her grandson, who knows nothing about it at all, will concoct a hypothesis out of thin air to counterbalance the genius Proudhon attributed to her. "She created a lot of socialist stuff," he said, although acknowledging that he could not untangle fact from fiction in the hearsay which was all he had to go by, and then he adds that "nevertheless" she was "a very pretty and noble lady." *Bas-bleu* does not imply ugliness in this instance, but rather the very antithesis of *cordon-bleu*, which is just as serious. From this sketch, we can conclude that whenever a woman shows some talent for ideas, an automatic reflex is triggered: ipso facto and gratuitously, she is judged somehow deficient, unable to satisfy certain male expectations, whose legitimacy, moreover, is never questioned.

Because the Puritans, who thought they were working for the republic, were committed to sobriety in clothing and demeanor, we can be sure that an intellectual woman has no taste whatsoever when it comes to dressing well or keeping a good table. Of course such a flaw is still reprehensible today, even when the expression "she's dressed to the nines" would provoke guffaws at every level of society, and even when lack of culinary talent is easily forgiven in those who have no other abilities either. We come to the heart of the problem when we realize that those qualities which used to be thought incompatible with intellectual activity have themselves become optional for women. One of these days, no one but *agrégées** de philosophie* will try to be attractive and display their housewifely talents, as if they had to redeem themselves. But from what? And the most irritating thing is that this suspicion never dies out. Recently I invited a good seventeenth-century scholar to a conference, and was showered with compliments by colleagues with whom I usually go for a drink after the seminar:

> "Thanks for inviting such a nice woman!"
> "Etc., etc."
> "And besides, she isn't a bluestocking at all!" one woman marvelled.

Hence my recourse to the dictionary, at a time of night when scholars of both sexes are asleep and dreaming, sometimes, but not always, in each other's arms.

1. How Intuition Came to Women

Are women—are we women—reliquaries or dustbins of history, especially for unflattering language? A word was born of the antagonism between Roundheads and Cavaliers; in the normal course of events, once the antagonism had faded or taken on a different form, the word should have

---

*An *agrégé(e)* is a person who has passed very competitive examinations (*concours*) to earn the *agrégation*, and is therefore qualified to teach in the upper two years of the secondary school system or in the lower ranks of the university.

become a linguistic cast-off, but in this case it acquired a new life, and a new referent, just as it was about to lapse into disuse. Of course, that is one more reason for irritation: the insults hurled at us were not even made to measure for us. But let us pose a theoretical question: anthropology (by which I mean any project of knowing human beings as they are supposed to be—as empirical givens) examines the sexual division of labor, functions, responsibilities, characteristics, and so on, in a particular society, frequently with the aim of finding one or two good reasons to show that the division is as it should be, the raw being the domain of one sex, the cooked belonging to the other, or vice versa.* As if, given the identity of one sex and the other, anyone could understand why something is symbolically attributed to one sex and something else to the other—for example, tailored to men, flowing to women, in the order of thought as in the world of fashion. But if we can show that there may be slippage of a symbol from one sexually identified category to another within a given society, then it is superfluous to try to justify the association of ideas, that is, the link between sex and symbolic attribution. Instead, it now becomes possible to speculate that the slippage is regulated by certain principles or laws that should be elucidated. By this I mean it would be pointless to analyze the image of the bluestocking by trying to explain why the color and reference to legs are associated with women, since the term was originally coined with respect to men. But perhaps the transfer from the first application (to male politicians) to its later one (to intellectual women) obeys some sociosymbolic law. You may object that I am offering only one example. Certainly in good logic a single instance suffices to destroy the theory to which it poses a contradiction, but not to establish a new one.

This is not a single instance. Take the concept of intuition, which in classical language designates a mode of immediate apprehension, a direct intellectual grasp of something true, which is distinct from, though not necessarily radically opposed to, mediated knowledge achieved through reasoning, discussion, internal debate, dialectic, experimentation, deduction, language, applying or trying to apply some form of proof . . . in short, what is generally called discursive knowledge. For a long time, intuition was considered, first, as an important and valid mode of knowledge; second, as one that can work in cooperation with other modes of thought; and third, as either the best possible form of knowledge and the completion of a process of discovery, or as the form of knowledge without which nothing would take place because it is what sets the process in motion. For example, Descartes says: "By 'intuition' I understand . . . the conception of the pure and attentive

* "The raw and the cooked" refers to the title of Claude Lévi-Strauss's important work in structuralist anthropology. Lévi-Strauss argues that the binary pair (i.e. the raw and the cooked, feminine and masculine) is the basic, universal structure of all human cultures and significations.

mind which is so simple and distinct that we can have no further doubt as to what we understand; . . . thus everyone can intuit in his mind that he exists, that he thinks, that a triangle is bounded by three lines. . . . " Descartes thinks the first principles of metaphysics and mathematics are known in this way, yet the extended consequences drawn from these principles can be known only by deduction.[2] For Plato, the philosophical itinerary is different: the process begins with debate, failure, working toward a definition, suffering, reasoning; and it has its outcome, if indeed it has an outcome at all, and its reward in a direct, clear grasp of the True. Some of Plato's disciples will even say "in an ineffable and unintelligent contact with Being," which is not necessarily everyone's ideal, but to each her or his own. Plato distinguishes *noêsis* (generally translated by intelligence) from *dianoia* (reasoning or discursive knowledge), but, even though he ranks these modes of knowledge—*noêsis* is superior to *dianoia*—he posits their coexistence in the cognitive activity of anyone, man or woman, who undertakes the long apprenticeship that leads to philosophy.[3]

In the long history of philosophy, discursivity and intuition are not inevitably contradictory or antagonistic, nor is this duality projected onto the duality of the sexes. Moreover, according to philosophers who write in Latin, *intueor* may simply mean "to consider," and *intuitus* an opinion; this vocabulary refers to a looser usage, and the related terms have no particular positive or negative epistemological value. Finally, I can assure you of one thing even though it cannot be verified: if Saint Thomas Aquinas had heard anyone use the term "feminine intuition," he would certainly have recoiled in horror, and more than a few others would have done so too. Hence a question to put to historians of ideas, or should I say pertaining to a history of ideas that are never examined because they are considered too silly, but which carry considerable weight in the debates that sometimes obliquely determine our destinies: how did intuition come to be attributed to girls and women? And beyond this question, should we not be troubled by the fact that thinking about what thought is—about what it is to know—functions in mythical mode, as though there were an epistemic imaginary that is a law unto itself, regulating our perception of what it is to think, to know, to have knowledge, and so on?

This question must be turned into a more complex problem: when the difference between intuitive and discursive modes of thought was accentuated to the point that each of these modes was attributed to one and only one type of being, sexual dualism was not immediately invoked to attribute superior discursive powers to one sex, while assigning only a mediocre or obscure intuition to the other. Jean-Jacques Rousseau draws the distinction along different lines: "God is intelligent; but how? Man is intelligent when he reasons, and the supreme intelligence has no need of reasoning; for it, there are no premises or consequences, there are not even any propositions; it is purely intuitive, etc."[4] Decide as you will whether or not "man" as Rousseau uses it includes women. It will make no difference to intuition, since it is literally divine; or perhaps it is more appropriate to say that divine intelligence is intuitive, which is not exactly the same thing. There is something slippery in the grammar of the adjectives used to qualify a substance; God's intelligence is posited as intuitive, which does not necessarily imply that intuition is part of God's essence nor that only he is intuitive. But the language slips from the attribution ("God's intelligence is intuitive") to the idea of an essential property, one belonging exclusively to God, and thus the quality becomes substantive. It would follow, then, that every intuitive act would become divine; when a human being "intuits", supposing the possibility of such a thing, that act implies some kind of deification.

Though he was perhaps not the first to propose a radical distinction between intuition and reason, Rousseau does not regard it as a sexual difference; for him, this distinction refers to the duality between God and man. However, the problem takes shape in his philosophy, since he posits a stark dichotomy between the two modes of knowing, as though they were no longer complementary, nor did they coexist in the same mind, and from that moment on, it had to be a matter of one or the other. The German Romantics took up this opposition, affirming that the Absolute must be intuited and not conceptualized—probably a recurrence of the neoPlatonic idea of an ineffable and unintelligent contact with Being. This affirmation was in fact a Pyrrhic victory for intuition, because soon afterward, philosophy placed itself at a careful distance from Romanticism, to the point of defining itself in distinction from it. Before long, *The Phenomenology of Spirit* effectively ruled out intuition of the Absolute, which Hegel taxes with being "a view which is in our time as prevalent as it is pretentious."[5] This same Hegel was to replace intuition with the painstaking labor of conceptual analysis as the norm of philosophical thought, and many people endorsed his view that this method should be the only admissible way of doing philosophy. "This intuitive perception which does not recognize itself is taken as a starting-point as if it were absolutely presupposed; it has in itself intuitive perception only as immediate knowledge, and not as self-knowledge: or it knows nothing, and what it perceives it does not really know. . . . ": thus runs his radical critique.[6] As far as I know, he did not go so far as to utter the ultimate anathema—"intuition is feminine"—but he came within a hair's breadth of inventing it. For he limits women to "taste," "elegance," and he writes that "women correspond to plants because their development is more placid and the principle that underlies it is the rather vague unity of feeling."[7] Now, according to him, a plant "does not attain to a being-for-self"[8] and he recognizes that at its best, intuition, *which does not know* *itself,* "consists of beautiful thoughts, but not knowledge."[9] Thus, moving from botany to the lack of self-knowledge, one may establish a more or less adequate transitivity: intuition does not know itself, a plant never achieves being-for-itself, woman is a plant. Let knowledgeable people of both sexes decide, as they wish, whether the connection is valid, and whether it is therefore possible to attribute to "woman-as-plant"—this anthropological fiction—a discredited way of knowing: intuition, devalued to the point of having lost its status as productive of knowledge. A century later, Anna de Noailles[*] initiated unanimism, "it is not the meadow, but rather my eye, that is in flower." In the fullest sense of the term, she actualizes the Hegelian figure of the woman of taste and refinement, producer of lovely plantlike thoughts intuitively spreading throughout Nature, thus obligingly leaving philosophy, science, and politics to those who claim them as their rightful domain; she cultivated a form of poetry that the public forthwith labelled minor, but charming.

If intuition came to be synonymous with unprovable allegations or un-justified claims, it no longer had a place in the real philosophy taught in institutions of learning under the name of theory of knowledge. For from the moment rivalry emerged between the intuitive and the discursive, the die was cast, at least in the academic world: since intuition can hardly be taught (unless of course we turn our lectures and seminars into transcendental meditation sessions!), it was a foregone conclusion that discursivity would win out wherever learning is transmitted. In point of fact, one could speak of a "field effect": when a given conflict occurs in an environment structured in a particular way—and universities are places structured in a particular way—it is inevitable that the structure will shape the outcome of the dispute. Today, the word intuition might survive only as a relic of antiquated philo-sophical discourse, a term that takes us back, as many others do, to notions of which we no longer have any idea: vegetative soul, spermatic Reason, or the Absolute. It is true that Descartes's oeuvre always figures prominently in school curricula, and the passage in the *Regulae* that elaborates the dis-tinction between intuition and deduction and articulates one with the other appears frequently on examinations. How can one make sense of this pas-sage if one believes intuition is mere whimsy, a woman's affair, "woman" being the antithesis of "the learned" about whose sex there can thus be no doubt? It is a mystery; but, as a matter of fact, we manage to make sense of this passage when the curriculum requires it without considering Cartesian views in the light of what we commonly assume in other circumstances.

"What we commonly assume in other circumstances" (the category extends beyond the single issue of supposedly feminine intuition) tends

---

[*] Anna de Noailles (1876–1933): French poet and novelist who combined romantic themes with neoclassical forms.

nevertheless to slip into commentaries and translators' choices, inflecting the discourse bit by bit; from one approximation to another, the history of philosophy succeeds in propagating rumors that blatantly contradict the texts themselves; in such situations, "common assumptions" always triumph. Thus, a colleague on the other side of the world explains that the influence of seventeenth-century rationalism is such that the term "intuition" refers to "a thought style that is not sharpened and systematized in the manner of which Cartesian method is the paradigm." And she continues: "Intuition, inevitably, has come to be associated with specifically *female* thought styles."[10] With respect to the history of philosophy, this is a mistake, because intuition cannot be set up in opposition to Cartesian method, which in fact incorporates it as a primordial element and indispensable anchoring point. Anyone who invokes Cartesianism must at least bear in mind that it presupposes intuition, to be followed by an articulation of intuition and reasoning. Moreover, from an epistemological point of view, Genevieve Lloyd's simplification is difficult to accept. Cartesian method is neither the only model nor the paradigm for any and every formalization of thought; there are other models competing for the intellectual space opened by the question: "how must one go about thinking and knowing with certainty, or with more certainty than usual?" Here in a nutshell is the effect of the dualism created, for example by projecting the duality of the sexes on to the question of knowledge: create two categories and simplify them both. Basically, all of this contributes to sustaining a reification—certain styles of thought are said to be specifically *women's* [*female*], and although the commentator appears to contest the identification of intuition with these modes of thought, she does not question the notion of "specifically" masculine or feminine thought. Or rather, in this instance, as so frequently happens, "specificity" applies only to the feminine, as if the masculine were the norm and the universal. "Field effect" again: when universities establish *women's studies* as a separate little world, defined only by specialization in feminine questions (while the rest of the academic world is busy with what?), the field is thus defined by the idea that specificity pertains only to the feminine. In the end, it devotes itself, and thus limits itself, to studying what differentiates us. Another disturbing corollary: in the guise of critique, all of this ends up once more flattering the masculine half of humanity, which takes comfort in the idea that there really is a "man of reason," systematic and methodical, from whom women who really are women differentiate themselves. As long as the equation of a crude notion of rationality with a class of individuals cursorily defined as "masculine" is not exposed as a myth, there is no point in valorizing or rejecting this hollow idea of reason on the basis of this equation. "Reason is masculine, and that's why I'm in favor of it" is as empty a declaration as "Reason is masculine, and that's why I want no part of it."

Neither has anything to say about what the issue of rationality might be, and both base a completely fantastical division of the sexes on a set of ill-defined questions.

Considered as nothing more than the direct opposite of reason, intuition could still have been useful as a foil: you can imagine philosophy courses explaining that there are various ways of knowing, some bad and some good, the value of the latter being all the more striking in contrast with the others. And since rumor already had it that women do not reason—a nice idea, suggested by Malebranche in a description of the fibers of the brain, developed by Rousseau, given added muscle by Hegel, driven home by Auguste Comte, lurking sometimes in John Stuart Mill's rhetoric, and still successfully pursued in works published less than twenty years ago—it became only too easy to evoke "feminine" intuition, condescendingly or otherwise. Both erudite language and ordinary language have done this, the latter under the influence of distant debates conducted by the former, whose ultimate significance eludes me somewhat. How is it that, one fine day, toward the end of the eighteenth century, people began to see such sharp contrasts between intellectual capacities, such conflicts between faculties and incompatibilities between ways of knowing, that one and the same being could no longer be said to contain them all? From a feminist perspective, beating the philosophical bushes flushes out a swarm of more and more interesting questions, even if there are no ready answers. And I cannot have an immediate response, since the very concept of "intellectual faculties" seems obscure to me.

Under the influence of Brouwer, a Dutch topologist, some mathematicians, especially in the English-speaking world, go to great lengths to claim that their work incorporates something like intuition, even though it also demands considerable intellectual labor. None of them has concluded that women alone can be truly creative in mathematics, though logically this is what should emerge from the encounter between common views of intuition and the epistemological position of these intuitionists. Must we infer that feminine intuition is not intuition after all? Or that there is no connection between what they say about mathematical objects (which must be intuited) and what is said in the folk epistemology embedded in everyday conversations?[11] Between the garden and the dining room, people take pleasure in detailing the supposed cognitive differences between women and men, without ever establishing even a minimal critical distance: how do we know these differences, and do we *know* them? Since we are discussing mathematics, let us note that the debate has a comic dimension. In francophone countries where Bourbakian constructivism prevails, intuition of mathematical objects is strictly forbidden: if after manipulating these objects for a long time, you begin to see them, do so on the sly and don't brag about it. In the anglophone world, intuitive or imagist representations of mathematical objects are legitimate; you may confess that you see a convergent series as a collection of small points racing off in a particular direction. From ridicule south of the Channel to relevance on its north shore, how amusing to note that epistemology is divided by an arm of the sea. Yet, on both shores, female mathematicians are equally marginalized.

2. Woman as an Object of Discourse: An Inquiry into Categories

Discourse on women's cognitive difference has little to do with what you and I are, and it is not even clear that the word supposedly designating us has a clear referent. This is easy to verify, thanks to the technological revolution that has changed how we do research in the history of philosophy and ideas, absurd or otherwise: with the advent of electronically accessible library catalogues, a vast array of references can be called up. In theory, the words of titles should offer the system a way of locating bibliographical information. If this were so, the computer would then quite neutrally spew out multiple references; for a single term, it would list novels, geography, poems, and commercial documents. In fact, the computer's responses are not organized in such a mechanical way. Sometimes editors add key words after an ISBN number, and sometimes librarians add something of their own. Not surprisingly, what we find are the classifications defined by the designers of the system. Call up the term "woman." If you unleash an avalanche of theological references and *A Vindication of the Rights of Woman* by Mary Wollstonecraft, while the plural "women" gives you a completely different collection, including novels written by men, indexed as "relations with," or statistics or census records, you will begin to realize that *women* is not the plural of *woman*, and a certain lack of referent will be apparent. Then, after many fruitless attempts, you will discover that to find even a trace of recent works written by women on the situation of women, which include the word "women" in their title ("in Eastern Europe," "and citizenship," "the rights of . . . "), you must enter "feminism" and not "women." Feminism is not a discourse that speaks about women, since these categories are mutually exclusive. A book written by a group of women, entitled *Women and Citizenship in Europe*, doesn't deal with "women"; it belongs to a discourse that is not defined by its object, but by its political stance. Perhaps it says nothing relevant about the object it claims to study. Thus this object remains the property of doctors, novelists, anthropologists, and statisticians, for literature, clinical studies, and highly empirical social sciences (but not political science) still co-own the term "women" in the plural, while the discourse of the theological old guard remains the sole legitimate owner of the singular referent "woman." And if neither "woman" nor "women" are call-words for a title like *Women and Citizenship in Europe,* the logical conclusion is that both refer to some inert object, lying there to be discussed, while in an expression like "women and citizenship" you can hear that the object of study would have its own comments to make, would make them, and does.

What is the significance of the fact that when women become objects of study, they must in addition be *inert* —and by this I mean passive—objects of study? Here is an additional misunderstanding, if not the fundamental misunderstanding. An object of study is not a figure carved on a tombstone, frozen or docile, merely to be noted, imagined, or manipulated by theory. And I am not protesting in the name of the "human" character of the object of the human sciences, which, being free, could not be known as a thing, or which, as a speaking, reading, thinking being, could in its turn very well be the judge of what is said about it. Not for the moment: it is my modest acquaintance with the natural sciences that makes me protest. To take a convenient example, let us remember that during the Renaissance, learned men tried to formulate the law of falling bodies by thinking they could cal-culate acceleration as a function of the distance covered. Now the object of their study—the law of acceleration—categorically refused to cooperate. The piece of chalk dropped by your physics teacher refused to obey even Leonardo da Vinci, thus demonstrating its resistance to what people wanted to say about it. When the wrong variable is selected, the mistake is obvious: you do not lay down the law, even to a piece of chalk. Then came Galileo, who had the idea of expressing acceleration as a function of time, and this time the object acquiesced; that was it, that still is it. At about the same time Bacon, taking into account the obdurate character of the realities with which scientific inquiry is confronted, declared that for everything pertaining to nature, one should consult nature herself. In the natural sciences, one can-not say just anything at all about the object of study. The scientific enterprise presupposes a certain stability in its object, but this stability should not be taken for infinitely malleable passivity. Furthermore, a scientific object is stable, but *that which is stable* is not necessarily what ordinary perception sees as "the object." *What is stable* may be a law of movement, or of alter-ation or transformation, whereas observable states of things are subject to metamorphosis.[12]

If we bear in mind these two simple features of scientificity as it functions in the classical natural sciences—stability, not necessarily that of the initially perceived phenomenon, and resistance of the object to what may be said about it, and if we now turn to the human sciences, then we cannot help but notice that they currently have less respect for their object than do the natural sciences. First, far from questioning the categories of ordinary per-ception, the social sciences allow these categories to determine their objects of study. Thus, in ordinary thought, there is a category named "woman" and another called "women" and we have seen how they function. At the very least, research in the human sciences should concern itself with the consistency of these categories and with possible criteria of relevance. In fact, the very opposite occurs: the same intellectual operation establishes woman or women as objects of discourse, and sets us up as objects about which you can say just about anything at all. In contrast, some feminist sociologists emphasize that, instead of focusing on "women," their work is about the social relationships between the sexes, which is a different approach altogether. These researchers remain isolated in their disciplinary community; moreover, I have just reinforced the separation by designating them as feminists. Yet, simple, cutting-edge methodological principles can be formulated as soon as one concentrates on social relations rather than "women" as the object of study. During the 1960s, Andrée Michel proposed one such simple idea to deal with the sexual division of labor: in any given society, women perform the tasks that men disdain. Forget about symbolism, about women bound to their fountains or hearths, to cooked rather than raw, liquid rather than solid, or whatever! Forget about the notion that the most demanding labors require masculine muscular strength and that, because of our weaker arms, women are restricted to less heavy or less dangerous tasks, which are therefore (according to this argument) quite normally accorded lesser value. Thanks to a heuristic principle like Michel's, we begin to see something that was previously invisible: rather than reasoning in qualitative terms, tying the supposedly feminine quality of a particular task to the female essence of the person performing it or the masculinity of another task to the maleness of its performer, we should focus on the *variable* social value of tasks. Obviously, such a principle may then need refining or redefining—that is the fate of interesting principles—but we can already cite some revealing examples. In the early 1990s, Spain was the European country with the largest proportion of women holding professorships in the sciences. The reason was that professorial salaries in Spain are very low; men who are highly trained scientists prefer more lucrative activities, whereas women with the same training are prepared to settle for low-prestige academic positions.[13]

Although the natural sciences acknowledge that their objects may resist the proposed theory, since this is the basis of their scientificity, the traditional human sciences study women without allowing for such a possibility. The first symptom is that as soon as a particular inquiry credits women with an ability to act, criticize the status quo, advance their cause, or sees them as initiators of some process, *then* the inquiry no longer counts as a study of women, but as a discourse expressing the political opinions of its author, and consequently (how hard this consequence is!), the proposed analysis falls outside the domain of scientific inquiry! The most common symptom is that it is possible to say anything and everything with no need to verify it. And the currently most fashionable symptom is to claim "a distance from the object": if you are a woman studying women, be sure to keep your distance to avoid "excessive identification" with your object! If a theory proposes that both sexes are free de jure and women are not objects to be manipulated at will by discourse, it will be treated as political opinion rather than scientific inquiry, or even as something that defies classification. Thus it is easy to understand why I could not find a keyword that would call up works like *The Second Sex* or a recently reissued pamphlet purportedly by "Jane Anger" (probably a pseudonym) containing this sharp assertion: "Wee are contrary to men, because they are contrarie to that which is good: because they are purblind they cannot see into our natures, and wee too well [though] we had but halfe an eie into their condition because they are so bad."[14] A young colleague handed me the bibliographical information across the back fence: clearly, good neighbors are essential to research, especially when it involves going off the beaten track in search of items passed over by an established structuring of knowledge that may prove inflexible. Your library's electronic catalogue yielded no information about women doctors: even after considerable effort, all you could find was a modest bibliography on female medical students (women have been studying medicine for a century, but it seems that none have finished *yet*) alongside a copious section devoted to female mediums.

The technological revolution in bibliographical methods offers one advantage: the computer allows you to track down lost works, isolated from any tradition, apparently without predecessors or successors; precisely because they are solitary witnesses, these works can shed new light on a question. Call up "intuition." Mathematical works, as you might have expected, works about Aristotle, also predictable; a recent work on the art of reconciling feminine intuition and masculine rationality: the only surprise being that there are not twelve dozen of them. But also—and at last something you hadn't expected—a certain Reverend John Frazer's *Deuteroskopia* [*Second Sight*], published in Edinburgh in 1707.[15] The gift of second sight was linked to intuition by twentieth-century librarians, something their predecessors of the classical age would not have done. We are not going to protest; this collection of picturesque stories provides one of the missing links for anyone trying to understand the necessarily multiple genesis of "feminine intuition." I found the previous link through a completely different connection. Over the last twenty-five years, thanks to feminist scholarship, the work of Gabrielle Suchon (1631–1703) has gradually been rediscovered. But for her I would never have imagined I could be interested in the concept of "infused knowledge"* (directly inspired knowledge) as a way of studying the genesis

---

* "Infused knowledge" traditionally signified a nugget of knowledge God gives directly to certain chosen persons; in colloquial French one may say mockingly, "tu crois que tu as la science infuse?"—"Do you think you know everything already?"

of intuition contrasted with reasoning, or with anything else for that matter. The notion had never been of any interest to me except as a quip directed at those who thought they knew everything. Suchon contrasts knowledge "which is the fruit of reasoning, study, and daily practice" with a God-given inspired or infused knowledge that requires no human effort because it is given freely by grace and favor. "God gives these gifts to chosen people less because of their saintliness than for the good of their neighbor."[16] Thus infused knowledge is defined by contrast and is a gift God gives to some men and some women alike: the spirit bloweth where it listeth. This religious reference allows Gabrielle Suchon to posit cognitive equality between the sexes within a broader inequality among people. For she recognizes that in the realm of knowledge acquired through study, people have unequal talents: not everyone has the same capabilities. But departing from the ideology of her time and of so many others, she denies the claim, so frequent in her own time as in so many others, that this inequality can be interpreted as sexual inequality. The reference to infused knowledge allows her to focus on a maximal distance from the ordinary or the average, since nothing is more singular than this infused knowledge, which allows immediate apprehension of God's will for a particular time and place. With respect to this extraordinary mode of knowing, both men and women who partake in it have the same advantages. Thus there is no need to worry about less dramatic variations in ordinary intellectual capability among human beings. These variations are nothing more than individual differences, and thus not marks of a sexual distinction.

Do not imagine that the ancient theologians had given much emphasis to the notion that infused knowledge was equally valid for both sexes (*épicène*).[17] But ecclesiastical history could allow this assertion if someone so desired. Can we move from there to the historical production of "feminine intuition"? With respect to philosophical understandings of this concept, we might suppose that feminine intuition is a transposition—laicized, anthropologized, attributed to just one sex—of ancient infused knowledge, both being defined by the same contrast. However, it is still necessary to look for the mediating factors: enter John Frazer. As he describes it, second sight is certainly a less dignified, more prosaic and everyday version of infused knowledge, with neither the approval of ecclesiastical authority nor theological legitimacy accorded to it, yet with the same mixed-sex character. "That such representations are made to the eyes of Men and Women, is to me of no doubt,"[18] he writes, citing the example of a woman who prophesies that if a certain gentleman takes a certain young boy on a journey with him, she "sees" that the boy will not come back alive. She warns an employee of the gentleman in question, but he is reluctant to annoy his master with such an unverifiable allegation, and refuses to transmit the message. As soon as something is labelled an "unverifiable allegation" others, inevitably and as a matter of course, acquire the authority to filter and sift it before deciding whether it merits consideration. In the *Deuteroscopia*, it is not only women who are not believed; it is the common fate of all those who prophesy and thus discredit themselves in the eyes of both ecclesiastical and civil authorities. Frazer's book offers evidence of a nascent sociocognitive disdain: these visions are *unaccountable*, he says—one cannot explain them oneself, they verge on popular superstition and therefore are not to be taken seriously.[19] If there was a historical transition from "infused" knowledge to "second sight," then feminine intuition may well be another name for this "second sight." This synonym came into use when intuition had lost its grand philosophical status and when the male half of humanity—illiterate men included—who had been dissociated from the infused knowledge formerly valid for both sexes, came to be identified with the cult of putatively rational knowledge.

3. Values/Countervalues

A point of view I find strange is often defended in debates about equality between women and men: since women do certain types of work, are associated with certain things, are quite simply this or that, have one kind of talent and not another, *then,* instead of trying to gain admission to traditional male roles, instead of breaking away from odd associations of ideas that bind us, of remaking ourselves, or developing other talents, it is better to validate or revalidate our own activities, talents, and ways of being. As if women's value rose or fell according to what is associated with us, as if the value of these things could be decided by an act of pure will, and as if our worth could not simply be affirmed! Thus, to return to the example of intellectual faculties, we sometimes hear it said that if intuition or empathy, its modern equivalent, were given fair value, then women would ipso facto be revalued. And likewise housework, mothering, and so on.

Such a project is vulnerable to all manner of critique: to begin with, the concept of intuition is unstable; it is impossible to claim that anything that might be called intuition exists in itself, prior to any epistemological theory, no matter how imprecise. In your garden, you see hydrangeas, roses, and geraniums as distinct and different from each other, and you think these distinctions among species exist prior to your awareness of them, and independently of it. It is not theory that produces the difference between a tulip and a hyssop plant. Only the catch-all category "weed" is an artifact that refers back to a merely functional connection. But bindweed will continue to be bindweed, and the ground elder will never be a dandelion, even if you do pull them all indiscriminately. By contrast, the constitution and distribution of modes of knowing does depend on the theoretical frame of reference you choose. You can have binary theories or theories comprising more than two terms; "intuition" may or may not be part of the nomenclature; sharp divisions, oppositions, or simply hierarchies may separate the various modes. As a result, the idea of reclaiming the value of intuition, with the promise that we will revalidate women in so doing, has no fixed point; its term of reference—intuition, to be reclaimed—does not function outside a general theory of the ordering of modes of knowledge.

Moreover, the idea of recognizing the value of women by restoring respect for intuition is invalidated by the following counterexample. Schopenhauer, a contemporary of Hegel, assures us that, unlike Kant, "I start from direct or intuitive knowledge."[20] He finds a way to connect intuition and reason while subordinating reason to intuition, since intuitive knowledge, according to him, is more highly valued than conceptual knowing and discursive reason. Very well; will he reach a conclusion favorable to our sex? Don't even dream of it! "Reason is feminine in nature; it can only give after it has received. Of itself it has nothing but the empty forms of its operation."[21] There it is! Women lose on all counts; no matter what the philosophical framework, women are always on the wrong side. If intuition is devalued, it is said to be feminine; if reason is judged uninteresting, then suddenly it is reason that is deemed feminine. Whether it was Schopenhauer or Hegel whose stock was higher in the philosophical marketplace, the result was inevitably the same and women were associated with the deficient faculty. Yet another counterexample: Bergson wrote at a time when the expression "feminine intuition" was a fully fledged lexical item. He foregrounds intuition; you might imagine that he draws first-rate conclusions about women's intellectual worth and that philosophically he rehabilitates the mode of cognition that is supposedly ours. Don't imagine anything; read him! According to him, what is funny about *The learned women* in Molière's play by the same name is that "they translate scientific ideas into the language of feminine sensibility: 'Epicurus is charming,' 'I dote on vortices.' "[22] It is enough to rearrange the conventional signs just a little—now that intuition has regained its positive connotation, "feminine intuition" becomes "feminine sensibility," and there you have it. Everything remains in an order more fundamental than the arrangement of signs. Once again, a man has made a mockery of women, of characters created by a man, but purporting to represent real women whom you or I might meet, since "feminine sensibility" is a term applicable to both theatrical characters and living women. It may be noted in passing that the duality suggested in *Laughter* between supposedly serious "scientific ideas" and ostensibly comic "feminine sensibility" may not correspond exactly to the structures of Bergson's philosophy of knowledge. If this duality has nothing to do with the epistemology Bergson attempted to advance, then we can be delighted by the example since it forces us to conclude that a philosophical system imposes no constraints on anyone, not even its author, who can always find a way to say what he wants, no matter what he might have thought elsewhere.

Questions with far-distant origins—the British parliament of 1653, if you can imagine such a thing, or the inability of philosophy to house intellectual faculties in the same brain—come back to haunt us in the form of vague ideas with forgotten origins, to which everyone nonetheless still subscribes. The identity imposed on us is made up of cast-offs—could there be any greater insult? If we believe Hélène Monsacré, even our tears attest to a similar historical mechanism. In Homer's time, heroes wept; but, then it became unacceptable for a warrior to cry, and so men, not knowing what to do with their tears, presented them to women.[23] We are the little sisters who get the broken toys, the worn-out ideas, and the signs that are being discarded. However, the gift is snatched back when what appeared to be an ordinary stone is revealed as a diamond in the rough or something that could pass for one. The practice of attributing these negative values to women is constant in form, even if the precise content varies ad libitum. Women can be taxed with anything at all, in a way that is both arbitrary and not accidental, provided that at some point in history it has had a negative value. This phenomenon did not escape the attention of Gabrielle Suchon, who notes in 1693: "When desires are seen as marks of need and poverty, they will be attributed by the score to women and girls, since people are always ready to turn unpleasant things over to them."[24] She has discerned a kind of law, to which we may add a corollary underscoring the historic fluctuation of these gifts. In the seventeenth century, desire was in disrepute, and so women were said to have it in excess; today, it has been revalued by psychoanalysis, which even sees it as a sign of mental health. Since then, it has become a male characteristic, even in the writings of female psychoanalysts. Thus, Helen Deutsch places "woman" at a pole of absolute non-desire. Whereas with animals the sex drive of the male depends on female fertility rhythms, in the human species "the male could free himself from his dependence upon the feminine rhythm and take sexual possession of the female even without her consent . . . among all living creatures, only man . . . is capable of rape in the full meaning of this term. . . . "[25] It is true that if one sex is constituted as the only subject of desire, and the other as the object of desire of the first, the configuration comes close to being an apologia for rape, which, in contrast to animals, thus becomes the defining characteristic of man's human nature.

Deutsch repeatedly insists that a woman in harmony with her nature has only intuitions. Thus we find this delectable passage:

> Woman's intellectuality is to a large extent paid for by the loss of valu-able feminine qualities: it feeds on the sap of the affective life and results in

impoverishment of this life either as a whole or in specific emotional qualities. The intellectual woman is not Autonoë, the Wise One, who draws her wisdom from the deep sources of intuition, for intuition is God's gift to the feminine woman; everything relating to exploration and cognition, all the forms and kinds of human cultural aspiration that require a strictly objective approach, are with few exceptions the domain of the masculine intellect, of man's spiritual power, against which woman can rarely compete. All observations point to the fact that the intellectual woman is masculinized; in her, warm intuitive knowledge has yielded to cold unproductive thinking.[26]

If there is a relationship between an apologia for rape and a condemnation of woman's intellectuality in a work that addresses these two issues, then what exactly are we talking about when we discuss women's relationship to knowledge and the intuition that is said to be typically ours? Are we talking about the cognitive faculty that we think we understand, or about a general status of passivity to which women are confined? In any case, Deutsch confirms our idea of *déshérences* (cast-offs); she goes on to affirm that the following passage from Goethe applies especially to intellectual woman: "Believe me, a fellow who speculates/ is like a beast on an arid heath/ Led 'round in circles by an evil spirit/ while close by a green meadow lies."[27] According to Deutsch, the green meadow "stands here for feminine affectivity and the 'arid heath' for the speculating intellectuality to which woman is led by her masculinity complex."[28] Isn't this wonderful?! In typical German Romantic fashion, Faust's self-criticism is aimed at "the reasoner." For the poet, those who reason are dry, but nevertheless they are men. Deutsch doesn't hesitate to displace this characteristic on to women, and to write that the man who reasons too much, is in fact an intellectual woman. We must analyze shifts of this sort with great care, no matter how much such analyses are blocked by the smoke-screens of our age, of which one notorious example is the question: "is there a fundamental cognitive difference between women and men?" If we want to investigate the position of women and men in the order of knowledge, it is vital to free ourselves from this question so that we can see phenomena of a different order of complexity and the hidden processes that accompany the construction of whatever is recognized as knowledge—as something worth learning.

4. Knowledge and Power

We have advanced the hypothesis that historically, "feminine intuition" had its genesis as a residue. To argue this further, we can enlist the help of Kant's *Conflict of the Faculties*, a work that, despite the apparent frivolity of its tone, nonetheless scrupulously upholds some fundamental traditions. Here, the term "faculty" refers to the administrative divisions within universities; Kant portrays the disputes between the philosophy faculty and the faculties of medicine, law, and theology. Raising the following question: "is human nature progressing constantly toward perfect goodness?"[29], he goes on to say that to answer it one must make a detour via a more theoretical problem: is a prophesying or divinatory history possible? He replies that knowledge of the future is possible if (but only if) the seer himself constructs and organizes the events he predicts. He offers three examples: the prophets of Israel, politicians, and men of the Church: these men of power prophesy the catastrophes they are in the process of orchestrating themselves, whence the fulfilment of their predictions. The prophets foretold the decline of the State which they themselves were making inevitable by their stubborn insistence on imposing an impossible constitution. They had the power to ensure that what they said would come about; all they did was to prophesy what, with their nefarious powers, they were already bringing about.[30] *Quod erat demonstrandum*... If reliable knowledge of the future depends on the power to fashion that future, then obviously people without power to influence the course of events can make no accurate predictions. Women or the lower classes can have all the divinatory intuitions they wish: these are merely caricatures of the knowledge the powerful have of the future they concoct. I am the one drawing these conclusions from Kant's ideas; in fact, he, who was delighted by the French Revolution, says nothing about the inability of the common people to know the future for, as that period had just discovered, the common people can make history. But he is at pains to designate, meticulously, just who would be incapable of predicting the future. Ridiculing those who "meddle with divination," that is, who get involved in it with no qualifications—the term indicates ineptitude and an absence of official status—Kant gives some examples of bungling futurologists who, curiously, are all women, from prophetesses to gypsies. Does this mean he is decreeing a general equivalence of knowledge and power? Is his ridicule of female prophets a symptom of his intention to use the full weight of his speculative authority to support women's exclusion from the spheres of knowledge and power? In raising the question, we touch on a point our era has difficulty addressing openly, despite constant harping on a collusion between knowledge and power. *The Conflict of Faculties* might, in its way, clarify this problem, which is in fact two problems in one: is it legitimate, in general, to assimilate all knowledge to power? And should every attempt to exclude women from knowledge be interpreted as a brutal or underhanded project of ensuring our radical and ongoing disempowerment?

From Kant's point of view, there is certainly no such thing as knowledge *tout court*. On the contrary, he distinguishes sharply between professional knowledge, which is purely about regulations and necessary for the exercise of a delegated authority, and other forms of knowledge that have minimal implications for power but count, nonetheless, as real knowledge. Because rational knowledge of this or that bit of reality does not fall within the purview of the faculties of theology, law, or medicine, whose function it is merely to train agents or instruments of government, priests, magistrates, or doctors merely exercise an authority delegated by the State and apply its rules concerning spiritual, social, and bodily well-being according to governmental conceptions of these forms of well-being. The faculty of medicine does not concern itself so much with human physiology as with sanitary regulations, or even, says Kant, with medical policing, although it happens to take an interest *also* in a knowledge of the body and in the laws of nature that govern the living human being. In general, the instruments of government formed in these three faculties "have legal influence on the public and form a special class of the intelligentsia, who are not free to make public use of their learning as they see fit, but are subject to the censorship of the faculties."[31] By contrast, the faculty of philosophy is free insofar as it does not prepare its students to govern or influence the people by applying certain doctrines. According to the author, philosophy includes disciplines as diverse as history, geography, humanities, mathematics, the metaphysics of nature and of mores . . . , all of them forms of knowledge that it subjects to critical analysis. Since this faculty exercises no authoritative function, government "leaves [its teachings] up to the scholars' reason."[32] Philosophy is to be left free to display its doubts and objections in public. So, on the one hand, knowledge derived from reflection on issues that precede or stand apart from government regulations is not dispensed, or only coincidentally dispensed, by the three faculties that delegate political power to their members. On the other hand, the faculty that does not confer power is the only one engaged in working toward knowledge of aspects of nature and human nature, problematizing and critically analyzing them through free inquiry. Kant's text thus advocates a radical disjunction between an apprenticeship for power (itself always subject to a central power) and the acquisition of true and truly reflective forms of knowledge. One can understand that with respect to knowledge of the future, Kant associates knowledge with the power to act: in this case, but only in this case, power and knowledge coincide.

To probe the question further, we must refer to some basic elements of epistemology: logically speaking, two temporal dimensions, the past and the future, are necessarily distinct. Philosophical language carries an equivalence between the dimension of the past, "what is done" (before now), and factuality (meaning the facts with which the protocols of objectification are concerned). If, for example, one speaks of "natural history," it is because it describes things already there. *Factum* in Latin, *fact* in English, *fait* in French: the three languages equate what has been done with what is really there, an equivalence that Aristotle also mentions: "It is to be noted that nothing that is past is an object of choice, e.g. no one chooses to have sacked Troy; for no one *deliberates* about the past, but about what is future and capable of being otherwise, while what is past is not capable of not taking place; hence Agathon is right in saying '*For this alone is lacking even to God/ To make undone things that have once been done.*'"[33] From Kant's point of view (and Bacon's, whom he follows in this), politically free knowledge must practice at least a minimal respect for facts. That does not mean that it accumulates and arranges them willy-nilly, even less that it makes a fetish of them, but that at the very least it postulates that to claim power over what *is done* is to engage in fantasy, and to assume a discretionary power that not even a poetic-philosophical deity could claim. Thus, equating power and knowledge is valid only when dealing with the future and with spheres in which there are no (ready-made) facts to be acknowledged, but rather programs of action or political agendas of one sort or another. The so-called learned professions (medicine, law, and theology) are concerned with the immediate future, even if this future amounts to no more than maintaining an established order; it is a matter of ensuring that tomorrow, in a few minutes, immediately, this or that state-defined health, social, or religious policy, will be enforced. From this point of view, jokes about fortune-tellers, even with no theoretical justification, have an allusive but universal appeal since they suggest that women could not have power—as doctors, lawyers, or clergy— nor be the agents of state decisions concerning the immediate physical, civic, or spiritual well-being of the public. Here nothing is explicitly said about women's access to such problematized knowledge as geography, the metaphysics of morals, history, or mathematics. However, in the epilogue to the work there is a remark about wretched printers who produce books in gray ink and characters that ruin the eyesight. This is unkind to male readers, says Kant, and even more so to "the now large number of" female readers, "who may feel more strongly about the nuisance of glasses."[34] Knowledge of Greek was supposed to give you a beard; reading will make your profile ugly because of your spectacles. Kant makes no link between the imaginary repression of women's access to forms of knowledge unconnected with sociopolitical power and the sarcasms he directs at powerless fortune-tellers incapable of predicting the future. Yet, whether or not forms of knowledge have some bearing on the exercise of power, there are enough colorful asides in his prose to indicate that they are no business of women. Since he is unable to offer a basis in reason for something that has none, he uses images to insinuate either that women's knowledge is false or that it diminishes their sex appeal. But the fact that there is an exclusion in both instances does not augur well for the distinction he posits between two types of knowledge. And how is he positioning himself when he supports the exclusion of women from all knowledge, whether or not it is linked to power? When a philosopher who, in theory, is on the side of knowledge without power uses negative images to argue that women's exclusion is normal and desirable, he is indeed engaged in social engineering, whatever he may say elsewhere.

What exactly are we talking about? Is it women and knowledge *or* women, knowledge, and power? Today we still must tackle this question that recalls an objection evoked by Anna Maria van Schurman as early as 1641, and taken up by Poullain de la Barre: one of the common objections to allowing women access to knowledge is the fact that since they are rarely entrusted with any public, political, ecclesiastical, or academic role, no purpose is served by their acquiring knowledge, and, of course, there is no sense in embarking on a useless project. To this, van Schurman replies, "in the speculative sciences women are by no means frustrated of their goal; even in the practical sciences . . . if they do not follow that primary or public goal, nevertheless they pursue the secondary and, as I would say, more private goal of these sciences."[35] Poullain de la Barre attacks this objection directly: women are no less capable than men of employment in society. They are capable of teaching, assuming ecclesiastical functions, drafting legislation, presiding over a parliament, being queens, and even commanding an army. So there is no reason to exclude them from knowledge. Fine, you'll say, from now on we have everything we need: on one side, van Schurman who insists on what she calls the sublime and delectable acquisition of knowledge in its purely speculative dimension; on the other, Poullain who thinks it is entirely suitable for women to have access to practical knowledge and to exercise a profession. Do we want anything else today? Would it not be better to consider that the question has been settled in theory, ever since the seventeenth century, which provided us with arguments adequate for us to believe in the possibility of equal access to knowledge for women and men, and therefore to reject the arguments of the venerable Kant, who, a century later, failed to take these remarkable theoretical advances into account? What do I find missing in this argumentation? Am I being difficult when I find something unsatisfying in these texts that certainly announce what we all want, what many people would like to see settled once and for all, or what too many think has already been achieved? These essays do indeed prefigure our contemporary situation, but with all its hesitations and ambiguities; closer reading of them allows us to understand some of today's uncertainties more clearly.

We can propose several precise criticisms of these essays. Without a murmur, Anna Maria van Schurman accepts women's containment within a private and entirely domestic sphere. Even though her insistence on the purely speculative succeeds in avoiding reductionism (any operation that accords knowledge only practical value is by definition reductive) and she successfully illustrates the significance of an intellectual life for a woman, she seems to remain content with a niche in a systematic sexual division of roles, which she neither examines nor criticizes. Women's access to knowledge is conditional on nothing changing too much, and therefore does not lead to anything outside itself. She concludes that parents have a duty to instruct their daughters, and this is not a negligible conclusion. But this thought seems to turn in on itself; as a painter, she left self-portraits, and her writing also tends to be self-reflexive. As for Poullain, the cognitive equality he posits between women and men is only an element in a strategy intended to produce an endorsement of Cartesianism. On the one hand he wants to explain (and explain the value of) doubt as the unavoidable negative passage between the method of the vulgar and the acquisition of a "sound knowledge" composed of clear and distinct ideas: "With the intent of establishing so important a principle, we have believed it best to choose a specific, striking subject in which everyone takes an interest. . . . "[36] Challenging the received idea of masculine superiority thus becomes a peculiarly pertinent and appropriate example for apprenticeship in the practice of Cartesian doubt. On the other hand, Poullain claims to have questioned women from every walk of life, in both city and country, about their thoughts on God, on the relation between their soul and their body, on the circulation of blood. . . . It would seem that Cartesianism had been instilled in all of them, since they all spontaneously gave responses that conform to the broad outlines of the *Meditations*. "They understand things as well as if they had received the best education"; they have none of the prejudices and confused ideas that are "so common to cultivated men."[37] The mutual exclusivity of the two categories, "women" and "learned," is thus maintained, as if no woman had ever been educated. In short, women are used here as a pretext, the value of their intellect serving only to prove the absolute truth of Cartesianism. The affirmation of intellectual equality between the sexes is destined to show the *sçavants* that they must practice Cartesian doubt; it is therefore part of an argument addressed to men. And if women's intellect has any value, it is insofar as it belongs, innately, to Cartesianism, which can then claim to represent the innate good sense of humanity. The women he claims to have questioned might just as well be fictitious characters, constructed as the antithesis of the figure of the learned man, and not far off from that of the "noble savage." Moreover, one must wonder why it would be necessary to teach women anything, since they already think so well and are always already on the side of Cartesianism, which Poullain considers to be the philosophy of natural reason!

Over and above specific criticisms of the texts, today's reader must work out a more difficult problem. True, we may well applaud an initiative that would put van Schurman's *De ingenii muliebris ad doctrinam et meliores litteras aptitudine* and Poullain's *De l'égalité des deux sexes* on the [French] secondary school philosophy curriculum, so that our adolescent girls and boys will at last discover that the idea of equality between women and men is not a recent invention. Nonetheless I must confess that these two authors leave me with an impression that something has not been thought through, and that the problem of the relation (or not) between knowledge and power remains at an impasse. In their work, the very question of women's access to an intellectual life seems to be limited from the outset, unable to find its own terms, or discussed against a background of constraining, tacitly accepted but unexamined principles that undermine the very effort to open the world of knowledge to women. We shall come back to this problem more than once. For the sake of offering an immediate, provisional response that can be expanded as the inquiry proceeds, we must note that our two authors conceive of a *conditional* access to knowledge for women. Poullain would allow women access to knowledge only if they remain strictly within the framework of Cartesian thought and swear allegiance to it. As for van Schurman, we have noted that she looks for gaps in a predetermined sexual division of roles. Both of them fully recognize women's rational capacity, but they do not envisage rationality as a form of autonomy, still less as a critical autonomy. Poullain thinks that women adhere immediately to the results of Cartesian thought, and he does not see them engaging in methodological doubt. The rejection of prejudices is for learned men only, in principle because they alone are in error; but, this division should be interpreted in the reverse direction. If women can exempt themselves from the practice of doubt and free inquiry, it is because it would be inappropriate for them to take it up.[38] And when van Schurman posits a strictly speculative acquisition of knowledge, she is careful to say that she does not intend it to imply equality between women and the luminaries of thought. Thus these treatises depict a kind of "second rationality" for women that takes its principles from elsewhere and adopts them as results.

Unless some notion of intellectual independence or critical reevaluation (accessible in law and in principle to everyone) accompanies the idea of cognitive equality between the sexes, the idea is nothing more than a hollow gesture, because its effect is to recognize intellectual activity in women only if it bears on knowledge already constituted or predigested for their uses. In other words, it allows them a merely secondhand intellectual vocation. Moreover, these are seventeenth-century texts, written at a time when the concept "second reason" had some meaning: it referred to what reason can extract from the principles, maxims, and regulations established by revelation and religion (and secondarily by the law) and to their application to human affairs, these revealed principles being themselves exempt from reason's critical scrutiny. Second reason is an art of logically deriving the corollaries from a discourse based on authority. It marks the dividing line between revealed truth and the study of nature, in which the principles themselves are examined.[39] Thus, when van Schurman and Poullain envisage women's access to knowledge or reason, they in fact presuppose a relationship that, in their century, is precisely fashioned as a so-called rational relationship to truths established on a principle of authority or articles of faith.

It is not just a matter of imposing a double standard or tacitly reviving the idea that women's access to intellectual life is merely conditional, but also of a cautious secondary admission of women into a tribe, be it the tribe of Cartesians or of the learned in general. Deemed worthy of *belonging* to a particular or general clan, women figure in the discourse as objects that might be appropriated. Nothing lends credence to this idea more than a remark of Descartes's about our Anna Maria: "This Voetius has also spoilt Mlle de Schurmans: she had excellent gifts for poetry, painting and other gentle arts, but these last five or six years he has taken her over completely so that she cares for nothing but theological controversies, and all decent people shun her."[40] The man who regrets that he does not *possess* Demoiselle Schurman, and who declares her ostracized by polite society, simultaneously reveals his definition of women's normal relationship to the life of the mind: pleasantries, trifles, nothing of great import. He will be more friendly to van Schurman's school friend, Princess Elisabeth of Bohemia. But didn't she have the good taste to become a disciple of Descartes and not of Voetius? Descartes was no stranger to possessiveness. When he writes: "Science is a woman; as long as she stays modestly next to her husband, she is respected; if she belongs to everyone, she is degraded,"[41] he is saying that everything that can be appropriated is like a woman. A generation earlier Bacon, flattered by the attention paid to his work by the Queen of Bohemia, mother of Descartes's friend, sent her one of his books, praising her "singular ability to read and judge of them", that elevates her "above [your] sex."[42] Women, you are outsiders in principle. Nevertheless, if you are willing to accept my tutelage, we might reconsider. Exclusion in principle seems to function as a formidable method of forcing dependence. And it is indeed a choice between "being on the outside or perhaps at my heel," conveying first an exclusion in principle, and then conditions for secondary entry, rather than the reverse, "at my heel or on the outside," which would indicate first a frank authoritarianism and then punishment for insubordination. The dictatorial tone that I believe can be detected in some seventeenth-century discourse echoes my own experience. It is still like that in the intellectual world, and the persistence of the discourse excluding women from the life of the mind could find an explanation here. This is an explicitly foregrounded discourse which leaves open the secondary possibility of an integration more tacitly permitted, on condition of docility and perfect subservience. To be included, a woman— women, all women—must meekly acquiesce to the status of disciple or helpmeet. There is nothing like excluding a class of people on principle only then to make them accept monstrous conditions. The treatment of immigrants, harassed or threatened with expulsion and thus constrained to accept even more arduous working conditions, shows that women are not alone in this. And I have read Monseigneur Dupanloup* for you: he draws upon the work of Joseph de Maistre, whom he criticizes. He rejects de Maistre's satire of "knowledge in petticoats" but not without recounting it at length, and then easily slides into saying that "women are made above all for Christian learning."[43] All their knowledge must relate to God and to France: they must not condemn themselves to ignorance of "the wonderful things that God has wrought in the world through France."[44] A will to maintain the appropriation of women by both a religious and a national community expresses itself through the bizarre construction of two forms of closed knowledge, Christian and patriotic learning. But is there really such a thing as closed knowledge? When there is closure, it means that individuals have been appropriated by knowledge; they do not possess it, they are possessed by it.

We must nonetheless insist that in the seventeenth century and beyond, people who were required to be bearers of knowledge, without exercising either their intellectual independence or their critical faculties in their relationship to knowledge, were men. This exercise of second reason with respect to revealed truths was valid for the learned professions (theology, law, medicine), themselves the intermediaries of power, that were endorsed at that time almost exclusively by men. Obedience to dogma, unquestioning acceptance of received wisdom, is the conduct prescribed for those designated to control society, not for those they control. For common people can remain as ignorant as they please, give or take a catechism or two. Thus, the intellectual subordination proposed to women who, in spite of their initial exclusion on principle, wanted to occupy at least a back seat in the world of thought is nothing out of the ordinary or made to measure for them. Nevertheless, at that time in history, a few men declared this type of mental activity absolutely worthless in both the sciences of nature and the "speculative sciences," and they advocated free inquiry in all forms of knowledge that had nothing to do with regulating society. For themselves, they no longer wanted the status of passively obedient clerks, trained as uncritical knowers and destined to serve as assistants to those in authority. They wanted something quite different: creative work that passed through the negative moment of doubt or rejection. At the end of the eighteenth century, Kant reveals himself as the direct descendant of the classical age when he describes

---

*Monseigneur Dupanloup (1802–1878): French prelate, member of the French government (Chambre des Députés), senator, member of the French Academy, violently opposed to the ideas of Renan, Taine and Littré. Author of catechetical works and a famous pamphlet in support of Pius IX's *Syllabus of Errors* and encyclical *Quanta cura*. Among many other ideas, the *Syllabus* condemned socialism, rationalism, pantheism, and liberalism.

the freedom of philosophy in contrast to the submissiveness required in the learned professions. Consequently—and paradoxically—the best that van Schurman and Poullain offered women was a relationship to knowledge that, though disdained by some men, was still typical of the very learned professions from which women were in fact excluded. Is it not strange for the "Star of Utrecht" (van Schurman) to have claimed such a mode of learning for women in the speculative sciences?

All of this prompts me to return to the theme of *déshérence*, since at best the relationship to knowledge proposed for women is precisely the one some men no longer want. And in general, it is possible to trace the production of this double standard to the classical age by examining the vagaries of a regulatory myth that, until that time, had rigorously controlled access to a free intellectual life for everyone, women and men alike, and that, according to certain thinkers, no longer prevailed except for women. Even those who champion education for women have had reservations about their free access to knowledge. I will try to analyse all kinds of reluctance as residues with which we must be satisfied, and I hope at the same time to illuminate some of today's many affirmations of women's lack of aptitude for knowledge—our nonaccess to reason, knowledge, sciences, and so on—or the innumerable claims that for us such things are vaguely indecent. There is an unlimited supply of such profound thoughts. Even as we discuss them, others are undoubtedly on their way into print.

5. Anti-intellectualism

A vague and ponderous prohibition on knowledge is all too familiar. The culture that for want of a better name is called European owes something of its structure to the Judeo-Christian religious tradition, whose attitude toward human attempts at knowledge production is, to say the least, ambiguous. The possibility of condemning all miserable human knowledge goes back at least as far as Solomon, who wanted wisdom above all but, as is well known, lamented the dreariness of knowledge, observing: "he that increaseth knowledge increaseth sorrow." Saint Paul added that *scientia inflat,* knowledge makes us swell up, with pride no doubt.[45] The possibility, in a traditional culture, of developing a totally negative view of thought and knowledge acquired through human endeavor is the repressive counterpart of that other fundamental religious idea: revealed truth. There you are! Since the Bible, the apostles, and their authorized interpreters are delivering you the complete truth, ready made and all wrapped up, why on earth are you trying to make another truth for yourselves that will necessarily be a deviation from true knowledge? The mandarins of the medieval Sorbonne, authors like Cornelius Agrippa, Sanchez, or Pascal, who dwell upon the vanity of human knowledge, would seize on this opportunity to denounce every independent or creative intellectual endeavor. In the sixteenth century, certain Puritans displayed an even greater practicality by burning books and manuscripts—thus the Oxford University library was ransacked. Everyone I have mentioned had learned, as something beyond the shadow of a doubt, that original sin was the sin of wanting to know. The good doctors of the medieval faculties, who on one day would declare a certain proposition about universals to be anathema, on another day a certain thesis about the infinity of the world, could condemn *either* this *or* that, all in good conscience because in their cultural horizon, free intellectual endeavor was universally and imprecisely condemned. The licit, the tolerated, or questions considered open to debate were mere exceptions granted by special permission against the background of a general prohibition. A generalized, floating condemnation legitimates all possible censorial precision, not to mention even more finely honed excisions.

Moreover, it is worth noting that the object of the prohibition does not necessarily exist prior to the operation that condemns it. It is the prohibition that names its object, or rather that fails to name it precisely. We are in a realm of mythical regulation, where things are forbidden outright and with broad strokes: knowledge in general or knowledge of good and evil, rational activity, or, in the story of Noah, failing to be embarrassed by the nudity of a drunken father . . . In fact, it is often difficult to know what the prohibition bears upon; it applies to a sort of conglomerate or a whole range of cognitive endeavors, which, according to the whims of the moment, may be branded as pretentious or as evidence of a desire to escape divine authority or its earthly representatives. One never knows at what point culpable pretension, or in other words, the sin, begins—to what extent something is more or less permitted, and where the threshold of error and guilt lies. A vague, undefined idea of "enough is enough" seems to be the counterpoint to every permission. Now these characteristics are also to be found in the discourse of modern phallocrats and of what is known as "second wave" feminism, based on the idea of sexual difference, in contrast with the first wave, which was characterized by humanistic, emancipatory values.[46] Whether the oppressive discourse implies women's unfitness or a delicious, radical exoticism, the taboo it involves sometimes encompasses a vaguely-defined conglomerate (truth, science, objectivity, education, possibly beginning with literacy), sometimes an imprecise, floating object—some form or any form of rational enterprise, "the theoretical", learning, the sciences of nature, physics alone, high culture, or perhaps only philosophy. And it is almost impossible to be sure about what is culpable and what might not be.

One fine day you come across some vast generalization consigning us all to the men in white coats. Thus, a woman "who wants to be educated is forced to let a little man grow inside her" and to "let a man who reasons as a man in the world of men cohabit, in the depths of one's self, with a woman who refuses to abjure her own judgments and uses them to gauge the alternatives proposed to her. . . . The woman who makes this effort is necessarily schizoid and, we might add, a hermaphrodite."[47] This point of view, articulated in 1976, strongly resembles that of Joseph de Maistre, "a woman's greatest defect is wanting to be a man; and wanting to be learned amounts to wanting to be a man." Certainly, "it is acceptable for women to know that Peking is not in Europe and that Alexander the Great did not ask to marry any niece of Louis XIV," but nothing more than that because "as soon as she wants to emulate a man, she is no more than a monkey."[48] And here you see how difficult it is for them to state precisely what we are not allowed to know and what we are, since legitimate knowledge is itself grotesquely characterized as just "knowing-that-not." Another day, instead of a hyperbolic condemnation of every woman who wants to educate herself or know anything beyond the fact that Beijing is not in Europe, instead of being threatened with schizophrenia or apishness, you will come upon a pointed critique of none other than your humble servant, who will naturally seize this opportunity to respond. It would seem that she reads classical philosophical texts in an appropriate fashion, with patience and due attention to detail; her respect for them attests to a disgraceful intention to salvage philosophy, and a tolerance for "a masculine rationality," just when the historical mission of feminist subversion is to break with all that by casting philosophy and rationality to the four winds.[49] These remarks are not objections but rather downright rejections. The "reply to my critics" mode would be an unsuitable means of responding; and my answer must proceed by highlighting the perversity of the claim that, as you will have realized, yet again characterizes rationality as "masculine." What irritates me most in the writings of difference feminists is that their way of designating a form of femininity radically separate from philosophy, rationality, education in general, the capacity to read texts accurately or even to read at all, goes hand in hand with the most flagrant sycophantic attitude toward the masculine half of the university world. Thus Claudine Hermann does not just think that education obliges a woman to be inhabited by the equivalent of "a man who reasons as a man," but she also notes "I had excellent [male] teachers."[50] Where on earth did she find them? Unless the only way to find masters "fascinating" and university studies wonderful is to situate oneself on the margins? The same thing is true of Elizabeth Grosz, whose book opens with a deferential summary of the philosophy of a few Parisian demigods, all men of course, and of their predecessors, the great (*sic*) antihumanists of the nineteenth century, Marx, Freud, and Nietzsche, the whole lot described as "the intellectual background and theoretical context of contemporary French feminisms."[51] In other words, "good" subversion is carried out under the tutelage of a cohort of male thinkers, and the rhetoric about the incompatibility of women and education, or of women and clear thinking in the history of philosophy, amounts not merely to praising these men on their own terms but to placing *even feminist discourse* under the authority of men thus designated as the legitimate managers of the entire realm of French philosophy. A realm seen from a great distance, it is tempting to note, but never mind; the real point here is that the structure of her discourse is perfectly revelationist. There was a generation of male prophets in the nineteenth century, another generation in poststructuralist Paris. A woman who fails to recognize that this is the context of the thought she is trying to construct is in the wrong, and it is just too bad if we do not know exactly what to reproach her with!

The point at which women are judged guilty is apparent in the general disapproval of women's education just as it once was in religious denunciations of knowing too much. Which diploma transforms a woman into a bluestocking? What more is she permitted to know, beyond the fact that Alexander the Great made no attempt to marry a niece of Louis XIV? If all of this is the imaginary residue of an older and more sweeping prohibition, we can suggest that religious tradition condemned knowledge for people of both sexes, except in carefully controlled doses; any specific condemnation of women's knowledge is a leftover from the once global and epicene condemnation of all knowledge. It is what remains after men—or certain men—have been granted permission to know a little of this or a lot of that. Such permissions have from time to time been granted. Consider some examples. To go straight to the author I know best, at the transition between the Renaissance and the early modern period, Bacon was engaged in demonstrating the innocence of important parts of knowledge. In his introduction to *The Advancement of Learning* (1605), he dismisses the centuries-old notion of original sin in order to shield the sciences of nature from prohibition on religious grounds. Bacon goes quite a long way in defending certain forms of knowledge against the accusation of sin: since humanity is "part of nature," knowledge of the human body and of what we call the human sciences are also innocent areas of inquiry. However, in greatly enlarging the realm of legitimate knowledge, Bacon did not call for complete abolition of the possibility of declaring certain aspirations to knowledge unsuitable or illicit. Far from challenging the very idea of any knowledge whatsoever being prohibited, the text perpetuates the view that some knowledge is unseemly, and that something should be left shrouded in mystery. As usual, in its Baconian formulation this notion has no precise content; it remains intrinsically vague except for one or two small indications; however, the souls of kings must of course be considered inscrutable.

In *The Advancement of Learning*, rehabilitation of knowledge does not initially seem to be tainted with sexism; fields of knowledge, not knowers, receive a certificate of innocence thanks to the absolution from sin Bacon grants them. Things deteriorate a little later, when he comments on the international friendship that ought to prevail among institutions of knowledge. Unfortunately, he refers to this friendship as a "brotherhood" and a "fraternity," recalling that fraternal contracts are the foundation of artisans' guilds and also serve to unite bishops and religious orders even across national divisions.[52] Then, when we come to *The New Atlantis* (c. 1623) and to the description of a learned community working for the advancement of the sciences, we discover that this ideal community is composed exclusively of men related to one another like *brothers,* under the pastoral tutelage of members who are called *fathers.* Membership in this community is not merely restricted to men, it is structured according to the bonds of kinship similar to those that bind men to each other in everyday society, and which were already in place, metaphorically, in that prototype of sexual apartheid, the monastery. Thus the philosophical operation that lifts the burden of sin from certain kinds of human knowledge is progressively narrowed, implicitly or even surreptitiously, and restricted to the male half of humanity, or rather to a small fraction of it: there is nothing here that could prevent Bacon's admirer, Voltaire, from writing that "we need ignorant paupers."

Today, in the anti-intellectualism recommended for women both by men and by "difference feminists" who dismiss the available intellectual heritage and rationality as such, often with a single stroke, I hear the echo of an age-old wish: that original sin had never been committed, or at least that Eve had never bitten into the apple. And let us not be blinded by the active role *Genesis* attributes to Eve. According to the Scriptures, the fruit of the tree of knowledge was forbidden to both Adam and Eve. It is both Adam and Eve who commit an act of insubordination against divine authority in accessing this knowledge (which is not really described, but designated as a mythical mass). But if it has been understood since the Renaissance, at least in secular learned circles, that Adam can nonetheless legitimately study zoology, just as Solomon can study botany, Galileo astrophysics, and other men philosophy, then only Eve is left in the wrong. Although please note that for Galileo things were not so easy either. His recent rehabilitation by the Catholic church is almost as disturbing as his condemnation in the seventeenth century by the same church. He was pardoned because the prelates came to recognize that, all things considered, he was right, or rather that today no one would challenge the Copernican hypothesis he was defending. What of those who, in exercising the same freedom to know nature without reference to the Scriptures, have made a few mistakes in their calculations or hypotheses? The principle of freedom of knowledge is no better acknowledged when the only beneficiary of rehabilitation is the scientist whose findings are uncontested.

That's an old story, you will say. Today approximately 95 percent of people born into the Judeo-Christian tradition practice no religion at all. Perhaps not, but religious material is recyclable. Note the undertone of sin that resonates through Helene Deutsch's text. Still, many questions remain unresolved. If the myth that has been at the very roots of culture from Constantinople to Iceland and even as far as California equates access to knowledge and freedom from authority (in its divine form, but other forms express themselves through it), it must involve something other than pure religion, if indeed there is such a thing. To put it another way: in the cultural universe that happens to be ours, there is a regulative idea—perhaps of the order of pure belief, perhaps of general principles that can reasonably be agreed upon—that assures that wanting to know, on one's own and without supervision, is a form of insubordination. If some men have benefited from a philosophical reassessment (duly handed down by certain combative communities of scholars), exempting certain domains from the taboo associated with knowledge, where is the act that recognizes the free exercise of intellect for everyone, including women? This frustration should prompt us also to define what is fundamentally problematic in Bacon's model of knowledge and his defense of it. Anyone tempted to take up the cudgels again today, not against theologians but against those who repressively sexualize access to knowledge, ought to be aware of a problem: in order to combat anti-intellectualism and conceptualize the value of people's access to knowledge, a philosophical program focused on the value of knowledge alone is not enough, for it makes knowledge and not knowers into an end in itself. It is vague at the outset about who should be responsible for ensuring the progress of knowledge, since the overriding concern is the development of knowledge. But none of this remains vague for long: it is scarcely an accident that anything that acquires value is absorbed into the heritage of those to whom everything of value is attributed, whereas anything that has lost value is off-loaded onto those whose lot in life is to accept other people's hand-me-downs.

These cast-offs were relatively insignificant in the seventeenth century. However, they do highlight what women were never permitted to do, namely, doubt, question, or explore. For the point of extricating knowledge from scriptural authority and from proscription of the will to know was not to defend existing knowledge, but rather knowledge yet to be established. Rather than the right to acquire existing knowledge, what was affirmed was the freedom to extend the boundaries of knowledge and of the freedom to doubt, to challenge past errors or destroy pseudoknowledge. Existing knowledge was sometimes declared a fiction, or its inadequacies exposed;

at the very most, it was deemed valid only for practical applications and learned professions. The Kantian distinction, articulated to promote free philosophical inquiry, originates here. If, from the dawn of modernity to the Enlightenment, intellectual thinking has emphasized critical reflection, it was with a view to further exploration or the discovery of new knowledge, whereas the acquisition and reproduction of existing knowledge took on secondary importance. If knowledge derived from Aristotle is exempted from free examination, says Bacon, it will never surpass the knowledge Aristotle himself had: critical examination is an essential springboard toward the as-yet-unknown. And he underscores the need for a pedagogy specially adapted to the knowledge presented to children, or more accurately, to the sons of science (the researchers-to-be): it should be delivered, "if it were possible, in the same method wherein it was invented."[53] The essays of Anna Maria van Schurman and Poullain de la Barre thus bypass the issue of precisely what constitutes intellectual liberation, both in their time and perhaps in ours. They do not admit the possibility that, in their search for things as yet unthought, women might challenge parts of available knowledge or elements of Cartesian philosophy. They must enter the world of knowledge as guarantors of the value of existing knowledge. It is troubling to find this same line of argument even in the feminist discourse to which we have referred; Elizabeth Grosz's work is one such example. She believes feminists' duty is to complete the subversion of reason initiated by Nietzsche, Freud, Marx, and their twentieth-century male disciples; including Jacques Derrida, whose generous views about women's relationship to truth we have already cited, a certain Louis Althusser, and one Jacques Lacan, whose fine remark "woman is not" or "there is no such entity as woman" is sometimes used to dismiss you when you want to create a program in women's studies. Even if their work proved kinder to us, the main issue nonetheless persists: is women's access to knowledge worth any effort at all, if it comes without intellectual independence?

6. Essays on Original Sin

If the myth of original sin survives in texts prescribing that women's existence be uncontaminated by intellectual effort—if we have moved from a universal prohibition on the will to know to a residual version, for women alone—then the too rare attempts to reexamine this myth take on new significance. Such an attempt appears in Gabrielle Suchon's *Traité de la morale et de la politique*. Having declared: "To me, knowledge is the greatest privilege of the state of innocence; it repairs the nature which has been wounded by sin, it partakes of the intelligence of the angels, and is the beginning of beatitude," she cites the book of *Genesis*—God having put the tree of life and the tree of knowledge of good and evil in the earthly paradise, he expressly forbade Adam and Eve to eat from it—and slips in a delightfully heterodox interpretation of the episode of the apple: "Divine wisdom, whose aims are only the highest, determined that this tree should be the object of man's knowledge by engaging the mind in a process of reflection thereon."[54] Occupying but a tiny space on the page, and somewhat eclipsed by the italics of the Biblical quotation, the commentary was quite likely to escape censorship, as indeed it did. But as it is caught in a textual network affirming the value of self-instruction—"one does not always need a teacher in order to study; someone who can learn nothing without instruction lacks ability"—its meaning is unequivocal: the relevant idea here is that knowledge of the tree should result from *the reflections that the human being would undertake,* not simply from picking and eating the apple. The passage insists on conceiving knowledge as an act, not as food consumption: "God gave us intelligence to force us to seek knowledge of things." The will to know did not cause the Fall, but the punishment was ignorance. This argument implies that redemption is within reach. Suchon proposes a validation of the innate seeds of knowledge given to us all, that allow us to shake off ignorance and sin, if only we cultivate them.[55] Intellectual effort is an act of repairing a human nature wounded by sin and the more personal the effort, the greater the personal reparation. Far from being a sin, then, knowledge is a duty and a means of salvation.

One can understand this point of view thus: when, beginning with Adam and Eve, God granted the human mind sufficient powers for every single person to find knowledge on his or her own by thinking a little, our first ancestors cheated like lazy schoolchildren taking a peek at the teacher's book instead of putting their brains to work as God had commanded. It would seem that God is a schoolmaster engaged in active pedagogy.[56] In any case it is clear that the act of insubordination amounted to having eaten the apple instead of struggling to understand good and evil by thinking them through; but one can also understand that ingesting the fruit bodily, eating it, demonstrates a complete misunderstanding of the very nature of knowledge: "the soul begs for the bread of others because it has neglected to seek nourishment within itself" and it pursues earthly goods because it takes no account of the goods of heaven, Suchon writes, attributing the idea to St. Bernard. Knowledge is food for the soul, for the mind rather than for the stomach, while all the other fruits of the Garden "were to feed the body."[57] Her attempt to limit the force of the prohibition inherent in the myth is obvious, and the way she proposes to treat the issue of curiosity illustrates this point even better: she will direct three objections against herself, she announces, to show that "the desire to know too much is dangerous," but she adds "I raise these objections only to protect myself in advance against the contrariness of those who pride themselves on censuring what they do not understand [. . .] and I use them to reinforce the truths I am proposing." Indeed! Reminding us of these potential criticisms of curiosity is for her a strategy to praise it more highly.[58]

It is not just a matter of engaging with the myth by interpreting it: her position is linked to a very clear epistemology and to equally clear practical projects. In the acquisition of knowledge, the main thing, for women or men, is the attempt to understand on one's own: it is this effort that is the formative process. "We frequently see [male] fools and ignoramuses in the schools, and they will never be anything but ignorant," which shows clearly enough that if there is no self-development of the capacity for reflection in the first place, nothing happens. Basically, learning is always autodidactic: one does not *receive* knowledge, but one re-creates it by acquiring it. Suchon herself exemplifies the truth of her thesis. She devoured books and, quite idiosyncratically, nourished her thinking with the Church Fathers. From her various readings, which might otherwise have been merely pious, she draws the idea that the founders of the Christian church, just like the Greek philosophers, were all uncompromising feminists who advocated freedom, knowledge, and authority for women. Everything is grist for her mill. Nonetheless, through the support she finds in these ancient writings, she claims for everyone what was liberating about the epistemic model of her times: not the passive acquisition of ready-made knowledge, and even less a version edited *ad usum delphini* or *ad usum feminae*. She deplores the fact that women are permitted to read only a few little books cobbled together by modern writers, who include only what they see fit: "Since the nourishment offered to them has been predigested by others, it repels them rather than satisfying hunger or stimulating their appetite."[59]

She knows that in acquiring knowledge, women are left to their own devices. Even though she is scandalized that they are denied entry to places of learning, she manages to represent autodidacticism as better than second best. Yet again we must "incite women and girls to wake from their slumbers and pull themselves out of the ignorance in which they spend their lives." Intending to address the subjectivity of her readers, she devotes herself to removing barriers and demonstrating that even the most concrete obstacle is imaginary: certainly women are forbidden entry to institutions of knowledge, there is no public schooling for them, but no matter, for they can create their own, at home. Above all, an ideological obstacle has to be dispelled. In order to keep schools, universities, and academies closed to women, allegations are circulated that also thwart their most private access to thought and books; hence the need to discredit these pretexts as "flimsy and misleading" since they reflect the biases of those who prefer unenlightened women. The solution offered by schools established at home fits with the hierarchy of knowledge she proposes: the highest ranked is knowledge residing in the human spirit, then knowledge locked away in the books that act as its guardians and trustees, and finally the knowledge dispensed by Professors and in the Schools and learned disputes. The real basis of knowledge is in the human spirit: reading and education may add to it and foster intellectual development, but no more than that, and, in any case, reading is more important than attending school. Suchon reads the expression *to cultivate reason* quite literally: reason must come first, followed by the means that allow it to develop fully. And, she insists, the means are there—books, which are more important than schools. Certainly this does not erase the sense of grievance. "If there were schools to teach women, many would be good humanists, eloquent rhetoricians, fine poets and very subtle philosophers" she affirms; the example of one Juliane Morel demonstrates that women fortunate enough to have been educated by their parents have been successful in humanistic studies.[60] But an exhortation, "Women, you have only to will it" runs through the essay, permitting her to formulate a generalization that does not depend on Providence or privilege of birth: every woman can begin to educate herself by creating a school at home in which she thinks and reads. Books always come before university. Women can then form societies for the purpose of thinking, arguing, and debating with one another, and teach one another what they have learned in secret, because exchanging the knowledge they have acquired will bring them new enlightenment.[61] This collaborative work, which marks the end of each woman's Robinson Crusoe-like isolation, corresponds to the exercise of logic and dialectic. Since these necessary and profitable modes of knowledge are forbidden to women, "they know nothing about definition, categorization, description, argumentation, and everything that serves to perfect reason and discourse, and it seems that the aim is to keep them in ignorance by depriving them of everything that might nourish their intelligence."

"Natural law derives its force from within itself alone, and can be observed everywhere in the same way."[62] Relying on this definition, Suchon suggests that freedom "is not subject to time or laws or to the whims of custom." The same applies to knowledge, which is a practice of freedom; the fullest exercise of this freedom, conversely, requires both clarity of ideas and the intelligence needed for deliberation. There is no better way to represent access to knowledge as the exercise of a natural right whose strength comes from within than to make self-instruction central to the process. The very method of the book is consonant with this idea. In the preface to the *Treatise*, among various pronouncements about the Old and the New Testaments (a veritable haystack hiding the needle from the censorship of which she was always mindful) Suchon writes that "Reason, truth, study, and experience" brought her into being as a writer, and not the ideas and concepts of good writers who before her have dealt with freedom, knowledge, and authority or who have written in praise of women. Reason, truth, study, and experience: too bad for those good Church Fathers and for the Greeks to whom she attributes so much! She regrets not having had a predecessor, "no one has yet written on this subject, since men have preferred to enforce women's deprivation rather than discussing it on paper." Since women have not yet taken up their pens to defend their cause, she says she is forced to seek a way of entering "this endless field of women's suffering, tangled with brambles and thorns,"[63] thus laying claim to all existing knowledge and adding to it knowledge of women's suffering. Oppression has to be described and theorized; only then will remedies be devised. This is the new field she wants to explore; it will involve an understanding of good and evil, and of good things and bad things. There is no doubt that in the course of this treatise she speaks liberally about knowing God. This reference to God is necessary for several reasons, among which is this one: she wants to open the totality of knowledge to women, and God is the name of the upper limit of the sphere she proposes or, more precisely, the object of the most sublime knowledge. She achieves her purpose by having Saint Jerome condemn "these semi-erudite men who cannot bear the fact that women may be capable of the most profound knowledge of Christianity."[64] When access to the sublime is blocked, and women are prevented from studying the loftier forms of knowledge, their spirit, "a fire whose flame constantly seeks new materials," is confined at the level of base thoughts and trivia that consume their time because they have no means of occupying themselves with more worthy matters.[65] Thus, instead of condemning coquetry, she proposes a genealogy of it. Knowing has to do with the sublime and the soul's fulfilment: on this point she concurs with van Schurman. Nevertheless, her project is to create a new knowledge, touching on women's lives and the deprivation of liberty, knowledge, and authority that afflicts them. It bears also on the only two institutions that, in her time, were open to women: matrimony and the cloister, with all the miseries they held in store. The "new knowledge" initiated in her work challenges the social order and is like a "knowledge for oneself." The notion itself is not particularly original; the *Discourse on Method* announces "an excessive desire to learn . . . in order to see clearly in my actions. . . ."[66] And, in the expression *sapere sibi* Bacon designates the knowledge necessary for conducting a life. But neither Bacon nor Descartes took the project very far, whereas it occupies the whole of Gabrielle Suchon's work. In order to know *for themselves,* women must appropriate all existing knowledge and construct a new knowledge that can come only from them, since they alone have a cognitive interest in the matter.

The way women are oppressed (Suchon says *oppressées,* suffocated) by deprivations stems less from established discourse than from non-verbalized practices, even though allegations that are no more than frivolous pretexts may contribute to their oppression. The wordlessness of this oppression challenges what men may have said about women. Knowledge of these deprivations has yet to be produced and it is not structurally analogous to existing forms of knowledge—the way Suchon envisages it could form the basis of a serious critique of our social sciences. In fact, before description is possible, there must be a theoretical understanding of the values informing analyses of concrete situations. Such a process requires a moral reflection that will reconfigure the received hierarchy of values, to define good and bad in themselves, and, furthermore, to give a full account of the good and bad character of particular things. Thus, on the subject of freedom she says that instead of offering an initial summary of what can be said about women on the subject, she will first develop "a long discussion of the essence, nature, different varieties, characteristics, and advantages of freedom," which leads her to make some remarkable statements about freedom of place, and the right to travel and choose a place of residence. Her readers were not to adopt her concepts ready-made, but rather to engage thoroughly with theoretical questions connected with the concepts they were about to use, so that they expressed thoughtfully-considered values. Likewise, moral reflection requires quite an original metaphysical analysis of deprivation: deprivation is not a simple absence or negation, but a mutilation with consequences. Considering pure deprivation as a cause with its own effects is by no means a standard approach. Traditionally, the mixture of possession and deprivation is said to be dynamic; a midpoint between science and ignorance can stimulate true knowledge.[67] Suchon sweeps all of that away by using a rustic or horticultural metaphor to present her metaphysic of deprivation as something productive only of negativity: a fallow field is not inert. The deprivation of knowledge means not only the absence of knowledge but also its prohibition and overall repression. Deprivation of freedom means not only the absence of freedom but also its violent removal and the substitution of slavery for it. There is never an absence pure and simple, but violence. In that, she concurs with Marie de Gournay, who said that men strip the feminine sex of its share of the best advantages, the inequality of bodily strength being "the cause of such a theft" and of the fact that women put up with it.[68] We were wondering whether there was a link between educational inequalities and cognitive barriers in ordinary life: by reminding us of prohibitions, these two seventeenth-century philosophers offer the concept that enables us to see a connection. School does not make all its knowledge available to girls, ordinary life dissuades women from understanding the relations between the sexes. In these two cases, deprivation stems from prohibition.

"Deprivation is a field that yields such an abundant crop of woes that its products are infinite; to comment on all the bitter fruits it offers to women would be an endless task."[69] If deprivation produced no effects, the injustice to women would be less. But Suchon so effectively demonstrates the disastrous consequences of the deprivation of freedom, knowledge, and authority and establishes so convincingly that slavery, ignorance, and powerlessness produce an unbearable mode of existence that in a sense she had no need to show that since freedom, knowledge, and authority are good things, it is therefore unjust to deprive women of them. But there is nothing between these two extremes. To have no access to knowledge is to be bound to live in intellectual and moral dependence on someone else, a point she illustrates vividly with respect to religious knowledge: anyone without personal access to texts becomes subject to a spiritual director. Not to be free is to be under someone else's domination. And none of that is without consequence. According to her, absence is defined by the presence of something else; being-without results from an act intended to deprive women and *thus* to impose on them the very opposite of what they should be able to develop themselves.

7. A Knowing Subject in Process

Men know nothing about the oppression they inflict. Suchon's way of thinking clearly dissociates knowledge and power—one *can* without really knowing—and this disjunction gives knowledge the advantage. Suchon draws on Seneca who considered that the opportunity to study should not be denied even to the lowliest of slaves, who "even though he was proscribed from all public office in states and republics, could not be prevented from becoming a great philosopher and a good man." And this champion of autodidacticism advances an argument based on fact: there are examples of people who, without the help of a master, have trained themselves intellectually and become authors. Her observation, which amounts to an incitement to do without schools, also affirms that power is not a condition for knowledge and that those who are destined to govern are not the only ones to seek knowledge. On the contrary, as access to knowledge increases in this world, power decreases. Reading the Bible and the Church Fathers for oneself makes it possible to do without a director of conscience. This is a paradigm of intellectual and moral emancipation, and thus of a general lessening of ambient power. Moreover, ignorance of the range of our sufferings leaves us vulnerable to suffering, just as ignorance of marriage is what allows such an institution to persist: no one with any foreknowledge of married life would have any part of it. Knowing the structures that produce suffering is thus integral to the project of emancipation. The fundamental hope of this enterprise is that even in the depths of misery it might be possible to understand one's own oppression, to know it theoretically and not just empirically and to explore it with the aim of finding "protection against the servility of constraint."[70] Knowledge is not power, but resistance to domination by others, considering that such domination is sustained by the ignorance of the dominated. Men, she says, deprive women of a just freedom and the means to acquire knowledge; they claim exclusive ownership of intellectual life in order more easily to dominate those "whom they want to keep in a state of dependence."[71] Each step forward into the order of knowledge makes it possible to become less dependent. Inspired by the Greek philosophical model of resistance to adversity or the vagaries of fate, Gabrielle Suchon broadens it to include resistance to oppression; such resistance also opens the possibility of new and potentially happier forms of life.

There is a difference between the *Traité de la morale et de la politique* and *Du célibat volontaire*: the first work assumes the existence of a knowing subject who, in the midst of subjection, struggles to find a way out of it. Suchon makes use of biographical material to convey the conviction that underlies her *Traité*: oppression is the lot of all women, including the one who is writing about it; but conversely, and this is what matters, the one who suffers from it can and must reflect upon it. Far from situating herself outside her object of study, she adopts the stance of a knowing subject, which is not at all the complacent point of view found in a *Suave, mari magno*... (by which I mean a description from the safety of dry land of the storms by which others are buffeted).[72] But, in *Du célibat volontaire*, Suchon, who had left the convent after many years and had never married, writes about matrimony and the religious life; she describes sufferings she has never experienced. And she is already experiencing the joys of celibate life, she announces.[73] As might be expected, she defines the object of study in the second, more traditional, treatise as "knowledge of the sufferings of others." In other words, rather than examining her own struggles, she proposes to study those of others. Suchon had advanced a more persuasive argument in her first book, the *Traité*: that it is possible to construct a theory of subjection even from the midst of subjection, and that the oppressed should attempt to understand their oppression. In the *Célibat* she depicts a way of life not yet generally accepted, more attractive than either the cloister or matrimony; this second work is nonetheless the successful culmination of the first. The *Traité* seeks a means of liberation. Its intellectual reward is the ability, at least theoretically, to offer an image of a better form of life: celibacy as a mode of existence that makes it possible to live in freedom, knowledge, and self-governance. Women of the past seem neither to have written laws nor proposed ways of life that break with tradition; thus, to find within oneself the resources to articulate a sociopolitical proposition or introduce a custom is like winning a battle. It is a genuine reclaiming of the freedom to think and exercise authority in the best sense of the term.[74] That is also the purpose of the exercise.

"If the only ill effect of their powerlessness were the fact of not dominating others, women could easily find reasons not to feel sorry for themselves."[75] The authority Suchon evokes is not what present-day political women demand in the name of power, nor does it coincide with the Platonic thesis according to which both women and men are capable of being Guardians of the City State. For her, "the excessive desire to command is always a crime."[76] From that starting point, and although she claims to be inspired by the "divine Plato," it would be unthinkable for her to adopt the model of the *Republic*. For she does not have in mind a dominant elite that would govern public affairs and everyday life with authority: an elite whose only unusual feature would be to include women among its numbers. True, when she underlines the fact that women "are excluded from legislative processes and subject to the harshest laws," she is making a connection between this radical exclusion from politics and subjection to the most rigorous aspects of all forms of governance: laws, regulations, the Gospel, and the canons and decrees of the Church.[77] Hence her emphasis on a few women in positions of authority or "passionate about the public good," and her reference to Plato as divine. Approximations of what she advocates have already existed both in fact and on paper; she can thus demonstrate the arbitrariness of women's exclusion. But the real originality of her thought is elsewhere: she assumes that in everyone there is a potentially "active reason, imprinted in the human heart," a principle of "rationality," in itself a law, and "queen of all mortals."[78] This law is a "legislative consciousness" that enables people to judge the goodness and justice of existing laws and to distinguish those that are absolutely binding from those that are not. Consequently, everyone possesses a capacity for reflection on both ancient and more modern laws. Moreover, she says there is a principle of equity even more constant than human laws, for these laws may err and legislators are fallible.[79] This principle drives the evolution of law and, in the public sphere, no doubt corresponds to the legislative consciousness she finds in every human being. The theory she develops is itself an exercise of this principle of fairness and of her legislative consciousness from her position as a woman and ordinary citizen of the world, if I can venture such a formulation. A major apologia for change and "becoming" emerges from this third part of the *Traité*: she says it is quite normal that laws should "sometimes be changed, moderated and even entirely abolished in order for people to establish more necessary and useful ones." Since this "becoming" must be founded on equity and clear knowledge, it must be explained and argued for rather than developed blindly. Consequently, to participate in bringing about such changes, women must become capable of "making laws and introducing customs," whether on paper as authors of utopias or in a debate that may seem difficult to situate: we can say only that Gabrielle Suchon wants it to be more wide-ranging than ever before.

The *Traité* clearly implies a dispersal of the legislative principle and a re-
duction of existing power rather than a division of political power over the
masses, to be shared among a few men and a few women. All the same, interpretation of this work is not always easy. It is undoubtedly no accident that
the precautions she takes to avoid censorship seem to culminate in political
discussion. Suchon swears she has no intention of encouraging women to
aspire to government, an idea she considers foolish and misguided.[80] Ostensibly she gives multiple examples of heroines and queens only to encourage
her female readers. At the same time, she notes sadly "that there is no kingdom, province, or city, however small, that is governed by women's laws,"
and observes that women "have no other defect that prevents them from
ruling, governing, commanding, and leading except the one that custom,
the laws and the absolute power of men imposes on them."[81] The only way
to reconcile these conflicting remarks is to distinguish between government
and legislation, insofar as laws can be proposed by people who are not necessarily in power. As for government by women, she merely pronounces a
nihil obstat; examples can be found in both pagan and Christian history.
Since Deborah led God's chosen people for forty years, divine will cannot
be said to have excluded women from government; Plato thought women
were capable of governing—clearly, wisdom can find no reason to reject
government by women! But she does not recall this fact in order to propose
access to government as a goal or to encourage her female readers to aspire
to it. Such aspirations would have been unthinkable in that time of hered-
itary monarchies—a woman is to govern only if she is born a princess and
heiress to a throne. It is women's collective access to legislative powers that
interests her, just as it is women's contribution to legislation that she finds
missing from History. Though she knows very well that some women have
exercised political power, she regrets that there is no city, however small,
that has been "governed by *the laws* of women" (my emphasis), and that
one can find no law "in [any] archive or library which bears a single trace
of them, since not one has ever taken it into her head to conceive
and formulate laws to instruct and organize the people."[82] Finally, if we look
closely, we see that her praise for Plato comes from the fact that he did not
want women to be unable to contribute to the public good by establishing
such *ordonnances* [legislation] as particular intelligence suggests to them.
She speaks especially of political and social imagination, about women formulating legal propositions rather than governing or exercising power over
others. She encourages her readers to invent laws, introduce new customs,
repeal or annul old ones, "to propose extraordinary ways of life," outline
novel modes of existence: it is moral and political creativity she wishes for
them, for which they will need "sound enlightened thinking" and a mind
of their own. Given her conception of a legislative consciousness and the

principle of equity that is to govern carefully-considered modifications of the law, it might seem that her philosophical aim is to encourage her readers to develop their legislative consciousness by developing themselves so that they can think independently about the social-political order and make their own contribution to it.

At that time, democracy was little more than an archeological artifact or an idea found in books. Venice and Geneva were but minuscule republican or oligarchic exceptions in a political landscape dominated by crowned heads. Moreover, Suchon notes that if royal birth sometimes gives women a role in the governments of monarchies, this is not the case in aristocratic, oligarchic, and democratic States, since these forms of government have always been established through the conniving of members of the first sex.[83] However, since she advocates a broad range of creative participation in the making of laws and customs, her views would have required the idea of democracy in order for her to locate her aspirations in a describable political regime. Given that her political model was as yet unknown, she could offer only approximations, among them the philosophical debate about the public sphere as she understood it in Plutarch's *The Dinner of the Seven Wise Men*.[84] And perhaps she had read more modern works than she wanted to acknowledge. From the Renaissance to the Enlightenment, numerous essays in political and legal philosophy attempt to do precisely what she is doing: propose new ideas on the functioning of the political community. In 1551, Ralph Robinson said that every day the writings of learned men develop proposals for furthering the public good, which is why he translated More's *Utopia* from Latin into English. Whatever we may think of their views, when Grotius or Pufendorf deal with human rights, their works also amount to a kind of theoretical intervention in debates of the day about law and politics. Closer to our own time, two books on the philosophy of law have recaptured the thinking typical of legal experts: one, by Helena Kennedy, exposes the everyday sexism of British legal practices; the other, by Odile Dhavernas, shows how thoroughly French law is permeated by the power of men. These are forceful interventions because they find the law wanting with respect to its major premise, the principle of equality: we must hope to see more books of this kind.[85] In any case, ever since the Renaissance, for the educated lay person books have been the vehicle for a debate that in itself is certainly not democratic, given how democracy affirms the *power* of the sovereign individual to exercise choice in public decisionmaking. All the same, this debate, which takes place only on the theoretical level, comes close to what we still hope for in democratic debate: Gabrielle Suchon has in mind a public intellectual debate that would include women, that is, a form of enlightened democracy in which laws and customs were debated in order to improve them. The project of volume 3 of the *Traité* is aimed at defending women's inclusion in such a debate, which can be as utopian or as reformist as one wishes, since the perspective is broad enough to encompass what for us would be utopia or reformism. She is a "meliorist," if my neologism is acceptable. *Du célibat volontaire* will put this idea into practice. The customs of her time recognize only two possibilities for women: marriage or the cloister, both of which are forms of oppression. A third possibility is needed: voluntary single life, a fitting way of life for those who might choose it, given, of course, that a vocation for the religious life or for marriage is also conceivable, and that one can try to ensure through a process of legislative reform that these two institutions do not become excessively oppressive. It would be good for a society to have a certain number of unmarried citizens; considered equity could not but approve the creation of such a custom.

8. Coherences

"Let us first consider women *deprived* of their liberty by the tyranny of men [...]"—this is no longer Gabrielle Suchon speaking, but the young Rousseau. Dating possibly from 1735 and from his first visit to Les Charmettes, some of his early drafts are astonishing particularly when one thinks of the status he later attributes to women in the *Letter to d'Alembert* and in *Émile,* for in these early drafts he speaks of iniquitous deprivation rather than difference.[86] Men's injustice has *robbed* women, not only of their freedom, but also of every opportunity to show their greatness of spirit; in the beginning, men *seized* thrones, functions, and positions, "by some natural right that I have never been able to understand and which may well have no other basis than force." Nevertheless, according to Rousseau, women have more major accomplishments to their credit than is commonly believed: history has deigned to remember only a small number of heroines. And Rousseau promises that some other time he will speak of the "women who have played a role in the Republic of Letters" (which he never did). The young Jean-Jacques seems to recognize some of the premises underlying Suchon's position, and he distances himself from the very concept of deprivation of freedom: it is an injustice, based in a right which he cannot understand. Likewise in the second volume of the *Social Contract* he refers to "the right of the strongest" as "inexplicable rubbish." To establish a possible relationship between these drafts and Suchon's *Traité,* two approaches may be taken, one based on the history of ideas and the other in the study of philosophical systems; or the two approaches may be combined. The simple history of ideas prompts us to wonder whether the young Rousseau might have read Suchon and endorsed her ideas. Perhaps, around the age of fifty, he reconsidered his opinions about the status of women and, although he reclaimed the values Suchon had developed for general application, he made them exclusive to men. For in Suchon's writings, rational self-education, personal autonomy, and an emphasis on conscience are good in themselves, for all, and not just as they apply to women. With respect to women, she conceptualizes something which is de jure accessible to all people; her frequent references to the notion of "person" allow her to generalize readily, since the French *personne* is grammatically feminine (though it applies to both men and women) she can move easily from discussing women's emancipation to the idea of emancipation for all. Likewise, the expression "the Holy Trinity" (also grammatically feminine in French) makes it possible for her to refer to the deity in the feminine while encompassing masculine characteristics within it. Nor does she hesitate to use the word "man" generically: when one can make either masculine or feminine words into universal terms of reference, one need no longer be troubled by this all-too-often dubious "neutral" term.

Philosophically speaking, it is troubling to find her writing about values and proposals usually considered typical of the ideas of the Enlightenment and the eighteenth century. It can be argued that when they are first established as values for oppressed women, but subsequently good for everyone, these values lend themselves more readily to a universal application than when they are seen as pertaining only to men and to European men at that—in Rousseau's works, *Caffres* [non-Muslim Africans] and Laplanders are no better off than Sophie.[87] Moreover, if what Suchon criticizes in women's lot and what she envisages for women as for everyone else corresponds to what Rousseau in his early drafts suggests about women (even though later, in *Émile*, he grants it only to men) then we can imagine a historiographical exercise aimed at establishing Suchon as a source of Rousseau's thought, however much he eventually distorted her ideas. Without venturing onto the shaky ground of possible sources, we can take a more philosophical approach. If we think in terms of freedom, individual conscience, moral knowledge, self-education aimed at developing rational capacity, and so on, and if by that we mean a good that may be stolen, lost, preserved, regained, what is more coherent: to see these values as valid for everyone once they have been established with reference to the most oppressed, or to restrict them to those who occupy a more or less dominant position? The problem posed by the restrictions Rousseau introduces into his philosophy is not merely ethicopolitical, rather, these restrictions destroy the internal coherence of his thought because they cannot be deduced, even dialectically, from the general framework.

Because I have seen so many female students read Rousseau with great interest while managing not to notice the sexist or racist restrictions built into his argument, I can suggest that the values outlined in the first books of *Émile* are very attractive to today's women: women genuinely recognize themselves in them. However, Book V, with its presentation of the education of Sophie, sets their teeth on edge, and they wonder why emancipatory values are reserved for men while the very opposite applies to this poor woman; why Rousseau relegates women to the status of sweet-faced ignoramuses, their husbands' disciples; why he asserts that young girls must be restrained from an early age and learn submission to the will of others. They wonder why, with respect to religion, women will be restricted to the rudiments of the catechism, while Émile will be granted an instinctual, god-like conscience—even atheists understand the enormity of this double standard. These questions cannot simply be brushed aside, nor is it possible to find excuses for Rousseau (was this not the prevailing wisdom of his times?) since in his youthful writing and even in *Émile* he demonstrates his awareness of another point of view: "On the other hand, women are always exclaiming that we educate them for nothing but vanity and coquetry, that we keep them amused with trifles that we may be their masters; we are responsible, so they say, for the faults we attribute to them. How silly! What have men to do with the education of girls? What is there to hinder their mothers educating them as they please? There are no colleges for girls; so much the better for them! Would God there were none for the boys. . . ."[88] This diatribe, which reads like a perversion of Suchon, proves in any case that at that time women were crying out (the word itself is a poem) for something other than what he envisages for Sophie. Rather than refute this other discourse, he dismisses it, declaring that neither men in general nor he himself admire(s) women who display the qualities of the *honnête-homme.* And since women's sole destiny is to please men, the subject is closed unless of course some woman sees how good it would be *not* to please men—even though she has a few lovers, some friendships, and at the end of her life a husband who will bitterly mourn her passing.

"[T]he most perfect education, in my opinion, is such . . . as is best calculated . . . to enable the individual to attain such habits of virtue as will render it independent. In fact, it is a farce to call any being virtuous whose virtues do not result from the exercise of its own reason. This was Rousseau's opinion respecting men: I extend it to women."[89] Today, *A Vindication of the Rights of Woman,* published in 1792 by Mary Wollstonecraft, is sometimes criticized for advocating the application of masculine values to women. Postmodern women's studies critical of Wollstonecraft do not feel it necessary to demonstrate that these values are indeed masculine; Rousseau is a man speaking for men, the poor unfortunate Wollstonecraft herself says she is extending to women what he has thought valid only for men. However, the *Vindication* could, on the contrary, mark the return of an idea to its point of origin, a return made more difficult by the imaginary of sexual difference, which, in the meantime, has sanctified the double standard and created the threatening term "masculine woman," to mean anyone who exercises independent judgment or indeed any judgment at all, has a sturdy physique, and is cultured and assertive. Sometimes Wollstonecraft attacks the myth while on other occasions she plays the devil's advocate: "wish with me, that they may every day grow more and more masculine,"[90] she writes, no doubt anxious to demonstrate that she has more serious concerns and that she is supremely indifferent to the epithet. She demolishes the special status reserved for women in Book 5 of *Émile* while reclaiming for women and men alike the ideas developed in the first four books. She maintains that domestic relationships—between a woman and a man, between parents and child—could only benefit from women being treated as adults, from their developing their understanding and acquiring the moral values that come from autonomy and a firm and stable character. This, she says, is the greatest hope. She calls for "a REVOLUTION in female manners"[91] which would precipitate a revolution in men's mores too. Women's liberation will deprive men of their traditional toys, bring an end to their status as overgrown children who take themselves for demigods, and force them to stop encroaching on others' lives. She appeals to "the advantages which might reasonably be expected to result from an improvement in female manners, towards the general transformation of society..." by counting on reasonable men to understand the benefit—including the emotional benefit—both for themselves and for society. She also hopes that the State will see how important all of this is for the improvement of its citizenry and that it will contribute to the project by creating mixed primary schools for children of all social classes. These would be day schools, since the family must not abdicate its own educative function; only the family can provide an education for domestic life. The schools she imagines have an ambitious program, including teaching botany, political science by the Socratic dialectical method, outdoor exercise, astronomy, and so on. The family and the school will share the task of teaching human reproduction and anatomy, a subject she considers particularly important.[92] Today, we would agree wholeheartedly with Wollstonecraft. Not only is this the quintessence of knowledge for oneself and for everyone but it is also, I believe, what authorizes all the others.

On one issue, Wollstonecraft's critique of Rousseau is incisive: "Men, indeed, appear to act in a very unphilosophical manner when they try to secure the good conduct of women by attempting to keep them always in a state of childhood. Rousseau was more consistent when he wished to stop the progress of reason in both sexes, for if men eat of the tree of knowledge, women will come in for a taste; but, from the imperfect cultivation which their understandings now receive, they only attain a knowledge of evil."[93] The allusion to the *Discourse on the Moral Effects of the Arts and Sciences* is harsh: when she reminds us that during at least one period in his life Rousseau launched a polemic against knowledge, she is recalling an anti-intellectualist phase in the evolution of his thought and, by the same token, insinuating (or perhaps this is my own interpretation) that the asexual anti-intellectualism of his 1750 writings (opposing knowledge for both sexes) resurfaces in the portrait of Sophie, this time with the intention of confining women and only women to an infantile state. Indeed, in the first *Discourse* Rousseau argues that women traditionally have had an affinity for the arts and sciences and a significant influence on public taste. Because of this feminization, the rebirth of the arts and sciences (the Renaissance and its legacy) has undermined traditional warlike qualities and the moral traits that incline one to duty and patriotism, not to mention virility, "famed Arouet, how many vigorous and strong beauties have you sacrificed to our false delicacy...."[94] It is essential to exclude an unworthy rabble from admission to the sanctuary of knowledge; only a few men should be permitted to devote themselves to learning, and those few should be made the counsellors of kings. Rousseau's polemic focuses more on political power than on social elitism; it is less a matter of limiting intellectual culture to a high or noble class than of restricting it to politically influential circles. And a footnote pays homage to Plato, the master who defended the idea that teaching women about virtue and greatness of soul helps men become great and virtuous. Surely Rousseau is not referring to the idea of a few women gaining access to philosophy, defended in the *Republic;* in the context of a deliberately crude diatribe against secular knowledge, libraries, and the dreadful art of printing, such a reference would have no meaning. It is more likely a reference to the *Laws* and to women's enrollment in the military, a possibility Rousseau takes up again in the *Letter to d'Alembert.*

9. Divine Plato?

In my commentary on Gabrielle Suchon you will have heard the echo of a present-day political preoccupation, since today certain political movements extol the virtues of an equal division of power between the sexes although in reality it is between a handful of men and a handful of women, as governors or parliamentarians. I have said elsewhere what I think of their arguments.[95] But the obvious criticism is that they do not examine the received concept of "power." According to our contemporaries, power is just power, whether it is exercised by women or men, hence the need to point out that in the seventeenth century a woman philosopher proposed something different. In fact, Suchon deconstructs the notion of power, neatly separating out what relates to the domination of others, which does not interest her at all, and what bears on the development of a capacity to address the issues of collective life, for women and others. Although she refers to Plato as "divine," in this respect she is no Platonist. On the other hand, our own era might be

Platonist without being aware of it, so much so that a meditation on Suchon and Plato together could shed some light on the division of power as it is conceived of today. This is my excuse for leading you on a journey through Plato's philosophy and its destiny, attempting to understand how the link between knowledge and power is made and unmade with respect to women. But why should an excuse be necessary? The *Republic* is studied by senior high school students in France, and in departments of philosophy, law, or political science everywhere. The people who will govern you tomorrow and who will make decisions affecting your life, perhaps without telling you, are at this very moment listening to a lecture presenting the broad outlines of Plato's thought, before moving on to Aristotle, Hobbes, Locke, and John Rawls. Is this not reason enough to be interested in what Plato said, and what he has been made to say or not say?

The *Republic* figures in a variety of curricula, while the treatise written in Semur-en-Auxois by a woman of modest social status assuredly does not; however, we should not think that their respective destinies were so different. Certainly, the *Traité de la morale et de la politique* has slumbered in obscurity; yet, until quite recently, Plato's theory about women's access to philosophy and politics did not fare much better. In hundreds of classrooms and lecture halls Plato's political ideas have been taught without a word about the fact that the *Republic* recognizes women as potential philosophers, able to participate, as Guardians, in governing the City-State. Much more often people gloss over this section as though it were a negligible or invisible detail. A few years ago, however, Julia Annas, a Plato specialist, devoted a chapter in her *Introduction to Plato's Republic* to the question of female philosophers and Guardians.[96] It is to be hoped that her initiative, which focuses on the difficulty of interpreting his argument, will establish a new norm for Platonic studies: no longer will you discuss the *Republic* without wondering how to understand this point. The admission of women to teaching the history of philosophy has had one beneficial effect: it has fostered a reconsideration of oft-reprinted texts that had never been adequately discussed. But if tomorrow the idea of power-sharing between representatives of the two sexes takes effect, Plato's argument risks becoming a commonplace. Summarily, they will claim that Plato's good sense prompted him to imagine the possibility of governance by women. No one will go on to ask whether something in his proposal should be questioned.

Annas's book is not merely a work in the history of philosophy. She carries on a discussion with Plato and expresses her opinion of his text. She admires Plato's contention that "the nature of women does not demand that women have different occupations from men" while regretting that the argument suffers from excessive generalization.[97] She has her own view of what can be said about women and politics, and she can also question Platonic thought while fulfilling her function as a commentator-teacher, which means explaining to students how to understand this aspect of Plato's philosophy. And when she writes that the claims about certain women's access to politics should not be interpreted as "an affirmation of women's rights . . . for Plato's interest is . . . with production of the common good, and a state where all contribute the best they can according to their aptitude," we see the specialist attempting to curb young women's enthusiasm for the opening the *Republic* might represent (but in contrast to what?). She pulls them back from the brink of a potentially serious misinterpretation.[98] Recalling that Plato has no idea whatsoever of the equal worth and dignity of human beings, which for her is fundamental to theories of human rights, she concludes: "He sees women as a huge untapped pool of resources . . . [and their subjection as] an irrational waste of resources."[99] Finally, reproaching him for not having recognized that there might be specific feminine competences and for having opened philosophy and politics to women, but not as they themselves might have wished, Annas concludes that the *Republic* is inadequate from a feminist point of view.

This conclusion has the virtue of encouraging further reflection, rather than assuming that a philosopher would have taken it upon himself to do all our thinking for us. Yet, however stimulating and learned Annas's interpretation may be, I am not sure I can concur with its broad outlines. It is disquieting to see Plato transformed into a nineteenth-century thinker, half-utilitarian, half-liberal, and more radically so than the Victorians who launched utilitarianism and liberalism. For these Victorians do not always take their reasoning to its logical conclusion—they do not say quite so bluntly that the subjection of women amounts to a nonuse of talent, nor do they conclude that it is urgent to liberate the full resources of human capabilities. Later we will discuss John Stuart Mill, who in my opinion does not go that far. How can we then accept the notion that Plato was a more coherent Mill than Mill himself? Moreover, it is implausible to credit Plato with the ideas of those responsible for recruiting today's new scientific researchers, who claim that they want to cast their nets as widely as possible. To me, Plato does not seem to be so preoccupied with broadening the magistrates' field of choice for future Guardians, or to be worried that a gifted person might be passed over, with unfortunate implications for the common good. Rather, he is primarily concerned to eliminate "without pity" those individuals who do not conform exactly to the criteria of selection.[100] While we must bear in mind the question Julia Annas poses to the philosophical community (what is this theory about certain women's access to politics, and what does it mean?), and although no one has a ready answer, we must stress that such a question is not limited to Plato specialists. Even today, it is an intellectual endeavor for citizens—both female and male—to try to understand the meaning of a proposal such as the one made in the *Republic*, if only to understand what preoccupies thinkers of our own time. But how do we go about initiating the debate?

If we are merely trying to account for Plato's having envisaged certain women's access to philosophy and to governing the Ideal City, a few remarks are in order. He had indeed seen women who loved wisdom, that is to say, true philo-sophers (lovers of wisdom). He acknowledges this fact in his comments that a particular woman is naturally gifted for medicine whereas another is not, a particular woman is impetuous whereas another is not, this woman loves wisdom (a *philo-sophe*) while that one despises it (a *miso-sophe*).[101] And since it is our century that interests us, let us look at some modern editions of this passage. In the Pléiade edition, Léon Robin translates "one woman who loves wisdom and another who despises it," indicating in a footnote "Should we have dared to imitate the Greek terms by using *philosophe* and *misosophe*?"[102] He did not dare: he preferred to relegate this sentence's most pertinent implication to a note at the end of the volume. In the Garnier-Flammarion edition, Robert Baccou translates "women who love wisdom and other women who hate it" and is quick to add a footnote citing Aristotle's *Politics*, which "maintains that the virtues of woman are not identical to those of man" . . . we certainly were worried![103] These reactions of the erudite of our own century show something that is often barely perceptible. Undoubtedly, the text one translates is by definition the work of someone else, but if the author is a member of the so-called founding fathers of the discipline, every one of his pronouncements tends to have a near-legislative value for the community of scholars and its functioning. The little sentence about women who were miso- or philo-sophers, recognizing a fact, is disturbing in its implications for those, and they are legion, who treasure the unsullied masculinity of the community of philosophizers. So translators balk at the fatal declaration, and manage to conceal it or to direct their readers' attention toward another "founding father."

Both in Plato's time and in the collective memory of his contemporaries there were several examples of women living in sects that were in point of fact schools of philosophy, on the margins of the larger society, where they lived a life quite different from that of bourgeois Athenian women. To name but a few, there were Eumetis and the female Pythagoreans. One generation after Socrates there would be Hipparchia. Thus, present-day commentaries affirming that "in Plato's time women were confined to the gynaecium" and therefore excluded from philosophy are somewhat misleading: they recall a historical fact, but represent it as being more generally the norm than it was, even in the families of the best citizens.[104] Moreover, there were foreigners, as well as slaves of both sexes; the norm of confinement was clearly meaningless for female slaves. In the *Meno*, Socrates has a young slave boy retrieve the solution to a problem in geometry; by the same token he could have held a dialectical discussion with a Thracian servant girl like the one who, in still more ancient times, cleverly made fun of Thales.[105] Thus if Plato notes in passing, in the *Republic*, that some women, but not all, display a taste for wisdom or philosophy, it is perhaps because he was not completely denying reality as he saw it. But then he limits this possibility to the Ideal City. So there is reason to wonder about the restriction he introduces—the possibility of women's access to philosophy pertains only in the Ideal City. We ordinarily expect philosophers' thoughts to be systems that generate each of their separate elements. Yet with respect to the question at issue, since Plato does not invent a way for women to gain access to philosophy, then what is of his own making—and therefore a likely part of his system—is having situated women's philosophical practice in an imaginary city, removed from real life. Moreover, since he believes that governing is an onerous task that the Ideal City will require of philosophers as a duty, asking why female philosophers would also have to govern the City amounts to being surprised to see that a philosopher has managed to be coherent. This question is not as ironic as it looks: male philosophers are not always coherent when it comes to applying the central ideas of their thought to women's social and intellectual situation. But if it is a question of an onerous task . . .

At this stage we could either say that the problem has been disposed of, or play with it to our hearts' content. Thus I, for one, would be tempted to discuss the idea of an epicene access to philosophy and politics in light of the Myth of Er. This myth, which occurs at the very end of the *Republic*, focuses on metempsychosis and the choices made by certain souls, between their previous life and the next one, about the circumstances of their next incarnation. The soul is not determined by the body it has had or will have, and the choice of sex one will have is shown to be a real choice: in the future life one will not automatically be reincarnated in the same sex, even if the events of the existence just lived weigh heavily in the choice of the next one, and thus possibly in the sex chosen or in the place one will occupy in the human/animal dichotomy.[106] Moreover, according to this myth, a philosophical soul knows how to choose a life that will be good in that it will make the soul more just; it will choose without being dazzled by riches, tyrannical power, honors, and other unworthy temptations of that nature. Similarly, Socrates's *Apology* concludes that there is nothing worse than preferring elevated social status to virtue, or believing oneself to be something when one is nothing. Hence, philosophical souls avoid destinies in which they would bring about unspeakable evils or suffer great ones in their turn, and they choose a middle way, free of excesses of any kind. This is all very well, but then why not choose a woman's life just as readily as a man's,

I ask you? The Myth of Er does not rule out the idea that a philosophical soul might choose a woman's destiny, and thus might already have chosen it, on condition of course that at least some women's destinies are exempt from too great sufferings, or are moderately happy. In the course of living out destinies of this sort a soul can cultivate its own justice. It is I who am thinking or dreaming with Plato here and articulating an idea formed in contact with his text by the young woman I once was. I thought that from a Platonic point of view it was a mistake to wonder whether a particular soul, already concretely linked to a particular destiny, could choose for or against philosophy, for the question of choice really poses itself the other way around. It is the degree of wisdom already attained that determines whether one chooses one's life judiciously or not, thus whether one chooses one destiny rather than another. Therefore, instead of wondering why women could gain access to philosophy or politics in the Ideal City, it makes better sense to wonder whether a philosophical soul, knowing in advance that a good life defines itself by the opportunities it offers for practicing justice, is likely to choose a woman's destiny or not—not necessarily the destiny of just any woman at all, but this or that particular destiny. Can a woman's life, in certain circumstances, be completely eligible for wisdom?

Such a question obviously falls outside the limits of Platonic studies; and the first responsibility of whoever formulates it is to assume the possibility of a response that engages her. If I imagine myself faced with this choice, I can reply in the affirmative and at the same time account for the broad outlines of the female destiny I have tried to live, taking things as they come and making the best of it. Like thousands of others, and with them, I have devoted a vast proportion of my leisure to "introducing a custom": access to contraception for all women and, when necessary, to safe abortion, so that every woman, myself included, could decide about her sexuality and liberate it from the tie that subjected it to procreation. How many hours spent thinking, either alone or with women of every imaginable social situation, about the stakes involved in what we now call reproductive rights! How many meetings and demonstrations (posters, tracts, etc.) were necessary to define a strategy for forcing government to confirm in law what our legislative conscience saw as a moral right for women, thus to create a greater measure of justice, rationality, and freedom for oneself and for other women. For experience shows that the more freely available abortion is, and the better the human conditions in which it is practiced, the fewer abortions there are.[107] In the terms of the Myth of Er, being born a woman in the middle of the twentieth century, in a country that already guaranteed civil rights and schooling (marvellously free, nonsectarian, and compulsory) while remaining singularly slow to recognize some fundamental freedoms, was a situation one can assess retrospectively, applaud, and understand as a possible choice. Moreover, it is always possible to choose to evaluate the potential of a given situation to foster the creative exercise of citizenship rather than to dwell on its drawbacks, discriminations, or risks. Long after French women's struggle for reproductive rights, many Algerian women dared to denounce both the family law to which they were subjected, and theocratic attempts to deny them the right to vote. Some came to Geneva to debate with my students: "Do not feel sorry for us or see us as victims: we have set out to win our citizenship, and that is all there is to it," said one of them, who had already received death threats.

When a basic level of freedom is guaranteed (though some heroic individuals can do without it), and if it is also possible for those still oppressed to conceive of solutions even with the mediocre means of action at their disposal, then the situation is not so bad, when practicing true citizenship is the objective. One might even say the situation is excellent if, as Gabrielle Suchon would have it, thinking about an oppressive situation from the very midst of it enables one to see its structures and propose improvements that those of the first sex would never imagine. Rejoicing in one's own situation as a woman today presupposes that, with respect to social and political issues, our circumstances might offer the cognitive advantage of enabling us to see injustices more clearly because we experience them and take them seriously. This cognitive advantage differs significantly from a talent for trigonometry, even if it might also be useful for many other purposes to have developed one's intellect by moving from geometry to trigonometry. Such a point of view also acknowledges our gratitude toward the thousands of women who in past centuries have thought about the question of equality or fought for access to the civil rights and education you and I have had from birth, thanks to them. Naturally, the version of history you have been taught in school will have passed over the epic of women's suffrage and the countless efforts to institute education for women. You will look endlessly and in vain for a trace of these energetic ancestors who have given you the means to be what you are. My generation continued the work of these early feminists and devoted a considerable portion of its leisure time to constructing the fundamental freedom represented in the mastery of our own reproductive lives, whereas others devoted their intellectual life to demonstrating the relevance of the thought of Simone de Beauvoir, Gabrielle Suchon and others. However, our efforts are already being severed from their effects. A book published last week attributes women's liberation from the "eternal servitude of procreation" and the transformation of "the female condition" to "the logic of postmodern societies."[108] As if it had all happened without us! And we are told that "woman (*sic*) is always being redefined," no doubt because being *defined* by others as this or that exposes women as the malleable creatures they are. To all of that the rejoinder must be that, regardless of its difficulties, a woman's life such as mine has been, until now, is cause for rejoicing because I have been able to think, act, know, and even attempt to analyze those who see us as inert beings.

Any bearded commentator of the classics who heartily thanks Providence that he was born a man, and who is proud to have his masculinity confirmed by his status as a philosopher, will shudder with horror at my interpretation of the Myth of Er. What? A wise soul would choose the destiny of a Pythagorean woman, an Aspasia, a Diotima, a Gabrielle Suchon, or a Mary Wollstonecraft, rather than that of a Thersites or some tyrant of Syracuse? Of course, but enough of this. I am not really explicating Plato here, but putting an ethical and philosophical question to you. Imagine yourself faced with this choice: what do you do? No doubt numerous male colleagues would be simply incapable of imagining how a reasonable soul could choose a woman's existence, and others equally numerous would prefer the everyday power conferred on them by their masculine status to the life of any woman philosopher. They see their intellectual capacity as a kind of extension of the power and prestige of the social status of maleness they have enjoyed from childhood. When their respective mothers would gladly have brushed their teeth for them every morning to save them five minutes and win them an extra quarter-point in the next mathematics test, they knew they owed it to the fact that they were boys. These men would immediately fail any examination conducted according to some Socratic principles that I am not inventing, or at least not entirely inventing.[109] Others, both women and men, would be astute enough to note that this choice is not offered in Plato's text; it is I who am slipping it in because I maintain that when someone is interested in working for justice, it can be advantageous to be born a woman, at least at certain times in history. More specifically, we must recognize that if such a choice were presented in Plato's texts, it would offer at most the life of Pythagoras's wife or Cléobulus's daughter, or of a woman philosopher in the Ideal City; at best, that of a divinely inspired Diotima who reveals to Socrates what love is all about but certainly not that of an Athenian Gabrielle Suchon or a Mary Wollstonecraft or a classical Harriet Taylor. These women invented themselves all on their own. Their destinies cannot be included in the myth, for what is completely lacking in the Platonic text is the idea of an ordinary real live woman who, with the cognitive capabilities of an ordinary human being, seeks philosophy, justice, and the Good, following the example of a Socrates or a Glaucon who struggles to find a shred of truth through the shadows. An ordinary woman, perhaps struggling with them sometimes, but not always like them or in agreement with them: such a character is not to be found in Plato's text. The participants in the conversations in the *Republic* who debate the constitution of the City, among other things, are exclusively male. It is almost impossible to imagine an older sister of Hipparchia, along with a few other women, debating with the men assembled at Polemarchus's house in Piraeus. Yet, how many dozens of interlocutors are included in the Platonic dialogues? And not a single woman? Surely we are not going to leave it there.

Recently, one remark in the *Apology of Socrates* has drawn more attention than it had received for centuries—it just goes to show you that the new mixing of the sexes in the philosophical community has made some small intellectual difference![110] Even today it may still help to explain the absence of women in the dialogues. At the end of the *Apology,* Socrates says that he is not sorry to die because in the Underworld he will finally be able to carry on discussions with the famous dead people he had always wanted to meet. Thus he will know who among them is really wise, and who only imagines he is. He can already imagine engaging "numberless others, men and women too" in the dialectic, and for him that would be an "infinite delight."[111] Thousands of men and women whom one could mention by name: did Socrates actually have in mind specific women who, in their lifetime, had had a name and about whom we could legitimately wonder whether they were wise? The received interpretation of this passage underscores the fact that in his lifetime he could not discuss philosophy in the street with women (understood to mean only the perfectly respectable spouses of citizens) since they were not allowed to be in public places or to participate in the banquets at which justice and love were debated. Now, Socratic philosophy takes place in the open air, in the agora, in public places, in the marketplace, and while people are strolling or feasting, the banquet being an element of public life. We should consider, then, that for Socrates the total absence of women in the dialectical debates he conducted himself could be attributed to a contingent social factor that he thought insurmountable in the real Athenian life of his time, but not in the Underworld. That is the substance of Gregory Vlastos's interpretation. However ingenious this interpretation may be, we must regard it as no more than a plausible, reasonable gloss; it is no more evident in the text than my brilliant idea which takes literally the principles guiding the wise choice of a way of life and concludes that there is something to be said for the idea that a philosophical soul might choose a woman's destiny, and therefore might already have chosen it. To tell the truth, the remark in the *Apology* might even tend to show that a wise soul may already have chosen a woman's life in the past and that the question extrapolated from the Myth of Er is not as crazy as it seems. However, in this case, the philosophical nature of this wise soul was not awakened during its lifetime; no one badgered it with questions, and we still have the problem of understanding why. Vlastos's reading rescues Socrates and exonerates him: he was not personally responsible for excluding women from his dialogues. However, if we do not try to acquit or justify the founding father of the discipline we claim to practice, we might just as well interpret the *location* of the philosophical dialogue, in the agora or banquets attended by one sex only, as a ruse based on more or less real social factors and deliberately designed to exclude women—or more precisely, women born into free families—from the domain of philosophy.[112]

There is a certain similarity between the approaches of Annas and Vlastos: they assume that in order to understand what Plato says, one must either go outside the text or explain what the text takes for granted, such as the pool of resources or the *gynaeceum*. What an extraordinary destiny for a work that is twenty-five centuries old suddenly to be exposed as incapable of saying what it means! For my part, and experimentally, I would like to give it a structural reading mixed with a pinch of suspicion, and to hypothesize that the author is willing to imagine that female persons could be capable of thought and the contemplation of truth, but only when it would be of no consequence: as for example on the model of divine inspiration, in the case of Diotima; in the Underworld, when everyone is dead and when it is only a matter of satisfying Socrates's curiosity; probably on Mount Olympus too, because according to *Phaedrus,* the gods throw themselves into the realm of Ideas which are food for the soul and the object of true science, all, except Hestia, "who stays at home alone."[113] If one allows that there were twelve important divinities of the Greek pantheon, gods and goddesses, it will be obvious that the cortege described in the *Phaedrus* is divided into eleven cohorts, twelve minus Hestia, the goddess of the hearth.[114] The other goddesses are included in the journey toward truth, or at least Hera is. But these are goddesses, not women like you and me, entangled as we are in the human condition and, it would seem, in forgetfulness of truth—even though at least some of us are eager, either by means of dialectic or reflective experience, to find a clear idea of justice and harmony that might include us. If we accept the following principle of interpretation—Plato imagines that women will have access to philosophy whenever such access is of no consequence—then we can return to a closer reading of Book V of the *Republic.* In the Ideal City, some women will be initiated into the practice of dialectic, but in this imaginary place nothing is of any further consequence for the basic organization of communal life. The broad outlines of this City—for example, that there will be three classes, not four, two, or none—have been decided by the men who were debating at Polemarchus's house in Piraeus. The dialogue depicts them designing the Ideal City together, well before male and female Guardians arrive on the fictive scene that ordinary men are creating; moreover, they design "the men's play" *first* and then, once it is well established, the women's play. The Guardians, male or female, will no longer have to invent the City or make major decisions. In modern terms, they will be administrators rather than politicians who would have to think and rethink the organization of communal life, and perhaps even reflect about what is at stake. Their function is to maintain a ready-made machinery of state rather than to make use of their own imagination or reflective capacities.

Moreover, they will receive the power to control the other classes, as "watchdogs," guardians of the flock, and thus to govern according to an authoritarian model that it is not their place to question. To show that Plato is no defender of equality in principle between women and men, Annas says, "he sneers at the prospect of equality between the sexes in any actual society as corrupting the natural hierarchy."[115] The text she is referring to does not say exactly that: criticizing the democratic State in which everyone is drunk on freedom, Plato particularly reviles "the extent of the legal equality and liberty [in the relationship between men and women]."[116] It is equal freedom, not equality in itself he is opposing here, and along with it the idea, which is nonetheless superb, of reciprocity in recognizing the freedom of the other. In calling all democracy "drunkenness" (particularly insofar as such a regime would encourage equal freedom and reciprocal recognition between the sexes) Plato performs an act of discursive violence. On the other hand, he has nothing against the equality of the sexes as long as it is a matter of envisaging an equal authoritarianism of male and female Guardians with respect to the flock they watch over together, following the structures prescribed by the founders of the City. The Platonic and Suchonian models are fundamentally opposed: Suchon locates the center of gravity on the side of the governed, not with a ruling elite, and thus she combines freedom, knowledge, and self-governance in a world that is in the process of becoming. Personal freedom is not a Platonic value; only for a ruling class are politics and knowledge united, and the major concern is that processes of becoming will cause the founders' model to deteriorate.

In this case, the underlying thought within Platonism might be as follows: provided that an agent's exercise of power is expected to occur at the end of an apprenticeship in knowledge and philosophy, it is possible to open the program to women and men alike. On the other hand, he does not envisage the possibility of integrating women into a freely conducted intellectual debate whose purpose is not to dominate. Stop women from thinking, unless you are also prepared to endow them with the power delegated by the founding fathers rather than with the freedom to challenge inherited models as they please or to establish a connection with the governed. In departments of political science or philosophy, wherever future governing elites are conditioned to believe that their primary task will be to maintain the social order and ensure that there is as little change as possible, few find fault with the basic schema of the *Republic,* which presupposes a hierarchy between a constitutive moment—the constitution of the Ideal City established with its main legislative activities at Piraeus—and a second moment when the City thus constituted is put into operation, but with the hope it will remain as it is. This is just how a number of countries today conceive of their political existence: in the past there was a founding or constitutive event followed by legislation or government; it is still possible to introduce prudent amendments or modest revisions to the constitution but only if a fundamental stability is scrupulously preserved. Our contemporaries will not find it strange if, according to Plato, the constitutive moment was purely masculine while day-to-day functioning admitted some women: that too is a present-day reality.

In the *Republic* the Guardians will even be required to lie to those they govern and to rule by means of fables, christened "noble lies," and supplied to them ready-made.[117] In effect, they will take over from the sorcerers who throw shadows onto the depths of the cave from which the future philosopher has been torn away. What would happen if a philosopher (male or female) in the Ideal City began to argue that it is wrong to lie, that one can govern by means other than lies fabricated to serve the ends of authoritarian conservatism, or that a classless society would be preferable? For the theme of the "noble lie" makes its appearance in the *Republic* when the discussants invoke the myth of the three metals to justify the division of the City into classes. Since no Guardian (male or female) is supposed to have the freedom to question the founding doctrines of the City, this can mean only one thing: that the philosophical dialectic into which they have been initiated in the course of their education is not entirely free, nor is it philosophy as one would like to practice it.[118] Power over others, with the aim of maintaining a social order created for all time, could in fact be the absolute antithesis of philosophy and not its ultimate vocation. In this case, women never really gain access to philosophy in Plato's theater. But, you will say to me, if this is the situation of the female Guardians, the same must be true of the male Guardians: logically, reflecting on the women's situation should lead to speculating about that of the men. Indeed it should, and it will provide an opportunity to clarify a question of method. It is always supposed that, in a society or system of thought, the people in a position of dominance represent the norm, whereas those who are excluded or dominated are regarded as deviations from the norm or as an isolated, specific, or exceptional case. It is a commonplace for the masculine condition to be considered the political-juridical norm—for it to require no explanation—while women are the exception. Similarly, when historians (female or male) study ancient cities, they tend to take the situation of free families as the norm, any deviation with respect to slaves being precisely that, an exception to be accounted for. To Hannah Arendt we owe a splendid reassessment of this way of thinking. She recalls that in Antiquity slaves were required to testify under torture, a practice her colleagues explain with reference to a belief they attribute to the Ancients: "a slave is unable to tell the truth except on the rack."[119] This is false, Arendt says. The Ancients believed that no one is capable of inventing a lie under torture, and therefore no one is sure to be telling the truth except under such duress. But since torture destroys freedom, it was impossible to inflict it on free citizens, thus only the slaves, and so on. In other words (but this is my gloss) what requires explanation is not the treatment inflicted on slaves since that fits in with a general system of beliefs, but rather the special treatment accorded to free men. This is a Copernican revolution to be constantly borne in mind, at least as a view that contests our assumptions about dualistic situations. It is possible that, in certain cases, what is made explicit with respect to women corresponds to an ordinary human condition, to a standard, and even to something universal, whereas an exceptional dispensation is provided for men in general or for just a few of them.

Annas regrets that, even as the *Republic* admits women into the political sphere, it fails to recognize that there are specifically feminine competences. We must understand her critique in light of what we have just said (when it is a matter of unusual features, it is always in women that a specificity is sought) and in the context of a currently popular belief, namely, the theme of sexual differences, which is in decline in the professional world and maintains itself in academia thanks to women's studies. It has also been rejuvenated in discourse about governance. Just when young women are feeling freer in their life choices than we were not so very long ago (your little female cousin wanted to be a truck driver rather than a hairdresser, the girl next door a pilot rather than a psychological counsellor, both delight in the novelty of their identity or laugh at traditional assumptions about their abilities), the division of power between the sexes is now argued on the basis of natural differences between women and men and thus, so they say, between a woman in politics and a man in politics.[120] There is no proof to support this belief, which is often expressed only with reference to the future, and is therefore not subject to factual verification. Women have exercised political power in recent or ancient history, but the prevailing discourse makes it sound as if the emergence of stateswomen were yet to occur. References to queens merely serve as proof of women's ability to handle power. If you evoke Elizabeth Tudor, Maria Theresa of Austria, Victoria, Margaret Thatcher, Benazir Bhutto, or Edith Cresson, declaring that there is little if any visible difference in their manner of governing, the answer is at hand: they were not woman enough, or they were male-identified. What I do consider serious is that no stateswoman has so far given any indication that she understands the real situation of women who are governed any better than her masculine counterparts do. Members of various grassroots organizations continue to deal as best they can with the knowledge of these difficult situations that politicians of both sexes prefer to ignore—as if these politicians' responsibilities were defined by a refusal to know what is not working or to understand progressive ideas.

I would be the first to rejoice if tomorrow a few stateswomen proved me wrong. At any rate, as long as the idea of gender-specific political capabilities has not been demonstrated in fact, there is no reason to reproach Plato for not having thought of it. All the more so as such a critique prevents us from taking account of a more important feature of Plato's views: in the Guardian class there is common possession of property, women, and children, since the male Guardians have common ownership of everyone and everything. Annas says that women's access to political functions is not the result of this thesis, which would have been perfectly possible without elevating women to the rank of Guardian. Agreed, but what about the reverse? A comparison between the *Republic* and the *Laws* shows at the very least that the two points are not unrelated. The *Republic* allows a few women access to intellectual life and the political sphere and for them it eliminates marriage, which is a form of subjugation of one person by another. In the *Laws,* everyone marries, but women's access to study and governing disappears. An education comprising gymnastics, dance, and music is given to children of both sexes; men are required to study mathematics and astronomy, advanced study of these disciplines being kept only for a "select few" of them, who are members of the nocturnal legislative Council.[121] Comparison of the two texts leads to the conclusion that, for Plato, marriage makes access to knowledge and politics either impossible or undesirable for *all* women. Not because married women are confined within the *gynaeceum* (there is no question of that in the *Laws*) but because for a woman, marriage to a man implies a form of moral submission. In fact, Plato credits Homer with having accurately described the family in the state of nature, still to be found among both Greeks and non-Greeks, when, speaking of the Cyclops, the poet says that "each man in his cave utters the law to his wives and his children."[122] Marriage is the appropriation of a woman by a man who rules over her, a fact that denotes the absence of real law and an exclusively executive power. On the other hand, the sexual commonality that the Guardians practice amounts to suppressing personal marriage, and it would be essential for the women of this class to receive an intellectual education and political responsibilities. But this commonality is nonetheless a form of marriage, or in any case an appropriation of all the female Guardians and children by the male Guardians as a group. If they possess women and children in common, would I have been mocking you just now when I asked what would happen in the Ideal City if the free practice of dialectic were to lead a philosopher—male or female—to think that it is time to abolish the class structure, and stop lying? Because the serious question the *Republic* leaves unanswered is this: what would happen if some of the female philosopher-apprentices rejected their mass appropriation by men, together with the form of marriage maintained for members of the other classes? I am not letting my imagination run away with me, or dreaming that this ideal city has become a reality with some women there inciting all women to revolt! I am merely expressing astonishment that no one has so far raised this question. Must we reproach Plato for not having thought about gender-specific political capabilities or for having advocated an appropriation of women as a group by men as a group? And would it not be instructive for schools of philosophy and political science to teach that according to him, marriage must be abolished in order to create even a hint of intellectual, and therefore of political, equality? *"Discuss with reference to Gabrielle Suchon: did Suchon propose a fully-developed theory, while for Plato, the idea was merely an intuition?"* And perhaps schools could teach that even that abolition would not be enough if mass appropriation were to take its place? A related question: what exactly are we talking about in discussing women's access to knowledge or political office? If we are talking about marriage, if intellectual life renders a woman unfit for matrimonial annexation, then we must analyse the bluestocking motif, and the imagery suggesting that an intellectual woman will lose her sex appeal, as projections onto all women of imperatives that in fact pertain only to wives and derive from the institution of marriage and not from some gender difference or other.

In the *Laws* the Guardians are men. The most important public office is that of director of education, for girls and boys; the person in charge must be at least fifty years old and the father of legitimate children. Everything that seemed progressive in the *Republic* disappears in the *Laws*. Of course, that matters little to you: you are not in a polling booth about to vote for or against the adoption of Platonism in the constitution. All the same, it is almost too good an opportunity to see which specific functions the author believes can be entrusted to women, a point that is certainly not mentioned in the *Republic,* although it is in the *Laws*. The husband and wife must get it into their heads that their duty is to produce fine children for the City, reproduction being an affair of the State.[123] Moreover, the interlocutors in the dialogue believe it is a mistake to enact political laws only for public matters. They criticize those who think it unnecessary to subject everything to a rule or to impose constraints on private behavior; they also criticize lawmakers who have enacted no laws governing the "most secretive and intriguing" female sex, which might as well be "abandoned to its disorderly condition through the perverse compliance of the lawmaker."[124] They proclaim that it is in the interest of the State to legislate *also* in the so-called private sphere. Thus there appears a group of female Inspectors, assistants who under the aegis of Eileithyia, goddess of childbirth, oversee young couples to verify that they are not using their sexuality for purposes foreign to the aims of the State.[125] They will "enter the houses of young people, and, partly by threats, partly by admonition, stop them from their sin and folly."[126] These Inspectors can also initiate a hearing to pronounce a divorce or refer the whole matter to the Guardians of the laws. So Plato did think about delegating to women certain functions that the reference to Eileithyia invites us to compare to those of the midwives in the *Theaetetus*. Too old to give birth themselves, they assist parturients; they can also perform abortions, when they think it necessary.[127] It is they who decide, not the woman involved. The functions of control and assistance are thus superimposed in this profession.

The figure of the matron as the official responsible for the reign of sexual order in society is not, strictly speaking, Plato's invention. One can sense that, in more recent times as well, a particular function is socially allocated to women described as "older." Saint Paul also describes a role to be assigned to the *presbitera*, the old woman. He enjoins women in general to be submissive to their husbands, chaste, and silent in assemblies "for it is not permitted unto them to speak," even if it were to ask a question; if a woman has a question she must pose it in private, to her husband.[128] But older women are allowed speech, which the Apostle carefully regulates: they must not be slanderers, but speak of what is good, so that they can teach young women good conduct and tell them to be temperate, to love their husbands and children, to be prudent, chaste, and take care of their house, and to be compliant and submissive to their husbands.[129] Thus women are forbidden to speak except when, having reached a greater age, they instruct younger women in their duty as it is ordained by the patriarchal order. To be able to generalize and give a name to what must be cast off, I propose the term *nomophatic* to designate a code that determines who has the right to speak, to whom, where, and on which topics, to say what and in what tone. The Pauline *nomophatic* quite closely resembles the one that codifies and is codified by the letters and fragments long attributed to the female Pythagoreans: Theano, Perictyone, Phyntis, Melissa, and Myia. A letter said to be written by Theano exhorts young married women to seek instruction from older women. Almost without exception, these texts bear on questions of conjugal and domestic morality and they sound like conservative directives addressed to young women: "You have beautiful arms," "Yes, but they belong only to my husband" would be one of Theano's replies. The fragment extends the directive to include speech: a restrained woman does not let everyone hear her voice. This literature evokes the death penalty that awaits the adulterous woman, although a good wife must valiantly put up with her husband's infidelity. It details the care to be given children and the respect to parents, criticizes luxury and coquetry, and continues in like vein.

The ancient and modern destiny of these texts is interesting. Clement of Alexandria, Stobeus, Henri Estienne, and Gilles Ménage seem to have believed that they really emanated from women who were close to Pythagoras.[130] It is true that Iamblichus's* catalogue says that seventeen women were Pythagoras's disciples. He names sixteen, a certain Theano among them. But then came Zeller, who in the middle of the nineteenth century classified these texts as Neopythagorean (thus later than the first century B.C.E.) and pseudonymous, thus implying that it was unthinkable that families in late Antiquity would have named their daughters after Pythagoras's female companion or after Perictyone, Plato's mother. In giving this subsection the title *Die Neupythagorische Schule, ihre Männer und Schriften,* "the Neo-Pythagorean School, Its Men and Its Writings" this mischief-maker insinuates that by excluding these texts, one finds oneself happily among men.[131] Considering their contents, I do not miss them at all, and I do note that Zeller's opinion does not refute what Iamblichus wrote, and thus cannot deny the existence of at least seventeen women in the School of Pythagoras: if they have nothing to do with the moralizing sermons attributed to them, surely this is cause for rejoicing? But this is not everyone's point of view. In 1932 a certain Mario Meunier published a French edition of these texts. Summoning all the resources of rhetoric to discredit Zeller's critique without opposing it overtly, he cites others who, like him, regret the lost authenticity of these fragments.[132] His oblique restoration of their status as authentic texts rests on circular reasoning: he thinks they are consistent with the most ancient traditions articulated by the first Pythagoreans on the same subject (woman); they must have been inspired by the teachings of the master and are therefore sufficient to give an idea of the Pythagorean theoretical and practical conception of woman. Finally, they are proof of Pythagoras's thinking about woman, that Meunier imagines by extrapolating from the general line of thought he finds in the fragments. What the supposedly female authors say surely reflects the idea of woman that could be attributed to Pythagoras, namely, that her subordination is required by divine order. And then he throws caution to the winds to speak directly of these texts: "this fragment of the book *On wisdom* that Perictyones wrote . . . " and so much for Zeller. The circularity of the reasoning is sustained by the commentator's agreement with a content and a formal principle: the *nomophatic* of these texts is certainly good, these women surely were their master's voice, and were thus real women.

Like Saint Paul and some others, Meunier raises a niggling question that we can reconstruct as follows: supposing we let women speak, just what should they talk about, and what should they say? From a logical point

---

*Iamblicus of Chalcis (c.250–c.330) appended a list, or catalogue, of all known Pythagorean thinkers to his *De Vita Pythagorae* (*The Life of Pythagoras* or *The Pythagorean Life*).

of view, at any rate, such an example shows the compatability between a problematic of difference, on the one hand, and conformity on the other. Those (women) who are required to look after their house and watch over their virtue are certainly different, and they show as much by conforming to what a master is alleged to have thought about a difference that amounts to subordination. Into the requirement of difference slips that of aligning oneself with the will of the master. From then on, one can just as readily imagine that these texts were written by men. I would make precisely this argument if the content of these texts were not so close to the discourse of Luce Irigaray. She exists, I have met her, and there are good reasons for believing that she wrote *Je, tu, nous: vers une culture de la différence*. This book is full of nostalgia for Hestia, symbol of "woman's fidelity to her identity,"[133] and the author muses a lot about Saints Anne and Mary; it suggests legislating the right to virginity and maternity, since they are components of feminine identity. The idea of equality between the sexes provokes a sarcastic "according to whose yardstick?" as though equal meant identical with, an idea that is conceptually false.[134] Everywhere you find references to nature and the mother, right down to the slogan: "rediscover respect for the mother and for nature." In fact, in her writing we find the three K's of Nazism, cooking with Hestia (*Küche*), children (*Kinder*) with the right to motherhood, and the church (*Kirche*) with leaden references to edifying (female) deities. The text thus is not very different from what the worst of men, and conservative women with them, have wanted for women, for National Socialism assigned the supervision of its girls to its female chieftains. *Speculum* includes a critique of Freud that resulted in the author's excommunication from the Lacanian school and the loss of her teaching position at Vincennes. Adopted then by the Heideggerian-Derridean-Nietzscheans, Luce Irigaray no longer runs the risk of critically examining the ideas of the men whose fellow-traveller she has become. But what has still to be explained is this: whereas in the 1970s only a few men championed her discourse, while female philosophy students were appalled by this postmodern submersion in the fonts of Saint-Sulpice,[*] nowadays some women seem to find value in what she says, whereas others, judging all of this absurd and historically inaccurate, are the first to contest the right of Irigaray's followers to speak for their generation. This divide seems to me to correspond to two possible outcomes of education. Those who feel strong and hope to find employment, a place in the professional world, and a satisfactory level of material independence prefer Simone de Beauvoir; those who are less sure probably need someone to talk to them in positive terms about a domestic destiny that might perhaps be theirs. For them, reading

---

[*] Saint-Sulpice is a church in Paris, begun in 1646 and completed in 1745. The allusion here is to excesses of religious piety.

Luce Irigaray would count as psychological preparation for what the current employment crisis will make of them. In any case, if one woman or a few take on this sort of task, men can certainly leave it to them.

What level of education would be required to perform the functions of a female inspector in the *Laws,* or those that Saint Paul entrusts to his *presbitera?* None, no more than to be enrolled in the Islamic women's brigades of today: it is a matter only of knowing and communicating the directives that must be followed. But the *Laws* proposes a concept of ignorance that has nothing to do with not knowing how to read or count. This ignorance is described, first of all, as being within the soul: it manifests itself when one detests something even while judging it to be good, or loves what one considers bad; in other words, when the lower part of the soul does not follow the higher part.[135] The line of reasoning then exploits the analogy between the State and the soul: such crass ignorance manifests itself when the masses do not obey the magistrates, the laws, or whatever is put in place to regulate society. Even an accomplished reasoner who manifests this sort of ignorance or unreason must be called ignorant. This description is given in the *Laws,* a dialogue that sketches a city established on a theory of belief: provided that one does not contrast pleasure and justice in presenting them, it is possible to persuade a person to lead a life of justice. Children can be made to believe everything, to the extent that a legislator has only to discover which belief is most useful to the State and instill it forthwith into the masses.[136] Thus what is described as ignorance is, in reality, the possible conflict with beliefs concocted by those at the top or an affective detachment from them. Values are fables to which one is supposed to give one's heart, and an astute legislator will give them an element of pleasure. If the city itself gives up knowledge in favor of belief, if the concept of knowledge dissolves into nothing but the interiorizing of beliefs, both women and men are deprived of an intellectual life, but women all the more so for just one reason, namely they are more subjected than men.

To return one last time to the question of *cast-offs* (*déshérences*): one passage in the *Republic* describes the Guardians "in the full sense of the word" and their function, which is to keep watch over the enemies without and friends within so that the friends will not wish to harm the City and the enemies will not be able to do so.[137] Thanks to a notable slip, Robin translates this passage to say that they are Guardians "as much against the enemies without as against the enemies within": he has understood that these "friends within," the governed classes, are friends only as long as they are under control. These classes correspond to the middle and lower parts of the soul, which are, respectively, a lion and a many-sided monster *within us.*[138] When they develop and can no longer be controlled, they indeed become the enemy within. Thus when Hegel writes that the community creates itself in what it represses and is at the same time essential to it, in femininity in general, he is taking up a Platonic concept. But the enemy within, sexually mixed as it was in Plato, becomes femininity in itself.[139] The eternal irony of the community is what remains when one believes one has engaged all men in it.

10. Eve's Awakening /Apollo's Ruling: Two Banquets Juxtaposed

> "*Lips closed, eyes too wide, cheeks taut, the face—absent from itself in concentration—listens. Eve listens to what? She listens to the birth of a listening. While her left hand wanders away, unbeknownst to her—she wants to ignore it—to pick the forbidden fruit, her right hand, above the elbow still immobilized in eternal clay, brushes her own cheek for the first time. With one hand Eve picks the apple, with the other she touches herself. A gesture so strange: the surprise, terror, pity of Eve discovering herself before saying "me." As if after a dream, an infinite absence, this right hand that touches herself, knows that it is touching. This touched cheek feels touched. Eve knows herself. She listens and knows that she listens.*"[140]

One evening when I was professor of women's studies at the University of Geneva, I was invited with a philosophy colleague to dinner at the house of Jeanne Hersch, and I was duly questioned about the so-called subject I was supposedly teaching. I told her about Elizabeth Gray and about how she had invented a remedy for melancholia. No, I didn't explain the formula in my classes. "Ah," exclaimed our hostess, "why should only the soul be poisoned?" Then, as I recall, the conversation turned to Gabrielle Suchon, with her marvellous idea of freeing women's thought from the disgrace of original sin; the conversation went on to include a few other women thinkers reclaimed from the dust of archives. After dessert, Madame Hersch went to rummage around in her attic and returned with one of her books, open to the first page of her meditation on a twelfth-century stone statue of Eve. Thus, in the author's own house and in her presence, I had the privilege of reading this essay in which a woman of today indicates her consent to Eve's gesture and follows her in thought, reliving with her this "tale that is henceforth immutable, but carried away among fairy tales and vulnerable to incredulity." In Eve's simultaneous gestures of reaching for the apple and touching her own cheek, Jeanne Hersch sees "everything that begins at once: consciousness and time, and the name of the beginning, the choice to live and the knowledge of death." So you see, if what bears the shameful name of original sin had not yet been committed, we would certainly have to commit it now. And oh! How beautiful Eve is as she emerges from her holy rigidity—in one hand, knowledge of the world, and in the other self-knowledge and, from her elbows to her knees, the birth of beauty and the first stirrings of charm.

For Jeanne Hersch, reliving the episode of the apple in this way, following Eve's gesture and its implications, amounts to accepting what she is, accepting the regrets, the fear, the expectancy, and the awareness, and also acknowledging the "movement of this rigid body in the process of becoming a woman's body," accepting a life that seeks or even brushes up against self-knowledge and knowledge of the world. In this scene there is no trace of Adam, nor any God, or at least of a wrathful and judgmental God—the old crank!—passing sentence: "in sorrow thou shalt bring forth children; and thy desire shall be to thy husband, and he shall rule over thee," and so forth.[141] Still more significant perhaps is the absence of a redeemer who might subsequently come to tell us how to do penance and earn redemption. The consequences of something that is not sin but an awakening to sin, exile, and existence are immanent and immediate, to the extent that they can scarcely be called consequences. But they are there forever, as are life, birth, love, and the knowledge of death. Now, readers, admit you are happy to know about Jeanne Hersch's text. Being born into knowledge is nothing other than reaching out with two hands to grasp the human condition—a condition that requires no redemption, a condition one can love, according to Jeanne Hersch, and that, incorrigible meliorist that I am, I believe one can also make more lovable.

Some day, quite by accident, you might come across a poem entitled "Blue-Stocking Revels" published in 1837, the year of Queen Victoria's accession to the throne of England.[142] In this poem, dozens of learned and literary women—and what a list!—"blue-footed charmers," have been invited to a banquet presided over by Apollo in person. Benjamin Stillingfleet is also present, wearing his famous stockings, and the guests are warned not to find fault. Apollo decrees that these charming women's stockings will no longer be blue, but violet—such a remarkable nuance! This transformation will hold as long as the women are well-behaved and good-tempered, and their writings conform to the triple norm he lays down: they must be unaffected, gentle, and affectionate. But women who think and write are duly forewarned: the minute you become solemn, scathing, or disloyal, your stockings will immediately revert to blue.

Since even a book can sometimes practice active pedagogy, I'll leave you here to your own thoughts, before leading you down other avenues of knowledge and power.

CHAPTER 2

Renaissances

Three women had wanted to study medicine at a London hospital. The authorities who turned them down issued a statement announcing that the objections to their enrollment would stand. They did not specify the reasons for their opposition. It is 1867, and an anonymous brochure entitled *Women Doctors* publishes an angry response to this peremptory and uninformative decision. What can the objections possibly be, asks the author who, intending to study medicine herself, declares in passing that, in the future, rather than limiting themselves to delivering babies, women practitioners will treat everyone and all kinds of disorders.[1] If you were to find a copy of this manifesto in your favorite library, you would see that a librarian of the day had pencilled in "midwifery"on the title page: the very opposite of the subject clearly announced in the title.

"From a distance, the square tower looks round"; "how can I know that this glass is really on this table?" the classical debates about knowing are still conducted using examples taken routinely from so-called everyday experience rather than from developed areas of knowledge. This square tower that looks round is two thousand years old, and yet, in all this time, entire epistemological projects have remained unexamined. Unless I am much mistaken, the tower and the glass on the table are small objects extracted from the perceptible world; they are reasonably stable and have ordinary names. The everyday simplicity of these *realia* hides the fact that prior to every articulated discourse of knowledge comes the task of constituting the object as such and determining the cognitive relationship: where is the knower and where is the known? A tower and an eye; a glass and an I: these typical examples presuppose an obvious, pre-defined, distribution of the poles of the cognitive relationship, given once and for all. The eye sees the tower, and clearly the reverse does not hold. I determine, rightly or wrongly, that the glass on the table exists. Neither the banal relativism, the subjectivism that is so fashionable today ("everyone is the measure of his or her own truth"), nor philosophical scepticism ever go so far as to wonder whether it is the tower that sees or the glass that thinks. Thus, they are of no help to us here. When a square phrase, "women doctors", is transformed into a round notion, "midwives", by a man's pencil (this brochure was added to the library's collection forty years before women began to be employed as temporary library assistants), it is quite a different matter, demanding different modes of analysis from those applied to questions of elementary knowledge. And because it is concerned only with perceiving or thinking "subjects", relativism would furnish too terse a response. It would suppose that there is an object (X) that a feminine subject would see or think about in one way, a masculine subject in another. Superficially, you might think this is what happened between the librarian and the author of the pamphlet. Yet such is not the case: here there is no common object, but two *successive* judgments, each producing its own concept, one pointing toward women doctors, the other reducing the question to one of midwifery, with the second quashing the first as if in a court of appeal. Moreover, these two judgments are logically quite different: the anonymous author who pleads in favor of women doctors is not making a factual judgment, but dealing with a possibility she finds worthy of consideration and whose value she sets out to demonstrate; on the other hand, the librarian who relates the work to midwifery fails to see it for what it is, thus committing the next thing to a professional error. He passes judgment on the document he is cataloguing: "this is about midwifery." Such a judgment is as likely as any other factual judgement to be true or false, and in this instance it is clearly false. It is not enough to talk of a difference between two subjectivities: he can decide that the author had no business saying what she did, and no competence to judge, and that therefore she has said nothing. By "(mis)knowing" (*méconnaissant*) her work, he denies her the status of a speaking subject, and transforms what she says into a small object about which only he can judge, since he is the arbiter of the established classification, equating woman to midwife.

If the question about who is qualified to judge is fundamental, the fixed simplicity of the relation between the two poles of cognition, in its classical epistemological form (something to know, someone to know) cannot simply be transposed to thinking about the construction of scholarly or scientific projects. If we imagine that this simple and apparently self-evident relationship structures knowledge itself, we might very well mistake for reality what may be only a vision based on tacit decisions and mistake for an "object" what has become sedimented from a particular way of looking. Critical analysis will sometimes allow us to go back to the guiding principles that have constructed the so-called object and to the broad distributions implicit in the ordering of the scene offered up to our gaze, as if everything were as simple as the glass on the table. This, at any rate, is what we are about to attempt.

1. The Intermittent Existence of Women Doctors

To take one example that will allow us to kill several birds with one stone, let us open *The Renaissance Notion of Woman*, published in 1983 in the *Cambridge Monographs on the History of Medicine*. The author, Ian Maclean, is a Fellow of an Oxford college; the journal *Renaissance Quarterly* praises "the rigor, depth, and scholarship" of the work; these are the kinds of favorable evaluations that current academic structures are likely to provide.[2] Reading this work may offer us an opportunity to think about the intellectual effects of this university culture: we can assume that it is not equally accessible to members of both sexes and we know that the tradition it has inherited is anything but inclusive. The book does offer some information, and we can learn something from a superficial reading. But it is structured around a questionable principle, which has remained invisible to male colleagues. Whoever gleans information from this book also risks accepting the a priori conceptual frameworks of the university community, intellectual automatisms that in turn will tend to direct and structure future reading or research. Indeed, this work presupposes as a self-evident truth a certain distribution that ostensibly constitutes the object. Thus, a long chapter is devoted to medicine. Now, before beginning to discuss "women and medicine in the Renaissance" you may choose among several questions: will you study what Renaissance women thought of medicine—which medicine?—or what Renaissance medicine thought of women—and again, which medicine? Or will you focus on how women gained access to medical care or how they dispensed it? Maclean does not debate these choices. As if it went without saying, he studies only the idea of Woman according to male doctors. One characteristic of the chapter will not be immediately obvious to anyone not versed in both Renaissance studies and feminist theory, though it will certainly make you flinch if you are familiar with these disciplines: Woman, in the singular, is exclusively considered as the object of medical discourse, never as one of the subjects who practice medicine, and even less among those who debate its validity. Maclean has compiled gynaecological treatises written only by men, thereby introducing a double limitation: Woman is only the object of medical theories, never the practitioner, and still less a thinker about medicine, and the female-object of medicine is gynaecology.

It is as if at that time, in the complex world of the art of healing, a woman could never be anything but the patient, suffering only from gynaecological disorders.

This tacit determination of the object forecloses everything else, even something you might already have thought about or that you could eventually have discovered. At the same time, in order to offer a critical view of this book, one must know something it completely ignores, for example, that in the Renaissance as in the Middle Ages or Antiquity and still in the seventeenth century, it was common for ladies or the mistress of the house to practice basic medicine. Some women, who practiced beyond the confines of their own households, were well-known practitioners who left a trace in collective memory, at least for a while. You might have found this idea suggested, though not extensively developed, in a book by Charles Webster, who cites three examples to support his point.[3] Your curiosity may have been piqued, perhaps you wanted to know more; at the very least, the idea generated a kind of category-in-waiting, where you could eventually file the name of a woman doctor encountered by chance in some book or in a small comment by Plato about women who, though they may be lazy about spinning, devote themselves energetically to caring for the sick of the household. A work like Maclean's will have the opposite effect ("women and medicine," ah yes, treatises written by male gynaecologists), which will either prevent you from taking note of what you may already have known, or even encourage you to unlearn it. It is a strange situation: the distinction between "having some knowledge" and "pursuing a critical inquiry" does not really hold if, in order to detect a dubious principle in the learned tome we cite as an example, we have to know that women did indeed practice medicine. If an informed critique is the only thing that allows us to reproblematize the "knowledge" offered to us, we would be ill-advised to desert institutions of knowledge or to opt for a tabula rasa. But we must admit that some learning does take place below the level of consciousness, and that the most learned environments can transmit a priori beliefs that in fact impede the acquisition of knowledge.

The historical existence of female medical practitioners is something we can still learn about today, even though the second half of the nineteenth century and the first half of the twentieth showed greater interest in them. Sandra Chaff's bibliography[4] lists articles and books on the subject, mostly published between 1860 and 1930. At a time when women were fighting for access to medical studies, it was important to find traces of female practitioners in earlier centuries; the old gave legitimacy to the new and the past gave some reasons for hope. The Kantian distinction between knowledge for the learned professions (*métiers savants*) and the free knowledge of facts (*connaissance libre de faits*) reveals its falsity as soon as we introduce terms such as hope or possibility and refer to persons who want to hope, to act, and to think about the possibility of what they hope for. The relationship between historical research and ongoing contemporary debates is sometimes made quite explicit by authors writing at the turn of the twentieth century: since this has happened once, it can happen again. The underlying reasoning is typically just what Aristotelians of both sexes would propose with respect to the possible: "about the possibility of things which have not yet occurred we are not yet sure; but it is evident that actual events are possible—they could not otherwise have occurred"; now, "what is relatively possible," and, in particular circumstances, time and place, is also *absolutely* possible, without reference to time, place, or circumstance; for if it were absolutely impossible, it would not be "possible in any respect or in any place or at any time."[5] Demonstrating that because something has happened in the past, it is therefore possible again today, tomorrow, or always is one of the logical strategies of feminism which, understood as thought that promotes equality and enhances occupational choices for all women, must inevitably grapple with the issue of possibilities. Research that either rediscovers or minimizes the figures of women who have engaged in interesting work must be understood in light of this logic. The best studies derive their significance from the extent to which they exhume possibilities from the past that hold promise for the future.

Before and after the Belle Époque, concern for enlisting scholarly research in the service of the questions of the day is evident in a preference for publishing articles rather than books, and in medical rather than historical journals. No matter how rigorous the methodology, their chosen mode of publication meant that in effect their research amounted to interventions in the debate.[6] If during this same period Zeller disputes the authenticity of texts attributed to female Pythagoreans, and if others painstakingly demolish Trotula (a professor of medicine at Salerno during the eleventh century, according to her medieval admirers), we cannot ignore their claims, even if we suspect the energy they devote to annihilating such figures stems from an antipathy toward women who wanted to study medicine or philosophy. At that time, it was a political choice to demonstrate that Trotula was merely a mythical figure or to write an article on Oliva Sabuco des Nantes Berrera, who in 1587 published a *New Philosophy of the nature of man, unknown to ancient philosophers, whose purpose is to improve human life and health.*[7] What is involved is a choice that can mobilise both women and men, since it depends on something willed rather than on a specific subjectivity, even though some men seem unable to go more than a quarter of the way. Thus, a certain J.-M. Guardia acknowledges Oliva Sabuco as a "doctor without a diploma," but he refuses to recognize her as a philosopher.[8] Claiming that uncritical admiration of her work would raise doubts about her authorship (if it is excellent, only a man could have written it!), he affirms "the complete failure of this brave woman who was the first to try to reduce human and animal nature to the nervous system"; but at the same time he validates Sabuco's thought as the subject matter of a doctoral thesis in the history of medicine.

Interest in the female practitioners of the past has not completely vanished today. It has levelled off or migrated toward a body of literature that academic reflexes tend to separate from ordinary knowledge by calling it feminist.[9] This interest in female practitioners is poorly integrated into research on the history of medicine in general, of whatever period; even a modest amount of attention to it is noteworthy. Writing about medicine in England at the beginning of the seventeenth century, Charles Webster alludes briefly to Dorothy Burton, Elizabeth Ray, and Elizabeth Grey, Countess of Kent; however, he provides no bibliographical information, and seems not to know quite what to do with them. Quite independently, you can find documents left by Elizabeth Grey[10]; but you would have much greater difficulty with the other two. In any case, it would be unjust to remember only famous practitioners, when we really should take note of a widespread, but far from universal, social reality. Very different from these famous women is the example of Sabine Saunders, "doctor to her whole family" during the Tudor period, whom you will find in Sandra Chaff's remarkable bibliography.[11]

From Antiquity we have inherited a distinction between two forms of medicine: the first, which was thought to be learned, was divided into various schools of thought and reserved for the treatment of free adult men who were heads of households; the second, practiced in the home, was for the care of children, women, servants, and slaves.[12] Today's expression "family medicine" is a distant echo of Latin *familia,* the group of people living under one roof or on one farm and subject to the authority of the same master or *pater familias.* This ancient division between two types of medicine still prevailed during the Renaissance.[13] For proof, you have only to open *The Patient,* a farce by Marguerite de Navarre (c. 1535). Three characters compete for the honor of treating the master of the house: his wife; a doctor who has not been to medical school but who can read Latin and therefore understands the treatises of those who have, and a pretty chambermaid who affirms that faith alone can heal. The two women subvert the established order of things by presuming to treat the master; he has insisted that the doctor be called, thinking it would be beneath his dignity to be treated by a mere wife. As for her, she considers her art to be effective, humble, and based on experience: "we little women know the little plants"; the diminutive metonymy transfers the lesser prestige of the practitioner to the remedy. But modesty is not enough to earn oneself a place in the sun. There is intense conflict between the two women and the Latinized doctor. Brandishing dire threats of repression, he is like a Diafoirus* who, as nasty as he is inept, vaunts his close relationship with those who administer control and punishment.

This literary source attests to the conflictual relationship between female practitioners and certified doctors. Not only does it show that female practitioners were a known phenomenon during the Renaissance since they were represented in a very successful play[14] but it can also teach us to read other texts for what they are, namely, productions, therefore representations to be interrogated. And since the author of *The Patient* is a woman, it shows that at that time a woman could judge the complex relationships among various healing arts: the playwright creates a situation and protagonists and establishes herself, in the courtroom of her theater, as the judge of three types of therapy. In the same way, Oliva Sabuco declares the uselessness of traditional medicine, which is two thousand years old, and argues that it must be completely rethought. If we are to believe that the Renaissance notion of woman is the one suggested in Maclean's book, a Marguerite de Navarre could not have functioned in her time, nor could she have staged a conflict between two women and a man, in which each person defends his or her point of view, speaks for him or herself, and resists the others, since none of them is a small object mastered by someone else. This is probably why Marguerite de Navarre does not appear in the chapter on medicine in this book we have been trying to assess in light of evidence that contradicts the author's claims. Elsewhere in the book, one short sentence indicates that the next generation of moralists criticized her for having dared to write about morals.

Some women historians claim that from the fourteenth century on, male doctors declared open war on female practitioners. Thus, in 1322, a certain Jacoba Félicie, or Jaqueline Félicie de Almania, was dragged before a court constituted by the Faculty of Medicine of Paris, and charged with practicing medicine illegally. She knew how to read, like the woman in *The Patient* who prides herself on having read books on basic medicine. She had received medical training, though we do not know how or of what sort, and her practice was not limited to "family medicine." Two charges were levelled against her: she visited the patients, and examined their urine just as doctors did, took their pulse, and examined their bodies, thus performing the rituals that were considered to be the prerogative of certified doctors; and worst of all, she had the audacity to cure patients whom qualified doctors had declared incurable. Although it was not a capital offense, the case was punishable by a heavy fine.[15] War against women doctors? We should not jump to conclusions on the basis of this one example. That year, the

---

*Diafoirus is the doctor in Molière's *Le Malade imaginaire*. His name has come to be associated with medical charlatanism.

Faculty of Medicine had drawn up a list of twenty-four people, including two women, whom it judged to be practicing medicine illegally. The Faculty was hoping for a papal bull threatening to excommunicate anyone who practiced medicine without a licence: their target was therefore both sexes. We can talk about the expulsion of women only if we take other factors into account. One is institutional. It was out of the question for women to receive a university education; therefore, restricting the practice of medicine to those recognized by the university meant eliminating women. The other factor is economic. Family medicine was practiced free of charge; neighborhood medicine was less costly than the services of certified doctors, even though it was no less successful. Jacoba Félicie did not charge for treatment; she received payment only when the patient was cured. All of this placed these women practitioners in a category apart from the general category of those practicing medicine without university endorsement. An article published in *Lancet* (January 18, 1908) points out that, in the sixteenth century, Henry VIII granted licences to women treating patients who were too poor to pay the fees of certified doctors, but who did not want to depend exclusively on charitable institutions. What, in 1908, could have inspired them to resurrect this Tudor decision?

The notion of war against female practitioners, to be treated with caution if we regard it as historical fact, appears in works on the history of women, which today are the only place where knowledge about female doctors of the past lives on. In examining this notion, we must also examine its neglect by mainstream historical scholarship. A corporatist war against those without diplomas, therefore against women; against providers of cheaper services, therefore against women; against those who based their knowledge of healing on experience and on successful treatments, therefore without doubt against women. It is quite plausible that all these factors found an echo in the misogyny of the corporation of certified doctors, who were also frequently men of the Church. But the idea of a war against women seems to stem from a persecutionist vision according to which men were conducting a war specifically directed against women while women practitioners were subjects constantly under threat of prosecution. The study of what they were is thus limited to an account of the difficulties they endured. Moreover, these representations of their existence tend to assimilate their practices to all of the outlawed practices in history and of alternative medicine today, from the most inoffensive to the most controversial. These ancient medical practitioners, who at the end of the nineteenth century symbolized women's will to gain access to official medicine, will soon be transformed into paradigmatic examples of the practice of alternative medicine. You will easily find a book (only one?) connecting them to the ethnoherbalism of today, without distinguishing between figures of legend and those whose existence is a matter of historical fact. Such are the effects of neglect: we would not have reached this point if ordinary historians of both sexes did not neglect women doctors when they write about medicine at a particular period, and if they did not leave the impression that no woman could ever have practiced the art of Aesculapius. Their negligence is even more obvious in their descriptions of medicine as a conflictual domain. From the Renaissance to the Enlightenment at the very least, the antagonisms between the social practices of the art of healing are well known. This oppositional diversity is not a simple matter of duality between experienced women and doctors with diplomas: the problem is that studies ignore the fact that the conflict had implications *also* for women. Thus *A General History of the Sciences*, edited by René Taton, reminds us that at the dawn of the modern era, the art of healing was practised not by one professional group but by several, who were never on good terms with one another; all these groups—approved doctors, with or without diplomas, surgeons, barbers, apothecaries, bone-setters, and so on—fought over practice and legitimacy. And once more, the women practitioners of day-to-day medicine are left off the list.

2. A Cognitive Norm

We can begin to understand a conflict that is both ancient and modern, and perhaps indeed endemic, if instead of thinking of the war against women doctors as a datable historical fact, we recognize that their existence, which has always disrupted an established order, troubles historians of today just as it posed a problem for the medical faculties of the Middle Ages. The sources Yvonne Knibiehler and Catherine Fouquet cite in their *Woman and the Medical Profession* show how an unsympathetic masculine medical view of women has persisted from Antiquity to the present day. Thus we can consider the question not just from a historical and social point of view, or with reference to the coercive pressure of the courts at certain periods in history, but also as a matter of an internal organization of knowledge as such. This point of view highlights a masculinist schema that allows us to distinguish the fate of women practitioners from the fate of men practicing without a diploma. In light of what the pseudo-gynaecological treatises had to say, it was essential for ladies and the humble female artisans practicing in the cities to disappear as colleagues, and not simply because they presented unfair competition. In 1928, Virginia Woolf noted that, even if women do not write about men, "woman" has always been a subject for male essayists and novelists, with and without diplomas, for men whose only visible qualification was that they were not women.[16] Since then, many documents written by women about their situation and their relationship with men have come to light; however, the second part of Woolf's remark still holds as an ironic description of a norm found in published medical treatises and in the language of today's historians, who could have discovered from available historical documents that the sexual division between knower and known is not as simple as they think. Reciprocally, if we juxtapose the discursive fact and the socio-political one, we may grasp that there really is a war, a conflict historians gloss over (and this suppression is nothing less than waging war by other means), in spite of ancient documents or literary representations whose message is nothing more than this: in the absence of knowledge, some men pontificate while some women and men act.

Bacon's sarcasm echoes Marguerite de Navarre's satirical accounts. He too recognizes the existence of female practitioners, while declaring that official medicine is still only a fictitious profession; it is not an application of knowledge since the knowledge does not yet exist.[17] Therefore, says Bacon, it comes as no surprise that witches, old women, and impostors have always been in competition with qualified doctors. Moreover, old women and "empirical" practitioners (those not recognized by medical faculties but whose competence is based on experience) are more successful in giving their treatments: they are more aware of the specificity of each disease, more persevering, and more methodical in their therapies. For the so-called learned doctors are inconsistent; their written prescriptions reveal nothing but incoherence and expedients determined as the need arises, with no definite plan. Moreover, these doctors are too quick to pronounce the case incurable and give up on the patient.[18] And since, ignorant as they are, they cannot gain mastery over the disease, they insist on controlling their patients. The diatribe is accompanied by an earnest plea for the proper establishment of a form of medicine which would at last know something, and this on the basis of experiment and method. Along with this call for a return to Hippocrates and for writing up case studies, Bacon encourages learning from empirical practitioners and old women, in order to go beyond them. But why old? There is a cultural cliché that "ages" any woman who talks or acts, as if language could acknowledge expertise only in women past childbearing age—women who were no longer really women.[19] In the same way, when we refer today to the female practitioners of former times, we have difficulty setting aside the notion that they were merely village bonesetters, akin to witches; prejudice associates them with heresy and illiteracy, which is far from accurate. Not truly learned?

Marguerite de Navarre and Francis Bacon thus weighed up the empirical practice of ladies and the practice of medicine by supposedly learned men. Marguerite de Navarre refuses to come out in favor of either: the lady is no better a therapist than the qualified doctor. Bacon, in polemical fashion, gives grudging recognition to the empiricists and to the women he describes as "old." Both indicate that there is conflict or rivalry, whereas Maclean proceeds as if the men who knew and published in Latin had always won and had, by the time of the Renaissance, already triumphed to such an extent that it was no longer necessary to study the conflict or useful even to acknowledge the existence of women who practiced medicine or who undertook to judge it. For him, as for the authors he has read, "woman," like an eternally wounded Amazon, is reduced to the status of a vanquished referent, the passive slave of spurious masters whose rantings appear in print; at best, woman is the object of academic debates among men. His book is a kind of *Suave mari magno* twice over, describing a deathly stillness and proposing a kind of estheticizing vision rather than a genuinely historical exploration. For the fundamental distinction between male subjects holding forth and the female objects of their (pseudo) knowledge is not simply an inappropriate cognitive framework; it transforms Maclean's work into something akin to painting. For he creates a tableau comparable to *The Death of Sardanapalus* or *The Eastern Slave-Market,* paintings analyzed by Linda Nochlin. Both works proclaim that men have power over women's bodies and that man the artist can offer the fantasy of even more power, in the form of pleasure by purchase or by destruction.[20]

3. Knowing by Dreaming? Object Versus Objectification

In his *Phenomenology of Perception,* Merleau-Ponty says that for a normal subject, the body of another person is not perceived as an object. The perception that might have been objective is in fact inhabited by another, more secret, perception, which, he says, accentuates the erogenous zones of the visible body of the other according to a sexual schema peculiar to the perceiving subject so that this body will call forth "the gestures of the masculine body."[21] He was speaking of the visible body in general, perceived by a normal subject; however, it becomes clear that this visible body is a woman's body, seen and redrawn by the gaze of a man, who before long will move unhesitatingly from gaze to gesture! Not only is the subject necessarily male, the visible body necessarily that of a woman, but also the gaze (of a man directed at a woman) can remake what it sees, to accentuate what he finds erogenous. A form of visual violence is normalized here in all its generality. On principle and as a general procedure, the (masculine) gaze re-creates the visible body of a (feminine) other precisely as it wishes.

If women are objects redrawn by each man's personal fantasy, then the individual is absorbed into a generalized structure of power. This is observable too in the gaze that is said to be learned, although at second hand. For example, speculating on female sexual pleasure, Lacan claims that one has *only* to look at Bernini's statue of Theresa of Avila to know everything about it. Thus a representation, sculpted by a male hand, serves to support Lacan's modelling of female pleasure. If we take Merleau-Ponty at his word, and say that a right to dream, opposed to any attempt at objectification, is affirmed in the essays that freeze us as objects or statues, then we could assume that there is an a priori, global schema, operative for each dreamer, without reference to a particular "field" or object. *The Renaissance Notion of Woman* verifies this hypothesis. Throughout the book, the absence of speaking women or of women practicing knowledge is flagrant, and even the masculine sources seem to be explored selectively. There is no female theologian in the chapter on theology, although without going beyond my own usual field of study I can name Anne Cook, a young woman who, with her energetic pen intervened in debates about the Church of England. She became Lady Bacon, and brought a certain small Francis into the world. Bacon's chaplain would eventually write that, although the men in the family had important political posts, the intellect was inherited from the maternal side.[22] Without exaggerating the volume of her works, we note that a dedication to her mother in her translation of Bernardino Ochino gave her the opportunity to comment on the education given to girls. Taking issue with the ornamental function of this education, she says she is happy to see her knowledge of Italian serve a useful purpose, namely, to translate Ochino, or in other words to prescribe which side the new Church should take on theological questions. Her translation of Jewel, the Bishop of Salisbury, elicited his dithyrambic praise of women's intellectual accomplishments. She wrote about theology; in her honor, a bishop produced a speech in which he favored not just women's education but also their active participation in the work to be done, and this is by no means the same thing. And yet in Maclean's learned work on the Renaissance notion of woman, this woman is nowhere to be found. Women are objects of male theological discourse, not writers, and not even handmaidens in a collective theologicopolitical enterprise; therefore, Anne Cook has no place in this book. But then, neither has Jewel, the author of comments on the participation of women, been considered a relevant source. The subject is therefore limited to the study of certain discourses. There are two brief references to Agrippa's *De la noblesse et excellence du sexe féminin*. In the first, Maclean claims that Agrippa's work is above all a rhetorical exercise, and in the second, he states that the idea of the superiority of the female sex would appear paradoxical in the context of the Renaissance—not surprising, when one thinks of how he describes this life! An a priori modelling of the object thus leads him to ignore any facts that contradict his thesis and to minimize the historical relevance even of some masculine sources. The *De nobilitate*, whose interpretation is complex, was a great success in its time.[23] If today a colleague marginalizes it, thus failing to take *all* the masculine gazes of the Renaissance into account, we need to take Merleau-Ponty's involuntary admission seriously: there is a fundamental postulate of the right to redraw anything at all, and within it, the possibility of idiosyncratic redrawing.

A sentence in a chapter of *The Renaissance Notion* devoted to morality, politics, and society makes the claim that there have been famous women mystics but very few mathematicians, cosmologists, or theologians, if any. There is a difference between very few and none at all, and here a distinction begins to appear: passionate love of God, possibly, but certainly no thinking. But no woman mystic is named. And it is not for me to know whether Theresa of Avila was a mystic or a theologian, or what meaning such a distinction would have had for her; in any case, this doctor of the Church, whose influence on matters of women's access to knowledge was felt as far away as Mexico, is never mentioned in this book. A philosopher and poet of the end of the seventeenth century, Juana Inès de la Cruz, following Theresa's lead with respect to theology, also praises secular knowledge, notably logic and *fisica*, natural history. She claims that in order to reach the queen of sciences, one must also take its handmaidens into account.[24] Thus the case for a much broader connection to knowledge could be argued through access to theology; Sor Juana espouses Theresa's criticism of those who, "misinterpreting Saint Paul," believe that women must neither teach nor play any role whatsoever in the Church. Thus one might conclude that Theresa intervened in the re-emerging Renaissance debate about the status of women.

When we consider how many real women who were notable for their words or deeds are excluded from the debate in order to prevent debate, we realize that *The Renaissance Notion of Woman* is not a book but a massacre. Christine de Pisan is also absent. Consequently *The City of Ladies* has nothing to do with the Renaissance notion of women? And since Maclean discusses political discourse, see if you can find Mary, and Elizabeth Tudor, whose accession to the throne is hard to miss. The chapter on politics includes a long list of masculine proper names, of which some, such as Aristotle, are still famous today, though others are considerably less so. One solitary sentence indicates that the opinions of these gentlemen explain the vehemence of the conservatives with respect to Catherine de Medici, Mary Stuart, and Elizabeth. But I would object that these women's exercise of royal power did not elicit exclusively hostile reactions, and that they themselves were more than mere objects of reaction. By limiting his interest to minor masters of political science, who generally had only negative things to say about women, the author manages to construct a notion that the "Renaissance" had of *woman*. It is exemplified in the idea that female sovereigns had no business ruling or being heard even when they expressed their own opinions of their status as women of state. Elizabeth reigned for more than forty years; as head of the Church of England, she also had to negotiate ecclesiastical questions. It is possible not to like everything in her injunctions and speeches, but that is not the issue. Today, expelled from Maclean's text, she is relegated to the cover design and to the book's conclusion, which, in stark contrast to the body of the argument, points out that "certain aspects of the notion of woman" change at the time of the Renaissance, although most Renaissance thought perpetuated the most negative medieval ideas. The study is based on a *petitio principii* and flawed inductive arguments: by choosing only male authors, we may conclude that scholasticism endured in the Renaissance and that in fact the Renaissance scarcely happened. Therefore, you will know neither the questions you owe to this period nor the awkward position it has created for you. And you will think the period has an "idea of woman" produced by men, with no connection to anything real women may have been, or lived, or wanted, or thought.

History does not always flow in the same direction. Had you been a student a few years earlier, you would have been required to read *The Civilization of the Renaissance in Italy* by Jacob Burckhardt, a book published in 1860, which offers a completely different view. Burckhardt maintains that the fifteenth and sixteenth centuries saw a resurgence of the term "virago," and he goes on to comment: "The title 'virago', which is an equivocal compliment in the present day, then implied nothing but praise. It was borne in all its glory by Caterina Sforza. . . ."[25] This heroine (1463–1509) succeeded her dead husband as ruler of a small independent city, and she mounted its military defense against Caesar Borgia; she was nicknamed the *virago,* and *la prima donna d'Italia.* Burckhardt assures us that such heroism was common among Italian ladies of the time. But what is the point of contrasting Burckhardt's vision with the one we have already examined, if not to underscore the fact that it is precisely a matter of visions, existing in the world of imagination and emotion? Women students emerge from a lecture in which the speaker explains that a *virago,* in classical Latin, is a woman with class, whereas in later Latin the term denotes a woman who exercises the functions [*officium*] of a man.[26] The same women students emerge depressed from a reading of Maclean or from a book by Paul Hoffman entitled *Woman in Enlightenment Thought,* which is also based exclusively on masculine sources.[27] But have them read the chapter on the rebirth of humanism in *A History of Their Own.* In it they are delighted to find dozens of educated women, but then they fail to understand why a problem has persisted right up to their own time.[28] We have to wonder what we are doing when we teach, and what the function of the university really is. Does our teaching have negative or supportive impact? Is it of any consequence for the future? For knowledge either breeds hope or crushes it when the past serves as a mirror of a desired future, or if one uses "facts" to define and defend a norm for today and for the future. In principle, for any branch of knowledge, an institution of learning must provide both a stock of basic information and, more important, cognitive frameworks that offer the student reference points and means of knowing, understanding, and continuing to explore on her own. In the sciences, the process is directed straight at the target, putting basic concepts in place along with methods of reasoning. Certainly, a solid formation in one discipline is no guarantee of success in another, and someone who thrives on geometry and algebra may be disconcerted by the transition to trigonometry. But this transition is easy in comparison with what you and I constantly encounter in the humanities. There, it is not just the intellectual mutation required for a transition from knowledge constructed on masculinism to the embryonic knowledge that recognizes the reality of women, but rather a kind of hesitation when it becomes apparent that the tools that facilitate learning can also impede the freedom to know, which in itself is a fundamental source of freedom to think and thus to form a sense of self.

If a learning process enables one to acquire a sense of the world and of oneself—schemata in themselves perhaps irrelevant to knowledge but able to apportion values and affective nuances—it will be clear why the bias of *The Renaissance Notion of Woman* concerns me. How is it possible, in our own day, to construct an object of study as Maclean does, when at the same time universities have become mixed, and when intellectual equality between the sexes is supposed to be a fait accompli? The book may simply be a *Je maintiendrai* (I shall uphold) addressed to young men in the education system: the fact that you have female fellow students certainly does not mean that men like you can no longer decide what a woman is. It is also symptomatic of a traditionally masculine community's inability to see that the work is based on a faulty induction. Merleau-Ponty's naive presupposition has lost none of its force. It implies that, because a man has the right to represent women as he wishes, a masculine intellectual community is incapable (even for the sake of scientificity) of refuting what a man says about women. It is traditional for men to talk about women. It is not at all traditional for them to want to *think* something about them or, with even a semblance of rigor, to take facts into account.

A similar idea crops up in the thought of Bertrand Russell. When he undertakes to demonstrate that the scientific spirit does not occur naturally in man [*sic*], and that at best, rational thought occupies only a minor place in the thought of a very few people, he often takes his examples from sexism. "The views of medical men on pregnancy, child-birth, and lactation were until fairly recently impregnated with sadism. It required, for example, more evidence to persuade them that anaesthetics may be used in childbirth than it would have required to persuade them of the opposite." "Aristotle could have avoided the mistake of thinking that women have fewer teeth than men, by the simple device of asking Mrs. Aristotle to keep her mouth open while he counted. He did not do so because he thought he knew."[29] However, when Russell tries to think through the relationship between the rational and the irrational, he proposes an image that marks the difference so strongly that it replaces a mere connection by a juxtaposition. He compares "[t]he mind of the most rational among us" to a stormy sea of passionate convictions akin to desire; this raging ocean tosses a few frail boats carrying scientifically tested beliefs.[30] I am prepared to recognize that this may be a description of the observable lack of relationship (the example is Russell's) between the logic of a mathematician when he is doing mathematics and the illogic displayed in his outbursts against real estate agents; but this model bypasses the most important issue. In the human sciences (including medicine), the appropriation of knowledge by one sex constructs objects, fields, and methods. It is not so easy to distinguish knowledge from the beliefs that bear it, all the more so as belief sometimes determines the outcome. Thus in 1994, on the occasion of the Cairo Conference on population, an article in *The Economist* began with an attack on a demographic study claiming that access to contraception accounted for 90 percent of variations in birthrates. *The Economist* declares that this argument cannot be taken seriously, and that it is ridiculous to consider the availability of contraceptives as the principal factor in birth rates. "Over the long term, the single most effective and enduring way of moderating population growth, even more than by the diffusion of contraception, is by giving women more and better education."[31] As if it had to be one or the other, as if one solution pleased the publishers while the other did not. The article is illustrated by a diagram based on statistics compiled by the World Resources Institute entitled "A little learning," which is supposed to show that birth rates fall as female literacy increases. So it is possible to criticize one set of statistics and prefer another. The twentieth century believed in the authority of scientific knowledge but evaluated it through the prism of its own preferences. Moreover, statistics are not always reliable even from a mathematical point of view, since their authors often neglect to verify the independence of the variables. Thus we find reasoning of the following type: people who pay more than 8,000 francs in rent ski more than other people; if we raise rents, winter sports will become more widely accessible. *The Economist* does not ask whether the variable "education" is independent with respect to a global situation that includes access to civil rights and reproductive rights, education, skilled work outside the home, and a certain freedom of speech, both domestic and public. And why "a little learning" for girls, rather than equal access for both sexes?

Another example, also demographic, is that of the National Demographics Institute (INED), founded after the liberation of France in 1945 on the
ruins of an organization created by the Vichy regime; natalist ideology (our
women never have enough children) is common to the entire French political class. Both the Neuwirth Law, which legalized contraception in 1967,
and the Veil Law provide for an annual report to the French parliament on
the French birth rate, a provision implying that if the birth rate were judged
insufficient, basic freedoms might be revoked. It just so happens that, for
years, the figures provided by the National Demographics Institute have been
manipulated in alarmist fashion; thanks to methods of calculation invented
for the occasion, the mistaken notion of a demographic decline was created.
All that was needed in order to arrive at the much publicized results—1.8
children per woman—was to include all women of reproductive age, between 15 and 45, in the calculations and to concoct a "short-term index."
However, if we count the children of a particular generation of women when
this generation reaches age 40, we find that ever since contraception came to
be readily available, French women have had on average 2.15 children each.
In 1990, when the doom-crying of the National Demographics Institute was
feeding the rhetoric of the National Front Party, researcher Hervé Le Bras
leaked this information to the press. But the far right is not the only group to
exploit misinformation by blaming women for making immigration necessary, and for the difficulties in paying for pensions that will apparently
follow. And had there been no conflict with the National Front, would there
have been anything for the demographers to say about this myth of decline?

4. Construction of an Object or Definition of a Field?

Judging from what we know of the Roman *medicae* whose practice was not
limited to obstetrics, of Jacoba Félicie who, like the *medicae*, treated both
men and women, of the German ophthalmologists of the fifteenth century,
or of Sabine Saunders who, in the sixteenth century, looked after her entire family, we can formulate a simple hypothesis: not one of these women
tried to define a distinct medical specialty called gynaecology, to which
she and other female practitioners should limit themselves. For them, the
disorders peculiar to women were an integral part of medicine in general.
This point is corroborated by the "old women" who, according to Bacon,
compete with certified doctors, and also by the compendium of remedies
written by Elizabeth Grey. Oliva Sabuco proposes a global theory of health
and disease (happiness promotes health while sadness undermines it) for
human beings in general. And the anonymous author of 1867, who defends
women's right to treat all patients and the full range of diseases, revives this

tradition, whereas the librarian who notes "midwifery" on the cover page of the manifesto maintains the opposite point of view. For this librarian, it would be unthinkable for women to practice medicine, except perhaps and at the very most as assistants at confinements. Similarly, the women doctors of earlier times did not construct "woman" as an undifferentiated object of knowledge, distinct from the rest of humanity, with specific characteristics and reducible to a matrix; they did not suppose that everything that happened to a woman happened because she was a woman. Their object was organized around a plurality: diseases and their remedies. Elizabeth Grey's *Choice Manual,* which has no section specifically devoted to obstetrics, proposes treatments for a whole range of distinct disorders, such as dog-bites, hemorrhoids, difficult pregnancies, gout, hysteria..., without organizing them into specialties. She uses either a "masculine neuter" or a "feminine neuter" pronoun of reference.[32] Her language, which refers to her patients either in the masculine or the feminine neuter, shows that she thinks she is treating patients whose sex is irrelevant except in determining the dosage of medication, in the same way as a pediatrician of today takes the age and weight of the child being treated into account. Of course, following the example of her fore-sisters (*prédécessoeurs*) who among other things had knowledge particularly useful to women, the Countess of Kent, also among other things, knew how to bring about the expulsion of a dead fetus, or treat crises thought to be spasms of the uterus. In other words, the integration of gynaecological questions into general medicine does not erase them, but merely removes the visibility that grouping them together as a specialization gives them.

Hence the issue I want to discuss is epistemological rather than historical. The (pseudo-)gynaecological treatises written by men, this truncated corpus that some would claim encompasses everything worth knowing about the relationship between women and medicine, could be symptomatic of a division that male doctors wanted, long before and long after the Renaissance. This division produced the treatises and, in so doing, constituted this so-called specialty. For after all, the need for gynaecology as a separate specialty is not immediately obvious, especially since at the time there was so little knowledge; the existence of a few disorders peculiar to only one category of people does not in itself justify creating a specialization. Because of the long voyages and consequent vitamin deficiencies, the sixteenth century saw the appearance of diseases that affected sailors in particular. No one created a specialization in nautology—that, moreover, would have been practiced by landlubbers only—even though around 1570 someone had the idea of military and naval medicine.[33] And seasickness has never found its way into the medical imaginary, whereas so-called phantom uterine contractions have long been a hot topic of medical chit-chat! We have not only to examine the construction of objects but also the constitution of a domain whose contours had been outlined as early as Antiquity, before there was real knowledge to locate within it, and whose possibility has persisted through years of debate. In its very construction, the category "gynaecology" may well encompass the unjustifiable postulate of a knowledge in which the direction of the cognitive relationship is from learned men to a woman-object reduced to nothing but her uterus. In which case it would be useless to ask whether women practice gynaecology differently from men.

5. Lady Trotula

To refute my argument, you might refer to a treatise dealing exclusively with questions of gynaecology and obstetrics, known from numerous manuscripts of the fourteenth and fifteenth centuries, written in different languages and with various titles, *De passionibus mulierum curandum* or *De curis mulierum*, or *Sekeness of Wymmen*, and so on. This treatise could be attributed to a certain Lady Trotula—or Trotulla—but there is some doubt.[34] The attribution was contested by learned men of the nineteenth century and had already been disputed once during the Renaissance: a learned text could not be the work of a woman! Instead of this nasty argument, we could propose another to the anti-Trotulists: what we know of female practitioners whose existence is documented suggests that they practised general medicine, and this could have included gynaecology (or ophthalmology). On the other hand, in ancient medical thought that bears the name of Hippocrates, the category of gynaecology appears as a learned male specialty, since the (male) doctor leaves anything resembling practical gestures to an intermediary: the doctor thinks, but he does not touch. Let us underscore the fact that these *Gynaecia* have come down to us *under the name of Hippocrates*. The attribution is without a doubt mythical, and the corpus, written over a considerable period of time, is the work of a school, not a single author. Here too there is a double standard: imagine that works on "Hippocrates" confined themselves, as is too often the case for "Trotula", to showing over and over again that the attribution is mythical, or on the contrary to proving the historical existence of this medical figure.

The three volumes of *Gynaecia* in the Hippocratic corpus are the work of a school of men; medieval gynaecological treatises that can be attributed with certainty are also the work of men. If then the medieval treatise known by various titles was really the work of a woman, Trotula, it would be the only instance, an exception within what is known about female practitioners and gynaecological treatises. I am not denying that there are exceptions, but my concern is to understand what is said about them. The debate about the sex of the author of *De curis mulierum*, or of *Sekeness of Wymmen*, and so on, catches us between two hypotheses, which, in my view, amount to the same thing: either it is the work of a man because a learned discourse is necessarily the work of a man, and immediately, some women students feel they have been robbed of a splendid figure to emulate, or, it is the work of a woman because *at the very most* a woman can practice obstetrics, and I can imagine such a hypothesis being written by a methodical man, obliterating with a stroke of his pen ("labor and delivery at the very most") the practice of general medicine by women. The debate over the sex of the author of *De curis* could very well be a psychodrama in which, even today, two negative ideas clash and reinforce each other: knowledge is for men, and a woman can, at the very most, know the things appropriate for her to know when she is delegated to care for women. Some commentators claim that "Trotula" was the intended recipient of the work, rather than its author. What this debate suppresses is the issue of women's access to 'medicine in general, to intellectual creation, to knowledge in general, and thus to astrophysics, maritime law or the history of the corn trade.

As guiding principles for reading *De curis* or as metaphors of women's access to any branch of knowledge, neither hypothesis—whether it is the work of a man or of a woman—is satisfactory. Do these hypotheses exhaust all possibilities? Of course not. This manual or practical guide is perhaps not the work of a single author in the way a sonnet or a novel is, but a composite production, anonymous, comprising successive additions, cobbling together elements of diverse origins to make a more or less coherent whole. The differences from version to version clearly show that each copyist feels free to excise, add, condense, or expand the version she or he uses as a model. Thus it may be regarded as a work whose very contours are indeed determined by an idea inherited from so-called Hippocratic medicine (gynaecology is a separate specialty; labor and delivery are the domain of female assistants), but whose content is also marked by pragmatic considerations. For beyond any theory, childbirth does exist and it is sometimes difficult. "How to assist expulsion of the placenta," "what to do if the baby is presenting badly": these are real questions and "Trotula's" answers are basically correct. Shaped by pragmatism, the content of the work is varied enough to have been taken from several sources, from teleological "theories," which were common and still are, to the knowledge (or opinions) of the empiricists, female practitioners, and midwives. The debate over the sex of the author supposes that there is *one* author, male or female, who was the author of the entire work ex nihilo, who had therefore read nothing, heard nothing, borrowed nothing in order to compose the treatise. On the other hand, we may postulate a compilation, a polygenesis, a patchwork quilt whose coherence does not stem from the masculine or feminine subjectivity of its creator but from its fundamentally practical purpose. This treatise is pragmatic, though supplemented with "theories", and it should be seen as the product of an accumulation, perhaps over several centuries, of ideas and empirical knowledge, accurate or otherwise. Such a product would be the work of a mixed group, and "Trotula" would then, in my view, be a title rather than the name of a person.[35] Bits of practical advice, some useful, others less so, products of an honorable intention to help women, may have become embedded in a category created through the influence of a masculinist Greek school of thought that insisted on isolating "knowledge" having to do with women and with the practice of midwifery. But there were midwives; midwifery as a profession has made it possible to accumulate experience. The knowledge about childbirth thus acquired could well have found its way into a document, first written by anyone at all, woman or man, and then rewritten by those who copied it over and over, with little attention to accuracy.

About the "theories" included in one version or another of the treatise, I will venture no opinion.[36] The interest of this prescientific manual lies rather in its details. Thus, in a paragraph devoted to "uterine cancers"—tumours, both benign and malignant, and ulcers—two points of view are described and shown to be unrelated. "We will make only passing reference to these diseases, since cures are so rare; indeed, doctors say that it is better not to treat hidden cancers than to treat them." The writer thus differentiates him/herself from those who are "doctors". They are the recognized authorities, qualified to define general principles, whereas the writer recognizes pragmatism as her/his guiding principle, affecting even the length or brevity of the discourse. It is doctors whose first rule is to decide when to treat and when not to, whereas the (male or female) author of the paragraph claims that it is nevertheless possible to treat the pain of cankers, and then in the imperative voice, describes how to go about it. Here we see the appearance of the idea of palliative care (which is of no small significance), presented as if it were almost an infraction or on the very margins of accepted medical practice. It is an act of independence on the part of the auxiliaries in defiance of the rule stipulating that patients with incurable diseases should not be treated. Relative to the philosophy of medicine, the writer is an innovator in suggesting that the assistance owed the sick also concerns their comfort and thus goes beyond the mere art of healing, a point that conservative doctors, rather too full of their professional dignity, still refuse to recognize. If someone managed to show that this paragraph could only be the work of a woman, this would add another fine ornament to the history of women practitioners. But the fact is that we just do not know. In our own century, so infatuated with the idea of an identifiable "women's writing" (*écriture féminine*)* no one has yet invented the chemical test that would allow us to identify the sex of an author without knowing his or her identity beforehand: instant verification!

"Even if Leucippus (is this a man's name or a woman's?) is little known, the work of Democritus is considerable."[37] It is 1988, the volume entitled *The Presocratics* has just appeared, and in the preface, Jean-Paul Dumont expresses a strange doubt about the identity of a philosopher known as "Leucippe" in French. The biography of this philosopher is indeed unknown, so much so that Epicurus and Hermachus claimed that such a person never existed. However, ancient doxography credits this author with the first formulation of the theory of atomism, which describes the universe as made of atoms and the void. Everyone, except of course Epicurus and Hermachus, says this theory was first advanced by Leucippus and then by a disciple, Democritus. The extraordinary doubt Dumont expresses creates a most unusual situation. When one discusses matters of *gender* in relation to a product of the intellect, the dice are usually loaded: the civil status of the author is known, and from there it may or may not be easy, depending on one's choice, to find a mark of the author's sex in the text. Since nothing is known about "Leucippe", perhaps we are finally in a truly experimental situation: can we guess his/her sex on the basis of the scraps of evidence provided by a very indirect tradition? I decided to read the fragments attributed to "Leucippe" and to "Democritus" with this question in mind. Comparison reveals a discrepancy: in what is attributed to Democritus, there are some allusions signalling a masculine complicity between him and a male reader, as if both parties knew without a doubt, say, that for a man it is insulting to be subject to the authority of a woman, or that a woman who reasons is detestable. On the other hand, in the very few lines attributed to Leucippus or to Leucippus-and-Democritus, there is no sign of the complicity anglophones call male bonding, the means men use to establish contact by talking about football or exchanging macho comments. Is this why Dumont suddenly began to doubt? Is it because male bonding is evident in the fragments attributed to Democritus but not in the few traditionally attributed to Leucippus that Dumont wondered whether "Leucippe" might be a woman's name? In 1988, this most faithful of friends still inhabited the world of atoms and the void. I pick up the phone:

> "Jean-Paul, you wrote that Leucippe . . . "
> "Yes, Le Doeuff, I wondered . . . "
> "Uhh . . . the theory of atomism might have been invented by a woman?"

---

*The concept is closely associated with the French literary theorist, novelist, and playwright Hélène Cixous. It refers to a nearly undefinable quality of language that reflects women's embodied experience, based on psychosexual difference. However, there is some ambiguity in Cixous's work about whether *écriture féminine* must *emerge* from a specifically female body.

"You're going too far; there were precursors. Remember Mochos the Phoenician
..."

"Don't quibble! According to the Ancients, Diogenes Laërtes in any case, Leucippus is the originator of the theory of atomism, so it's not just because it may
have been the work of a woman that ... "

Ten minutes later, he called back. "My mistake! I confused Leukippos
and Leukippè. The philosopher's name is Leukippos, a man's name." It
all dissolved into laughter, and yet, I still clutched a tiny but indubitable
fact: Dumont's slip-up shows how a man of today unconsciously, rightly
or wrongly, detects *gender* in a text. Masculine gender is marked by masculinism, without it, it is difficult to know (it is I who say this) whether a
text is the work of a woman or a nice man or the accidental result of the
preservation of just a few lines of text. But Dumont had settled the question.
Besides, let's look at the structure of the sentence: "if Leucippe (is this a
man's name or a woman's?) is little-known, the work of Democritus on the
other hand is considerable." What a strange sentence! Did Leucippus have
to be unknown for Democritus's work to be so well known? Perhaps, for
according to more than one Ancient, Democritus plagiarized the work of
Leucippus. Who other than a woman could be a source so little known, yet
plagiarized to such an extent by a disciple/friend?

Trotula is free of male bonding: the version edited by Beryl Rowland shows
how it could have been attributed to a woman and how to understand what
was at stake:

> Because there are many women who have numerous diverse illnesses—some of
> them almost fatal—and because they are also ashamed to reveal and tell their
> distress to any man, I therefore shall write somewhat to cure their illnesses. [...]
> they are ashamed for fear of reproof in times to come and of exposure by discour-
> teous men who love women only for physical pleasure and evil gratification. And
> if women are sick, such men despise them and fail to realize how much sickness
> women have before they bring them into this world. And so, to assist women, I
> intend to write of how to help their secret maladies so that one woman may aid
> another in her illness and not divulge her secrets to such discourteous men.

This extract, written by a woman or by a courteous man, names affects:
sickness makes woman undesirable and turns her into an object of scorn,
not only for a husband but also—and so we are given to understand—for a
male doctor, since the woman would be ashamed to reveal her ailments to
him, the doctor is more man than doctor. Thus, no matter how magnificent it
might be, the idea that a woman can help another woman intervenes here as
a lifesaving gesture in a context of scorn, distress, shame, and abandonment;
but, centred on childbirth, this idea tends to save only the woman giving
birth.

Is nothing new under the sun? In objecting to the construction of gy-naecology as a specialized branch of medicine, I thought my critique was original; however, from Antiquity on there has been a debate over the legitimacy of separating gynaecology from the rest of medicine. Doctors of the empirical school considered that women's diseases are specific to them, while those of the methodical school believed that the same principles govern the diseases of both sexes.[38] The definition of the specialty is far from clear. Moreover, unlike the other Hippocratic texts, the *Gynaecia* contain lists of remedies and recipes that would continue to be transmitted even among those who no longer subscribed to Hippocratic beliefs. It is as if a pharmacopoeia unrelated to the Hippocratic doctrine had infiltrated its writings and evolved quite independently of the "theories" themselves, since theories and practices seemed to be separable according to whim. If this duality recalls the masculinist division (theory for learned men, practice for the female assistant), then critical study should focus not only on the construction of objects and fields but also on how the art of medicine is actually practiced. Even more: there is no reason to suppose that any aspect of the "theories" of the *Gynaecia* was justifiable "theoretically," or that a single remedy had a real pragmatic effect or that so-called empirical knowledge had been empirically tested. What the history of ancient medicine shows is a series of empty boxes, "theoretical," "pragmatic," and "practical," put in place and defined well before any content filled them. Knowledge was still in its infancy but its categories were already being established; an ordering of the cognitive relationship precedes all knowledge, and *woman,* the object of a special knowledge supposedly possessed by men, guaranteed men their theorizing function and their status as knowing subjects, even though they still knew nothing.

If we consider how women today practice routine gynaecology as part of general medicine, we see further evidence that the classification of gynaecology as a specialty is an artifact rooted in men's appropriation of woman as object of the so-called theoretical function and the medical profession. The reintegration of gynaecology into general medicine distinguishes generalist practitioners clearly enough according to their sex: a woman general practitioner often deals with requests for contraception, or the mycosis contracted during a seaside holiday, or the Pap test that detects cervical cancer, just as she vaccinates her patients and treats bronchitis; her male colleague almost always refers his patients to a gynaecologist for treatment of these disorders. At the same time, thanks to the initiative of women generalists, a new field of knowledge is developing whose name I borrow from a British manual, *Women's Problems in General Practice.*[39] Questions related to obstetrics are not addressed there, and thus women's existence is separated from their role as potential mother. Besides the questions already mentioned, the manual contains sections on bulimia and anorexia and premenstrual problems, many observations on the social and familial environment, and even more important, indications in each case of when a specialist must be consulted—more often in a hospital-based department such as endocrinology than a gynaecologist in private practice. One might conclude that in a way gynaecology is a false specialization: either the problems it treats are ordinary enough for a general practitioner to treat or they are complex enough to justify consulting a more sophisticated and technical specialization. Moreover, new perspectives are appearing as old stereotypes are reexamined: it has been demonstrated that male doctors see their typical female patient as someone who does not work outside the home, is blessed with two children, is more or less neurotic, and complains of vague symptoms. Recalling that only 5 percent of women could correspond to this cliché, the manual counters these ideas with facts: female manual workers who are also single mothers constitute the social group most likely to suffer from stress and a poor state of general health. In a variety of ways, a woman in a household has the responsibility for the health and well-being of everyone, including elderly parents, and therefore more worries and anxiety. And since the environment rather than the soul is a major factor, the manual proposes some remarkable new directions.[40] It foregrounds general practitioners who reflect on what they see in their practice rather than merely applying the knowledge they have received through their training. For female patients, the implications of such an approach are significant. The reintegration of everyday gynaecology into general practice allows each woman to assimilate her sex-specific problems into the more general framework of her body and life experiences. Since it is less expensive to consult a general practitioner than a specialist, it is possible to improve access to contraception among poor women and young women, who are almost always poor. And since the reintegration of "women's problems" into general medicine encourages greater attention to the social situation of the patient, "the object" is no longer "woman," an essence defined in male rantings, but rather the living debate between women and their environment.

There is more. So-called learned gynaecology did not enter history because it involved knowledge complex enough to justify creating a specialty, but as maverick medicine, linking everything to hysteria and hysteria itself to a perverse will connected with the lesser or defective status of one half of humanity. *Woman* was constituted as an object not merely of pseudoknowledge but also of learned scorn. Faced with this object, the preeminence of male doctors allows them to strike poses of unparalleled presumption, take the worst theoretical approaches, and commit the worst diagnostic errors. Oncology departments are filled with women who had initially been assured by a gynaecologist that there was nothing wrong (it was all in her head), although they were often reporting unequivocal and blatantly obvious symptoms. After consulting a notebook containing an abridged medical history of his patients, Léon Schwartzenberg has told me that half the women he has treated for breast cancer had previously been reassured once (twice, three times) by their gynaecologist who, in a spectacular refusal to acknowledge reality, caused them to lose potentially precious months. "Women complain not because they have something wrong with them, but because they are women": corporate ideology plays a role in this refusal to recognize the reality of the disease, while claiming an objectivity that should astonish us. "As for me, I have always thought of gynaecology as a branch of veterinary medicine": twenty years ago this witticism uttered by a president of the French national gynaecological society could be found as the epigraph on xeroxed course notes for both male and female interns. The maxim, taken up by the profession as a rule of thumb, stipulates that what women patients say about their bodies is of no account because they have only fantasies to tell, so they might as well be treated like mute farm animals. The refusal to pay attention to what a woman says, presented here as an objective principle, is not just a fake method or a methodological posturing. Refusal to hear is already a scornful annihilation of the person; such a refusal to recognize the other opens the door to authoritarianism and a denial of reality. This point of view is not only misogynist, but also scientifically unacceptable. Moreover, this beastly president was flattering himself: veterinarians have more precise obstetrical knowledge and more reliable diagnostic skills than most gynaecologists, to such an extent that it is sometimes said that ewes and pregnant giraffes are in better hands than the female of the human species. The difference between a ewe and a woman is that the authoritarian pronouncement enjoining women to see themselves in a certain way has no effect on the ewe, whereas in the human world, woman is expected to be obedient and to conform to the image the world has of her. When Lévi-Strauss talks about symbolic efficacy, he evokes a shaman who uses incantations to cure a woman: it is a time-worn scene, a sha*man* tells her to get better, a *male* ethnologist notes that *she* really does get well. Despotic subjectivism can evolve from "be as I want to see you" to "you are exactly as I see you."

In case we lose sight of the norm—a woman conforms to the image people have of her—a Victorian novel reminds us that being feminine is possible only through suppression of the self:

> Then Rosalind took up the delicate work that lay on the table, and when the gentlemen entered, was seated on a low seat within the circle of the shaded lamp, warm in the glow of the genial fireside, her pretty head bent a little over her pretty industry, her hands busy. She who had been the image of anxiety and unrest a moment before, was now the culminating point of all the soft domestic

tranquility, luxury, boundless content and peace, of which this silent room was the home. She looked up with a smile to greet them as they came in. The brave girl had recovered her sweet looks, her colour, and air of youthful composure and self-possession, by sheer force of will, from the strain of the crisis in which she stood to maintain the honour of the family at every hazard. She had been able to do that, but she could not yet for the moment trust herself to speak.[41]

The heroine seated in the midst of such a peaceful scene has just faced a very difficult conflict. A disaster is imminent, but all trace of distress "must disappear before the gentlemen came in": one never shows men anything that might upset them. They will know nothing about it because a woman conforms to what men want to see. A woman must therefore be able to suppress her own reactions and take her expected place as an element of the decor, and the novelist evokes "that strange art which comes naturally to a woman, of obliterating herself and her own sensations."

6. Being as One Is Perceived

In May 1984, Jacques Le Goff gave a lecture entitled "What is the history of the imaginary?" The text was published, with the minutes of the ensuing discussion, in *Sens et place des connaissances dans la société*. What a wonderful title, and how we wish we could find a good book on the subject![42] An initial question from the floor provided an opportunity for Le Goff to reiterate his argument: "We must get rid of the prejudice that claims the imaginary is not a historical reality. The imaginary *is* a historical reality." Point taken, and I heartily agree. Up to this stage we are dealing with the categorical affirmation of a thesis open to coherent discussion. I will agree with it and even note that the affirmation is anything but superfluous: the twentieth century has been marked by the views of Jung, Bachelard, and Mircea Eliade, all of whom posit an atemporal, ahistorical, essentially primitive imagining soul, existing outside cultural, linguistic, and social variations. According to them, the same "dream data" are to be found in a medieval Japanese poem, a Scottish legend recorded during the Romantic period, the dream you had last night, and an Inca story recorded by some missionary. It is gratifying to see a historian contest this dominant point of view, even if we also note that the thesis affirming the historical existence of the imaginary has as its corollary the claim that the imaginary is properly the domain of historians, not of dream analysts. Le Goff's argument thus includes a corporatist benefit. Yet another object of study is drawn into the purview of historical science, but it is nonetheless a good idea, all the more so as it has already proven its usefulness in the Hellenist studies of the school of Jean-Pierre Vernant, Nicole Loraux, and others.[43] Thus, with no doubt whatsoever, "the imaginary is a historical reality."

A second question follows: "As a historian, do you think there is a specifically feminine imaginary?" It is a typical formulation, since it supposes that if there is a feminine imaginary, it is specific, any other imaginary being considered as the norm. But it is strange to ask him to say, as a historian, whether there is a distinction: his purpose is rather to explain that the thirteenth century imaginary is not the same as the imaginary of Antiquity. In all intellectual honesty, he should refuse to answer the question. However, Jacques Le Goff refuses nothing. He plunges in and everything he had constructed to that point collapses. "Yes, without a doubt," he answers, "And why? First of all, because I think there is an imaginary that is linked to the physiological situation of woman, which is not that of man." Is he serious? After stating that "the imaginary is a historical reality" we now move to physiology? And how, "as a historian," can one have any special insights into physiology and its possible connection with an imaginary? Are we to understand that women's imaginary is a product of their physiology while men's imaginary is a historical reality? For goodness sake, that may be the presupposition of the entire debate, if indeed there is a presupposition capable of being be so clearly formulated. Rather, we have the impression of someone who has been challenged and, in response, delivers random bits and pieces of a speech and mobilizes fragments from here and there. The original speech published by the Éditions du CNRS* is not so much a snapshot as a film that captures how a question can set a whole series of reflexes in motion. A truly admirable denial follows: "I'm not going to go back to a biological causality, but there are syndromes!" For goodness sake (once more), we have already had physiology, which refers to the functioning of a healthy organism, and now we're talking about "syndromes," a term that evokes pathology. He elaborates: "I think certain forms of the imaginary are already linked to the specificities of feminine anatomy and physiology." Note that it is we who are specific, and moreover this is what the question implied; and it is quite possible that this specificity is a deviation from a norm, so that the physiology of woman ("which is not that of man") amounts to a pathology.

The most egregious is yet to come. "The problems pertaining to woman in the domain of the imaginary are among the most interesting—but they are the most difficult, because there is a tendency to adopt ready-made ideas, whether they are old or new, and one must be cautious. I spoke of Satan a while ago; Christianity's second great creation is the Virgin Mary. That is a point which fascinates historians." The historian has managed to confuse the imaginary women are supposed to have (fruit of our imagination, which

*The Centre national de la recherche scientifique is a publicly funded French organization dedicated to using science for the public good—its motto is "la science au service des hommes" ("science in the service of men"). CNRS Éditions is an affiliate of CNRS that publishes books in the social as well as the physical sciences.

in turn is governed by our anatomy), with icons or figures of women, the imaginary of femininity, in this instance a Christian imaginary. The slippage is so extreme that we might overlook the choice of example—the Virgin Mary juxtaposed with Satan, thanks for that, but only as the "second great creation," thanks again. And let us note that if Satan is named first, then the Father, the Son, and the Holy Ghost are not creations of Christianity. In Christianity, even as it is seen by a historian, some characters are creators and others creations—couldn't Father, Son, and Holy Ghost be seen as cultural productions in the same way as Satan and Mary? The sex-based identification between a learned man and the three masculine principles of Christianity creates an epistemological obstacle, and it diverts the historian from historical inquiry into a discourse of belief. From a Christian point of view no doubt, Christianity is the work of these three masculine principles; but, for the history of civilizations, these figures are no more than products or elements of a particular religion.

Le Goff has moved imperceptibly from women as imagining beings or subjects (subjects invented by him, but that cannot be helped) to women as they are imagined or are objects of a collective imaginary. Thanks to this confusion, history reclaims its position, "among the Greeks, in Byzantium", "in the West", and so on and so on, and the answer ends with a self-satisfied "So I think there really is a feminine imaginary, for the reasons I have indicated, and these reasons are not too 'ideological.'" He had presented himself initially as a spokesperson for erudition, warning against ready-made ideas old or new, and recommending caution. To conclude with a decree that his reasons are "not too ideological" is to place himself once again in the camp of "science," without seeming to realize that whatever is scientific cannot be self-proclaimed. *Dura lex sed lex,* what is scientific is what is established according to protocols that can be verified by someone else (by anyone at all), and that therefore can be passed from one to another, even to an unknown person; or, it is what could always be written in the second person—take a board and roll a marble down it, and so on. Read this passage from Plato in relation to some philological data or other, or some point in art history, and you . . . and so on. This is not enough to ensure scientificity, but without it, we find ourselves in a discourse that is most definitely not scientific.

Moreover, there is a certain heavy-handedness in presenting "the Virgin Mary" as a "point that fascinates historians" without saying a word about theological works, as if she were the exclusive property of historians. In 1984, when the conference took place, male theologians and at least one female theologian, all of whom, it must be said, had some passing acquaintance with the history of religions, had for some time been studying the historical invention, not of Mary, but of her virginity. For the mother of Christ did not enter hagiography as a virgin, even less as that thoroughly solidified construct, the-Virgin-Mary, which recalls the excesses of nineteenth-century religious fervor, more than Christianity at its apogee. The early Gospels know nothing of this virginity, which seems to have appeared between the second and fourth centuries as the result of a series of confusions that mixed together a translation error in the Septuagint, the Greek Old Testament (the Hebrew term *alma* was translated by the Greek *parthenos,* which shifts the idea of a young woman to that of a young maiden), the identification of Jesus with the child promised by Isaiah, and God only knows what else. In fact, ever since the Reformation, Protestant theology has made it possible to doubt the virginity of the mother of Christ, thus opening the way to questions about its historical construction. In the nineteenth century, a Protestant, David Friedrich Strauss, tried to shed some light on the debate. By an irony of history, however, it was a female Catholic theologian, Uta Ranke-Heinemann, the first woman in the world to occupy a chair in theology, who produced the most comprehensive analysis of the construction of the virginity of Mary as part of a systematic reflection on the fate the Catholic tradition reserves for sexuality.[44] Ranke-Heinemann's earliest work on the question had prompted her dismissal from her chair in New Testament studies, though the university made up for it by appointing her to a chair in the history of religions. In principle, this is the dividing line between theology and the history of religions. In theology, beliefs determined by orthodoxy make it impossible to exercise one's judgment freely, even if it means sacrificing what is scientifically knowable; in studying the history of religions, one is free in principle, academically free at least. Thus, even though Ranke-Heinemann's book, *Eunuchs for Heaven: The Catholic Church and Sexuality,* which she wrote as professor of this discipline, resulted in her excommunication from the Church, as far as we can tell, it created scarcely a ripple in the University.[45]

To make the production of a myth intelligible, it is essential to search for an interpretive principle. Returning to the philological and historical scholarship on the virginity of Mary, Uta Ranke-Heinemann gives it a new center of gravity: what about the Church and sexuality? This question makes it possible to interpret the virginity myth, not by linking it to a "masculine" imaginary, said to be "masculine" in general, outside any precise history and social configuration but rather to a phantasm of those "eunuchs who made themselves eunuchs for kingdom of heaven's sake," as the Gospel of Matthew expresses it.[46] It is a fantasy of monks rendered neurotic by their self-imposed rule of chastity. Its production stands on the same sexophobic platform as the articles of canon law against contraception and abortion or the recent encyclicals on the same subjects. Following Ranke-Heinemann's lead—excommunicated as a heretic for the scientific rigor and creativity with which she proposed such unthinkable notions—we can push our analysis of Le Goff's speech one step further. To a question about a specific feminine imaginary, he replies with a reference to the Virgin, a figure whose construction is linked to a prohibition of sexual relations, most especially for clerics. Thus, a question about women's imaginary takes us from physiological difference to pathology to the negation of our existence as imagining subjects, leaving room only for our status as imagined objects. In the final analysis, we are objects imagined on the basis of a prohibition of sexual relations. And Le Goff will certainly have played havoc with the physiology reputed to be ours if the phantasm of a woman without anatomy obliterates it and if we end up disappearing, first as subjects and then as real bodies. For the body of the Virgin is rather a sublimated envelope, in tones of ivory or lily or more rarely ebony, emerging from draped silk, a pure receptacle whose function is only to carry someone else, in her arms or below her waist, a double shell empty of human physiology, a body whose surface is reduced to the visible, and an abdominal swelling beneath her robe that is said to be infinitely more interesting than she is. Mary is not one of us; she is not equipped with a digestive system, elbows, lungs, internal organs existing independently of their role as carrier of a future being, or legs that are so very useful for moving from place to place. When "women" are reduced to "woman", the patient and acquiescent object of a phantasmagoria that empties us of our being, nothing remains but a place to receive whatever is more important than woman herself. And any manifestation of ourselves that might be a bit more than this *nothing* is quite out of place. The same gesture seems to seal us within the status of object (not to know but to dream of) and to create the conditions for a radical non-knowledge, since the object itself has disappeared in the very process of positing it.

Merleau-Ponty's text dates from 1945, *The Renaissance Notion of Woman* was published in 1983, Le Goff's lecture was delivered in 1984. A Victorian novel shows explicitly how women conceal their misery from men—who have the right to see only what they want to see—a habit that corresponds to what a manuscript of *Trotula* pointed out four centuries earlier. It is not easy to determine precisely when it was first permissible for those who believe that the seeing and knowing subject is masculine to deny the reality of women's lives or to relate their refusal to any particular doctrine. Everything happens as if the very possibility of determining the validity of a "theory" and the factuality of an "object" resided in power—a point Hannah Arendt noted with respect to government propaganda at the time of the Vietnam War. Ignoring reports filed by the secret services, which exposed all sorts of facts contrary to the government's theories, the experts and decisionmakers of the Pentagon invented nonrealities, thus closing themselves off in a solipsistic logic of disinformation.[47] Sexual power conforms to the general logic of power, and it would be pointless to blame something as vast as "Western culture." One day, someone gives you an edition of the *Muqaddima* of Ibn Khaldun, born in Tunis in the fifteenth century, commenting that "he is the great Arab rationalist."[48] Naturally, the volume opens at the page where the rationalist explains that it is an error to believe that hunger causes death: eating is a habit, and if one gradually becomes accustomed to doing without food, everything will be fine. Men have been known to tolerate a forty-day fast. Two women who had not eaten in two years were presented at the sultan's court; they were put to the test, the facts were verified (*sic*), and they continued to fast until they died. The forty days of masculine fasting are epic exaggeration and heroism, the definitive fast of the women a denial of reality, in this instance, bearing on fundamental needs.

In his article "More than 100 Million Women Are Missing" Amartya Sen notes that although there are more women than men in the developed countries, the opposite is true in Asia, China, Latin America, and Africa.[49] Taking the statistics of the wealthy countries as an indication of a genetic advantage, he calculates a higher rate of female mortality in poor countries, variable from one poor country to another. Where resources are scarce, women receive even less food and medical care than men, and birthing conditions are deplorable; but the overall degree of poverty is not in itself the deciding factor. The extent of women's independence from family structures is another factor; a very poor sub-Saharan country in which women have access to independent work has a lower mortality rate than a less-poor country where they are completely dependent on their families. Sen explains that with greater independence, a woman can negotiate a better domestic deal for herself, and the status of the girl child, the food and care she receives, varies according to that of the adult woman. We have attempted to show that without recognition, there can be no cognition. Sen encourages us to add that without independence, there is no recognition, and therefore no awareness of even the most urgent of needs. But even when there is independence, recognition and therefore knowledge do not necessarily follow.

7. Legal Counsel on Strike

A recent legal example illustrates the refusal to go beyond the disorders to which woman is susceptible, and to know also her needs and rights and make them known. French legislation permits abortion under certain conditions. Since the end of the 1980s, commandos protesting against this right have been attacking abortion clinics. In 1993, the Neiertz law responded by creating a new legal concept, that of obstructing abortion. There were trials; the grounds of the courts' decisions constitute the ensuing jurisprudence. However, until very recently this jurisprudence was never properly constituted, that is to say, collated and published, a phenomenon unique in legal history. Usually, in response to a new law, specialized jurists, who are usually professors of law, allow very little time to elapse before publishing the jurisprudence that clarifies the implications and limits of a particular law. This process shows how a law passed by Parliament is treated by judges and lawyers, who are the legal technicians. In this case, however, two years passed, twenty judgments were rendered, and the specialists who collate judgments to identify their general tenor still neglected to publish the jurisprudence that provides necessary information for the courts, since a judge takes previous decisions into account in rendering her or his own verdict. Lawyers for the plaintiffs had to photocopy details of previous decisions in order to pass them on to new judges, and this continued until the French bar association became irritated enough to compensate for the lack of ordinary publication circuits by producing a brochure.[50] You do not need to be especially clairvoyant to predict that this jurisprudence will not appear any time soon on law school curricula. Why is it so difficult to include the jurisprudence confirming women's right to abortion in the legal knowledge published and taught? The French bar association responds: "the technical press is generally hostile to the rights of women and especially to the right to abortion." That is quite obvious. I would propose an additional interpretation that will take us back to the question of temporality. Teaching these facts to practicing jurists or law students presupposes both a recognition that abortion has a future, and an awareness of the thinking developed in various courts during the hearings. Legal decisions are not compiled for the pleasure of writing their history, but because tomorrow or in ten years, courts will need them. However, the legal mandarins seem incapable of persuading themselves—if indeed they try—that the Veil and Neiertz laws are here to stay, that they have a bearing on the future, and that therefore both the laws and the decisions they inform should be published and taught, just like laws against vandalism and smoking. From their point of view, these are temporary, transitory, or experimental laws; this was indeed the case for the Veil law between 1975 and 1979. They are thought to have no future—they cannot last. Thus the adversaries' position is the one assumed to have an (illusory) future.

At the heart of the problem is a wide-ranging scepticism about the future of laws recognizing women's rights. Attacks against clinics by antiabortion militants are prompted by this scepticism: these vandals claim that recognition of a right for women is nothing more than a misunderstanding, an error that acts of petty violence can dissipate, since such a right is powerless against their strength and capacity to intimidate. It would seem that the Veil law was never promulgated; no one can believe it. When the attacks began, the vigilantes counted on the passive complicity of the police and the authorities; they were right, alas. Mounted policemen would arrive at the scene hours after the attack and leave without having verified the attackers' identities. The government encouraged the family planning organization to respond with the most cautious inaction, as if the Veil law were basically debatable. People had to get involved and force the politicians to act.[51] Then came the Neiertz law; when the attackers were sued, they developed a new form of guerrilla warfare, this time on the judicial front. They were not merely defending themselves, as was normal; rather, they hoped for a jurisprudence that would condemn the law (*contra legem*) and judges who would condemn the lawmakers ("the judge"refers to the persons constituting the successive tribunals that hear a particular question). Your Honor, the Veil and Neiertz laws are incompatible with the rest of French legislation, don't you agree? Surely incompatible with the international treaties that France has ratified? And do they not include terms or categories that are not part of recognized legal language? The twenty opinions contained in the brochure published by the French lawyers' association show that these arguments were groundless—the terms of the Veil and Neiertz laws are perfectly compatible with the rest of the legal arsenal—but the fact remains that the antiabortionists hoped for a jurisprudence that would annul the legislation. Moreover, the various courts hearing the cases (and one notes their gender mix with pleasure) paid close attention to these matters and proposed extensive reflection on all aspects of the right to abortion, with the result that it emerged from the trials stronger than ever.[52] Let us quote one of the grounds of the Paris court of appeal: "the judge must not give a ruling outside the framework of the law [. . .] he would flagrantly exceed his role were he to do so, risk setting himself up as a moralist or a philosopher [. . .] eminent scientists have been unable to determine the beginning of human life precisely and unequivocally [. . .] the judge has no alternative but to accept the law."[53] We are delighted to hear this. From the judge's perspective, the law exists—it *is*, without any doubt, but the public must be reminded of it, forcefully and insistently.

The legalization of abortion in France is still a fundamental issue whose significance extends well beyond the practical needs it addresses. It was obtained by a broad-based activist movement that brought together women from all walks of life, and included a few men. In an interview in the magazine *Lunes* (1997), Simone Veil acknowledged that she had not really initiated the law that bears her name. Interior Minister Michel Poniatowski, fearful that members of the movement for free access to contraception and abortion might occupy Mme Veil's ministry and carry out abortions there, urged her to act without delay. Not only did this struggle require an enormous display of militant energy but it was also the occasion for professionals to volunteer their professional skills in the service of political ends. Women doctors, dentists, and nurses carried out abortions; others, who had studied the human sciences, wrote analyses and tracts that made full use of their expertise; women journalists risked quarrelling with their editors in chief; lawyers pleaded in show trials, and intellectuals like Simone de Beauvoir appeared as witnesses. A hitherto unknown phenomenon occurred. Women who had studied in the traditional fields of medicine, law, sociology used their knowledge and know-how to defend something that concerned all women, and women who had been called mere paramedics sometimes taught everyone a lesson. Thus the equation emerged: sexual solidarity, plus knowledge and even traditional know-how, challenge the patriarchal order. For reproductive rights change something in the balance of power in heterosexual couples. They shift the focus from "conjugal duties" to sexual pleasure. Women's access to knowledge or skills does not always lead to such a major upheaval; but, if a crucial issue arises, and if there are educated women capable of female solidarity and equipped with the relevant training and intellectual resources, then the knowledge and skills they and some men possess pose a threat to the established order. There was no need even to wait for the passing of a law: women in civil society discovered they could be subversive by using their own skills. However, Mme Veil and her staff deserve recognition for having formulated the legal principle so well: "The woman who feels that her pregnancy places her in a state of distress [...]." It is she who decides, and not some committee. By acknowledging her as the judge, the law asserts that no one knows better than she does what she has to do, and the formulation marks the entry into law of the principle of an equal freedom of conscience for all women.

In publishing and distributing the legal precedents, female and male lawyers for the plaintiffs acted in a manner similar to that of professional women who struggled to obtain legislation. But the positive message (there are good legal precedents; women and men lawyers are still giving their professional talent to the cause) circulated only in certain milieux. The major print media, whose role is not to publish the technicalities of judgments, have focused on attacks on abortion clinics, all the more so as the attacks themselves were intended to attract attention. The public was thus informed that an attack was followed by a trial and almost always by a sentence. However, comparison of the transcripts of court proceedings with the narrative provided in the daily newspapers reveals a discrepancy: in the press, the attacks were presented as an interminable and repetitive novel—a sentence, another attack, "the right to abortion repeatedly challenged." The newspapers announced an endless struggle that underscored the fragility of our rights, whereas to read through the legal precedents is reassuring. Except that we came close to knowing nothing about them, and shrewd lawyers-in-training are the only ones who will know how to find them.[54]

Here is a parallel that may seem far-fetched, but I offer it for your consideration. A sentence in a *History of French Feminism* states: "Taking up what was only intuited by Christine de Pisan, Cornelius Agrippa unambiguously attributes women's inferiority not to a different nature but to the education they receive." It is hilarious. Once again a woman's thought has been characterized as "nothing more than intuition," an intuition developed over more than two hundred pages, while a man's thought is described with reference to its firmness. There is something more insidious in this, however: while Christine deals with women's dignity, and Agrippa with their superiority, and both include views about equality in their discussion, our contemporaries refer to their ideas by their antithesis, "the problem of inferiority." Women are inferior and it is a problem to be debated. Thus dignity and equality, objects of positive discourse, are replaced by something sad and unsightly, woman's (*sic*) inferiority, though no one identifies to whom or to what they are inferior. Moreover, the comparison implies that Christine is inferior to Agrippa, although the two authors are remarkably in agreement about intellectual equality.[55] Has our culture inculcated a systematic tendency to deprive women of positive representations, and thus of authors and information that might support us?

8. *Verum index sui*

"I know the difference between the sexes: men don't understand anything," exclaimed a female student at the end of a particularly animated seminar discussion. Since I cannot ratify such a categorical statement, I propose this one instead: some men, filled with self-importance, do not understand anything; and perhaps, instead of wondering what a woman can know, at some point we will have to elaborate the concept of masculinist unknowing, which could prove to be useful even in the history of philosophy. How else could one explain the astounding proposition Spinoza advanced at the end of his life, an argument that he claimed was founded on experience but that took no notice of the facts? "But perhaps someone will ask whether it is by nature or by convention that women are subject to men. For if this is due solely to convention, we have excluded women from the government without any reasonable cause. However, if we consult actual experience, we shall see that it is due to their weakness."[56] *Ex earum imbecillitate*, it is a matter of their lack of spiritual and intellectual strength, since Spinoza argues that in the human species, moral and intellectual strength is the basis of power, and therefore of right. Now according to him experience would tend to show that if women are excluded from government and subjected to male authority, it is because of a natural weakness of spirit, for "nowhere has there been any instance of men and women ruling together; but whenever we find men and women living together, we find that the men rule and the women are ruled, and that on this basis both sexes live in harmony." Of course, among the legendary Amazons, women ruled, but that was because they did not tolerate the presence of men in their territory. Spinoza goes on to say that if women were naturally equal to men, endowed with equivalent strength of spirit and intellect, it would follow that among diverse countries, there would be some in which both men and women might rule, and others in which men, governed by women, would receive an education designed to limit the exercise of their intellectual qualities.

Thus, Spinoza proposes that *ingenium* is an innate characteristic and that women naturally have less of it; but when he encounters the hypothesis envisaging the possibility of men's subjection, he suggests that the education of those destined to be ruled is based on a mutilation of their intellect. The so-called experiment refutes the disturbing hypothesis: government by women "has nowhere happened, [therefore] I am fully entitled to assert that women have not the same right as men by nature, but are necessarily inferior to them." According to Spinoza, equal access to governing power by both sexes is neither possible nor desirable, for men's love for women is merely sensual, and they are jealous; therefore, equal power would threaten civic peace. Beneath the question of state rule we must also read that of domestic power, as if the conjugal subordination of women to men (to allay male jealousy?) were guaranteed only by the masculine monopolization of the State.

When equality is pronounced impossible and undesirable, one must sus-pect that the desirable, which is to say, desired by the author, determines what is possible. But what is odd is that Spinoza claims to base his argument on empirical evidence and to have observed that among "so many different nations," government by women was unknown in human history. He wrote this in 1677, in a year when the long reign of Elizabeth I of England was cer-tainly still a matter of common knowledge. Perhaps one might forget Mary Tudor or Christina of Sweden, but Elizabeth? Spinoza has denied reality. He had no opportunity to retract his statement; after ending the chapter with a "But I have said enough on this topic," he died, and the editions of the *Tractatus Politicus* all bear the fateful indication, *unfinished.* It may well be: after all, the poor man was old, and perhaps the page in question was only a draft. But where is the edition of this treatise that adds a note saying that "Spinoza's error is no doubt attributable to his fatigue" or "oddly enough, he has overlooked Elizabeth Tudor and Mary Stuart"? Generations of trans-lators and commentators have passed over this chapter and no one has seen that, with respect to the most basic factuality, the theory that claims to be founded on a *nullibi factum est* is untenable. When a theory signed by a famous gentleman collides with a historical fact, the theory wins. A group of Danish women campaigned against the Maastricht agreement because, as they insisted, it had been developed by a handful of men appointed by the executive level of government of the member countries rather than by a mixed assembly elected by a mixed electorate. They went on to propose an analysis of the treaty's weaknesses with the ironical comment: "but Father of course always knows best." Don't trust your judgment or what you know; a blunder signed by Spinoza or Hegel must remain invisible. "When women hold the helm of government, the state is at once in jeopardy, because women regulate their actions not by the demands of universality but by arbitrary inclinations and opinions."[57] Hegel did note the presence of women in government, and it is through his interpretation of fact that he whittles away at the facts themselves. It is difficult to see what threat was posed to Austria by the reign of Maria Theresa; and if England was in danger in Elizabeth's time, it was not because of her or her government. When a Spanish king declares war on you and sends an Armada he calls invincible to invade your shores and when three popes excommunicate you and the third encourages your subjects to become dissidents and join forces with the king of Spain, these are indeed dangerous times. It is not this danger, however, to which Hegel refers, but rather a risk inherent in the deeds of women who rule. Since, as women, they are not qualified to rule correctly, the State is in danger. Hegel must have forgotten the mad kings, who are not exactly rare in European history, and the protections extended to monarchs so that madness would be of little consequence. Spinoza denied that women had ever ruled; Hegel corrects this position somewhat but not completely, denying the value of government by women. Denial of value replaces the denial of reality—and yet no one dismisses either of these men as fools.

Curiously, the danger Hegel denounces echoes the 1588 "deposition" of Elizabeth by Pope Sixtus V, who claimed that the kingdoms of England and Ireland had degenerated to an extremely precarious state; moreover, they had become infected and contagious limbs threatening to infect the entire body of Christendom. Here the discourse is practically self-referential: England is in spiritual danger because it has separated from Rome, says Rome; the Pope claims that Elizabeth cannot govern because she does not have the support of the papacy; and since he himself calls on Elizabeth's subjects to revolt against her, he can then proclaim that England is in danger because he is making every effort to ensure it is. This proclamation amounts almost to a performative utterance: it creates what it names, as does a declaration of war. And we could almost allow a *verum index sui* (truth is its own indicator), but not quite. For the one who declares war does not necessarily win it, and the future knows something about that. From the quasi-performative of Sixtus V, uttered in the present tense (in 1588, year of the Armada, he states that

England and Ireland are in danger), to the philosophical-historical thought of Hegel who, fully two centuries later, announces in the eternal present (when women rule ...), we move from a statement that is about to sink with the Armada but has not yet sunk at the moment of its utterance, to a construction that can be proven wrong—in fact, to a false proposition. The Pope could base his argument on a future whose outcome was as yet unknown, whereas Hegel ought to have known that the major but external danger was dissipated by a storm and by the English fleet. It seems to me that Sixtus V, Spinoza, Hegel, and their commentators and the routine concerns of philosophy must be taken together as evidence of a cognitive chimera rather than a real allergy to rule by women. They all conspire to sustain the dream of a discourse that would be tangential to the papal performative, as if the aim of discourse were to produce itself in its entirety, even to the point of fabricating its own referent, as if paying attention to reality degraded this ideal and therefore caused suffering. Here is a good example: if ever a theologian of the political sphere was seriously embarrassed, it was John Knox. In 1558, he published a short work whose title summarizes its entire argument, *The First Blast of the Trumpet against the Monstrous Regiment of Women* ("regiment", here, meaning "government"). He argued the thesis in general terms, although in fact he was attacking only the Catholics Mary Stuart and Marie de Guise. Then suddenly Elizabeth became queen; she was of a religious denomination that Knox approved, and the Protestants needed her. Although he was happy she was on the throne, Knox neither withdrew his argument nor openly disavowed his book. Anyone who thinks he knows everything about a particular object wants to believe in his pontifical or even divine infallibility. It was Calvin who apologized to Elizabeth's government for having allowed the publication of the *First Blast* in Geneva, by advancing a theory that allowed him to maintain his position as arbitrator and have the last word: since rule by women is unnatural, only divine intervention could have called Elizabeth to the throne.

In the philosophical world, it is common to joke about "the empty eyes of the Greek gods." Mistaking the modern-day appearance of the ancient statues for their original state, Hegel philosophized about the vacuity of their eyes without knowing that originally they were painted. It is laughable to see such a false element fit so perfectly into the Hegelian system—it is as if they had to be empty so that the complex structure of the Hegelian system could unfold unhindered. Why then do we not laugh at the statement that "if women are at the head of the government, the State is in danger," a thought that flies in the face of the historical information available to the author? Without recognition, there is no cognition, and if acting and thinking women are omitted from the encyclopedia of human knowledge, it is because dull factual knowledge has already undermined the myth to such an extent that if, on top of everything else, we now have to acknowledge the reality of the noble deeds of real women who are subjects under the law, only dreariness remains. One more proof.

9. Interlude

A philosophical encyclopedia was being prepared, and the group responsible for the section on "English philosophy of the seventeenth and eighteenth centuries" was meeting at the Sorbonne. Everyone engaged in cultivating this particular garden was there, and a professor of English literature had also been invited. The aim was to ensure that no important author had been overlooked, to find volunteers to write about the philosophers who had not yet been assigned, and to determine the number of pages to be allocated to each one—so many for Locke and so many for Shaftesbury, ah, no, he deserves at least fifteen more lines! The haggling went on, and it was impressive to see the institutional value of each one being weighed up and quantified. Lucian of Samosata had imagined philosophers obliged to sell themselves one day in the slave market: at that auction, Stoics had a high value while Epicureans were worth nothing at all. Another day, another currency; now we establish the respective value of our authors by typographic space. Since Bacon had been assigned to me, I was part of the group. The group leader ran through a list of proper names, and there was a lengthy procession of Peter Adams and Anthony Jones of whom neither you nor I know anything. Our encyclopedia promised to be instructive! These Thompsons and Davises who would be summarized in a paragraph or two were perhaps "levellers", nonconformist theologians, and with a bit of luck, republican militants. If I could judge by the earnest expressions on the faces around me, I was not the only one to think it wise not to ask who these people were, in case there might be one among them who really was a philosopher and more or less important. We arrived at the letter "W", and I woke up, because one name that matters to me had not been mentioned. "There should be an entry on Mary Wollstonecraft," I said.

"Mary who?" asked the learned assembly with one voice.

"Mary Wollstonecraft," I repeated, glancing gratefully at the English literature professor, who had nodded.

"Who is *she*?"

The question came from all corners of the room. For the two previous hours, anyone could have insisted with impunity on an entry for a purely imaginary "William Marshall", and I was sorry I had not thought of it. But everyone has the right not to know who a Mary might be, to say so, and demand an explanation from whoever was impertinent enough to want to include her in an encyclopedia. So I began cautiously—her book on the rights of man, her debate with Edmund Burke (who had just been allocated two pages), her membership in the rationalist group known as the Dissenters, but I did not say she was the wife of William Godwin (three pages), even though the mention of the Dissenters sparked a glimmer of recollection in my neighbor: "She wasn't Godwin's wife, was she?" I went on to mention her interest in the philosophy of education, without specifying that it was the education of daughters, for even the education of girls is still education. Finally, I took the plunge and said that her most classic work, the one reprinted across the Channel for use in the schools, and on which, across the Atlantic, dissertations are written, is a treatise on the rights of women, in which she uses the conceptual legacy of the Enlightenment to contest the subjugation of women, thus—and I will not pass over it in silence—becoming one of the first feminist theorists.

Roars of laughter ("maybe you'd like an entry on women's lib while you're at it?"), jokes and giggles, while the professor of English literature says softly, "She *is* very important." He says it quietly, just as I had tentatively explained the reasons for Mary's enduring reputation. Neither of us was quite at home in this gathering. To claim that women exist in the history of philosophy, that the question of women's rights is as philosophical as the question of the so-called rights of man, and that moreover these questions might be seen as one and the same, is to set oneself apart and to take on the status of the Anglicist whom *we* had invited to join *our* group of philosophers. The laughter died down, the group leader wiped her eyes, and since she rather likes Bacon and me, she said, "All right, Michèle, but the shorter the better." Later, having looked into the matter, she finally recognized that this Mary was very important after all, so important that I would not have believed she needed me in order to exist. The following year, *A Vindication of the Rights of Woman* was on the curriculum of the *agrégation** in English. What did I tell them! And much later, the director of a group that included ours as a subgroup called me to say, "Just wrapping things up here, we're a bit short on women . . . , could you suggest a few?"

If we can judge by Mary Wollstonecraft's misadventure at the Sorbonne (although it all ended happily ever after), we must conclude that prior to the act of knowing, there is a judgment or a decision about the importance or lack thereof attached to re-cognizing the existence and value of this or that. If recognition must come before knowing, we must postulate that knowledge is ordered by a much more elementary structure than all imaginable a priori frameworks of perception or judgment: anyone who sees and judges has already deigned to meet the object halfway. In the case I have mentioned, a feminine name was enough to announce the place of a work, or rather

---

*See translators note p. 3, above.

its lack of place, in the initial division between what is and is not worth knowing, before the theme of the author's thought had even been indicated. One is perfectly entitled not to know of a Mary's existence or work; it is not so bad to admit one's ignorance publicly. And if someone wants her to be recognized as a woman of thought, it is prudent to see what she is about before she is perhaps allocated a small place. Let my wise reader make no mistake: Mary Wollstonecraft was lucky. Thanks to the airborne mediation of my words, my colleagues generously allowed the object to be submitted to them and subjected to their judgment. What happens in meetings in which a committee must choose between male and female candidates for a position? Is a feminine name enough to produce a reaction like the one that greeted the name of Mary Wollstonecraft? Does someone whisper to a neighbor, "Is that Godwin's wife?" marriage to a colleague conferring a legitimation by association? And if the poor woman is notorious for supporting women's rights or shows some degree of solidarity?

10. Masculine Foreclosure of Knowledge

We have talked enough about Elizabeth I to ask her what she thought of this female solidarity:

> 1. The Quene's Majestie consideringe howe the Palaces & Howses as well of Cathedrall Churches as of Colleges of this Realme, have bine, bothe of auncient and late Tyme, builded and inclosed in Severaltie, to sustayne & keep Societies and learned Men professing Studies and Prayer, for the Edification of the Church of God, & so consequentlye to serve the common Weal; And understandinge of late, that, within certeyne of the same Houses, as well the cheiffe Governours as the Prebendaries, Students and Members thereof, being married, do kepe particular Housholde with their Wifs & Children & Nurses, whereof no small Offence growth to the Entente of the Founders, & to the quiett & orderlye Profession of Studye & Lerninge within the same.

> 2. Her Majestie hath thought mete to provide Remedye herein, least, by Sufferaunce thereof, the rest of the Colleges (speciallye such as be replenished with younge Students) as the very Romes & Buildings be not aunswerable for such Families of Women & young Children, should folloe the like Example:

> 3. And therefore expressly willeth and commandeth, that noe Manner of Person, being either the Hedd or Member of any Colledge or Cathedrall Churche within this Realme, shall, from the Time of the Notification hereof in the same Colledge, have or be permitted to have, within the Precincte of every such Colledge, his Wife or other Woman, to abide and dwell in the same, or to frequent & haunt any Longinge within the same Colledge; upon Payne, that, whosoever shall do the contrarye, shall forfeit all Ecclesiasticall Promotions in any Cathedrall or Collegiatt Churche or Colledge withim this Realme.

4. And, for Continuaunce of this Order, her Majestie willethe, that the Transcripte hereof, shal be reputed as Percell of the Statuts of the same, and be so observed.

5. Yeven under oure Signet, etc[58]

This text corresponds so poorly to what we hope for today from women's access to government that we may be tempted to think it a fake, like so many other documents. I thought it wise to double-check: the original, attached to a letter from Elizabeth to William Cecil, Chancellor of Cambridge, as well as three copies, are found in Ipswich, in an absolutely reliable archive, and registered in the *Calendar of State Papers* for August, 9, 1561. At the very most one may wonder about the Queen's status as author. It is possible to suppose that Cecil himself instigated the injunction, relaying the complaints or simple concerns of Cambridge dons. In 1549 the clergy had been granted permission to marry. This innovation threatened the university as an all-male bastion, whereas until that time, the celibacy of the learned had been assured by the simple fact that they belonged to the clergy. Elizabeth didn't much like married people, and dealt carefully with her academics. During a royal visit to Cambridge, she was asked to make a speech in Latin. What? I no longer have the right to speak English to My subjects?? She finally gives in to the argument that the university world wants to hear nothing but Latin: *Etsi foeminilis pudor* ... although feminine modesty may make me hesitate to give an unprepared speech before such an assembly of learned men, my good will..., the speech was a success.[59] She had done so little to turn her male subjects against rule by women that the conspirators in the Gunpowder Plot, who attempted quite literally to blow up her successor, intended to install a little girl on the throne, hoping to transform her into a good Catholic. What shakes England in the sixteenth and seventeenth centuries is not the question of whether the State is governed by a king or a queen; rather, the specific religion of the person who holds the sceptre is the most important issue. Symmetrically, the papacy supported Mary Tudor and Mary Stuart, both Catholics. Moreover, the English conspirators showed a decided preference for potential queens. While her half-sister Mary was alive, Elizabeth is said to have been the intended beneficiary of a plan for a coup d'état; the same was true of Mary Stuart during her imprisonment in London, of Lady Jane Grey, whom the Protestant faction wanted to have succeed Edward VI, and of Elizabeth Stuart, who would have reigned if the Gunpowder Plot had succeeded. Those women, who reigned or who almost reigned, were descended from kings; if genealogy was a major factor, sex seems not to have been decisive in a country that had rejected the fictitious "Salic law." Unless of course we have to say enough is enough and that the plotters' mania for putting women on the throne should be questioned: were they hoping to exercise the real power themselves vicariously through a queen who would be more accommodating toward factions than a king? It is probably to the English Renaissance that we owe one devious idea: when a woman reigns, high-level (male) organizations, religious factions (*idem*) can more easily manipulate the central power.

But why talk so much about the Renaissance, when specialists of art history, philosophy, or ideas do not agree among themselves about its exact dates, and when the usefulness of cutting up history to make a slice called "Renaissance" is sometimes contested? The old debate is complicated today by a question that touches on geopolitics, namely, that of the emergence of a European culture as such. The dominant doctrine claims that the reign of Charlemagne marked the beginning of the continent of Europe, with ancient, Biblical, Germanic, and Celtic traditions apparently having blended together at that time.[60] Today's European federalism chooses to find its reflection in the empire of the ninth century, a choice that augurs nothing good for the mixing of sexes: for Charlemagne, with his florid beard and his schools, presented as schools *for boys,* is said to have decreed that convents of nuns, and their abbesses, were to be placed under the control of bishops, that is, of men. And we want to represent him as founder of the world of tomorrow? If we consider how historical periodization can serve political ends, and if we prefer a world inclusive of both sexes, and we also believe in the importance of women's access to knowledge, we must propose a different periodization. Antiquity ended in Alexandria in 415 with the assassination of Hypatia, and the Renaissance—a reappearance of ancient ideas whose possibilities and limitations are still relevant today—begins with *la vaillant Christine,* as one of her fifteenth-century colleagues called her, a poet-philosopher who stands for some of what we must hope for from Europe.

11. *Epikleroi*

Some of you may not have heard of Hypatia, who at the beginning of the fifth century taught mathematics and philosophy in Alexandria.[61] Young people from the four corners of the known world flocked to her classes. She was the daughter of Theon, a philosopher who owed to her his nickname "father of a divine child." Then came Lent, 415. A certain Cyril, bishop of the city, sent monks to burn the synagogues and assassinate Hypatia, which they did with an abominable display of sadism. Antiquity had known thinking women. In the seventeenth century, Gilles Ménage was to compile a catalogue of them, without managing to reintroduce the idea into Western culture that women have been able to be, and can be, philosophers. Even in 1992, George Steiner claims that in the entire history of the West there has been only one, Simone Weil, and, according to him, she paid for it with her health, her body, her femininity, and her life, which makes her a spectre to brandish before the eyes of all women.[62] If we divide history into periods according to the possibilities available to women, Antiquity ends with fair Hypatia, and for our colleagues who will never emerge from the Middle Ages, she is as dead as if she had never existed.

It is not easy to disentangle the role sexism may have played in this murder. At the time, both female and male neo-Platonists were persecuted by a Christianity administered by men who in principle had no sexual life and who, if they had read Saint Paul (some, too ignorant for that, had only heard about him), might argue that a woman must be silent in public places and assemblies. Since 313, when Constantine had promulgated an edict confirming Christianity as the state religion throughout the Roman Empire, there had been confusion between a spiritual mandate and the exercise of temporal power. According to some historians, this confusion became the defining characteristic of the Middle Ages.[63] One of the issues in dispute between Cyril and Hypatia is said to have been that, as bishop, Cyril considered himself the political authority of the city against the Roman prefect who, curiously, continued to distinguish politics from religious authority. Hypatia was of the same opinion as the prefect, for which she deserves credit: confusing a religion with the State produces the strongest possible structure of intolerance since other religions are thereby excluded from society, and with them atheism or free thought. When, in addition, the only authorized belief is administered by communities of men who force women to keep silent, the structure amounts to state sexism. The assassination of Hypatia marks the enacting of a dogma and the end of a possibility that had been partially available, if not to all women, at least to a few.

To that point, although political and social life in the Hellenic world had been marked by an undeniable marginalization of women, some, called *epikleroi,* were better off than the others. The term means "a girl who is part of the inheritance." Not, strictly speaking, an heiress, since a girl could not inherit, but a girl to be taken with the inheritance because she was born to a father who had no son. In Athens, if she was not married when her father died, this girl, who found herself on the margins of an inheritance or who was part of the inheritance, automatically became the wife of the real heir, a close relative of the father; in Sparta, she became the wife of whatever man he chose, even of a stranger. With local variations, this practice is documented everywhere in Greece and the Greek world. And without being exactly the heiress, this girl without brothers was more or less the guardian of the inheritance. Otherwise, Aristotle would not have written that one of the problems in Sparta was that too much land belonged to women, because of the large number of *epikleroi* and the custom of giving large dowries.[64] Starting from this principle of property transferral, we can propose the concept of a literate *epikleracy,* for in the Hellenic world talents could be regarded as property: knowledge and know-how constitute an inheritance that allowed one to live.[65] Just as fathers without sons leave their material property to their daughter, so philosophers or learned men transmit their store of knowledge to a daughter. This practice appears as early as the time of Cleobulus, one of the seven wise men of ancient Greece who taught philosophy to his daughter Eumetis, "blessed intelligence", also called Cleobuline. She, who never married, became director of the school after her father's death. I will leave it to those more knowledgeable than I to determine whether, in all instances of girls initiated into knowledge, there was no brother; I can say only that I have found nothing to invalidate this hypothesis. Hypatia is typically a philosophical *epikleros;* even if she was sent to school in Athens, as some believe, education within her family was the core of her learning process. Her assassination by a gang of brutish monks marks the beginning of a time when knowledge will no longer be transmitted within the family but rather, when indeed there is knowledge, within closed masculine communities; and it will be narrower, less open knowledge, clerical and limited to religious tradition. Schools for boys— including boys of lower-class origin—associated with Charlemagne, then the universities, will produce clerics, administrators, and priests, not learned men. Special reference will be made to the poor schoolboy. Helping poor men gain access to studies was an issue; so very many clerics were required to teach in their parishes that, as Saint Augustine says, contraception is a worse sin than incest with one's mother—the endowments that were to constitute the rich colleges of Oxbridge had this poor schoolboy in mind.

Christine de Pisan represents the resurgence of the literate *epikleros.* She was the daughter of an unfortunate astrologist-doctor who had no son (she herself underscores the fact), and who transmitted to her a part of his knowledge, only crumbs, she regrets; but judging from her work, they were tasty crumbs. Or rather, the quantity matters little: fatherly teaching had obviously encouraged her to educate herself. She gives evidence of highly sophisticated reading. We might call "Renaissance" the period marked by the reappearance of a class of literate laity, possibly married, fathers and sometimes fathers of daughters only, as if the family, the book, and secular knowledge were taking revenge on the monastery, school, or university. And if you accept my concept of literate *epikleracy,* all of a sudden you can envisage a Europe swarming with ladies and female members of the lower bourgeoisie who are "nurtured by literary culture" thanks to a family situation in which the education of daughters is all the more careful if there are no sons. In the sixteenth century Thomas More created a little school in his house for his children and his wards because of just such a situation. His only son was mentally handicapped, whereas one of his daughters was brilliant. His action set a new precedent: during the sixteenth century everyone talked about More's daughters, and Anna Maria van Schurman was still talking about them in 1641. A letter to William Gonell, a tutor, shows that he is thinking particularly about his daughters. He writes:

> Education, along with virtue, has more value to me than a king's ransom; but if it is separated from innocence, it produces only a suspect reputation. And this is even more true in the case of a woman, whose learning is so often mercilessly attacked, since it is a new phenomenon that reflects negatively on male laziness; men see *belles lettres* as a natural evil, and they imagine that they can extract enough from the vices of cultivated people to allow their own ignorance to pass for virtue.[66]

A new phenomenon, says More, but widespread in the milieux affected by humanism, and severely condemned. A good century before him, Christine de Pisan, in writing of unworthy men who have known or met many women whose intelligence and noble behavior exceeds their own, notes that they have become bitter and rancorous, and out of jealousy have held these women up to public opprobrium.[67]

We can also remember the attacks against two sisters from Verona, Isotta and Ginevra Nogarola, and the tissue of fantasies aroused by their mastery of humanistic knowledge.[68] Isotta complains that the entire city is laughing at her; an anonymous pamphlet has even gone so far as to accuse her of egregious sexual excesses, claiming in passing that no eloquent woman is chaste. As for male humanists, their perception of the situation is far from simple. First, we find Guarino's enthusiastic praise in a letter to Foscari who had sent him some of Isotta's essays and then in letters to others who are also men; but when Isotta is bold enough to write to him, he does not reply, as if she interested him only as a subject on which he could hold forth interminably in conversation with his colleagues or disciples (men), and not as an interlocutor. The poor woman sees this as a situation linked to her sex and, persisting, asks if he has been shocked by her transgression of the "laws that require a woman to be silent." What happened to her sister Ginevra after her marriage—male humanists lost all interest in her—shows even more clearly the tyranny their fantasies imposed on literate women: one of them, outlining to Isotta how much Ginevra has been changed for the worse by marriage, fantasizes about virginity and the loss thereof, as if virginity were a necessity for women to have any sense of the humanities.

Thus More takes note of a social reality—erudition in a woman is attacked—and tries to understand it. Two reasons are evoked: it is something new and, one might note, not yet assimilated by the social context; it is a bare fact, which simply emerged without the supporting justifications that might have allowed it to take root in social life. Everything seems to take place as if the humanists gave their daughters access to the high culture of their time—Latin, Greek, prosody, philosophy—without really knowing why. There is knowledge to transmit; are we perhaps to think it was the stock of knowledge itself that wanted to find someone to inherit it? Since they are laymen, there is no reason for them *not* to pass on what they have to their daughters, like the Greeks whose daughters were a kind of recipient of their legacy; the "new fact" arises, not because secular milieux discover a compelling motive for educating their daughters, but simply because an obstacle has disappeared—the barrier constituted by the stranglehold over intellectual life maintained by closed masculine communities like the monasteries and universities. And if the reason for educating one's daughters was not immediately apparent to the fathers themselves, it is because the question is basically "why not?" In the third-world countries that gave themselves universities after independence, thus creating a class of intellectuals more or less out of step with their society, we can see the phenomenon that marked the Greek schools and the Renaissance. It would take a lot for an educated man from Bamako or Delhi not to allow his daughter a higher education, especially when he has no son and basically because he has no reason for refusing to do so. He himself may have had a scholarship in Paris or Bristol, since the colonial period imitated the medieval model and gave assistance to men. Now, we have women colleagues in every discipline in every part of the world. However, universal education, for all girls and all boys, has not yet been achieved and there is no parity: 70 percent of children who do not go to school at all are girls. Is that a reason to imagine, as happens all too often, that all women in the developing world are illiterate? Under the Taliban, the great leap backward had the effect, among other things, of forbidding women doctors to continue to practice. That should have shaken the prejudices of public opinion in developed countries and forced a recognition that before Kabul fell into the hands of the Taliban, there were women doctors in the country. And why would there not have been?

And whie nott so? This is how a seventeenth-century *epikleros*, Martha Moulsworth, judges the fact that her father taught her Latin[69]—and why not? she says before going on to look for justifications in the imaginary, and a sexual solidarity between muses and women of this world. Undoubtedly there were no justifications except in the imaginary. Whereas the education of men led to an occupation, nothing comparable was available to women—whence the chapter devoid of triumphalism that Lisa Jardine devotes to women's access to humanist culture, *Education for what?* Moreover, Martha Moulsworth notes: "Lattin is not the most marketable marriadge mettall." If finding a husband is the essential standard, then knowledge has really neither purpose nor functionality. If she had not had a dowry of a more solid material sort, she adds, she would have remained unmarried. A dowry in money or in land is given to the husband, whereas one must acquire knowledge oneself in order to possess it—might this be one of the reasons for male resentment of intellectual women? Martha Moulsworth nevertheless takes pleasure in her intellectual dowry, and she hopes other women will have a more institutional access to culture: "Two universities we haue of men/O that we had but one of women then/O then that would in witt, and tongs surpasse/All art of men thatt is, or ever was," *art* in this instance being understood as everything that is a human creation. The ultimate consequence of women's institutional access to knowledge would be a spectacular surpassing of existing knowledge. The poem is elliptical, as if the author were experiencing some difficulty in specifying the effects that would follow from a university for women. The vision is not detailed, but this very lack of representation makes space for the lyrical certainty of the writing subject. During this period there is a collective difficulty in proposing an adequate representation of the meaning of women's access to the world of knowledge, but let us take careful note of the force of the question, *and whie nott so?* High-level instruction for what purpose? asks Lisa Jardine, and why not? replies Martha; if these two contradictory questions, left without a precise answer, occupy a certain reemerging consciousness, we should not be surprised that, in the Renaissance and beyond, the theme produced endless reflections or rantings. The bare fact (some women are educated) for which a suitable location is sought within the cultural milieu generates considerable discussion, sometimes in an unstable way.

Thus Thomas More proposes two different justifications, one appearing to take back what the other grants. He declares that humanity, reason, and study include both sexes: "the designation of human being is suitable for either sex and it is reason that distinguishes human nature from that of animals; the study of the humanities is suitable for both, a study that improves reason and makes it fertile like a ploughed field on which has been sown the seed of good precepts." But he goes on: "And supposing that the feminine earth is not fertile, that it produces more weeds than good crops (an opinion common to many who seek to deter women from study), I would think it necessary to give all the more care to cultivating a woman's spirit through literature and wise precepts, in order to correct a vice inherent in her nature." The two justifications, one by the validity of reason for both sexes, the other by the correction of a specific vice, together legitimize education for girls, but philosophically they are out of step with each other. The first alludes to the general program of humanism, which supposes that human nature is not given but is infinitely perfectible; it is therefore possible to develop humanity in oneself by reading works of wisdom. The Renaissance will coin the term *Litterae Humaniores*, humanities that make humanity more human. The second justification is a reminder of the gospel metaphor of the barren ground, in this case feminine, a hypothesis that, ironically, More would be prepared to concede. It confirms his project (if this is the case, it is all the more necessary to educate women) but renders the point of view inconsistent: the education given to young girls will either develop in them a nature that already includes reason or will correct an innate vice. Two contradictory reasons for educating daughters (it is a recourse to the dilemma: if A therefore X, and if not-A also therefore X), two opposing judgments of the being-that-is-woman for the sake of one certainty: teach my little girls, and you are right Gonell, "not to want to clip the wings of the noble and elevated spirit of my dear Margaret." If then it is possible to propose two opposing ideas of the ethical-ontological status of women on the same page, the education project surely does not derive from an idea of "woman." Anthropology neither precedes nor commands the decision to educate.

Not all men are sure of what they say, not all pronounce dogmatically on "woman"; if More hesitates between two possible assessments, the first affirmed as a thesis, the second as a hypothesis that he will concede if necessary, this hesitation is then the most salient feature of what he says. He has no very clear idea of what "woman" is, but he wants his little girls to be able to contemplate sublime things, hoping that they will find in them a "serenity and peace of the soul," and no doubt strength of character as well, if thanks to that contemplation they will not allow themselves to be "hurt by the stupidity of the illiterates who mock the study of the humanities." With the disease comes its remedy, since women's erudition is attacked as "an accusation of masculine laziness." For More, the allegedly difficult relationship between intellectual women and bodies of knowledge stems from men's aggressively projecting on to women their own shame at not being learned. Let us bear this diagnosis in mind: the monks of Hypatia's time were ignorant, the young murderer in the Montreal massacre was an academic failure. In a culture that either overvalues knowledge or sees it as a sin, one idea endures, namely, knowledge should at least respect the social hierarchy of the sexes. When this does not happen, the rejection of all challenges to the dogma can even include murder.

The thought developed in *Utopia* (1516) shows no interest in an anthropology of "woman". The Utopians have ample leisure, since joint property ownership means that work is organized to the best effect; each person works only a few hours a day, and this arrangement makes time available to be used at the discretion of each. Both men and women play, listen to music, and attend lectures or readings. They read Plato and Plutarch, revel in the persiflage of Lucian, enjoy Aristophanes, Homer, Thucydides, and the tale does not suggest that the texts should be expurgated for women. The first part of the reasoning presented to Gonell reflects this utopian lesson: education is valid for both sexes, culture is honest pleasure, contemplation of truth is pleasing, and these pleasures constitute the meaning of life for both sexes since nature wants everyone, male and female, to have a happy life. In this context, "woman" is said, not as the object of an anthropological theory, but as an end in herself, just as "man" is, since persons are ends and not means. Each in her or his own way, they give themselves (or not) to the things of the spirit. But within the family, they cease to be ends. Wives are subject to their husbands, children to their parents; parents chastise their children and husbands their wives; and More slips in a remark about the dizzy spells common among pregnant women, as if pregnancy were an excess or an imbalance. "Woman" and "wife" are not strictly synonymous. A woman is a human being of the female sex and there is a commonality of nature and vocation between the two sexes; a wife is tied to a man by marriage. More, who sees this subjection as appropriate, maintains a conception of the patri-archal family with a husband-father as head; within the family, women who have become wives or future mothers are represented as needing correction or chastisement, and as susceptible to the vagaries of pregnancy. Woman is therefore abstracted from the being-that-is-wife, since conjugal subjection does not affect the status of the being-that-is-woman. He had no reason to propose an anthropology of the feminine, since, beyond conjugal life, a woman lives an ordinary human life that he does not define as analogous to what he could observe of masculine existence. Utopians of both sexes detest war, know nothing of duels, and abhor animal fights; three of the reference points of virility are thus challenged. In separating the concept of woman from that of wife, More recalls Christine de Pisan. *The City of Ladies* is centered on the notion of a human being of female sex whose dignity Christine reconstructs. But the closing comments addressed to the reader reintroduce wives: you who are married, do not disdain being subject to your husbands. Let the woman who has a sensible husband thank the Lord, let her whose husband is neither good nor bad be thankful that he is not worse, and let the woman with a wicked husband put up with him.[70] One thing, however, distinguishes Christine de Pisan from More and Saint Paul. She does not feel obliged to say that subjection is right, she limits herself to recommending patience, and she does so only in the post scriptum to the reader, thus almost outside the text. And to demonstrate the value of women, Lady Reason resorts liberally to what one might call "proof by widows", for they in particular have shown the capabilities a woman may have. But if the magic formula is to be a woman and to have been a wife, then this is clearly because a problem has not found its solution.

The time of the *epicleracy,* which has not ended anywhere, produces some notable contradictions. One of them is to allow a few women of select families access to intellectual life without changing the average or everyday situation. Such access means that these women are seen as existing beyond—therefore outside—their sex. Yet not even a fine collection of cultivated and learned women abolishes women's exclusion in principle from knowledge, even if some of them are henceforth well placed to think about what might improve the lives of all women. The major contradiction continues to be a wish to institute equality of access to bodies of knowledge without at the same time questioning marital and paternal power; consequently, *woman,* a subject who is free to roam in the world of knowledge, is differentiated from *wife,* who remains subordinate. What happens to a woman's subjectivity when she is free (in principle) in her intellectual life and subjugated (in practice) in her family? Let us not imagine that the problem is obsolete, even if to all intents and purposes in our own societies the legal principle of marital authority was abolished scarcely a generation ago. Masculine domination persists in the domestic sphere; inequalities in the workplace prevent many women from renegotiating their domestic agreements, and these inequalities are carefully maintained by the (male) managers of the workplace. Being free in principle in one sphere, and dominated in practice in another, cannot help but produce some strange effects. When women whose potential material independence is tied to intellectual work experience some difficulty in being, everything encourages them to conclude that their problem lies in their feminine essence (which is incompatible with that sort of work), and they have no means, except within themselves, to make them aware of the structures of the learned world and of how their active presence might effect some positive change in it. A significant proportion of the women who have been admitted to the intellectual world are still *epikleroi.* Being born a woman, and working class, is still a difficult combination, not because of the sum total of disadvantages, but because the institutionalization of knowledge continues to exclude women, although it makes a few exceptions. This phenomenon is on the increase in Europe. Until recently, for example, attending university cost almost nothing except the price of lodging and meals. Today, however, universities are raising tuition fees. "E = MC3, the cost of everything is going up, even universities." To use Virginia Woolf's phrase, this move will accentuate both material and immaterial barriers since financial difficulties can be psychologically dissuasive for both men and women whose presence in university is not already legitimized. In response to protests made on behalf of young people of modest means, the authorities promise to allocate funds in recognition of academic performance rather than financial need. But should we believe this promise? If we estimate the administrative cost of an operation requiring the submission and review of application files, we must conclude that once the secretaries and faculty are paid out of the tuition revenues, little money will be left, and assistance to the children of the working classes risks being meagre indeed. Moreover, daughters of working-class families have never been part of the discourse or of any plan; there is a risk that the Carolingian preference for sons will reappear. And among those who are neither rich nor poor, it is the son who will be encouraged from birth, even though for the moment there is no need to think fifteen years ahead about how to send a child to university. If the proportion of women in the student population were suddenly to decline, there would be significant consequences, even for those not eliminated by the new system. If I can believe my own observations, what altered the spirit of university study, even for the *epikleroi*, was the entry of girls from average or working-class backgrounds. During the 1960s, two types of women students could be contrasted. On the one hand, those from upper-middle-class families, who had gone to private confessional schools, were studying while they waited for marriage; on the other hand, those from a more modest milieu, whose mothers had paid employment, and who had been educated in public primary and secondary schools, were determined to put their education to use in some occupation and to work for a living. But one day, I began to see the daughters of ministers, ambassadors, or doctors enroll in university with plans that to that point had been more typical of poorer daughters.[71]

12. Three Headscarves

When we think of the countries that, from the Renaissance to the present day, have allowed only a few women to have access to knowledge, we can see that the *epikleros* has no certain destiny. Nothing determines in advance what use she will make of her intellectual inheritance. Margaret More, who is still known for her translation of the *Commentary on the Lord's Prayer* by Erasmus, was her father's *alter ego*, as if she were repeatedly duplicating her relationship with the father figure without being able to go beyond it. Others have lived their lives completely oblivious to the collective situation; "I have never felt oppressed" being the typical justification for such an attitude. A quick look at *Femmes en tête* (1997) is enough to confirm the possible (though not automatic) persistence of "things have always gone well for me," which is not even always true but is thought to be the right thing to say in a context in which every criticism is seen as a recrimination.[72] Christine de Pisan deserves our admiration: although she could have identified herself with the paternal source of her culture, she used it instead to defend the cause of all women "of high, average, and humble situation," calling for schools and legal training to enable them to defend themselves. Four centuries later, Mary Wollstonecraft was obliged to repeat the demand by calling for mixed schools for everyone. Thinking about an issue does not guarantee achieving one's goals; but for women who have inherited knowledge to realize that they must think on behalf of all women, is a fragile, unpredictable phenomenon that occurs only intermittently, in our own era just as at the dawning of the modern age, and potentially everywhere. For example, Algerian women with university diplomas are working to bring literacy to women of the lower classes, while at the same time, a Yemenite woman, completely veiled in black, who drives her car and delivers her lectures in a faculty of law, considers it right for women found guilty of adultery to be put to death (although she does concede that stoning is not the most humane method). Women anthropologists in India have exposed an abomination they call wife burning (if the in-laws are not pleased with the bride or her dowry, they may stage a "domestic accident" that is in fact a murder). African women campaign against female circumcision wherever it is found, and they find themselves in conflict with an insipid cultural relativism, applied only to women. For no one cares a bit when a nuclear power station is built in India, when Geneva and the Emirates have the most cordial banking relationships in the world, and when an African monarch has an epidural anaesthetic for prostate surgery. However, when Egyptian women protest against the construction of a seventh mosque in a city that claims it has no money to build the very first school for girls, they are unfailingly labelled as having sold out to the West, and never mind the fact that the mosque is built using techniques with nothing Egyptian about them. Localism and the transformation of cultures into superficial folklore both work against women's access to progress and fail to prevent the importing of Western tools of power or amenities for the privileged sectors of society. Awa Thiam, a Senegalese philosopher, testifies against female circumcision at a trial in Paris; the Mali defense lawyer in turn accuses her of being a victim of ethnocide and says she has "nothing African left except a few negroid features"; he himself had come to France by plane, and called a French woman, supposedly an anthropologist, to testify in favour of female circumcision. People imagine that in the Third World the emancipation of women is not even about to begin, although it is claimed to be a fait accompli in Europe. As a critical transformation of any culture and the creation of conditions of equality, women's emancipation is possible everywhere, because educated women and women's movements exist as its foundation and because everywhere so much remains to be done. Where I come from, cultural relativism posing as a pretext for sexual domination is just one of many things still to be unmasked.

As long as it is a matter of subjugation rather than liberation, any religious or national culture can demonstrate its readiness to integrate elements it may find exotic, without questioning their possible origin. In Istanbul at the end of the nineteenth century, a certain Dr. Zambaco introduced cauterization of the clitoris with a red-hot iron as a way of dealing with masturbation in little girls; commenting that he had learned it at an international medical conference in London from a certain Dr. Jules Guérin, he said, "when I returned to Constantinople, I had no difficulty persuading the family to accept the advice of the learned academician."[73] In the sixteenth century, Vivès, of whom we will have more to say, deplores the fact that some widows do not mourn their husbands enough; he offers the example of the Thracian and Indian widows competing for the honor of being cremated with the deceased.[74] This point allows us to judge the kind of enclosure he has in mind in *De Institutione Feminae Christianae*. We might think he is attempting to confine the women of his tribe within local religious law so that they will belong to this religion and no other; but such is not the case, since when he extols the virtues of Indian or Thracian wives he forgets that Christianity forbids polygamy and suicide. Furthermore, since 1989, a psychodrama unfolding in France enables us to understand that allergy to other cultures is not a simple matter. During the first trial for female circumcision (and not for homicide by clitoridectomy), the "headscarves affair" exploded, and attracted much more attention. With respect to female circumcision, the response was indifferent cultural relativism—"that's their culture", or, in its Left-Bank version, "this custom is not incompatible with republican social order and therefore should be tolerated"[75]—and then comes silence in the face of this violence aimed at destroying the libido. The response to the headscarves was a call to expel the schoolgirls in the name of a vacuous secularism. "We'll liberate these girls," said some who had never done anything for equality of opportunity or for making sexual information available in schools, and who now wanted the schools to force their pupils to be free. "Schools have the right to insist on discipline," said others, while a young man old before his time came out with the comment, "I want to see what I'm trying to pick up." Everyone, it seems, agrees that women should submit—to discipline, to a man's desire. By the thousands in France, and by the millions throughout the world, little girls are circumcised or live under the threat of it, while at the same time inspectors in the *lycées* report there are almost no girls wearing headscarves in schools. None of this is to the glory of our opinion-makers or of the international image of France. Yet the headscarves affair is ongoing in spite of the astoundingly disproportionate attention it has received, whereas only a handful of militant women and legal experts, entirely on their own, continue the struggle against female circumcision. Even if it is a matter of anti-Islamic prejudice in the case of the headscarves (Jewish boys' skull caps and Catholic holy medals are still allowed in schools), the whole affair shows that girls' right to education is not a right, since a simple piece of clothing can justify expulsion. As for the right to bodily integrity and sexual desire, no one even talks about it.

In order to understand the rare scarves that are headline news in the French media, and the more numerous scarves to be photographed at Istanbul University, I think we must take the fragility of girls' right to education as a starting point, and leave the Islamic setting aside. I propose to interpret the scarves with reference to those seen in Montreal after the massacre of women engineering students by a man who attacked them for being feminists; the victims were buried in white coffins and their fellow women students, who had denied the accusation ("we are not feminists"), walked in the funeral procession wearing white scarves on their heads.[76] It seems to me that this is about protesting one's innocence with respect to education: we are students but our intentions are pure; we are not trying to upset the established order; we still do what is expected of us. The women students of Istanbul and the two or three French high-school students who defend wearing headscarves are making the same argument as the Quebec women; they want to swear that their acquisition of knowledge will not compromise their loyalty to traditional values, and they promise to put their knowledge to work within the boundaries of established beliefs. The headscarf is a profession of faith that bothers me, of course, all the more so as in Istanbul it is female medical students who demonstrate in its favor. But aside from the fact that such promises may not be kept for an entire lifetime, are headscarves a reason to deny these students an education? And it is absurd to see in such a gesture an implication that they and their families are rejecting the education system of the French Republic, while in fact they are showing just how much they value it. Muslim fathers do not say why they want their daughters to go to school. Perhaps it is the same for them as for Thomas More, the will to educate daughters preceding the idea, which is yet to be found. We can, however, suggest something to think about. In the Maghreb it happens that girls wear the veil until they have their *bac*,[*] after which they are allowed to do as they please. In the middle of the twentieth century, in several Muslim countries, groups of girls tore up their veils, always when they had acquired a professional education that would provide them with a livelihood even if they did not marry. The scarf, which certainly helps in the search for a husband, is perhaps a form of survival insurance, in the event that education does not lead to paid work. At the beginning of the 1970s, when the *bac* was a guarantee of employment, the educational prowess of young North African women impressed everyone; and they could be seen choosing, from among their grandmothers' traditions, those they wanted to

---

[*]The *baccalauréat* is the French equivalent of a secondary school diploma (of A levels in Britain).

keep and those they would abandon. The youth employment crisis has currently made it more prudent for a young woman to hold onto the possibility of a traditional marriage.

Moreover, is it not precisely because the school system might possibly be a liberating influence that families are so insistent on demonstrating their allegiance to the sexual-religious order while educating their children? Conversely, believing that education cannot liberate without imposing freedom is tantamount to saying that it is not a liberating influence at all. I believe it has so much potential to be liberating that from a conservative point of view due precautions must be taken before allowing a woman to learn to read. I also think learning to read could have been a means of disciplining her. To understand the ambiguity of education, we must reread an old author, always bearing in mind that the fact precedes the idea.

13. The Jailer's Catechism

From the Renaissance on, the mere existence of *epikleroi* created a certain unease that must be addressed; and if a few women's access to knowledge was a fact that had to find cultural acceptance or be tamed, the negative reaction to it, alas, won the day. In 1523, Vivès wrote *De Institutione Feminae Christianae*, which went through several printings and was translated into Castilian (1528), English (1540–41), French (1542, followed by two better translations), Italian (1546), and German (1566). Like *The Book of the City of Ladies*, the work was read all over Europe. Its author, a Spanish humanist engaged by the English court to take charge of the education of Mary Tudor, belonged to the same circle as Erasmus and More, whose daughters he knew. His list of *epikleroi* is five pages long, and there are so many "daughters of…" that the list could serve to back up our concept of *epikleroi*. He rhymes off: Cleobulina, daughter of Cleobulus, the daughter of Pythagoras who directed the school after her father's death; Theano of Metapont; the empress Eudoxia; the five daughters of Diodorus the dialectician; Hortensia, daughter of Hortensius; Spanish princesses; and even the little daughters of his friend, whose theories he amends. More wanted his daughters to have access to culture because it is a good thing; but, since educated women are subject to ridicule, it is all the more important, he says, that they be of irreproachable morality. Vivès twists the logical connection: "their father was not content that they be chaste but also took pains that they be learned, in the belief that in this way they would be more truly and steadfastly chaste."[77]

In this way: indeed the text slyly instrumentalizes the question of cultured women. The cohort of famous women, each more chaste than the others, whose existence the author recognizes, is used to illustrate an opinion of Plutarch's: we have almost never known a learned woman to be immodest.

"The study of literature [...] occupies a person's whole attention [...] it lifts the mind to the contemplation of beautiful things and rids it of lowly thoughts, and if any such thoughts creep in, the mind, fortified by precepts and counsels of good living... dispels it... 'Never,' said Plutarch, 'will a woman dedicated to literature distract herself in dancing.'"[78] As a few examples will show, chastity thus becomes an end in itself and studying a means to this end. In the argument affirming that studious women are more dutiful than others, we should read an apologia for humanism by a humanist: when one is engaged in defending a culture, as humanists were, there is nothing like affirming that study fosters virtue in men, and even—just imagine!—in women. Here women are a mere pretext for singing the praises of the humanities. And the idea of study as a kind of chastity belt offers some hope of connecting the two concerns: the self-apologia and monogamous morality. It is a vain hope, though, and a discrepancy will emerge with respect to the *epikleroi:* it is a matter of high culture. They wrote stories, conversed in Latin with ambassadors, or taught philosophy, all of which presupposes access to non-domestic public space. However, when Vivès moves on to outline a plan of education, the scale shrinks considerably. For in place of the erudition appropriate for famous women, he substitutes a minimalist program notable for its restrictions, and one thing is axiomatic: the best way to keep women virtuous is to seal them up at home. Chastity, which was the argument of the thesis supporting education for girls, thus becomes the antithesis and the principle that restricts the program. "But in what kind of literature should a woman be versed? [...] the study of wisdom, which forms morals in the way of virtue [...] I am not at all concerned with eloquence. A woman has no need of that; she needs rectitude [*probitate*] and wisdom [*sapentia*]," and the chapter devoted to what she must read focuses mostly on what she must not read.[79] Libraries are full of immodest books, and "books in the vernacular, written in that tongue so that they may be read by idle men and women, treat of no other material than love and war"; reading them is dangerous.[80] So a woman will not read Tristan, Maugis, Flamette, Lancelot of the Lake, Melusine, or Ovid. She will read the Gospels, the Epistles, and the Acts of the Apostles, Seneca, "moral stories," and "moral doctrine." Whereas philosophy, rhetoric, the writing of stories, and Latin had been included in the praise of women who were both learned and chaste, nothing is left but edifying literature.

What is worse is that, having been kept on a leash even in her home library, a woman must not try to understand books by herself but must rather take counsel from serious men, without being so imprudent as to follow her own judgment, *nec temere suum judicium sequetur femina* for fear that having sampled the humanities, she might consider false and pernicious things to be true, healthy, or acceptable.[81] A woman is not free to interpret the little she is allowed to read. Her reduced horizon will then shrivel to zero. On feast days, returning from Mass, she will first look after the housekeeping and then, if she knows how to read, she may read a page; if she does not know how to read, someone will read a page to her. Literacy is therefore not necessarily included in the program. The underlying question in the book is really this: what must she be taught to ensure that she knows nothing other than what is relevant to her conjugal duty and her fear of God, as if all culture were dangerous. The argument against freedom to read and to know is first given in a form valid for both sexes: "Pernicious is the view of those who wish their children not to be ignorant of both good and evil"[82]; as the story of Adam and Eve demonstrates, one ought not to know evil at all. His conclusion, which does not apply to both sexes, is that a girl must remain ignorant of evil, even the most minor evil: she must not learn to utter lustful words or to make unseemly gestures or facial expressions.

Women as women have been ousted from the thought presented in the book, since that thought is organized around the situation of wives. The book is divided into three parts, devoted to the virgin, the wife, and the widow; the virgin is the woman being prepared for marriage, the widow the one who must mourn her husband assiduously; and the central character in the treatise is the husband who will come, is there, or is no more. A woman is only a wife and she is entirely molded to conform to the expectations of her lord and master. The book is maniacal in the detail with which it regulates women's lives so that they never exceed the prescribed limits of their destiny. The chastity of the young girl and the fidelity of the married woman are conditioned from the moment of birth and overseen throughout their lives. The dedication to Catherine of Aragon says that if men take care of both public and private affairs, "a woman's only care is chastity,"[83] and therefore the question of her education can be dealt with through a limited number of principles. But the book is not as short as all that, for the *unica cura feminae,* which is nothing but an absence of action, is a work that occupies every moment. The poor woman must think of it constantly, and the author thinks of everything—she should wash her face with pure water and without soap, frequent fasting will calm the ardor of youth—could the anorexia of young girls have precisely such a disciplinary function? At the same time, the theme of maintaining chastity becomes all-encompassing since it shapes and directs everything: clothing, reading, use of the hands, confinement within the home. Cooking is the sole feminine activity not connected with chastity. A woman must develop culinary talents in order not to be hated by her husband and to discourage him from turning into an habitué of the tavern; any woman to whom this happens has only herself to blame. Thus the wife even carries the guilt of her husband's misdeeds.

Throughout the entire book, it is the potential for misdeed that justifies educating women thoroughly; the text is punctuated with critical comments about misbehavior, insolence, vice, anger, among others. The book allows us to understand how a negative image of the being-woman is produced by the very wish to rule her completely. She is always on the verge of falling into error because, according to an expression of Alain, "the jailer is never happy." Moreover, Vivès is not the last one to blame women even for male alcoholism. In the regional press in 1983, a pathetic psychiatrist from Quimper published a series of articles on the theme "Men drink because women wear the pants in the household,"[84] as well as a book entitled *The Psychological Matriarchy of the Bretons*. Psychological: someone must have pointed out to him that the observable features of Breton society are as marked by masculine domination as any others; so he moved the inquiry to a nonobservable soul, which he claims is known to him and perhaps to him alone. There is no law against incitement to sexist hatred, but we might dare the publisher to read a few pages without blushing, or remind him that if such things were published about an ethnic group, and not about women ("Breton men and women drink because the French are so horrible to them"), the MRAP.* Would certainly have something to say about it.

If Vivès considers studying, to be done at home, as one of several means of keeping women in their place in the sexual order, it is first of all because it reinforces other ways of imprisoning them: "it was a national custom in Egypt that women did not wear shoes so that they could be confined to the home. So, if you take away from a woman her silks, linens, gold, silver, jewels and precious stones you can more easily keep her in the house."[85] And naturally, he praises women who do not leave the house without a veil. Aside from the function of the veil in more than one culture as an intermediary between the interior and the exterior, and therefore a sign of loyalty to the interior even when a woman is outdoors, the *De Institutione* allows us to understand how a particular visual theme became a classic: a woman, at home, is bent over a book. The motif must be interpreted not as a symbol of liberation, but rather of domestication, since the location and position of the body in these scenes are identical to those of a woman spinning wool or doing needlework. But if they are closed in, what could possibly be the risk of adultery, whether or not these women are literate? Vivès's project, which does not validate women's culture as such, exploits it as a means to realizing his program: idleness is dangerous, and reading prevents it much as needlework does. "Therefore she will learn together

* MRAP: Mouvement contre le racisme et pour l'amitié entre les peuples. One of a number of anti-racism movements formed in the past thirty years in France. One of the best-known of these is S.O.S. Racisme, whose slogan is "hands off my buddy (touche pas à mon pote)."

with reading how to work with wool and flax [...] when she is tired of
reading, I cannot bear seeing her idle."[86] Thus affirming the equal value
of studying and spinning* for the maintenance of chastity, he devotes long
pages to describing the virtues of ladies' handiwork, especially necessary
for those whose social standing relieves them of domestic duties. Since two
methods are better than one, N + 1 control mechanisms being by definition
better than N, reading is a welcome redundancy. Otherwise, an idle woman
"will converse with men, I suppose, or other women [...] Perhaps she
will think. About what?" Alas, "a woman's thoughts are swift and generally
unsettled, roving without direction, and I know not where her instability
will lead her,"[87] a comment reiterated elsewhere: "A woman's thoughts are
inconstant and they do not remain easily fixed in one place [...] [Publius
Syrus, the writer of mimes, was right in saying] 'When a woman thinks
alone, she thinks bad thoughts' (*Mulier quam sola cogitat male cogitat*)."[88]
Let us understand what he means: she has amorous desires and she thinks
about them. Healthy readings will prevent her from straying in this way. For
it is not enough that a woman be chaste in deed; she also must devote her
inner life to this virtue. Her education is designed to make her internalize the
norms of the sexual order. She will be stronger in her chastity if she knows
to what extent it is ordered by all the authorities, and her faithfulness is not
only the appropriation of her body by the husband but the colonization of
a mind that must have absorbed the lesson of appropriation and be focused
only on that. She must know her duty in every detail. With appropriate
references to Saint Augustine or Saint Jerome, it will be explained to her
that a woman has no rights over her own body, not even with respect to the
good that is abstinence, for it is not she, but her husband, who has power
over her body; she can choose abstinence only with his permission. Thus
chastity, which is extolled in this book, has nothing to do with freely-chosen
abstinence but quite to the contrary, it consists in a woman's complete and
exclusive subjection to her husband.

"When a woman thinks alone, she thinks bad thoughts": the idea that her
thought is unpredictable and lecherous is located in a "moral" rather than
an epistemic register. It is not that she would reason without logic if she
were left to her own thoughts but that she would have evil thoughts. One
hypothesis can be drawn from this: the controversial theme of a specifically
feminine mode of thought, which today is declared to be epistemic, may
have been a transposition into the cognitive domain of a theme initially
developed to address issues of conduct and sexual morality. Reading the
pages Malebranche devotes to the fragility of the fibers of the brain, you

---

* *Hipparchia's Choice: An Essay Concerning Women, Philosophy, etc.* (trans. Trista Selous. Oxford: Blackwell, 1991),
is the title of an earlier book by Michèle Le Doeuff. The French title, *L'Étude et le rouet* (Paris: Éditions du Seuil,
1989) literally means "studying and the spinning wheel."

may wonder whether beneath this text, which seems to deal with cognition, there is a subtext, erased but still decipherable, as if it were a palimpsest:

> ... the delicacy of the brain fibers is one of the principal causes impeding our efforts to apply ourselves to discovering truths that are slightly hidden [...] this delicacy of the brain fibers is usually found in women, and this is what gives them great understanding of everything that strikes the senses. It is for women to set fashions, judge languages, discern elegance and good manners [...] Everything that depends upon taste is within their area of competence, but normally they are incapable of penetrating to truths that are slightly difficult to discover. Everything abstract is incomprehensible to them.

Next, with one hand he offers to a few women something he proceeds to deny to women in general:

> If it is certain that this delicacy of the fibers is the principal cause of all these effects, it is not at all certain that it is to be found in all women [...] some women are found to have stronger minds than some men [...] There are strong, constant women, and there are feeble, inconstant men. There are learned women, courageous women, women capable of anything [...] In short, when we attribute certain defects to a sex [...] we mean only that it is ordinarily true, always assuming that there is no general rule without exceptions.[89]

The exception proves the rule for cases that are not exceptions, for in describing women who, in his opinion, are exceptions to their sex, Malebranche depicts a supposedly standard characteristic: the majority of women are inconstant, weak, cowardly (these are moral rather than cognitive givens); their intelligence is particularly well adapted to "whatever appeals to the senses" (an accusation of sensuality?) and to trivial things. The "fragility of the fibers" seems to be another name for moral frailty (*oh frailty, thy name is woman*), a flaw that justifies keeping women under supervision. A related question: where has he seen fibers, and has he seen any at all? We are floundering in the imaginary here, so much so that, in order to confuse the issue further, you have only to mention subtlety, which is surely necessary for discovering somewhat obscure truths. This is the imaginary he protects in suggesting the possibility of exceptions; if he recognizes that some women have solid intelligence, he can maintain his "theory" of brain fibers against all counterexamples and offer it as an admirable synthesis. It guarantees the virility of the inquiring mind, declares women's lack of capacity for theory, and justifies placing them under surveillance.

A French translation of Vivès, reprinted in 1891 for use in the fight against secondary education for girls shows the extent to which, even at that late date, sexual morality motivates the argument in favor of a minimalist curriculum. Although characterizing Vivès's program as somewhat skimpy, the author of the preface nonetheless denounces the excessively rich curriculum envisaged at that time: "Our young *lycéennes* of fourteen or fifteen, assigned such topics as the comparison of Plautus's *Amphitryon* with that of Molière by teachers with no regard at all for what should and should not be said, would not be satisfied with this intellectual nourishment. But today, are we not going too far when the curriculum planned for them includes an encyclopaedic coverage of human knowledge, enough to terrify a member of the Institut?"* This gross nonsense (the curriculum of boys' *lycées* becomes an impossible encyclopedia when it is offered to girls) must not mask one juicy detail— *Amphitryon* is a play about adultery!

14. A Little Learning

When girls' education serves a disciplinary function, everything outside the curriculum is said to be useless, harmful, and impossible. This idea, which until very recently has left its mark on Europe, explains why so much pedagogical discourse creates the category of what a woman should not know, and therefore is not able to know. A quick look at Fénelon shows that learning cleanliness, which to him is essential ("Never allow girls to have anything soiled or untidy"), is also what gives meaning to literacy: teach a girl to read and write correctly; it is shameful but not unusual to see women who do not know how to pronounce what they read; they are even worse at spelling; teach them to draw straight lines, to form their letters neatly, to use the right words, to explain their thought in orderly fashion and with brevity and concision, then they will be able to teach their children to speak properly, but at the same time they must be shown how incapable they are of understanding the difficulties of the law.[90] What might pass for the acquisition of a skill, such as literacy, is nonetheless an apprenticeship in the virtues of order and cleanliness, and then the figure of the legitimate beneficiaries, who are these women's children, appears. When you think of the sloppy scribbling of more than one classical author, their casual attitude to spelling, the messy condition of some manuscripts, you might well wonder whether there is not something important at stake. Descartes proclaimed his disdain for spelling—let his printer decide whether or not a *p* is necessary in *corps*, he could not care less, as if intellectual creativity were more comfortable with a certain messiness.[91] In any case, what is denied to women is the right to the tiniest amount of disorder, or even the possibility of disorder.

*The Institut de France is the "parliament of the learned" that is said to reflect the state of the art of French intellectual life. It comprises five smaller "Academies" that represent the major disciplines. Its mandate is to promote the artistic and scientific disciplines in France and ensure the advancement of human knowledge. Its academicians are regarded as the highest representatives of academic knowledge in France. Common critiques of the Institut de France are that it is highly conservative and that it counts almost no women among its members.

In our own day, women students would probably dismiss Vivès, Fénelon, and the others as dinosaurs. They would burst out laughing at the idea that they could be locked up at home and kept barefoot, sent to school to learn chastity, restricted to the study of edifying literature, and expected to show their cleanliness in the way they write. But girls and women who went to school in the mid-twentieth century will surely have understood that in my analysis of these texts, I have been trying to produce a crude image of what we ourselves experienced to varying degrees, a schema that still corresponds too closely with what too many masculine authorities in this world have in mind. As is clear from the *Economist* article I have mentioned, the fantasy that a little learning can be used instrumentally to define a small part of culture, whose boundaries are deliberately determined, is still with us. There is a link between using knowledge as an instrument and seeing it as a predetermination that both affirms and denies, allowing one thing and refusing another, with the result that anything more is seen as useless, harmful, and therefore impossible. What these old texts also show is that the practice of determining women's intellect or lack of it operates according to an idea, not of gender, but of correct sexuality; it is not a matter of a masculine/feminine opposition involving two independent terms but rather of precise views on sexual relations and procreation. We have inherited a culture in which the value of women's intellect is thought of in relation to sexual morality and to the seductiveness required of us, not to mention the possible contradictions between morality and seduction at times when we are required to be pleasing, but only to the husband. When Helen Deutsch associates the feminine (intuitive and not creative) with passivity and masochism, she means that a truly feminine woman accepts forced marital sex and pregnancy, passively and masochistically. When at the end of a war women who had been put to work are expelled from their jobs, they are to be relieved (*sic*) to give the work back to the men, and they must hurry back home to busy themselves with the increased birth rates that follow wars and to prove retrospectively that if they accepted work while the men were at the front, it was once again because of a masochistic submission to imposed directives.[92] The construction of an image of gender (the feminine as lewd or masochistic) projects norms, aims, and concerns that focus on sexuality and the reproductive body onto an idea of feminine nature.

Even today, it is very difficult to make some people understand that it is possible to discuss intellectual life without connecting it to sexual issues, and to argue that there is no necessary connection. For at least twenty centuries, the link between intellectuality and sexuality has been manipulated in every imaginable way, without anyone thinking the two terms could be posited independently of one another. No eloquent woman is chaste; a studious woman is more chaste; an educated woman is a bluestocking with no seductive power whatsoever and it serves her right; a studious woman does not think about decking herself out, and that is a good thing; one and the same law forbids women to aspire to knowledge and to wear cloth of gold, or pearls, or carefully arranged braids, it is one and the same passion that attracts them to books and to finery (quotes from Saint Paul or Fénelon: take your pick); the same acceptance of a masochist identity leads women to renounce the theoretical domain and tolerate conjugal rape. These gentlemen and forewomen (a forewoman is a female foreman) of the patriarchal order are not always in agreement among themselves about the so-called logical connection between intellectuality and acceptable sexual conduct—if A then B, if A then not-B, A & B, A & not-B (you can continue the series yourself)— but they are all quite sure that there is a link. In the psychoanalytic debates of the 1970s, it was said either that uneducated women have an untroubled sexuality, unlike college girls, or that women students have more orgasms than working-class women. There were even debates over two kinds of orgasm, one vaginal and the other clitoral, and efforts to relate the first (generally judged healthy) to the situation of the married woman in the home, and the second (often called toxic) to the life of fully-qualified amazons.

Meanwhile, and leaving these debates to those who were still swayed by the idea of a causal relationship, women of my generation fought for all women's control of their fertility, so that sexuality could be purely a matter of pleasure. From personal experience, we knew that there is nothing like the fear of becoming pregnant either by accident or through the unilateral decision of the male partner to spoil your fun. If you who are now twenty years old have difficulty in understanding why I am exhuming all these ridiculous writers, it is because your sexuality has changed so much that you can envisage a relationship to the world and to knowledge, without taking sexuality into account. Whatever your sexuality may be, it is no longer bound up with procreation; because of this fact, it can be whatever you manage to negotiate with your circumstances. Moreover, the positive psychological and cultural effects of contraception play themselves out across two generations: when a mother stops thinking of herself as a potential victim of her sexuality—for the consequences of unwanted or repeated pregnancies weigh on a woman's perception of herself as a woman—she can enjoy a better relationship with her daughter, without transmitting a negative imaginary of what it is to be a woman. In this regard, one could also rethink the issue of domestic violence and urge the authorities to act quickly and decisively. Moreover, by dissociating sexuality from procreation, we also made it possible to recognize female homosexuality. Male homosexuality has always had an ambiguous status, generally condemned but validated in some spheres of power and in closed masculine communities. For women, heterosexuality—without desire and not necessarily pleasurable, as appropriation of their body by men—has until very recently been the only norm. Winning reproductive rights has led to the idea that women have a libido separate from the desire for children or acceptance of an imposed pregnancy. As a result, lesbians cease—or begin to cease—to appear as an incomprehensible monstrosity. A heterosexual libido that has the means to separate its pleasure from pro-creation and a lesbian libido no longer differ in anything but their choice of object, and the heterosexual way of life for a woman differs less and less from that of a lesbian. And since the imaginary of the self plays itself out over two generations, the young women of today, hetero or lesbian, are in a similar situation: their mother's reconciliation with her own sexuality plays a part in their liberation.

Vivès has something else to teach us: if we examine a few translations of the *De Institutione,* we see that through the interplay of mistranslations, prefaces, or corrections (one of them removes a particular woman from the list of famous women, and the other adds a certain male author to the list of works a woman may read) the translators each put something of their own into the text, inflecting it in one direction or another as if it belonged as much to the translator as to the author, and as if the translator could therefore substitute his authority for the author's. It is true that we know of other translations that are too free, but in this case we can sense that each translator is claiming the right to say what he wants to say about women, and using the act of translation to express himself, as if the original text were nothing more than a source of inspiration. It is similar to the case of the American translation of *The Second Sex* by a retired male zoologist who added sentences and cut out large chunks of text. A translation of Vivès that Pierre de Changy prepared for his daughter is virtually an original work; the preface to an anonymous translation, published by Linocier Press in 1587, is much at variance with the author's thought.[93] When Changy's transla-tion is reprinted in 1891, the writer of the preface, an admirer of Joseph de Maistre, calls on other authors, insinuating that, according to the univer-sal testimony of at least the masculine half of humanity, it is not wise to teach girls to read. He goes so far as to attribute opinions to Vivès: Vivès might have been of the same opinion as so-and-so; he might have said, as another so-and-so does, and on it goes. The book's circulation shows its extraordinary plasticity, though it remains within the scope of a constant premise: it is up to men to define the purpose and content of girls' educa-tion. Evidence? No, it is rather a pedagogical *aporia* (impasse), for even if the discussion always leads back to marital obedience, the husband's wish itself is not always entirely predictable. When Vivès assures us that making a woman studious is the best way to dissuade her from a taste for finery and high living, he also specifies that if her husband wants her to be sumptuously dressed, then of course she must obey his wish. Since it is always up to the husband to decide what he wants from his wife—the age of the Cyclops and the caves being still with us—no stable pedagogical discourse is really possible. An author can provide general advice but not replace the husband's final and true authority. Fénelon stumbles over the same obstacle: a woman must only learn to "obey her husband without reasoning why." Instead of gnashing our teeth, let us try to understand: he means that she will be subject to an executive rather than a legislative authority, an arbitrary will wanting unforeseeable things that may differ from or contradict each other, simultaneously or at quarter-hour intervals, to the point where it is impossible to say with certainty what kind of education she needs. But what is clear is that reasoning and judgment must be prevented from developing. Arbitrary personal power creates chaotic situations for women who are subjected to it; an order can be countermanded and constraints can become a double bind. A capacity for judgment or reasoning might risk compromising everything by making it possible for women to contest chaos or incoherence.

15. The Judgment of Christine

Fair daughter, have you lost all your sense?[94] Lady Reason's questioning of the author creates the initial dramatic impulse of *The Book of the City of Ladies* and it enunciates a difficult problem. Christine has represented herself as a studious woman who, after a day spent in her study, opens a lighter work for relaxation. Reading it upsets her and brings back memories of other misogynist works—it is almost impossible to find a text about mores that does not contain some chapter or paragraph commenting negatively on women's nature and behavior: how can it be that so many illustrious men have all made the same error in the same way? By rekindling her deference toward authors who are better known than Matheolus, her dismay prompts her to think there may be a semblance of truth in what they say: if they all have said that we are unworthy creatures, "it was ... truly fitting that such was the case." Self-loathing, consternation, tears, until three ladies arrive on the scene. The role of the first, Reason, is to insinuate herself into people's minds, to shake them up, just like Socrates's demon. Against opinions laden with prejudice, she attempts to bring Christine back to her own judgment (what has become of it?)—to her *scens* and culture. Christine has read the philosophers, she knows that they criticize one another, quarrel with one another, and make mistakes; why has she allowed herself to be impressed by them? It is because of a gap between knowledge and judgment, between the intellectual training acquired through study, and the possibility of using it at the very moment when it might be most necessary. Christine knows everything can be criticized; when, under Reason's direction, she sifts through misogynist opinions, she will find them baseless; she should have seen them immediately for what they are, a mass of defamatory lies and nonsense. And yet she has become distraught, forgetting even what she knows, from personal experience and with complete certainty, about her body and her being as a woman. She says she was endowed with strength by a double knowledge, one derived from books (everything can be examined) and the other from existence, and with a capacity for judgment; yet her judgment gave way in the face of authority and the collusion of famous men. *The Book of the City of Ladies* reveals the paradox of a type of mental functioning that is not pure cognition: the way we think in our daily lives and about important questions is in part a-rational. Reciprocally, restoring personal judgment to the center of thought cannot be achieved simply by decree. It requires a long effort of dialogue. And, modest as she is, Reason seems to know that the task requires more than she alone can give, whence her order to Christine that she build a city peopled with worthy women in order to give us a safe place in our imaginary. Among these figures, some excelled in their discernment or good sense, others in their mastery of a particular branch of knowledge, such as Novella Andrea who delivered her papa's lectures on canon law when Papa was busy with other things[95]; still others have shown their exceptional tenderness and courage, others their ability to invent new techniques or fields of knowledge. Because the portrait gallery offers such a wide range of possible ideals, it does not close the gap between knowledge and judgment: it is possible to have one without the other, though, says Christine, it is better to have both at once. Why is *scens* so weak, and what must be done to strengthen it?

Not all the conditions that affect the exercise of judgment are derivable from knowledge; not all are rational. To understand this point more clearly it is interesting to examine a recent parallel to what Christine says. According to Hannah Arendt, throughout the Vietnam War, Pentagon experts, the military, and game theorists, calculated but never *judged* either the situation or the possible implications of their calculations.[96] Their premise was the chimera of double omnipotence—the military superpower of the United States and the power of publicity campaigns. They thought they could break the psychological resistance of the enemy without knowing him, and sell everything to American public opinion just as they wished. If we take Christine de Pisan and Hannah Arendt together, we can begin to see, not that the thinking subject can be marked by gender, but—and this is more important—that every subject is caught up in an imaginary network of self-representations, authorizations, or inhibitions more significant than the mere intellectual conditions of thought, and error can result from too many of these just as easily as from too few. From this perspective, the question of gender is fully functional as a social construction that inequitably (to say the least) distributes the psycho-imaginary conditions for the exercise of thought. Men are given fantasies of omnipotence that prevent them from thinking, just as women are prevented from thinking by a self-image of unworthiness. Conversely, the subject who is capable of judgment could be seen as a mid-point between extremes, based on a positive but moderate self-image that legitimates the very act of judging and makes it necessary. Such a subject would be capable of understanding the equal reality of itself and of a situation or of taking an object into account as fully as it does itself and vice versa.

It is possible that for both men and women the acquisition of knowledge has nothing to do with the formation of judgment; a vexing idea, to be sure, but we should take serious note of it before we overestimate knowledge. Past and present guardians of the world of knowledge who perhaps feared that, having become learned, women might be able to examine their condition critically, could after all have slept in peace. Something more is always needed. If we consult Christine de Pisan on this point, we can indeed see that much more is needed. Thought may be blocked by a negative imaginary and freed by an interlocutor (in this case a lady) who provides the beginning of a magical cure. Christine drinks her consoling words like dew, and then this Lady, an allegory of rational dialogue—two people are therefore involved—takes the time to talk with her, inviting her to grasp the tools of interrogation and to use them. It is by being an active subject, questioning and building for all women, that she will rediscover her own dignity. Her work produces an imaginary—the city populated by respectable women who are psychological supports for all women—a poetics that is both an ethics and a mode of resistance. By choosing to be "deserving" according to the noble principles of the city, they all have the possibility of extricating themselves from the socioreligious norm of "turning the other cheek"; in their naive goodness, and following the divine precept, women patiently suffer the devastating insults directed against them "wrongly and to their detriment, relying on God and their own will"; but this resignation resembles the slavery Pharoah imposed on Israel, and is not part of the laws of the new city.[97]

Thus, to change women's situation for the better, we need consolation, dialogue, active pedagogy, and the creation of a poetics that is also an ethics. For men too, something has to be changed, but Christine does not give us a complete recipe. Lady Reason links misogynist fantasies to the circumstances of men's lives, suggesting that our opponents' nonsense does not originate in men's thought but in unfortunate circumstances, negative experiences with women, or no contact with them at all. The less frequently a man meets women, the more he makes defamatory and stupid remarks.

This is a bit simplistic, for it is possible to encounter women without recognizing them as real; Christine leaves us still looking for answers, but we can supplement what she says. The illusion of omnipotence, which so damages men's exercise of judgment, does not derive only from the postulate of an American military superpower, for instance, have you noticed the psycho-legal position that husbands occupied for so long? And the possibility for men to deny needs, wrongs, and facts as they wished, or to invent them as they pleased?

"*The I took issue with the World as a conspiracy mounted by itself against itself [. . .]. Descartes called into being an I-God, and already the Universe was no more than a expanse on which the I might sit [. . .]. Husserl teaches us now that "the object constructs itself within the ego" [. . .] now the Universe is completely swallowed up.*"[98] Catherine Pozzi is describing a subject who believes himself to be absolute, and then—immediately thereafter—she challenges its very existence: "*But does the I think? [. . .] perhaps thinking needs no I [. . .], perhaps it thinks in the same way that it rains. [. . .] If it thinks through the I in the way that rain might fall on a sponge, the I does not exist at all [. . .] it is feeling that needs the I, and the two are needed for feeling, dear master. But don't upset yourself, the other is perhaps only a table [. . .]*" In this satire, we must recognize the aporia of the subject of pure thought, who presents itself as an absolute, requiring nothing beyond itself (*it needs only itself in order to think*), and possibly without being at all. The modern thesis that knowledge is a process without a knowing subject would be compatible with the idea of an absolute subject. In any case, what must be retained in Christine de Pisan and Catherine Pozzi is the challenge to the idea that JE [I] might need only itself in order to think. It is a challenge developed in a mixture of fable and analysis; rationality works hand in hand both with the creation of imagery and with the empirical analysis of the social. Besides, such a point of view makes it possible (which is no mean feat) to avoid reproducing the duality between the subject engaged in the work of reason, and its others, be they the masses, women, children, or another lesser Other to whom is off-loaded a remainder called myth, ignorance, or fable. Moreover, the I prides itself on being able to manipulate these lesser beings with ad hoc embellishments of the fables. According to Christine, everyone, starting with herself, is in the imaginary and, with a bit of luck, within rationality.

We have seen a ray of hope emerging in civic society, linked to the spread of a capacity to reflect and to act. In the professions, a more equal representation of women and men seems, daily, to promise that women's needs and rights will increasingly be taken into account while men's power will be diminished, something some men already welcome. When persons, both women and men, are taken for ends in themselves, when persons take themselves as finite ends, what counts most is the formation of a free and solid judgment, not the mere acquisition of knowledge, especially since that acquisition might prove to be inoperative or to play itself out only in an agonistic, competitive framework—know more, calculate more quickly, and too bad if the calculation is faulty. But I have spoken about very old things. Have I made it clear that only yesterday they were still part of our lives, and that, quite recently and not in the distant past, the example of just one of your own high school days could show you how knowledge is dispensed at the same time as its use is forbidden?

8:00 a.m.: Latin class. You failed to recognize a double accusative, and you are roundly scolded: lack of academic ability is a moral weakness, error is a moral flaw, the mediocre pupil suffers from weakness of will, and a reprimand can set it right. Thus, at 8:00 a.m., you are in the wrong. French class comes next, without even a pause. The same teacher leads the class through a line-by-line study of [Molière's] Les Femmes savantes. The rule of the game is so obvious that there is no need to explain it, since the reason for studying the classics day after day is to instil in pupils the art of reading politely and identifying themselves with the author's point of view. Molière does not recommend that women be learned, and the lady who teaches humanities at the girls' high school will glare at the pupil who has just absent-mindedly defended Armande, the female character with a passion for philosophy. Sheepish and speechless, you are still digesting the shame of a Latin translation that only an hour before was castigated as pure fiction. Next comes the sewing class. Still more trouble; you knew how to sew when you started at the lycée; you had done enough housework for that. No matter—you will not know how to sew a hem until someone has taught you.

Perhaps at the time you noticed something wrong with this picture; not knowing exactly what, you may have filed the experience away in your memory so that some day you might see how to interpret it. Today, thanks to an adult culture—but where did you get that?—you can see that this is the old double bind, dual constraint. Schoolgirls are subjected to contradictory imperatives: first they must thoroughly master Latin or Greek, then learn to make fun of women who are interested in ancient or modern humanities, then, thanks to the sewing class, they find themselves reminded that their destiny is not even to know their own destiny, but to understand that in reality they do not know what they already know. A good pupil must be able to do everything at intervals of only a few minutes, without asking herself any questions; a lady teaching humanities must be able to impose this on her (female) pupils without asking herself questions and without allowing them to ask her any. Whence her half-threatening, half-anxious look at your friend who said she thought Armande the more intelligent of the two sisters. Initially you defend Armande, and then there are no limits: you might even criticize the curriculum, not on grounds of political correctness, but for its lack of coherence, which is a more serious criticism. For it is truly incoherent to insist that schoolgirls spend their youth learning Latin and Greek if it is only to give them a devastating image of women who might know something: it amounts to making them ashamed of what is being demanded of them. School is for learning, a minister said one day, and the maxim is irrefutable. But for learning what? If it is learning to be ashamed of what schooling makes of us, then perhaps it would be better to learn nothing at all? No, you liked school, from geometry to hopscotch, and the conclusion is hasty. Let us wait until university to consider the question in all its implications. You have survived the contradictions of the *lycée* and have enrolled in a faculty of psychology where two-thirds of the students are female. You will sail through your examinations, including one on Helen Deutsch; you have not followed the example of your friend who, after dismissing *The Psychology of Women* as a punitive rhapsody strung together with parental threats— "there is nothing to learn from it"—and its author as an old dragon, left university to establish a series of books—for liberated women, she said. You wanted to see it through, and here you are meditating on how the story common to us all might end: one day, a young epistemologist, who had always done as she was told, made an appointment with a psychiatrist, and told her, "It's very hard to be an intellectual woman." The psychiatrist looked straight at her, burst into tears, and that was the end of the appointment. What is knowledge worth if it remains caught in the very problem it is supposed to solve, or if it makes someone dissolve in silent tears when its contradictions affect a knowing subject for whom the content of learning is indeed self-contradictory?

Your male cousin did not come up against the same obstacles. In Caesar's *Commentaries,* in addition to the Latin you also learned, he learned a way of being, that of the citizen-soldier who defends the motherland or expands colonial possessions. Precisely what the Republic had in mind for him! For him, it was amusing to read *Les Femmes savantes* and to burst out laughing. When he read in Hegel that freedom is being at home in an Other, he found the idea brilliant. And if he subsequently became a psychiatrist, nothing ever disturbed the closed intellectual coherence he had inherited. He even believed, and still believes, he could reign over the sciences, or rather, over the scientists. But he is aghast to see his young colleagues, including some (men and women) whom he has trained, turning to a kind of ridiculous environmentalism—they claim that fixed roles are toxic, and propose domestic work equal leisure as a panacea for everyone, men, women, and children. When a senior executive has a breakdown he is asked to tell about his eighteen-hour workdays, how he was hired on the basis of astrology and graphology, his team-building weekends spent walking on hot coals or jumping out of planes. These young psychiatrists then tell him to cook dinner every second night, and if it conflicts with his job, he should change jobs. Mothers who spoonfeed their sons are told this is a poor preparation for the active pedagogy that reigns in primary teaching. At this level, it is boys who fail at school: teach a boy to bake or to wash his own gym clothes and everything will be better; and you should return to your own studies instead of worrying about his. Things of that sort. Some featherbrain who works on your cousin's ward specializes in what she calls the little problems of educated women. Quoting Uta Ranke-Heinemann, she says that being excommunicated for heresy makes it possible to commune with other heretics. She has them recount the stupidities they have heard in their workplace and gets them to laugh. She claims that modern medicine owes two things to women: one is cinchona bark, brought back from South America by a certain countess what's-her-name who had been treated for malaria by the Indians, and the other is the smallpox vaccination, brought back from Istanbul by Lady Montagu, who had learned the technique from some old women. But wasn't it farm women who discovered that infecting oneself with pus collected from cows' udders (really!!) causes a mild illness that also prevents the serious one? This same featherbrain replaces psychiatry with morality disguised as epistemology. To hear her talk, you would think that when we stop considering the Other as a lesser being, it is amazing what we can discover.

CHAPTER 3

An Epistemology of Hope

The area of philosophy called feminist epistemology sees the scientific enterprise created in the seventeenth century as a masculine project of domination over nature, which is conceived as woman. Pierre Thuillier sums up one of its founding works, Carolyn Merchant's *The Death of Nature,* as follows: by looking to the past, we can identify a close relationship between the destinies reserved for both women and nature, an "observation" based on a linguistic argument—"in the major texts of the west, nature is grammatically feminine." Faced with "the fantastical and frightening universe of witches" modern science presents itself as an ordering of the world "reliant on a *'masculine'* philosophy in which reason is in control." As a result, women's knowledge and powers are devalued while "masculine competences are privileged."[1]

Various objections come to mind. First, in certain countries of Europe, just as many men as women were condemned as witches;[2] thus, to present witchcraft as a world of women amounts to a representation or invention after the fact. Second, witchcraft and the occult sciences thought of themselves as loci of power: it is therefore debatable to contrast them formally to a science that is also seen as powerful. Third, the ancient texts that depict nature biologically usually talk of it as of a living being, which is not at all the same thing as a woman. Fourth, even though the Aristotelians assimilated the *materia prima* to a principle that, to them, was a principle of femininity, I cannot see why I should have to identify myself with that principle or to make common cause with it. Fifth, when Marina Yaguello speaks of the sex of words, she is greeted with a storm of protest: she is confusing sex with grammatical gender.[3] However, this approach is acceptable when others use it, and associate it with the idea that there are good reasons why girls do not succeed in science studies. Sixth, have you noticed that the good old phrase about masculine-philosophy-making-reason-rule has been slipped in as a self-evident idea, but in quotation marks? Whereas Thuillier implies that Merchant's view about the femininity of nature might be reductionist and should be invoked with caution . . .

"I know very well . . . , but all the same": according to Octave Mannoni, a belief can persist even while it is being repudiated and can spread precisely because of its repudiation.[4] "I know very well" that it is not really true that nature is a woman but I say it to you all the same, summarizing the discourse of someone who thinks that it is. And by putting "masculine" philosophy in quotation marks, I indicate that my belief has been shaken but (all the same!) there is certainly something like an affinity between masculinity and reason, science, philosophy, orderliness. . . . When Thuillier relates Merchant's thesis about the sex of nature without validating or critiquing it—a thesis that allows him to insinuate a relationship between the masculine and the rational—he is in fact simply having a woman provide him with an argument confirming what some have already thought for such a long time.

Feminist epistemology is, essentially, a psychology of the scientific mind, which it relates to an aggressiveness that is supposedly characteristic of the first sex: the invention of forceps in the seventeenth century and the penetration of miners into the bowels of the earth, as described by Agricola, could serve as paradigms.[5] However, this line of thought fails to address the social structures of science, the recruitment conditions in laboratories, or the ongoing and ordinary systemic discriminations in scientific life, or it does so only to spark discussion. Moreover, we cannot help but wonder whether it does not encourage a misinterpretation of the ecology we so badly need: in the name of sexual solidarity and against the sciences, it proposes a defense of Mother Nature, as if we had no need of the sciences to analyze the problems of industrial or automobile pollution; as if your children, after swimming in a pond naturally saturated with microorganisms, did not come back to you one with a tonsil infection, another with a fungus infection on a shoulder blade, a third with a bad case of diarrhoea from swallowing the water.

To examine the functioning of feminist epistemology at its highest level, let us consider Evelyn Fox Keller's 1987 contribution to *Daedalus,* and also the chapter she devoted to Baconian science, two years previously, in a landmark work *Reflections on Gender and Science.*[6] The example is crucial, for feminist epistemology is now representing Bacon as the male chauvinist founder of modern science. Too bad for him; he deserves it, but not for the reasons she gives. According to Keller, Bacon established that "the new science required a 'virile' mind, properly cleansed of all traces of femininity."[7] Unfortunately, none of his texts encourage the reader to regard the Idols—of which the mind must purge itself—as feminine: *idolum* is any element that stands as an obstacle to knowledge; for example, the mind has an unfortunate habit of wanting to find more order and symmetry everywhere than there really is, whence the astronomers' tendency to believe that the stars moved in perfect circles. The femininity of such a quirky notion is not immediately obvious; nor is the image of science as the will to impose order since Bacon describes this will as contributing to error. After this simple example, let us move on to the complex.

1. Take an Aspirin

The *Daedalus* article recalls some twenty years of reflections on the relations between science and sexual duality. Keller cites the views of Bruno Bettelheim and Erik Erikson, published in 1965, and Nancy Hopkins, published in 1976.[8] These accounts, together with what she herself says, show how susceptible the connection between "science as science" and the sociology of scientific institutions is to diverse interpretations, and how a double discourse can function, even in quoted texts. Quite ingenuously, Bettelheim, cited thus by Keller, recognizes that he does not know very much about the sciences: "I wish I knew more about physics and engineering, so that perhaps I could spell out for you how the specific female (*sic* and without quotation marks) genius can find its realization in these particular fields of human endeavour."[9] This comment articulates a dogmatic certainty based on a professed ignorance. I know nothing, but I can still tell you that if I did, I might be able to tell you how a specifically feminine genius—something of which I do have a clear idea, and whose existence I do not doubt—could realize its potential. It is as if, in 1965, no woman had ever earned recognition in the scientific world. As for Nancy Hopkins, she marks the distinction between the scientificity of science and its institutional reality, but with quotation marks to signal the instability of both poles: "The intellectual processes involved in 'pure' science are as natural or as unnatural to women as they are to men. On the other hand, science as a 'profession' has been constructed by and for men."[10] Keller, on the other hand, notes that it may no longer be fashionable or acceptable "to openly equate 'scientific' with 'masculine,' but contemporary science nonetheless carries the history of that conjunction in the operative norms that guide its choice of questions, institutional structures, and methodological and explanatory structures." Moreover, she affirms: "This conjunction between the scientific and masculine norms (no quotation marks) has been historically functional in guaranteeing a sexual division of emotional and intellectual labor that effectively excludes most women from scientific professions and simultaneously excludes all those values that have been traditionally regarded as 'feminine' from the practice of science."[11] However, it is by marking a distance that Keller evokes the idea of an integral connection between the two aspects of the scientific enterprise, institutional and theoretical: neither Erikson nor Bettelheim, she says, claimed that what they called "female genius" would lead "to different laws of Nature."[12] So be it, they did not go so far, but how far did they propose to go? Alternately rejected and taken up again, the idea of a fundamental difference between the relations of the two sexes to the sciences hovers in the background: something internal to the sciences and that cannot be anything but the masculine has excluded women. Keller seems to have found a principle of equilibrium in the social-cultural domain. Explaining that she has abandoned the idea of "male and female natures" in favor of the ideology of *gender*—thus of cultural beliefs about masculine or feminine natures—she now proposes to examine how these beliefs might affect science itself.[13] But the argument really does not work: the naturalistic belief she repudiates reasserts itself in a displacement typical of the so-called *gender* perspective: we no longer believe in sexed natures, all of that is culturally constructed, but by whom? Ah, by men, and of course, since they construct the culture rather than being constructed by it, it is masculinity in itself, for itself, and real, that determines cultural productions. In turn, marked as they are by masculine norms, these cultural productions exclude women.

So contemporary science incorporates this historical conjunction between the scientific and the masculine, with or without quotation marks, "in the operative norms that guide its choice of operations, institutional structures, and methodological and explanatory structures." Such a pronouncement has a certain initial plausibility. That the decision-making structures of the scientific world are dominated by men is a given of present-day experience. The higher the level in the scientific hierarchy, the fewer women there are; in their training, young women researchers receive less attention in the laboratory than young men. It can also be argued that the choice of questions in the applied sciences often ignores both our basic freedoms and women's interesting existence in this everyday world. Submit a proposal to a research institute for an interdisciplinary project on contraception or on women's role in the construction of Europe, and you will see what happens. I wager the response will be that the application was poorly presented. And what about military research or military objectives concealed within so-called civilian or even basic research programs? However, I am less convinced when Keller refers to "methodological and explanatory preferences." As a scientist and a historian of science, she should have provided at least one example because the examples I can think of fail to illustrate her point.[14] And I disagree entirely when I read her argument for the "historical conjunction" between the scientific and the masculine as the article presents it with reference to Francis Bacon's masculinist (*virilophile*) rhetoric. Undoubtedly, sexist elements abound in Bacon's work; but, recalling Keller's words, can one really base any conclusions about *operative norms* on a particular rhetoric or even on a philosophy?

The *Daedalus* article refers us back to the chapter on Bacon in *Reflections on Gender and Science*. There too there are two levels of discourse: she carefully emphasizes that the Baconian model is more complex than its detractors are prepared to acknowledge and she takes account of the fact that the Baconian perspective on the domination of nature is a dialectic between domination and submission. However, and with respect to this very dialectic, another discourse comes into play and reintegrates a sexualized metaphysic: "The imagery of submission is in noteworthy contrast to the male imagery of mastery that Bacon typically used to describe the relation of mind to nature."[15] As though it were necessary to hear the nonmasculine in every submission and especially in the watchword "submission to the things themselves." And Keller cites the following thought, attributing it to Bacon, "the empire of man over things depends [wholly] on the [arts] and sciences. For we cannot command nature except by obeying her" a thought that according to her reading fixes the poles of knowledge; *man* would refer to a masculine subject while nature would be *her*, a "she" and thus not neuter.[16]

Now, if instead of reading Bacon in Anderson's translation as Keller does, one were to refer to the *Novum Organum*, one would read: "*Homo, Naturae minister et interpres, tantum facit et intelligit quantum de Naturae ordine re vel mente observaverit, nec amplius scit aut potest* [...] *Natura enim non nisi parendo vincitur.*"[17] That text names *homo*, the human being, as the subject of the enterprise. As for the term "nature," it is not repeated as a "she," marking the feminine as with *her*, but with an *ordo naturae*: "Human beings, who are the auxiliaries and interpreters of Nature, can do and understand so much and so much only as they have observed in fact or in thought in the course of nature: beyond this they neither know anything nor can do anything [...] Nature to be commanded must be obeyed."[18] The emphasis is placed on the *nec amplius* "nothing beyond that"; the intention is to inscribe knowledge within conditions and limits ensuring its humility, thus challenging the megalomania exemplified by Giordano Bruno and others. And there is no sexualization here unless, as Spedding proposes, one reads the aphorism in the light of a maxim of Publius Syrus, *Casta ad virum matrona parendo imperat*, the chaste matron commands her husband by obeying him, a reading that places the knowing subject in the situation of a wife, and nature and its order as an inflexible but maneuvrable husband. From time to time Bacon personifies nature as masculine: it is a Proteus or a Pan.[19] And, in *The Advancement of Learning*, discussing natural induction which he considers superior to what the logicians describe, he speaks favorably of the human mind, and refers to it, exceptionally for him, as grammatically feminine, "the mind of herself by nature," a *mind* that is like a bee gathering pollen.[20] Finally, if we insist on playing on the sex of words, let us note that a passage about the marriage of mind and nature says quite specifically, *Thalamum mentis humanae et universi,* the marriage of human intelligence (feminine) and the universe (masculine).[21] The least one can say is that when it occurs, the allegorical-grammatical sexualization of the poles of knowledge is less than precise. And Bacon complicates things by writing sometimes in English, sometimes in Latin: in the English works we find "man," an ambiguous term with both a generic and a specific meaning; we also find the adjective "human." The Latin texts use *homo,* the human being without specification; the English or French translations of the Latin works generally, but not always, use "man" or "*homme*" for *homo.* Thus we are confronted with two philosophical languages in the original texts, one ambiguous, the other not. Each has the potential for generating quite different ideas. Moreover, in the contemporary debate, we must take the language and style of the translators into account. One thing at least is clear: in the Latin works, *homo,* the unspecified human being, serves as much to describe the mind as it is, ill-suited for scientific labor and prone to error, as it does to designate the subject who should be interested in the development of the sciences. So here is the problem: while admitting that for Bacon the mind is full of errors and must be cleansed, Keller claims that the reformed mind, purged of its illusions and errors, would be powerful in itself, virile, and thus capable of begetting—an idea she returns to in a more developed form in the *Daedalus* article, which describes the scientific mind as "cleansed of all traces of femininity."

The claim that science requires a virile mind is tenable only if one has read nothing but English translations of Latin works, or glosses written by our male contemporaries. The first problem is that when we study these texts we encounter the imaginary of recent Baconians rather than that of Bacon himself. Moreover, no one attempts to determine the extent to which Baconian metaphysics and "his" imaginary are compatible. It is as though the imaginary could substitute for the philosophy as such. Finally, and although she refines her own thesis extensively, Evelyn Fox Keller maintains that through this imagery (which presupposes a masculine subject seeking aggressively and violently to know a nature-that-is-woman), Bacon has provided a truer description of "the scientific impulse" than is generally provided by the defenders of science.[22] Keller's intention therefore is not to engage with the history of philosophy but to credit Bacon with depicting the true state of the sciences in a way that is valid even today. We are drawn into a strange game of mirrors here: she never cites the English works she could have read in the original to support her interpretation, but only Latin works in translation, paraphrased or with commentaries produced by our male colleagues. Since, compared with the originals, these translations seem either to pick up on the slightest hint of sexualization or to be blatantly inaccurate, we cannot help thinking that she is in fact discussing the imaginary of such mid-twentieth-century scholars as Anderson or Farrington. All of this, of course, offers a remarkable perspective on the mentality of our esteemed male colleagues and proof positive that history does not always flow in the right direction— men of the twentieth century have felt the need to embellish it. However, they most certainly cannot pass as founders of early modern science; their fantasies could have no influence on the course of any scientific practice whatsoever. Thus, it is only by projecting these twentieth-century scholars' fantasies onto seventeenth-century texts that one can posit a connection with the sciences themselves. And the unfair criticism levelled at Bacon, especially when more serious charges could have been brought against him, inscribes in the sciences themselves the impossibility for women to have any interest in them, because they generate a certain unease or mental distress— even Bruno Bettelheim, psychiatrist or psychoanalyst, has been asked what he thinks about it.

Instead of being surprised that these undeniably sexist elements of Bacon's thought have been neither denounced nor even mentioned, let us examine how the allegations leading to this flawed indictment have been fabricated. Keller cites Farrington's interpretation of the title of a short work by Bacon, the *Temporis partus masculus*: "that older science represented only a female off-spring, passive, weak, expectant, but now a son was born, active, virile, generative."[23] What we have here is merely an interpretation that certainly does not explain the title of the work, but serves at the very most to reveal the masculinist biases of a colleague who has no regard for his female students. Like many others, Bacon says that truth is the daughter of time, *veritas filia temporis:* time, represented in the iconography as a bearded old man, is a father who gives birth to a truth-daughter.[24] Thus the title can be read literally: he announces a masculine birth of time. Moreover, in a passage cited by Keller, Farrington adds one significant word. Bacon says that marriage with the things themselves will produce *beatissimam prolem vere Heroum,* a blessed race of Heroes; Farrington adds "or Supermen."[25] There would not necessarily have been any doubt as to the sex of the progeny who would combat humanity's innumerable miseries, even though the offspring could be discoveries rather than persons. In any case, adding "Supermen" betrays an interest in placing the accent on sex, and not, for example, on the fortunate character of the scientific enterprise. Keller has thus allowed herself to be manipulated by the language of Farrington, who not only represents the purified mind as virile but also returns to the vocabulary of the sexless human being when it is a matter of criticizing the unpurified mind. Thus, when the *mens humana*, swollen or aroused with observations, produces all sorts of errors, Farrington translates it as "the human mind"![26] And when Bacon mentions the legitimate humiliation of the human mind, *spiritus humani humiliatio*, Farrington unfailingly translates it as "of the human spirit,"[27] he who in more positive statements invariably translates *homo* as *Man*. What makes this all the more inexcusable is that, as a Bacon specialist, he should have known that the purging of the understanding is used more as a regulative concept than a description of a real project: my son, "no matter how much you might wish to, you cannot rid yourself of idols simply because I have told you to, or without knowledge of things. Obviously, you cannot write anything new without erasing the old; but the opposite is true for the spirit: until you have written something new, you cannot erase the old."[28] Assimilating the purified mind to masculinity (the mind purified of all femininity!) seems to be quite a recent proposition, superimposed upon Baconian philosophy, whereas for Bacon himself this idea of a purified mind is a regulative ideal, not a concrete possibility. What must be done, and in this instance can be done, is to attach a weight to human understanding: "The understanding must not therefore be supplied with wings, but rather hung with weights, to keep it from leaping and flying," by imposing methods that will be like ballast.[29]

As far as nature is concerned, translators also produce an oversexualization by using "her" and introducing metaphors of their own invention. Thus, in Spedding, we find the locution "to follow and as it were to hound nature in her wanderings." The expression offers the image of a vagabond nature that must be tracked down. Citing this passage, Keller comments that nature may be coy but she can be conquered—as though this hunt were an amorous pursuit. Yet the text offers a much more benign *naturae vestigia persequaris*. It invites you—because it addresses itself to a "you" [tu]—only to follow the traces of nature's footsteps when she spontaneously departs from her usual course, so that when you will, you can lead her back to the same place.[30] This "pursuit" will culminate in the enslavement of a nature that is "indubitably woman," says Keller, this time citing Farrington who offers the translation *I am come leading to you Nature with all her children to bind her to your service and make her your slave* (in the Latin text this is a much paler statement: *naturam cum fetibus suis tibi addicturus et mancipaturus*, "I reward you and give you nature and her children").[31] The image of capture does occur in Bacon, but he criticizes it. He reproaches Aristotle for having displayed a captive experience rather than consulting it in all its freedom and, indeed, of having twisted it to conform to his own predilections and thus made it captive.[32] And the image of tracking or of the hunt could well be a misunderstanding of the philosophical parable of Pan's hunt: all the other gods were looking for Ceres; he was hunting and quite by chance he found her.[33]

Basing her theory, I think, on a paraphrase, Keller affirms that scientific knowledge and the mechanical inventions it leads to do not merely exert a gentle guidance over nature's course; they have the power to conquer and subdue her, to "shake her to her foundations."[34] This is somewhat surprising since for Bacon the laws of nature are the laws of God, and he would not overstep them without a very good reason.[35] In fact, in the passage Keller mentions, Bacon takes issue with two major, symmetrical errors: the first is to think of artifice (*ars*) as something totally different from nature, with the result that natural and artificial things must be kept separate; the second, and subtler one, consists in thinking of artifice as a simple addition to nature, able to complete what nature has begun, or to improve upon it when it deviates, but not to transmute it or shake it to its foundations.[36] The power to *in imis concutere*—shake its foundation—is denied by a doctrine unequivocally rejected by Bacon. However, we should not infer from this that the expression describes precisely what he affirms. In fact, he continues, "things artificial differ from things natural, not in form or essence, but only in the efficient; that man has in truth no power over nature, except that of motion—the power, I say of putting natural bodies together or separating them—and that the rest is done by nature working within."[37] One could not read into this any affirmation of a superhuman power, virile or otherwise, since nature completes what artifice begins; scatter some manure at the foot of a tree, nature will do the rest. Moreover, this is why one must know nature's laws in order to make it do anything.

2. An Offensive Philosophy, but to Whom?

Bacon's English texts can be interpreted as saying a lot of bad things about the nature of the mind of all men.[38] Moreover, throughout his works in both Latin and English, he cites exclusively masculine examples of bad method or theoretical folly: Plato, Aristotle, the Aristotelians and the Scholastics, Cicero, Cardan, Gilbert are called every name under the sun. We could even claim that the unreformed intellect has precisely the characteristics Keller attributes to masculinity. Obsession with power belongs to the pseudo-sciences; twisting experience to suit oneself, as Aristotle does, is deplorable; dogmatism manipulates facts, pushes aside those that do not correspond to whatever theory is being defended, and advances its cause by using only facts that support it, as if these facts were Roman lictors or sergeants deployed to remove obstacles. Dogmatism thus amounts to a form of violence against those toward whom the theory is directed.[39] Moreover, when Bacon doubts the existence of *men*'s genuine desire for knowledge, he underscores the extent to which good knowledge, which he calls "dry," is contrary to their nature: "generally men taste well knowledges that are drenched in flesh and blood, Civil History, Morality, Policy, about the [*sic*] which men's affections, praises, fortunes, do turn and are conversant." The shortcoming he denounces almost amounts to a specificity that at that time was masculine, honors and fortunes being the key questions for ambitious courtiers. The dry light of theoretical work "doth parch and offend most men's soft and watery natures"; and "seemeth but a net of subtility and spinosity"—and all of this is about *men*'s nature.[40] Furthermore, Bacon's philosophy of scientific knowledge offends the pride or narcissism of men of science, who in his scheme are merely laborers in the collective enterprise. In his view, the veneration of inventors stands in the way of progress; what counts is not the eye, the hand, nor the natural mind, but instruments like the magnifying glass, the compass, or the inductive apparatus. Stop using facts dogmatically, he urges, be humble, allow yourselves to be guided by the things themselves, and know that your experience is valid only if it is communicable. Thus, strictly speaking, there is no subject of knowledge but only methods, experimental protocols, instruments, and therefore "there is no significant inequality among human intellects,"[41] whence the figure of the anonymous laboratory assistant who performs experiments dreamed up by others or that of "anybody at all" as the subject who carries out the experiment.[42] But there is a double subject involved in verification, not the author but the reader together with nature, the unknown reader addressed by a book that unpretentiously sets out the schemata of experience: it is *you* who will verify what I say, by testing my words in nature. For *omnino scientia ex naturae lumine petenda*, science in its entirety should be sought in (or drawn from) the light of nature and "for what pertains to nature, nature herself must be consulted."[43] It is nature who has the last word, so go and ask it; nature is the one to be consulted, rather than established authority, the Bible, Aristotle, and so on, and still less our (my, your) phantasmagoria. However, this nature cannot be read like an open book, otherwise there would have been no need to invent sophisticated scientific procedures. One of Anderson's sentences quoted by Keller is more or less accurate: the *De Augmentis* says: "the nature of things betrays itself more readily under the vexations of art . . . than in its natural freedom."[44] A certain instrumentality precedes scientific work, and technology is not merely an application of discoveries. For example, you might wonder whether distance from the earth would not cause the weight of a body to vary. To find the answer, you would set up the following crucial experiment: take two clocks, one with weights, the other working by compression of a metal blade, set to mark exactly the same time and carry them to an elevated place. If the first starts to slow down in relation to the other, or if they continue to run in the same way, you will have the answer. Compressing the blade may be a little like torture; the metaphor of *natura vexata* sends us back to the detestable legal practice of putting the accused to the question [the rack]. However, in this case, the sadism is in the language rather than in the compression of a blade, and it is not nearly enough to be the basis for articulating a crucial experiment. The amount of imagination required to set up this experiment is infinitely greater than the element of metaphorical cruelty that might be involved in winding up a spring.

Truth is not the daughter of authority: is it for this reason that the universities have taken so long to expand their self-definition to include sciences and research? For to provide a home for the sciences, various state structures interested in scientific development had to create the Royal Society, Academies of Science in the seventeenth century, the École Polytechnique in the Napoleonic era or a CNRS (Centre national de la recherche scientifique) in the 1930s. All these bodies were created outside the traditional sites of learning. Universities' opposition to them has been as vigorous as their resistance to the admission of women; moreover, sciences and women were admitted at more or less the same time. They remained marginalized or were regarded with suspicion for a long time and in the same way, as if they signalled a new definition of the institution, a new function with the power to supplant the old identity defined by the discourse of authority. This discourse seems to have been central to the rejection of science and women. It rejected science because scientific work contests authority, and women because society at large requires a form of social thought that denies women any possibility of authority. Furthermore, if authority depends on the symbolic status of its spokespersons, it formally distinguishes itself from scientific knowledge, which is regulated by the principle of anonymity and of equality between the person who invents and the one who verifies. A form of knowledge that, because it claims objectivity, grants the capacity to act to anyone who possesses it, ultimately depersonalizes the knower, and erases personal identity. Thus, following the laws of nature (which presupposes knowing them), *one* can hope to make use of natural possibilities for whatever ends one determines. To understand this point and my use of "one", we must make a detour through Baconian metaphysics.

Nature is likely to exist in three different states. Either it is free and reveals itself according to its usual course, when it moves by its own efforts freely and without hindrance; as happens with celestial bodies, animals, plants; or it is torn out of its own state and demolished by material irregularities and the violence of obstacles, as happens with monsters; or, finally, by artifice and the human hand (*ministerio humano*), it is harnessed (or put in chains), fashioned, transplanted, and so to speak made anew, which happens with artificial things. Thus natural history treats of the freedom, the restless wanderings or the ties (*vincula*) of nature.[45] Bacon thus offers a triptych, not a diptych like that of commentators who contrast nature with human intervention and who transpose onto this intervention the vocabulary of violence he uses to speak of the production of monsters. Indeed, certain texts suggest a parallel between the nonhuman production of monsters and the human production of artifices, but the second is in fact said to copy the first, and thus the three terms are maintained. Moreover, seeing a duel between man and nature bypasses the essential: what characterizes nature is its mobility in its three states and from one state to another; when it is free, it moves by its own efforts, and the essay "Of Gardens" presents it as unstable even in its "natural" state—a wasteland must be maintained or it degenerates.[46] Agreeing with this view, the *Valerius Terminus* mentions "the calculation and ordination of the true degrees, moments, limits, and laws of motions and alterations by means whereof all works and effects are produced."[47] For the laws of nature are precise, not indefinite, laws of transformation, and this fact explains the possibility of alteration by human intervention; what could anyone do, faced with a frozen or petrified universe? Correlatively, human intervention is possible only within the limits of the laws of nature; since there is a law or a rule-governed passage between movement and heat, you can transform movement into heat and vice versa. Furthermore, if rapprochement or distancing is possible, producing an interesting effect, then

> it matters not whether it be done by art and human nature, or by nature unaided by man [. . .] when gold is found pure in the sands, nature does the work for herself just as much as if it were refined by the furnace and human appliance. Sometimes again the ministering office is by the law of the universe deputed to other animals; for honey, which is made by the industry of the bee, is no less artificial than sugar, which is made by man.[48]

One page of *The Advancement of Learning* observes ironically that other animals are perhaps capable of invention. The intrinsic mobility of nature also explains why human intervention can occasionally be described as something that contains and binds: arts and technologies *retain* those transformations useful to human life. Finally, the effect of this mobility is that the same "thing" can present itself in various states; consequently, scientific process consists in working backwards from observable phenomena, which present themselves as distinct from one another, to rediscover their common form, and thence the law that governs transformation from one to the other: for example, there is no doubt that the transformation of movement into heat follows the laws of nature.

A sexist imaginary was certainly not the inevitable consequence of this Baconian metaphysic: if the agent of knowledge and action can be just anyone at all, including animals other than human, and if nature can transform itself, there is no reason whatsoever not to imagine women in today's laboratories or in the House of Solomon. Since, however, *The New Atlantis* depicts this center of research as populated only by men, there must have been a deliberate sexist choice and Bacon has no excuses. This is the source of my disagreement with *feminist epistemology*. To critique Bacon as Keller does is in effect to grant that both he and the founders of the Academies were right to confine the sciences within a masculine enclosure: we are indeed indebted to virility for the sciences, since it is masculine impulses that are at work in the scientific enterprise! In my opinion, this is false and, in any case, if Bacon is dragged into the argument, it is important to emphasize that neither philosophy nor an irresistible imaginary gave him any reason to argue that a fraternal contract is the foundation of the learned community, thus making an indubitably sexist claim that goes unnoticed even today. And I have explained elsewhere that because he knew many women of intellect, he cannot be excused with a dismissive "that is just how it was at that time."[49] If he has no excuse, he can be reproached for excluding women by fiat and putting into circulation a facile idea that is as hard to refute as it is easy to repeat.

3. Sciences, Humanities, and Philosophy

In many ways, I have a certain affection for the sciences. I enjoyed those that I studied at the *lycée* and they taught me a certain liberating rigor. In mathematics, biology, physics, and chemistry, you are not asked to take anyone at her or his word; the exercises and practical applications are there, so that even as a child, you can verify an adult's claims—wouldn't that be reason enough to bless the sciences? And too bad if it has unfortunate consequences for a certain type of literary teaching and if, having had a taste of the sciences, you decide to see whether close textual reading will support those professorial pronouncements. Sometimes you will deflate hollow generalizations ("Racine paints men as they are and Corneille as they should be") that are far removed from what these authors in fact give us to read or see on stage; but, above all, you will understand that the purpose of literary studies is less to put you in contact with literary works than to communicate a discourse. This discourse is undoubtedly about works, but just barely: it substitutes itself for them and serves other purposes. As you will have realized, the purpose of a certain type of Baconian studies in the twentieth century was less to understand Bacon's project to create scientific research than to rewrite it using twentieth-century clichés. As a hypothesis, one could also propose that there are more nationalist values in Lanson or Lagarde and Michard,* more sexism and conformity among literary critics in general than in a novel or a tragedy, as if the literary work itself had little tolerance for cliché while critical discourse makes strenuous efforts to reduce bold or exploratory literary experience to simple social forms.

Consider Jane Austen's novel, *Mansfield Park*, published with a learned preface from which we learn that it is "the story of a girl who triumphs by doing nothing"—really!? There follows a long development in which Tanner, a Cambridge professor, explains that Fanny is an unpleasant character, that she is "a very unpopular heroine" and "a prig," although you may perhaps have admired this poor cousin's stoicism and have believed that the purpose of the novel was to contrast it with bourgeois pettiness. The function of the commentary seems to be to induce the reader to adopt Tanner's unjust, cruel, and certainly stereotyped vision of a fictional woman, a perspective he would extend to women of flesh and blood. His point of view may pass for wise or learned, but it barely conceals its amateurism, for Tanner concludes: "nobody falls in love with Fanny Price."[50] There you have it! the only function of the heroines of a novel is to allow a male reader to fall in love: if one of them fails to fulfill that function, she is in the wrong. All the same, Tanner will redeem the novel, not without wondering what "such a poor sort of heroine is doing in such a great book," he who prefers other heroines and who lumps this string of marriageable young women together like debutantes sitting in a row at a ball, there to be chosen by a husband-reader. Putting himself in the place of a possible suitor who finds some of them more seductive than others, the commentator confers upon Jane Austen the status of mother of marriageable daughters, noting quite ingenuously that she was not incapable of creating attractive heroines; two, he says, are adored by the public. In the end Fanny appears as the ugly duckling of Mrs. Austen's covey. Now although this is meant to be a learned academic reading, the commentator brings to it a ready-made schema that he has not acquired through critical reflection but from his own social experience. For only a man who assumes he can look at young girls and choose from the display as a potential buyer would do could read a novel in such a way. Must we simply conclude that it is a

---

*André Lagarde and Laurent Michard are the authors of a series of widely used manuals of French literary history from the Middle Ages to the twentieth century. Each manual focuses on a period (the Middle Ages) or a century (16th, 17th, 18th, etc.) and comprises a chronological presentation of significant works and authors (as defined by Lagarde and Michard), excerpts from the most important works, commentary on main themes and literary-historical importance, time lines of principal historical events, and many illustrations. Like Gustave Lanson, Lagarde and Michard present a strictly canonical national literary history.

matter of relativism—everyone reads novels according to his or her own experience? No, Tanner is one of the canonical interpreters of Jane Austen; his projection of a social structure onto the text amounts to establishing a norm, just as Anderson's and Farrington's readings of Bacon set the norm in countries where studies of the history of philosophy consist in reading commentaries rather than the texts themselves.

A currently fashionable literary theory affirms that there are no texts, but only interpretations or literary theories, a claim that seems to propose relativism as the only possible point of view. This assumption of absolute control over the text raises to the level of theory the possibility of doing whatever one likes with unique works and validates substituting an interpretive discourse for the works themselves, thus short-circuiting any possibility of critical analysis and ignoring the power structures that allow such an assumption in the first place. This interpretive discourse takes effect in a very specific institutional structure. There are more female than male students in the humanities; yet, the further one goes up the hierarchy in the professorial ranks, the fewer women there are. The most insightful among the female students say examinations often have little to do with understanding literary works themselves, but require conformity to a received interpretation, even if it is absurd. If your exam is conducted by a Tannerian and you do not show disdain for Fanny, you risk a bad mark. In the literary world, it is men who achieve the status of canonical commentators. The structure seems paradoxical if we are thinking only in terms of gender: there appears to be a pre-established harmony between femininity and literary matters at the level of the taught body, but strangely enough, a harmony between literature and masculinity at the highest levels of the teaching body. We may find this rather suspect, but the apparent paradox dissolves if we are mindful of questions of authority and the substitution of a cliché-ridden discourse for the literary work itself. A majority of women on the receiving end, an overwhelming majority of men producing canonical commentaries: could the purpose of literary studies be to make women ingest schemata administered by men?

Conversely, the universities' resistance to the natural sciences and their dismay at seeing women meddle in the sciences could be seen as part and parcel of an ultraorthodox position. Not only are the sciences exempt from the discourse of authority but they are also domains of knowledge that cannot be managed solely on the basis of belief, whereas beliefs themselves can be concocted and administered by structures of power, or they can develop along social lines. Until quite recently, the division between literary and scientific studies was highly sexualized, and it could refer back to a quasi-legal distinction between those destined to be believers and those authorized to function outside the confines of belief, at least in the laboratory. And the sciences have removed themselves from belief in yet another way: it is neither necessary nor obligatory to believe in them; you can learn something of them, and take pleasure in discovering that a few theories and a test tube can make the world partially intelligible, and later on you may be completely indifferent to science, or let forgetfulness, that radical form of disbelief, do its work. Contrary to Auguste Comte's view, there is freedom of conscience in astronomy, except for astronomers and school children who because of their status are subject to the constraints inherent in this scientific discipline. Forty percent of my compatriots believe that the sun turns around the earth even though the schools teach the opposite; it is their absolute right because they are not accountable for their opinions. On the other hand, if you entrust your eyes to a surgeon, she or he is expected to know everything that can be known about optics and asepsis, and to remember it all at the right time. Adherence to scientific methods and results is obligatory only when the social and professional responsibility of integrity and respect for others is at issue: it is a constraint that weighs only upon someone with a special power to act. Surely, it is prudent for the layperson (of whom I am one) to try to understand as much as possible of these things, and the democratic ideal would want everyone to be capable of examining what is going on in scientific research. But how? The daily and weekly press certainly includes sections on "Science" or "Research" but to the fraction of public opinion that reads the newspapers, they present an account of scientific works that owes more to fantasy than to intellect, as if scientific topics such as the origin of the galaxies and of humanity could pick up where the old myths about cosmogony and anthropogony left off. Only rarely do they provide elements of an informed judgment on the state of knowledge or the functioning of the institutions that dispense or add to it.

The division we have seen between literary and scientific studies is also internal to philosophy. One approach to teaching the history of philosophy is obsequiously deferential toward allegedly great authors and tends to substitute for the texts themselves a discourse that is sometimes a mistranslation or a reflection of extraneous values. Conversely, I remember certain classes with gratitude, for example, Georges Canguilhem explaining a page of Bachelard and grumbling about an idea or sentence whose lack of precision he summarized implacably. Sometimes an entire paragraph was consigned to sonorous inanity, or a whole page of Galileo, Pascal, or Claude Bernard was torn to shreds; but what remained after such careful sifting was all the more remarkable. Far from forbidding critical vigilance, Canguilhem systematically encouraged it, and you might surmise that if I spend so much time criticizing the universities, it is because the education they give rarely achieves the same level of free examination as his teaching did. However, I finally came to understand his displeasure at finding female students in his classes; he showed it so clearly that many called him misogynist *urbi et orbi*. I think he was especially misogynist when it came to philosophy, and wherever he communicated his critical acumen. He must have found it unseemly for women to come to him in order to learn how to read critically without being taken in. And what about his logician colleagues, all of whom at that time, at all levels of the hierarchy, were men? The exercises they gave us—count the logical fallacies in a military speech—were delightful, but their explicit purpose was to limit women to understanding propositional calculus but not predicate calculus; consequently, predicate calculus was thoroughly taught only in an *école normale* seminar which of course was closed to women.[*] One day I will enroll in a logic course to try to see whether the Sorbonne blocked my access to worthwhile intellectual methods, and if so, why.

4. Finalities

If in their daily lives women do indeed owe something to scientific discoveries, then postulating that science is male or virile makes our collective relationship with men one of indebtedness and dependence. While regretting that the history of science tends to deny the contributions of the Lady Mary Wortley Montagus of this world and that feminist epistemology disregards Marie Curie, we must indeed accept that, whatever may be true of the past, our indebtedness persists; is this a reason for wanting it to continue? When he refuted the widely accepted theory of spontaneous generation and invented microbes, a certain Pasteur rendered great service to many— women, men, children, and new mothers—because asepsis is crucial for childbirth and breast-feeding and bottle-feeding an infant. The implications of asepsis are far-reaching, and we women have to acknowledge that it was a man's scientific work that made us understand the need for such hygiene. Admittedly, puerperal fever did not disappear at once nor did bottle-feeding immediately become the most obvious solution when a mother could not or did not want to breast-feed. Scientific discoveries pass through a number of different filters, and it always takes more than mere scientific discovery itself for the potential of any particular one to be fully realized, especially for women. But until the discovery is made, it is impossible even to formulate requirements, whereas with a simple knowledge of scientific results, an ounce of common sense, plus a healthy dose of ethical consideration of people's material lives, we can begin to recognize that some things in this world are not acceptable. If, for example, every mother giving birth in Uganda or in a Delhi shanty town today could do so on a sheet that had been boiled, if she

---

[*]The *écoles normales* are among the most prestigious institutions of higher learning in France. Unlike the universities, they have highly selective admission policies involving rigorous preparatory courses followed by competitive entrance examinations (*concours*).

and the woman attending her had some elementary knowledge of hygiene, maternal and infant death would be less frequent. That should be the decisive criterion for judging medical practices. We should be working with the World Health Organization to define both a set of techniques aimed particularly at women's reproduction and realistic policies of sanitation that include access to care or prophylactic measures as a fundamental human right.

Here I am touching on a very sensitive issue, even from a feminist point of view. We see it in Ann Oakley's famous analysis of a conflict in rural India between what she describes as two types of control over childbirth, one traditional and feminine, the other modern and masculine. A medical assistant employed by the government arrives in the village to examine pregnant women; she comes into conflict with the loyalty of these women and their mothers to the local midwife. Oakley interprets this situation as a gender-based struggle for control of childbirth: "Although the health visitor is a woman, she is sent to educate the female community by a male-dominated medical authority," thus as a masculine attempt to exercise control over women.[51] We can comment only on the account we are given, not on the conflict itself, of which we have no firsthand knowledge, although we might suspect that in this case, as so often happens, there was indeed a clumsy and authoritarian intervention. We should also be working on respectful pedagogical models, appropriate for providing groups of women with information, knowledge, and the skills that matter to them. I would be willing to wager that the family planning counsellors from Villeurbanne or Seine-Saint-Denis could teach us all a thing or two, since their first principle is to validate what a woman already knows and encourage her to trust her own judgment. In any case, in Oakley's account, because the visiting nurse is the representative of modern medicine, she is denied her status as a woman, as if medicine were intrinsically masculine because it is dominated by men, and as if women should therefore shun it, especially with respect to such an emblematic issue as childbirth. You will have guessed that I categorically deny anyone the right to make an emblem of an event that engages the reality of body and life, or to make it the focus of a conflict over control, as if two powers, for the sake of their own glory, were entitled to argue over an unfortunate body with no concern for its possible fate. In this vignette, it is important to recognize that, face to face with medical power, not only does the birthing mother disappear as a subject with rights, but a fantasy of femininity emerges, cleansed of all connection to the masculine, symmetrical with the one Farrington, Anderson, and Keller attribute to Bacon. In the name of pragmatism and respect for the birthing mother, we must affirm our modernity on condition that it be beneficial, sometimes more with respect to hygiene than to high-tech medicine, but also with respect to high tech, when it is justified; there is no reason for women not to benefit from the practical advances that scientific work makes possible. If more women are needed in the sciences for the collective imaginary to entertain such ideas, then by all means let us work toward it! In fact, I refuse to believe that attributing numerous technicoscientific developments to men is a major obstacle to their applicability to women. In certain Muslim countries like Indonesia, boys are vaccinated but not girls because vaccination requires exposing a bit of flesh, and in any case a girl's death matters less. It would be of little or only indirect use to remind the parents that Lady Mary Wortley Montagu learned the principle of vaccination from the women of Istanbul. If women in the developed world could overcome their dualism and their allergy to the sciences, which like their male compatriots they believe to be masculine, then it would be clear to them that the benefit of scientific progress is, to say the least, inequitably shared, and that an alliance of educated women from both developed and developing countries could articulate the needs of all women and devise the political means of ensuring that international organizations and governments respond to them. This does not require us to object to Pasteur's beard or to see nothing but a beard in microbiology; but it does require us to challenge the dualism that always relegates the feminine to the traditional or archaic and thwarts political awareness of the responsibilities that fall to us when they are of no interest to anyone else.

Finally, we must contest the faulty logic that substantializes adjectives. Until now, more men than women have been involved in the scientific enterprise; but it does not follow that the enterprise itself must be masculine to the core, to the point where masculinity could graft itself onto another substance in alchemical fashion. For the ultimate transformation of substantialism is transsubstantiation: beginning with a statistical given—more men than women in the sciences, especially in decision making—we project it onto two essences, masculinity, and scientificity, declaring that the first determines the second. Then, when a woman dares to become involved in scientific work, the essence of masculinity, which had transplanted itself into the essence of scientificity, is supposed to migrate from there to this unfortunate woman. Thus, the Indian medical aide is reputed to resemble a man, a shameful transsubstantiation, of course, while the power exercised over women by her traditional counterpart, the midwife, is not seen to be exercised on behalf of the group of men, although I would nevertheless wager that it is. All of this completely misses a more significant, ethical, problematic. It is possible to want or not to want freedom for every woman, to see her as a subject of rights, or not, to respect or not to respect the reality of her needs and physical well-being. When anyone, male or female, supports this aspiration to freedom, respects bodily reality, and so on, this person acts well; when anyone, male or female, thinks of a woman only as an object of control or prey to symbolic conflicts, the result in either case is no more positive for the woman. Exploitation is exploitation, whether by a man or a woman. One day in the United States, I said as much about some of Simone de Beauvoir's liaisons (before writing *The Second Sex,* she was not very nice to other women), and I got into hot water: when they want to create a sisterhood, you must not criticize the sisters. I continue to maintain that Beauvoir became feminist through her writing, and there you can see an argument for active pedagogy if you wish. And I repeat: the idea of a feminist community is meaningless unless from the outset we reach agreement on a few ethical, and thus political, principles, which we must hope will come to be widely shared. One of them is recognition of the reality and freedom of every woman. Conversely, where could the dulling of the critical faculty lead us if not to what Bacon called a contract of errors: the distressing complicity he saw in the universities, although at the same time he failed to consider whether the closed world of masculine scientific sociability he proposed might entail the same risk. Question of fact: in the scientific world, are there no errors attributable to men's complicity among themselves? Then a more abstract question: how is contractualism in general a necessary but ambiguous custom in knowledge, a tightly closed contract being in itself disastrous? To illustrate the problem briefly: in order to think and know with others, we must accept certain minimal assumptions, points such as 2 and 2 make 4 or, most important of all, ways of discussing methods, which normally claim to be accessible to everyone.[52] But when such minimal understandings evolve into rigid pacts, explicit in their exclusions, implicit in their effects, we must wonder what fictions knowledge is instituting.

To put it as bluntly as possible: I differentiate between sciences said to have been founded by men alone, and sciences managed by men who refuse entry to anyone but men.[53] And I emphasize this distinction all the more because it allows me to highlight a problem that has gone systematically unnoticed: currently, campaigns for women's entry into the sciences (something that in my view has been in place for a long time) or for more equity (and there everything remains to be thought about) are based on the claim that the sciences would benefit and that new fields of study or new methods would appear. Now, even if that has been true in the human sciences ever since Gabrielle Suchon outlined a new body of knowledge, and less evident in the natural sciences, there is still a problem: women are looked upon as means, in this instance as the means to a scientific renewal—means, as usual, for achieving a good that would not initially be theirs. So to the extent that we must endorse the general idea that more justice for women will produce positive effects for everyone, we must also and first of all take women themselves as ends rather than means. People too often miss the point: even when justice for women would imply no particular benefit for anyone but them or for institutions, it would still be intrinsically valuable.

It thus becomes a matter of simple justice to make the scientific world more equitably mixed. Women enroll in scientific studies and find nothing there to encourage them; no mode of analysis allows them to decipher the social context in which they work, and they encounter a discourse telling them they have no place there, they will play subordinate roles in collaborative work, and—one of the greatest scientific hoaxes of this century—in any case "women publish less than men." A scholarly article (I include sociology, and other social sciences) is sometimes, signed first by the man or woman administratively responsible for the project (usually a man) then cosigned by the person who has contributed most to the work. To be a subordinate is potentially to see one's work attributed to someone else, thus sometimes to be exploited in perpetuity. Moreover (every cloud has a silver lining!), let my own unpleasant experience in an evaluation process underscore the point. One day, with five books and two dozen articles to your credit, you apply for something: the report credits you with one book. You start again with six books and three dozen articles; this time the writer of the report seems to have taken note of the previous report, and removes more from the list. For the nth time a biologist is a candidate for promotion; she is turned down but with assurances that she is appreciated: the committee has recommended her for an award, but she had received this distinction ten years previously and it was recorded in her dossier. When an evaluation glosses over the factual aspects of an application, it is clear that the pronouncement "women publish less" has no basis in scientific fact-finding.

The prevailing discourse assures us that science is virile, and naturalizes women's lesser capacity in science. However, it proposes no strategy for rectifying the situation; indeed, it prevents analysis of the relationship between overexploitation of women and their longer, more rigorous subordination. To describe the place allocated to women in scientific production, I borrow a term from old Parisian workers' language: in dressmaking workshops the apprentices, called *les arpètes*, were trainees who performed jobs or tasks that were beneath the dignity even of the seamstresses. Until quite recently, "to be treated like *une arpète*" had a precise meaning: someone who is ostensibly a trainee must nonetheless perform tasks without training value, even if they are useful to the community—sweeping the workshop instead of learning overstitching. If most women are the *arpètes* of scientific projects essentially defined by men, we find a structure of subordination, premeditated since Bacon, that foresees a body of male researchers and a mixed secondary or ancillary body: "As you can imagine, we also have novices and apprentices so that men involved in research can always be replaced; and these are in addition to a large number of male and female servants."[54] Today there are indeed female novices, but they can still be neglected.

Does this affirm or deny that if women had half the decision-making power, there would be undue risk to the male establishment and that an unfair advantage to a different kind of creativity would emerge from a community that at long last included both sexes? The only real response to this question is to make all decision-making agencies completely mixed, half men, half women: let's experiment and assess the outcome. Moreover, a history of scientific imposture might throw some light on the question, but who would analyze a particular discovery as if it were an imposture? The well-known examples, such as airplanes capable of detecting oil deposits, were exposed as soon as specialists in pure research could examine the alleged discoveries, which had captured the imagination because of their possible applications. Such applications either appeal to the imaginary or they do not, and I can propose an example with heuristic value even if so far it is poorly established. I spoke to a man and a woman, both engaged in pure research, who had been part of the team working on the potential applications of RU 486, a molecule being studied because of its promise for treating certain side effects of cortisone. Both testimonies concurred: at the end of the clinical trials, when they could not determine how to make the drug tolerable during prolonged treatment, the team decided to use a single dose to produce abortion. The result was positive. The female researcher was proud, but the male researcher spoke deprecatingly of this discovery: "it was rushed, we had come to a dead end, we wanted to buy some time by proving something at least." Even in pure research, the idea of a useful application (but who defines usefulness?) often originates at the margins of a project. So long as the scientific community is not egalitarian and happily mixed, hypotheses and ideas for applications useful to women will be neglected and lost every day. While we are waiting for the scientific milieu to change and shed its masculinism, scientific thought will remain linguistically sexualized: its metaphors, however superficial, make it impossible to formulate any demands, especially for egalitarianism. Science makes it imperative to leave alchemy behind, but the scientific community makes up for it with an alchemy of the Word.

5. The Alchemy of the Word

I think I have shown that Bacon's philosophy could have done without sexist metaphors and that his metaphoric itself is not constant in its sexism. How, then, to account for the fact that it is sometimes sexist and especially, as indisputable evidence shows, that the Chancellor's conception of the scientific community is clearly *virilophile* because there is not a single woman in the House of Solomon, except as a servant? One passage leads me to posit two things: first, a deliberate metaphorical strategy in his work seeking to play on all possibilities, and second, the exclusion of women that functions in part within this framework. "And if any one dislike that arts should be called the bonds of nature, thinking they should rather be counted as her deliverers and champions, because in some cases they enable her to fulfil her own intention by reducing obstacles to order; for my part I do not care about these refinements and elegancies of speech; all I mean is, that Nature, like Proteus, is forced by art to do that which without art would not be done; call it what you will—force and bonds, or help and perfection."[55] He doesn't care? Nonsense! He offers a choice by leaving the question of metaphor up to the reader's taste: whether one sees oneself as possessor or chivalrous defender of nature, it is all the same to Bacon, who cares a great deal about the imaginary inherent in the scientific enterprise, but only secondarily, because the dream must be pleasing. He labored over his writing in order to seduce his readers; for example, one day he proposed to write "an oration ad filios, delightfull, sublime, and mixt with elegancy, affection, *novelty of conceyt and yet sensible,* and [without] Superstition," thus making careful decisions about the tonalities of a discourse before setting out the argument.[56] He had to "sell" his project of developing a vast body of scientific knowledge of nature to a readership who he thought might support it. The ascetic nature of the project itself made it all the more difficult to sell. We have already seen the extent to which this philosophy is vexatious. Whence the construction of a laudatory discourse destined to accompany and acclaim the scientific work, distinct from operative norms. This discourse promises the learned a socioimaginary validation at the end of a labor that, itself, presupposes a certain humility: if you force yourself to follow scientific method, you will be able to imagine yourself as proprietor or liberator of nature. Be slow and deliberate, accept work broken down into individual operations, for the division of the labor of research will transform you into a worker focused on a small segment of reality. When you have earned the recognition of the Halls of Learning, we will erect a statue to you, sir, in the gallery of distinguished inventors that we will build in the House of Solomon, even though, philosophically, we have established that the veneration of inventors is a major obstacle to progress. "Sir" assuredly, not because scientific work might require male impulses but because, among other things, the laudatory discourse whose function it is to reward personal sacrifice uses the idea of a greatness that can be conferred upon the learned, all the greater because it will be reserved for men. Bacon is not really inventing anything new here; he plays on an existing social masculinism and transposes it resolutely into the sciences. A detour through philology and an examination of a scientific tale of Kepler's makes this point easier to grasp.

In Latin, *vir* has the descriptive or literal meaning of a human being of the masculine sex, and a laudatory meaning considered hyperbolic: *vir* is someone important, a personality, an individual who plays an important role in the city—as the Gaffiot Latin-French dictionary says, "a man in the full sense of the term"! *Mulier* also has a literal sense, that of a human being of the feminine sex, and a secondary sense that is alas pejorative: a weakling. Thus, to acknowledge a woman's heroism or her greatness, Latin uses another word: *virago*.[57] The simple effect of this structure is that men can be both named and honored through an identical term of reference, whereas a distinct term is required to designate a woman worthy of recognition. Now Kepler's *Somnium* shows that one of Bacon's contemporaries foresaw the possibility of the *virago* but was categorically opposed to it. The point of departure of the tale is the narrator's reading of the story of Libussa, "famous for her magic art."[58] According to the legend she was a queen, and the founder of Prague, who was said to have the gift of predicting the future and who figured in the episode called "the girls' war." She lived surrounded by exclusively female guards who, after her death, agreed to stay together and shut themselves away in a fort. Taking a dim view of their decision, the men declared war on them and exterminated them. The first concern of the *Somnium* is therefore to erase the very possibility of heroines, including scientific heroines; the hero, Duracotus, will learn astronomy in Hven in the insular and fraternal laboratory of Tycho Brahe, the counterpart of the fort to which the viragos had withdrawn. This Duracotus was born of an unknown father, now deceased, and a sorceress mother; the story and the notes added subsequently by Kepler make of her an allegory sometimes of ignorance, sometimes of secret knowledge, sometimes of the university as the refuge of the old ignorance, Kepler placing her everywhere he himself does not want to be.

This tale appears to be the story of an elimination: first remove the persona of the virago, then the figure of the father, then reduce feminine existence to the role of the mother, who is herself the global opposite of the sciences. She delays the son's scientific emancipation, trying to protect him against an explicit threat of castration by men. Evoking the condemnation of Copernicus's theory in 1616, Kepler comments: "They castrated the poet/Lest he copulate;/He lived without testicles./O, Pythagoras,/Whose thoughts survived chains:/They allow you life/After removing your brains." *They*, men of ecclesiastical or political power, castrate poets in the name of the moral order and remove the brain of the man of science. Given such threats, the mother teaches prudence: she exhorts Duracotus neither to write nor publish, telling him that *they* are numerous and formidable, *they* denigrate what their stupidity does not allow them to understand, they have people sentenced, and so on. Only the death of this protective mother will free the son to write, hence to risk brain removal, castration, and death. This tale conveys a serious message that, though expressed in fantastical mode, is without any doubt based in historical reality. The lesson of the fable could be that a man who would be a hero of the sciences must have neither father nor mother nor, above all, a female counterpart; this last requirement in fact comes first. A man will leave his father and his mother to go to a woman, the Old Testament said; putting himself in the place of the bride, Christ said "Leave father and mother and come to me." "To turn to the sciences" seems to be the early-seventeenth-century variation on this theme. The sorceress mother nevertheless brings as a dream something that knowledge itself could not deliver. Thanks to her affinities with demons, she will enable Duracotus to go to the moon in order to see the earth move, something that only the new astronomy allowed him only to think, not to see.

In the *New Atlantis,* the atmosphere is less tragic and the elimination of scientific women works according to a simple rhetorical process. The Father of the House of Solomon lists the groups of men of science who comprise the household, then speaks of domestic servants, male and female—since we are only ten lines away from the gallery of great inventors, it is high time to remove women to quite a different place. Moreover, the *Novum Organum* shows that Bacon restores the dual sense of *vir* to *homo:* "Again, let a man only consider what a difference there is between the life of men in the most civilized province of Europe, and in the wildest and most barbarous district of New India; he will feel it be great enough to justify the saying that 'man is a god to man,' not only in regard of aid and benefit, but also by a comparison of condition."[59] Here, instead of describing the power of science over nature, he describes its power to combat the misery of the world; and most of all he emphasizes the preeminence science ensures over those who do not possess it. If one human group in possession of knowledge has quasi-divine power over another, powerless, group, then clearly the exclusion of women, except in the role of servants, has a dual purpose: to flatter learned men by making them believe that at the end of an unrewarding labor they will achieve a supremacy one might call *virilodivine,* and to reinforce the power of one sex over the other. Accolades, and a restriction of the effective power of inventions to a sexually (and geographically) defined group, overlap perfectly, whereas the description of scientific work itself, makes use of a *you,* a *tu,* an *anybody* and outlines a process of depersonalization. But through its style, the writing moves straight from the scientific question of validation to the—imaginary—question of validating the learned person; and Bacon's determination to prevent random access to scientific work completes this conflation.

6. Phallomelancholia or Gay Science?

The language associated with the sciences has scarcely changed since the seventeenth century, even though the reality of scientific institutions is no longer the same. Now that science includes 30 percent women, we are no longer facing radical exclusion; nevertheless, the vocabulary of scientific discourse is still marked by a phenomenon I call a refusal to acknowledge the mixing of the sexes. It involves evoking or representing a group, a community, a body of people, which is in fact more or less mixed, as if it were entirely and essentially masculine. For some years I myself regularly attended scholarly meetings in France, and I have come to understand that such a representation of research is common among many male colleagues. Thus, invariably in the course of a meeting, a man will trot out the sentence, "research is not only a matter of money and equipment, but first and foremost of men"; a movement of the chin or shoulders always follows, to remove any ambiguity from the term: the colleague throws out his chest and utters the cliché inherited in all likelihood from military phraseology. On each occasion, I really hear "a force of greater strength in men and armaments" ("not only in weapons but also in men"), greater than what, I have no idea, undoubtedly greater than those with whom French research is in competition, since we are also constantly being told that "we must remain competitive," though with or against whom or what, they never say.

From time to time, I have urged my close friends to change their language: *Couldn't you say "a matter of women and men" once in a while?* Well, no, for "that makes it sound like an election speech" *Well then, "a matter that concerns us all"?* Not that either, because "that sounds long-winded and awkward" *Then why not "an activity in which people are personally involved"?* The colleagues who like the even rhythm "not only of funds but also of men" do not like the word "people" and they like the expression "people of science" even less; only a few academic women notice its analogy with "people of letters", "people of quality", "people of the sea", "honest people", and so on. As for saying that research is "not only a matter of funding but also of well-educated brains," I am assured that the expression is obscure or cynical (even if it underscores a certain responsibility toward female and male researchers in training). I have proposed other possibilities, have announced that one day, instead of debating, I intended to scream. Nothing came of it, not even the most flattering comparisons with General Bigeard. But what do they mean, then, by "a matter of men," if the expression they insist on is so untranslatable into ordinary language? For they refuse to give it up, even if the effects of this ritual pronouncement are anything but felicitous. In spite of all the posturing, the phrase is always uttered somewhat wearily; it wafts in melancholic fashion over the men while the women seem to have absented themselves mentally—and that does not gladden the heart either. For the men, everything happens as it does with nostalgia: it is an evocation of something that can no longer really be lived, and they do not even take any pleasure in saying such things. Proclaiming their belief in the masculinity of science, they seem to regress to a primary process in which a desire seeks instant gratification through the short-term expedient of hallucination, with maximum displeasure.

To find a notion of knowledge as the fulfillment of personal instincts and impulses, one must dig deep into the psyche. When the infant Gargantua undertakes "by long and painstaking experiments" to establish "a way to wipe my ass, the most lordly, the most excellent, the most expedient that was ever seen," impulses indubitably come into play along with the direct experience of the body, for he tries embroidered satin, velvet, lettuce leaves on himself. And the results are validated not by an anonymous, collective agency of verification, but by his father Grandgousier himself: "In these next few days I'll make you a doctor in gay science [or Doctor of the Sorbonne, depending on the French edition] . . . So go on with your ass-wipative discourse, I pray you."[60] These are the intimate pleasures one has to renounce in order to take part in creating the Republic of the Sciences, as well as the sciences themselves. But what has been discarded with childhood can be recovered in scientific discourse, which for the 70 percent of researchers who are gentlemen functions as compensation for a frustrated ego. Research, people tell them, is not for just anyone at all (equally educated), but for the man that you are, the [male] researcher, the [male] technician, *passionately* absorbed in their [male] activities;[61] moreover, you will all be known by name and you will all earn great recognition, just like your elders, who are men, real men. The fiftieth anniversary issue of the house journal of the CNRS did precisely this: "this demonstrates the importance of men to the CNRS," "leaders of men," "thanks to the men." *La Recherche* produced a special issue that elevated twenty-nine gentlemen to the status of representatives of the CNRS ("it is thanks to the passion and to the rigour of these men[. . .]") and not a single woman, not even Nicole Le Douarin—it is true that when she received an award for her embryological research on hybrids of quails and chickens, the CNRS periodical paid special attention to her fingers (the headline called them "golden fingers"), implying that the medal of the same metal had been awarded to a remarkable female technician,[62] an *arpète*, in fact.

An advertisement for a book entitled *Intelligence, passion honteuse* (*Intelligence, a Shameful Passion*) arrives in the mail. The illustration shows a naked, blushing fellow who has put a vine leaf on his skull. The publicity flyer insists on the notion of a *man* and since this person's genitals are fully exposed, there can be no ambiguity. Strange image for a book about the miseries of the intelligent being. Let us model the strangeness by tracing two lines of thought in the work. First, there are those who cannot resist alluding to an exclusive sexual identity (excuse the redundancy) and who, like Kepler, perhaps allude intentionally to an organ that surely does not replace a brain when it comes to doing research. Second, this reference combines with notions of melancholia. Verification of the model: in October 1990, under the signature of a young (male) researcher, the journal *La Recherche* publishes an article filled with interesting turns of phrase. First line of thought, "child of Sisyphus", "Odyssey of a man pushing back the frontiers", "hero in the front lines of combat", "leader of men", "heroic benefactor of humanity", "natural heir of scholars, he has established himself since the time of Galileo . . . ", "the battle of the monk and the warrior", "of the wise man and the Samurai", "a descendant of Sisyphus, that Greek hero who . . . ", "the modern man", "our life as a researcher and a man." Second line of thought: "often you meet only failure", "rage and even a certain despair", "disillusionment", "[society's] incomprehension", "laborer in the cause of knowledge", "science will lose its soul", "the balloon deflates", "the illusion of a victorious outcome of the battle, but soon the myth sank into the storm." What are they really telling us about here? Surely not about science, but about phallicism deflated. Phallocratic representations are widely supposed to satisfy phallocrats, and the affirmation of masculinism to include a benefit in the form of pleasure for almost all men, so much so that it seems inevitable for a man, when he is off guard, to spout male chauvinist theories or make idiotic comments, in the etymological sense of the term. Without rejecting this idea completely, we must emphasize how miserable masculinism really is. If some men insist on a configuration that nonetheless is as uncomfortable for them as for women, we must call it a symptom; and a symptom cannot pass for a valid theory of anything at all, particularly not of scientific work.

This dreary, empty symptom has persisted through time periods and intellectual fields. In 1808, Joseph de Maistre wrote: "Women have never created a masterpiece in any field. They did not create the *Iliad*, or the *Aenead*, or *Phaedra*, or Athaliah, or the Pantheon, or the Venus of Medici [etc., etc.]. They invented neither algebra, nor the telescope, nor the heat pump, [etc.],"[63] and we still find this belief in circulation, enacted in the structure of special editions of periodicals, in feature articles, and in anthologies. Thus at the beginning of the 1990s, *Le Nouvel Observateur* published an overview of French intellectuals, all men, and a book by Bernard-Henri Lévy took the same point of view; and in December 1985, *Le Magazine littéraire* brought out an issue entitled "Ten Years of Philosophy in France," containing a who's who of French philosophers. Sixty-three authors—we did not know that there were so many lovely flowers in the garden of French philosophy—but only two of them are women, Sarah Kofman and Angèle Krémer-Marietti. To find sixty-one French men worth discussing, it is impossible to overlook anyone, neither the retirees nor the most junior, nor the essayists whose books are not clearly philosophical, nor a few of the dead who still cast a shadow. To find only two women, one must deliberately set out to do just that. In another part of the issue, Isabelle Stengers, Élisabeth de Fontenay, Christine Buci-Glucksman, and Catherine Clément are called into service; their absence from the catalogue of philosophers "whose ideas will undoubtedly have an impact in the future" thus becomes more noticeable. They exist only as auxiliaries, brought in to write pieces on various topics in a special issue, a concoction that is doubly patriotic, French and masculinist. Thought is male in our country—the function of this type of special issue is not to inform people or to incite them to read, but to produce precisely this image. But by including one or two women in the list—what a pleasure to have the latitude to choose one or two from the full dozen one knows!—they evade any accusation of male chauvinism, which may nonetheless be levied against them, and in fact they draw even more attention to the weak representation of women. Two women in this issue, one and a half in the book by Christian Descamps on the same subject: Michèle Le Doeuff and, the half, Isabelle Stengers, who appears in the index after Ilya Prigogine in the form "and I. Stengers."

These feature articles or works of popularization have a specific role: they form a thread linking the university or the research world to a broader community, or at least to a fraction of it. Unless we subscribe to an ill-conceived notion of elitism, we cannot deny civil society the right to examine the world of thought. Unfortunately, this kind of literature offers something much less than a means of participating in debates about the life of ideas or in a definition of what is worth knowing, researching, or teaching. Moreover, the tenor of the images presented in these communications with the outside world reflects the internal fetishes and sedimented clichés of the academic world itself. We know that institutions, both those administering knowledge, and others, are resistant to change. However, we cannot attribute the ostracism of women or feminist studies merely to the existence of institutions or to institutional conservatism. The same principle prevails in the public view of university life, as though a global masculinist contract connected the managers of learned institutions with the managers of society. When one party yields a little territory on an issue, the other party comes to the rescue. *Le Monde* of February 17, 1994, gives us a remarkable example. An article by Colombe Schnek, the newspaper's U.S. correspondent, says that the movement its opponents call "politically correct" has begun to discover the rich origins of French culture, and to find them to be far more diverse than anyone in the Île-de-France might think. The list of authors (both female and male) considered worthy of study has been extended, French departments across the Atlantic are being repopulated, and their future is playing itself out through the interest of both female and male teachers and students in works by (female and male) writers from the Antilles and the Maghreb, women from France, homosexuals of both sexes, and so on. The tone is joyous, the broadening of intellectual horizons is reason enough for it to be so. The journalist does not initiate any polemic, nor does she say that Ronsard and Péguy do not enjoy a divine right to be taught in the rest of the world. She does not even intimate that everybody and his sister may tire of writing essays on Racine, who paints men just as they are. Anyone who knows American universities firsthand can corroborate her report: there, one can read Aziz Begag and Diderot, just as one can also read Jamaica Kincaid and Milton, George Sand and Merleau-Ponty, Madame de La Fayette with Monique Wittig and Christine de Pisan. Coexistence is not always peaceable, but so what? Have we never seen two Leibnizians at drawn daggers, each wanting the entire budget and all the influence? Journalists write articles, but section editors are responsible for composing the title; that is a completely different job, it seems. And too bad if on reading the title the reader is utterly mystified: Schnek's piece appeared with the headline and subheadline: "French booby-trapped by American multiculturalism. On certain campuses, the study of French is subjected to censorship by the 'politically correct' constraints imposed by ethnic and sexual minorities." *Censorship*, then, for a broadening of the program that makes it possible *also* to read Aimé Césaire, Simone de Beauvoir, Julia Kristeva, and Genet; a *trap*, recognition of the diversity of thought in the French language. As for the contemptuous expression "ethnic and sexual minorities," the journalist does not use it to refer to numerical minorities but to legal minorities who should know how to remain minor and keep politely to their marginal place. Our worthy *Monde* seems to be presenting a problem of logic: how have these editors been able to anticipate that a female reader or an ordinary male reader would unquestioningly equate broadening horizons to censorship? But this is not a matter of logic but of values and a call for order: things should not be like that. Of course it is France that protests against the fate of its favorite export, the French language. A certain definition of what must count as French literature is being defended in almost paranoid fashion—as if the inclusion of Simone Schwartz-Bart amounted to censoring Hugo or Vigny and as if the implied reader would undoubtedly agree. An opening amounts to censorship when the incumbent claims the right to keep the entire space for himself, in this case in partisan notions about what counts as literature (neither women nor Caribbeans nor North Africans wrote the *Lettre à d'Alembert*). What, then, is at issue in social representations when the entire intellectual world is no longer the sole possession of white men? It is the construction of this life as a sexual and patriotic totem, in which the men of the clan, even the uneducated ones, can forge their collective identity.

7. Duplicities

This is where the phallocratic ruse lies, I think: not in male bias coloring all scientific or philosophical values but in the art of pulling the wool over people's eyes, leading them to believe that the inflated language of cliché and masculinist phrases is a genuine commentary on scientific work or to believe that masculinist imaginary, which may be a comfort to both learned and unlearned men, could also define and contain scientificity. De Maistre did not invent the telescope himself, nor did he write the *Iliad;* but, when he affirms that the "masterpiece" is always a masculine product, he can imagine for an instant that algebra is almost his own creation. Generally, the exclusion of female creators from the mythic representation of inventiveness allows any man to take himself for Einstein or Leonardo da Vinci, without having to manipulate an equation or handle a paintbrush, and even without the slightest interest in painting or physics. For him, it is not a matter of taking pleasure in the works but of vicariously absorbing the idea of the "great man." I do fear that part of the feminist problematic of the sciences has simply fallen into the trap of this deliberate confusion produced by masculinism, so that it attacks only a virtual image of scientific work. For the subject, this confusion plays on the ambiguity of *vir* (man/great man); in so doing, it abolishes the gulf between a hollow or allegorical idea of Reason, on the one hand, and, on the other, a complex labor of establishing procedures and reflecting on concepts or experimental protocols. It is entirely possible to preserve the modest idea of rational endeavor in the sciences and philosophy, valid for both sexes and all nations, and to declare that the allegory of a hollow Reason is of no interest whatsoever except for someone seeking narcissistic benefit or a way of symbolically excluding a goodly number of Others from the debate: women, Eskimos, Carib Indians, and so on. If indeed this connection is fraudulent, this is what we must challenge. Thus duplicity becomes the charge against Bacon, for he welded a masculinist vision—the House of Solomon—to a theory of inductive labour that, in fact, could have accommodated everyone.

The *Lettre à d'Alembert* provides an illustration of the philosophical duplicity inherent in any attempt to represent rationality in the guise of a fetishized conception of Reason. The *Lettre* does not entirely bridge the gap between them, for it presents two layers of discourse differentiated by typography; one appears in the notes, the other in the body of the text. In the notes we find a fine, complex, and open theory of human reason, while the text itself imposes a closed and simplistic image with only a feeble claim to being philosophical.[64] Thus, in one note, Rousseau writes: "The intellectual world, without excepting geometry, is full of truths incomprehensible and nevertheless incontestable; because reason, which demonstrates their existence, cannot, as it were, touch them across the limits which arrest it but can only perceive them at a distance."[65] That refers to the existence of God, he says, and the reference to geometry probably alludes to the difficulties of the infinitesimal calculus highlighted by Berkeley: this calculus contains obscurities that would not be tolerated in theology.[66] Another note indicates: "human reason has no well-determined common measure and [...] it is unjust for any man to give his own as the rule to that of others. Let us suppose good faith, without which all disputation is only cackle. Up to a certain point there are common principles, a common evidence, and, in addition, each has his own reason which determines him; thus this sentiment does not lead to skepticism; but also, since the general limits of reason are not fixed and no one can inspect another's, here, with one stroke, the proud dogmatist is stopped."[67] For Rousseau, this list of givens is a "principle" capable of providing an adequate basis for religious tolerance; religions presuppose an acceptance of mysteries that are not all implausible absurdities but that an individual might find it difficult to believe if his understanding cannot encompass a demonstration of them. In any case a demonstration does not make a truth palpable. He posits these remarks as theses: taken together, they are the foundation of tolerance, but he provides no foundation for them. He says his principle could be well demonstrated but he does not attempt to do so, and admits that he merely sees it, or even has the impression he sees it. Basically, the notes advance a theory of reason whose salient feature is that it is incomplete. It is related to what individuals may have in common but it is always limited, and the extent of the commonality is not obvious. In each person, it does not therefore strictly coincide with what we all (female and male) have in common; commonality and diversity mingle, the boundary between what is shared and what is not being neither fixed nor determined. I am commenting here, seeing in this theory a rationalist hope that is perhaps greater than Rousseau intended it to be but that I am prepared to endorse: what is diversified has as much claim to being rational as what is common; for each of us, it is therefore worthwhile to explain ourselves and to debate. Since reason is not entirely the same in everyone, one person can produce ideas that appear at first glance to be at odds with received wisdom, but may evolve to the point of being communicable, so that it can be useful to express and debate them. Since no one has inspection rights over the limits of anyone else's reason, no one can claim before the fact that these views will or will not be endorsed by that other person. For if everything rational were always already held in common, we would have nothing to say to one another on the subject; conversely, if everything that is not a shared belief were a matter of pure opinion, a-rational and forever so, we would all be reduced to mere monologue. This conception of reason invites us to extend the field of rationality, opening the possibility and indeed the necessity of fostering in each person a rational capacity whose boundaries are not fixed. Situated between Gabrielle Suchon and Mary Wollstonecraft, our man Jean-Jacques is proposing a theory of the rational that contains within itself a necessity to work for its own growth. This amounts to a conception of the Enlightenment that from the outset involves a vision of the collective and individual progress of enlightenment, and it is comprehensible only where there is activity and movement. Note too that for Rousseau this principle is not sufficient; he adds a moral condition, "Let us suppose good faith, without which all disputation is only cackle," that also attests to the theory's incompleteness. In intellectual debates something more than argumentation is required, something of an ethical order. Fine.

However, a problem is already apparent in these notes: Rousseau thinks that such a principle will bring religious persecution and philosophical disputes to an end—an astonishing amalgamation that could also include all intellectual debate in the category of what is to be stopped. And he imagines that someone might ask him why he himself argues against d'Alembert: "I would answer that I speak to the many and that I am explaining practical truths, that I base myself on experience."[68] What are "the many" doing in this argument and how much dogmatism is implied in the reference to practical truths and to a form of experience that is not described but alleged? And if you skip the notes and turn to the text itself, you will find almost the opposite of what the notes suggest, not incompleteness in the process of becoming, but a static closure. Eulogizing the men's clubs of Geneva, Rousseau writes: "By themselves, the men, exempted from having to lower their ideas to the range of women and to clothe reason in gallantry, can devote themselves to grave and serious discourse without fear of ridicule. They dare to speak of country and virtue without passing for windbags; they even dare to be themselves without being enslaved to the maxims of a magpie."[69] He makes no secret of the fact that these clubs are derived from hunting or military clubs and that, like everything human, they have their disadvantages. He says: "They gamble, they drink, they get drunk...."[70] Now even if you and I harbor a few doubts about the intellectual level of the repetitive, carping, drunken conversations that take place there, these closed societies of military cronies are nonetheless described by Rousseau as loci of unadorned Reason; they *situate* Reason in a place that capitalizes on identity and exclusiveness: in these closed circles reserved for citizen-men, "they even dare to be themselves." And although the notes opened rationality to diversification and individuation, this picture of the Genevan clubs goes right back to a strict (one)-Self. In the notes there is no assimilation of rationality and commonality (*only to a certain point* are there common principles and a common form of evidence), but in the text itself citizen-men form an identifiable community that both supports an exalted Reason (one does not debase one's ideas by lowering them to women's level), and co-owners of a completely naked Reason. Finally, although one note states that no one may inspect other people's reasoning, the text reserves Reason for men, as if women's reason had been inspected and found wanting; in yet another note, he recognizes that they can "acquire science, erudition, talents and everything which is acquired by dint of work," that they can produce a piece of work, so long as it requires only taste, charm, philosophy, and reasoning;[71] and he praises [Mme de Graffigny's] *Cénie*, although this play is the work of a woman, for "it is not to *a* woman that I refuse the talents of men, but to women."[72]

Essentially, the *Lettre* sets out, deviously, to reject all the facts it notes and thus to disqualify women, sometimes by denying them genius, sometimes by locating reason in a place to which they have no access, sometimes by dismissing them as mere prattlers, which amounts to invoking ethics to exclude them, since idle chatter is antithetical to the good faith required for a discussion.[73] But all of that amounts to requiring Rousseau to sacrifice his own subtle theory of rationality in favor of a hollow symbolic of Reason, so hollow that one wonders why he assigns that name to the common property of the members of these men's clubs. In any case, we must choose between these two versions of reason, and I venture to say that one is philosophically interesting and the other utter rubbish. One says we cannot identify the common measure, the other merely indicates who possesses it and who does not. The first could be called weak, in the sense mathematicians give to this term: it is a minimal characterization that sets out some rules of the game and prompts people to turn either to the products or the processes of this form of rationality. The second, which is a crude form of sexo-sociology, attributes to men, at least to all men of Geneva and not a single woman, a form of reason in which no rule of the game is set out. This attribution has only emblematic value, and amounts to nothing more than the exclusion of women, when in the sketch of a theory of the rational, there was an entire and recognizable "intellectual world."

Two versions of reason; but only one, which *is not* a theory of the rational, is compatible with men's stranglehold on politics and with Rousseau's definition of an exclusively domestic life for modest women. Only one is compatible with grand statements about "the respectable rights of fathers over their children, of husbands over their wives, of masters over their servants."[74] Only this one is compatible with the masculine superiority conferred by making Reason into a hollow emblem linked to virility, itself derived from the laudatory sense of *vir*, which in Rousseau's text becomes a subject magnified by citizenship. The presence of an interesting and open theory of rationality in the footnotes shows that the hollow version does not attest to poor Jean-Jacques's deeply held belief: it is not true that "at that time" it was impossible to imagine anything else. However, the theory evokes a concept of rationality that is impossible to situate from an anthropological point of view or even that of an anthropological fiction, and it does not allow for any kind of magnification. It excludes no one from the debate, expecially not the talking and thinking women of the time, who are one of the targets of the *Lettre*. Actually, it is ironic to discover that there is not necessarily a preestablished harmony between a philosophical theory, even one articulated by a man like Rousseau, and the conservative interests of patriarchy. But when there is a clash between a philosophical point of view and these interests, it is philosophy that yields and is relegated to the footnotes; a concern to maintain sexual domination overrides any speculative inclination and declares itself openly in the body of the text. You might whisper to today's male philosophers-in-training that they would philosophize much better if they could shed their elders' preoccupation with defending the interests and symbols of domination. To them, as to female philosophers-to-be, we must also demonstrate that this determination to dominate has produced concepts apprehending nothing, but intimidating some women and sowing universal confusion.

In *Émile* the situation is exacerbated, for the interesting version of the rational expressed in the footnotes of the *Lettre* will be attributed only to men, based on a judgment of taste: a woman can certainly be as cultured as an *honnête homme,* but I would not have her as my mistress or my friend, so "the search for abstract and speculative truths, for principles and axioms in science, for all that tends to wide generalization, is beyond a woman's grasp; their studies should be thoroughly practical. It is their business to apply the principles discovered by men. . . . Woman should discover, so to speak, an experimental morality, man should reduce it to a system."[75] This is not about real women, but about those who conform to the ideal type defined by an "us" that is just as closed as a Genevan men's club, even though notions like "the search" or "all that tends to wide generalization" point to an intellectual dynamic, rather than to the patriotic tediousness to which the body of the *Lettre* refers. Having connected this hollow Reason to *vir* (man) inflated by citizenship, Rousseau reserves the work of reason, seen as research, for men. The exclusion of women links the totemic version of Reason depicted in the *Lettre* to the kind of intellectual work amenable to description. Such a dubious process persists to the present day and Derrida, for example, perpetuates it. In a lengthy note, he declares that a book by Lévinas "pushes the respect for dissymmetry so far that it seems to us impossible, essentially impossible, that it could have been written by a woman. Its philosophical subject is man (*vir.*)"[76] In the words of Catherine Chalier, writing on Derrida, "woman has been excluded from philosophy by the undecidable neutrality of the subject elaborated there."[77] It really takes several of them to refuse entry to philosophy to someone called "woman": a *vir* clinging to the homage he renders the patriarch in their shared respect for dissymmetry, and an undecidable neuter, insisting that "perhaps metaphysical desire is essentially virile, even in what is called woman."[78] Which . . .

8. Neutrality

The notion of neutrality has value only as a function of the process that creates it: it is a notion of rootedness that denies itself. Even if I were not as I am, I would, however, think, say, and want what I do, since I am the way I am. The ambiguity of the concept comes from the fact that it states a concrete particular in order better to refute it. I, Descartes, educated by the Jesuits, finding myself beside a wood-burning stove in Germany with nothing better to do than think, I produce an "I think" in which the *I* no longer refers back to these dubious biographical details; moreover, my body, if indeed I have one, could be a melon or a diamond, I do not really know just now. However, I think, and any *I* at all can see that he thinks, that he is, and various other more complicated things. The concrete biographical detail recalls itself in order to contest itself by means of the fantastical, the *I* placing itself face to face with the me-being-this and relegating the concrete traits of the individual to a poorly understood and contingent empirical domain. A similar game of the I (since we are in ludic mode) creates a play within a play in Shakespeare. I am not what I am, says Iago; I am not Romeo, says Romeo; I am not Juliet, says Juliet; even though I am called Snout, I am a wall, as this brick will prove, says Snout. Shakespeare, Descartes, and Hobbes produce the idea of a subject who says who he is by extricating himself from the natural individual. He becomes an actor or a legal entity, who can represent another legal entity and act in his or her name by virtue of a delegated authority.

To apply the idea of the neutral subject to knowledge is to repeat the process that, merely for the sake of contesting it, recognizes the knower or would-be knower as rooted in such concrete circumstances as biography. Nothing forces us to relate knowledge to a knowing subject, but since we are discussing a process that refers philosophy to an undecidably neutral *vir*, we must consider the question within the framework of subjectivism. It is truly nonsensical to posit the neutral, and thus to involve the I in a play on itself, only to block this play by clinging to a reference to a specific man while excluding someone in the name of neutrality. For the only sense that can be given to the problematic of the neutral, if we really want to take it up, is precisely that it does not exclude anyone from the game. When an archivist refused her access to the letters of James I, alleging that they were unsuitable for a lady, Catharine Macaulay, a mid-eighteenth-century Republican historian, retorted sharply "whoever engages with history has no sex." Her claim that her discipline is gender neutral has a subversive effect; for a woman who denies that her work is a *woman's work* breaks down a barrier, thus gaining access to a correspondence that clearly shows this particular king had morals whose very existence a lady should not even suspect. She will make the link between obscenity and James's absolute power but will set his morals aside—it is beneath the dignity of history to hold them against him.[79] Conversely, the problematic of the neutral amounts to a mis-knowing when a body of established knowledge, possessed by a specific group of people, claims to be neutral. A remark of Bertrand Russell's will help us to grasp this: the science of Classical Antiquity might well have been defined (Russell cautiously proposes) by an implicit principle of limitation to intangible objects; the most valued forms of knowledge were mathematics and astronomy, whose common feature is that they are inaccessible to touch. He proposes seeing this as an instance of the principle of the ancient *polis:* the citizens, free men, left manual work to others and their political status depended on their doing so. From this one might conclude that it is not the sciences conceived as forms of knowledge that are politically determined, but their limits, edges, or boundaries. Correlatively, an act that attempts to overstep the boundaries may well be endorsed by a new political will or the consciousness of a different group: but this does not imply that the new knowledge will be nonneutral or nonknowledge, pure opinion, or the folklore of this group. Thus there would seem to be a connection between political interests and either the desire to maintain a closed intellectual domain, or, on the contrary, to carry out research that will develop new knowledge. If the allegation of neutrality is connected to a will to closure, it proclaims that existing forms of knowledge have no boundaries needing to be crossed. Such an allegation is a form of mis-knowing of itself and its surroundings. On the other hand, when it is associated with a desire to increase knowledge, the allegation of neutrality indicates that, even if the desire belongs to someone, the methods and results will achieve the status of knowledge. There is a vast distance between a subversive, creative Catharine Macaulay and a Derrida who, under the guise of neutrality, seeks to maintain a male monopoly of philosophy.

In the preface to her monumental *History of England,* Macaulay theorizes her scholarly practice and criticizes the universities of her time: history is not taught there, or so little and so badly. With delectable scientific irony, she insists she has no firsthand knowledge of this institutional flaw: "here, as I am told and have great reason to believe, are taught doctrines little cal-culated to form patriots to support and defend the privileges of the subject in this limited monarchy."[80] As a historian accustomed to basing her work on original documents and sources, she considers that what she reports as happening in a place inaccessible to her is mere hearsay. University teaching does not encourage noble principles of independence; ancient languages are taught, but not the precepts that ancient peoples observed, with the result that these truncated forms of study are sterile. Young people are encouraged to love arbitrary government and become slaves of absolute monarchy: "The study of history is little cultivated in these seminaries; and not at all those fundamental principles of the English constitution on which our ancestors founded a system of government, in which the Liberty of the subject is as absolutely instituted as the dignity of the sovereign."[81] Now a knowledge of principles is as necessary for understanding the system as it was for constructing it, and the spirit of the constitution is lost when those responsible for maintaining it ignore all the principles that defend civil liberty against royal prerogatives. Let us understand one thing clearly: ignorance of the system of liberties destroys it, for civil liberties have to be re-created continuously; and this creation is impossible unless the history of their difficult construction is taught. Far from positing a contradiction between scientific rigor and political engagement, or from complaining about her exclusion from the universities, Macaulay analyzes the sidelining of the historian's discipline in political terms and, following the model of the annals and histories of the Roman republic, assigns to herself "the laborious task" of untangling the broad outlines of her country's constitutional history.

The caricaturists of her time had a field day. The *Monthly Review*, discovering that she was married, was delighted to note that "the woman has not lost herself in the historian." The republicans loved it and, with a few notable exceptions, the history of history gave her no recognition. The nineteenth century, for example, insisted on contrasting amateurism (often attributed to "society women") and a university discipline developed in closed male seminars; her archival experience seems to count for nothing in these opinions.[82] This dualism throws a veil of rose-colored silk over her and reserves the value-laden term "work" for men, their fingers soiled with the dust of books and brows furrowed by method. Similarly, Macaulay's political intentions stood in the way of accurate perception of her work. Since she was spurred on by republican motives, her books count as partisan literature, not a historian's (neutral) work. Such a dichotomy overlooks what is most subtle in her approach: she exposes a despotic political management of ignorance. On the other hand freedom is connected to knowledge. The republicans needed a conception of freedom and had to understand its principles in order to make it a reality: to maintain it, one must understand it. The object of study thus defines itself as a history of the conflict between absolutism and citizens' rights or civil liberties. In order to see anything nonneutral in her work, it may not be necessary to think of any and every object of study as inert and without freedom, but I am sure it helps. A dramatist of her time portrays her in a play and imputes to her the intention of turning the critique of political despotism into one of familial despotism.[83] She does none of this in her historical work, does very little of it elsewhere, and I see it as the best proof of her vocation. There is indeed a history of conflict between the republican movement and absolutism. There have not yet been enough conflicts between familial patriarchy and movements defending the freedom of women and children for it to be possible to write their history. Historians (male or female) do not create their objects out of nothing, even if history often limits its own scope of inquiry.

Defending a gender-neutral and universal notion of the efforts of rationality or distinguishing between scientific work and its self-aggrandizing discourse does not, however, amount to endorsing the thesis of neutrality in thought or scientific work. The problematic of the neutral—for or against—seems inadequate to me, for it focuses on the product rather than the debates scientific work generates, or the process of its transmission. Now circulation is essential to the scientific character of anything, if it is true that in order to be valid an experiment must at least be written up, published, and verifiable by others, thus taken up by an unknown person who is not determined in advance. If at this very moment a young Japanese man is discovering the work of a Breton woman biologist, verifies it, takes it up himself, and extends it while a Peruvian woman mathematician uses the zero that the world of numbers owes to the Arabs, it is because scientific culture circulates and passes from hand to hand. This culture can be understood only in process, because it creates the community in which it subsequently participates; such is undoubtedly the case also for many interesting ideas that are not strictly scientific. Unfortunately, this same structure also opens the way to exploitation of those (male and female) who are subordinated in the collective organization of research, and to the theft of results. It explains that Democritus may have plagiarized Leucippus, that the House of Solomon includes professional looters, and finally that scientific espionage, which has been understood as such since the seventeenth century, is so painful a reality. Let us return to the Baconian imaginary for one last time: on two occasions, it shows Jupiter appropriating embryos, devouring Metis, who is pregnant with the future Athena, or snatching the future Dionysus from the breast of Semele, in order to carry him in his thigh.[84] Bacon interprets the devouring of Metis, goddess of intelligence, as mythologizing the way the powerful of this world appropriate the good ideas of their counsellors, who are thus eclipsed as authors. The true violence of the intellectual world lurks in the ever-present risk that the work of some will be stolen by others, or in the authoritarian manner of putting subordinates (male or female) to work, much more than in a Sadean relationship to Mother Nature. However, when Bacon speaks of intellectual larceny on the model of a father's appropriation of the mother's role in procreation, with the progeny appearing to be the issue of the father alone, he is in effect claiming it is more normal to steal a woman's share of something than that of another man. Moreover, he so often uses the expression *filum labyrinthi* (the thread through the labyrinth) that we must recognize that he has a Theseus complex. (Theseus explored the labyrinth with the help of the thread held by Ariadne and then, having become a hero, abandoned the poor woman). Two present-day scholars, Colette Guillaumin and Nicole-Claude Mathieu, have noted the presence, in social practices, of men's appropriation of the products of women's bodies, and a scholarly legal justification of the assassination of women by the father of their child.[85] Once we understand how common is the appropriation of the fruits of labor, reproductive or otherwise, in the traditional relations between the sexes, we can no longer consider it exceptional. Even though women are not the only victims of intellectual theft, it seems to be more easily imagined or more self-evident when the victim is a female figure.

The question of the neutral, associated with the image of women as not neutral, takes us to a place where several different problems intersect. Here is Erik Erikson: "Is scientific inspiration really so impersonal and method-bound that personality plays no role in scientific creativity? And if we grant that a woman is never not a woman, even if and especially when she has become an excellent scientist and co-worker [beyond all special apologies or claims,] then why deny so strenuously that there may be in science also [(on the scientific periphery of some tasks, and maybe in the very core of others)] areas where the addition, to the male kind of creative vision, of women's vision and creativity may yet yield, not to new laws of verification, but to new areas of inquiry and to new applications?"[86] Here he is extremely prudent—his hyperbole seems only to deny a negation that no one would maintain. It is difficult to put one's finger on the flaw in Erikson's argument, which amounts to an egregious dissymmetry; what has happened so far is presented simultaneously as impersonal methodology and masculine creativity, with the result that men of science are credited with both virility and impersonal neutrality, whereas neutrality does not accrue to a woman since she is never nonwoman. Now it is not certain that science is precisely the subject at issue here, for there is a possible connection with politics: in John Rawls's *A Theory of Justice*, one page envisages the potential relevance of an unequal distribution of rights and fundamental liberties. Even though it is not a matter of cognitive differences, this problem will present itself as formally identical to what Erikson says.[87]

As a general thesis, Rawls maintains that justice as fairness presupposes an equal citizenry but different levels of income and wealth, a material inequality he considers desirable. Let us set these premises aside, even if they make us uneasy, and consider the following: "Sometimes, however, other positions may need to be taken into account. If, for example, there are unequal basic rights founded on fixed natural characteristics, these inequalities will single out relevant positions. Since these characteristics cannot be changed, the positions they define count as starting places in the basic structure. Distinctions based on sex are of this type, and so are those depending on race and culture. Thus if, say, men are favored in the assignment of basic rights, this inequality is justified by. . . ." Oh yes! we saw this one coming: as soon as an author mentions distinctions based on sex and fixed natural characteristics, we anticipate that the argument will focus on differences that favor men, rather than on a distribution that gives more rights to women. But the expression "fixed natural characteristics" is what interests me; it signals the appearance of some kind of anthropology in an argument alleged to be political-legal; curiously enough, the fixity of said characteristics (called natural) will be found among human groups to which the author does not belong. Nature as invoked here is a transcendent guarantee of discriminations and a thoroughly dogmatic form of reference (the cliché "it is not I who say this to you but the Lord" has evolved without much change into "it is not I who say this to you but Nature"). This thesis presupposes describable people with fixed characteristics, unlike the subject of reference in neutral discourse who has no special traits. According to the author, this justifies granting fewer rights to persons whose sex, race, culture (further along, he adds caste and ethnicity) gives them fixed characteristics than to those fortunate enough not to be so permanently defined. The whole page is astounding, but you will note that this "type of distinction" elevates sexual differentiation to the status of a paradigmatic example that allows a global category to be conceptualized; the others are posited by analogy, while the natural fixity of a describable feminine sex becomes a self-evident model.

In *Le Monde* of January 27, 1983, Christiane Chombeau provides us with a fragment of crude art that illustrates the widespread character of this type of schema. Yvette Roudy, then Minister for the Status of Women, meets a presiding judge of the Court of Appeal at Poitiers. The presiding judge: "I have no objection to your great principles of equality between men and women, except with respect to the judiciary, where women should be assigned certain responsibilities and not others. My own experience has shown me that women excel in cases about minors and deal better with issues of spousal desertion. On the other hand, only men are firm enough to be examining magistrates." Roudy: "Do you mean there are special genes?"

The judge: "Absolutely. Women must be given responsibilities appropriate to their nature." The speaker is not talking about the judiciary; he sees flesh-and-blood magistrates, and even women who might escape the confinement (to certain duties but not others) that is ensured by their proximity to their nature, and must be maintained. To his confreres he grants neutrality ("certain duties and not others" does not apply to them) and virility—for really, how are we to interpret "firm enough"? At the same time, the restrictions this imposes on female magistrates are expressed in muted form, theyshould-be-assigned-only, as a limitation without a visible limiting agent, a regulation with no regulative authority other than their nature. The credo of Modernity incorporates the idea of an oppression with no oppressor other than the nature of the oppressed (female or male); this nature is necessarily defined in a fictional mode, but an ingredient called theoretical incapacity is often part of the definition. Thus no theoretical challenge is possible.

From Rousseau on, humanity has been divided into two: on the one hand, the subject of the social contract, who is not fixed and cannot be since he changes during the course of the contract, trading his natural liberty for civil liberty; on the other, groups of people reputed to be different, assumed to have a nature and characteristics, thus to be objects of an anthropological knowledge that in fact is no knowledge at all but a product of the imagination. There was no need for Rousseau ever to have seen an Eskimo or a Carib Indian to be able to talk about them at length; a note from the *Discourse on the Origin of Inequality* even describes a savage whose country is not named, an archetype of the savage in general, explaining that this savage could well look at his own legs without ever thinking that he had two, and without knowing how to count to five, and, even if in placing his hands one against the other, "he could have noticed that the fingers matched exactly, he was far from dreaming of their numerical equality."[88] Anthropology begins in (human) science fiction and will long bear this birthmark. When Auguste Comte invents sociology, and says that it "will prove that the equality of the sexes, of which so much is said, is incompatible with all social existence, by showing that each sex has special and permanent functions which it must fulfil in the human family," he defines it in anticipation of its results, which clearly count as fictional.[89] In an early article, John Stuart Mill maintains that to know a general truth is always to discover it for oneself as a new truth (one needs as much intellect as Newton to understand every truth that is not apparent to the senses and as much genius to understand a work of Aeschylus or of Raphael as to produce it), and he goes on to say that cognitive genius is the product of a higher faculty than creative genius. To conceive of the internal ordering of someone's mind, to understand how the world and life are represented in the perception of a Greek, a Spanish peasant, a Hindu demands a greater effort than to create a fictitious person at will, for in this case imagination is subject to greater constraints.[90] Anthropo-psychology is even more difficult than fiction because its limits are less flexible! We notice that the world and life are represented in the minds of ethnic subjects without any apparent effort on their part, whereas understanding Newton requires as much genius as Newton himself employed. At the end of his life, Mill is no longer an ethnographer except about one group: "But, looking at women as they are known in experience, it may be said of them, with more truth than belongs to other generalizations on the subject, that the general bent of their talents is toward the practical. . . . What is meant by a woman's capacity for intuitive perception? It means a rapid and correct insight into present fact. It has nothing to do with general principles. Nobody ever perceived a scientific law of nature by intuition, nor arrived at a general rule of duty or prudence by it."[91] And so on: he still conceives of the internal ordering of a mind not his own and, since women do not have access to the general, they can scarcely challenge generalizations made about them, especially not the one denying them access to the general. The debate between women and men about women will not take place.

9. Factual Violence/Ideational Violence

In *L'Anatomie politique*, Nicole-Claude Mathieu returns to a distinction proposed by Godelier, and challenges its workings. Godelier asserts that real violence in relations between the sexes is relatively rare, whereas ideational violence is ever present. He adds: "men's greatest strength lies not in the exercise of violence but in women's consent to their domination; and this consent can only exist if both sexes share the same conceptions, which here legitimize male domination"[92]; I seem to remember some of Pierre Bourdieu's remarks, likewise affirming that it was high time we asked ourselves about women's participation in their own oppression, something that exposes the same schema at work. In response to Godelier, Mathieu points out that ideational violence is not a permanent part of women's consciousness, but it is a permanent part of the mindset of the male dominator. Certainly, she adds, for the woman who is dominated, "it is factual violence that is permanent."[93] If the debate between Mathieu and Godelier is really and only about the Baruya,* I have little to add to the discussion; on the other hand, if the debate can be related to a field I know, namely, the history of philosophy, I think I can pinpoint the exact political site that gives it its meaning. Let us go back to

---

*The Baruya, who live in the eastern highlands of Papua New Guinea, have no state structure and no dominant class. Yet inequality exists among them, particularly in the form of male domination. The Baruya's first contact with a white person was in 1952; beginning in 1960, Australia sought to "pacify", and then to govern, them. Godelier's first visits took place in 1967.

Rawls: "Thus if, say, men are favored in the assignment of basic rights, this inequality is justified by the difference principle...only if it is to the advantage of women and acceptable from their standpoint." Lesser rights, and that is supposed to be advantageous for the person who has fewer? Such an idea is as unthinkable as that of a square circle—and for whom other than women would they dare to propose a comparable conceptual monster? Or else it is a matter of religious prohibitions and not of legal or civil rights. American or French law allows people to eat meat and chocolate every day; on the other hand, devout Catholics (female or male) are proud of the prohibition against eating meat on Friday or chocolate during Lent. When it is a matter of religious identity, it can be beneficial to allow oneself fewer rights than others. However, such considerations have no place in civil liberties or state-defined fundamental freedoms: they are an interpolation that should be seen as the logical outcome of the highly debatable identitarian position imposed by the notion of fixed natural characteristics. Rawls sees a fixed female nature that makes it advantageous for women to have fewer rights than men—a nature best fulfilled only when it is constrained or at least when it has an inclination toward deprivation, and so it is with any specificity that can be encompassed within the framework of liberal democracy.[94] To give these comments any semblance of plausibility, one really has to be able to claim that there is a mysterious female nature, mysterious but well known to our esteemed authors. As for the second clause, "only if [the inequality] is...acceptable from their standpoint," it declares that those with a lesser share of freedom and rights must internalize their inequality; what Godelier calls women's consent to ideational violence is thus postulated as highly necessary.

Rawls tells us about a political model concocted in the United States which the anglophone world, with the exception of women and a few men, finds plausible. What is Godelier taking about when he writes, "men's greatest strength lies... in women's consent to their domination"? Baruya? Come on! "The stronger is never strong enough to be forever master, unless he transforms his force into right, and obedience into duty."[95] But if we grant this to Rousseau, we can say that Godelier is stating the obvious. When there is domination, there is a culture of domination that tends to produce at least intermittent consent, or at least a statistical resignation on the part of the dominated, whether female or male. We can find that he goes a bit too far: he sees women's consent to their domination as its main foundation and perceives it as voluntary servitude. I do not know what Baruya women think of this; in my view, this idea may well have been superimposed after lying in wait for them ever since the seventeenth century, lurking in a tradition of political philosophy we teach to European and American youth even when we are ostensibly talking to them about the Baruya. Godelier is hurling Locke at us (us, I say, because this discourse takes effect in the philosophical-political convictions or hesitations of his European or American readership); it is Locke who was the inspiration for Rousseau, Rawls, and so many others.

The first of the *Two Treatises of Government* engages in a polemic against Filmer and the metaphor of the power of the father or patriarch as the foundation of a political power that would therefore inevitably be monarchical. Now Filmer had maintained that in giving Adam supreme power over Eve, God had conferred the status of monarch upon him. Locke is bound to protest: if Adam is the absolute monarch by divine right in his family-to-be, any attack on the patriarchal foundation of power would be weak. However, and for reasons best known to himself, he does not really want to abolish the father's dominance over the wife and children in the family. Whence comes a subtle interpretation of the passage from *Genesis* that describes the conjugal relationship. "*Thy husband shall rule over thee*" is a curse that applies only to Eve and woman; God certainly did not confer any prerogatives upon Adam when he set out the wages of sin. He gives Adam no authority over Eve, he simply punishes Eve and women "but only fortels what should be the Womans Lot, how by his Providence he would order it so, that she should be subject to her husband, as we see that generally the Laws of Mankind and customs of Nations have ordered it so; and there is, I grant, a foundation in Nature for it."[96] So women are solely responsible for the domination to which they are subjected. In the ego of Adam and of men there is not a trace of the domination they practice, it is accidental (*sic*) to them, and this fact allows them to be normal and innocent, to have no divinely inspired penchant for patriarchal-monarchical authority, and to be able to create political societies established by an egalitarian and fraternal contract. As the contract is a fraternal alliance among men, each one being father within the family, the principle of the patriarchy is abolished at the level of government without being abolished in family law. To achieve such a tour de force, women must be held intrinsically responsible for their subjection and one must choose to ignore the fact that a masculine alliance controls the means of organizing their subservient condition by writing it into its institutions, political relations, social practices, and the production of ideas. The masculine alliance can, moreover, organize conflict among women themselves: we have seen that societies from the Mediterranean to the North Sea assign control of younger women and the right of speech that accompanies it to women said to be "older" and supposed no longer to have any sexual interest.[97] And I do not think this is a matter of age.

Locke's support for conjugal subordination (and the correlative absence of women in the fraternal political contract) does not simply draw on his particular reading of Genesis; it also grafts itself onto a thesis about inferiority in understanding: ""But the Husband and Wife, though they have but one common Concern [the children to raise], yet having different understandings, will unavoidably sometimes have different wills too; it therefore being necessary that the last Determination, *i.e.* the Rule, should be placed somewhere, it naturally falls to the Man's share, as the abler and the stronger."[98] The idea of differences in understanding is taken from the complexity of the language of the time, whether it is the simple fact of two people and two understandings, or of divergence, qualitative difference, or inequality, it does not very much matter. Man's understanding is what must prevail because he is more capable; he is the natural head of the domestic government and his judgment is law. Thus in Locke we find both the figure of women responsible for their own subjection closely associated with the idea that the husband's intellectual superiority naturally assures he will govern the family, and reference to a strength that is perhaps mental, perhaps not. Since marriage is based in consent, one can infer that, in the cultural sphere where these schemata define her functions, a woman's marriageability is judged by the consent she gives to domination by male intellectual superiority. Never had it been so necessary for woman to have a diminished intellect, to place herself outside reason and to recognize a masculine character in every mental product; never so timely to find a few headscarves to photograph ("women do not want to be free") rather than to see the women who are fighting for freedom. Never had it been more useful to develop human sciences confirming that the daughters of Eve carry in their soul a willingness to be dominated, or a psychoanalysis that recycles clichés, and not only from the pen of Sigmund Freud or Helene Deutsch.

In 1976 Le Seuil published *La Sexualité féminine* by Moustapha Safouan. The date is significant. Since 1971 the women's movement had been fighting for the right to contraception and abortion against political efforts to keep the birth rate high, against Catholic opinion and against those of our male companions who, traditional men that they were, defended their power to decide by themselves and without consultation, saying that they would "take care of it." We had some success when the application of the Neuwirth Law was passed, and again in 1975, with the passing of the Veil Law. Then, psychoanalysis took upon itself to declare our victory pathogenic: "Who does not know" writes Safouan, "that the birth control methods available to woman have reinforced her fixations and made the solution to the question of her desire even harder to find?"[99] Isn't this lovely!? Everyone is supposed to know it, so this exempts him from any onus of proof, and he is not criticizing contraception in general but the fact that its methods will be placed at woman's disposal, a practice so hostile to social order that he cannot imagine saying it in French, so he uses the English *birth control*. After Paul VI's

Encyclical *Humanae Vitae* explained that controlling our own fertility would make heaven weep, and after the astonishing notion of "the duty to be improvident in matters of contraception" was refined by theologians; after the howls of male politicians who swore France would be on the road to ruin if we stopped having unwanted children; after the medical association spelled out how much all of that is contrary to its professional ethics and therefore bad for your health, psychoanalysis joined the chorus in affirming that our control of our own fertility is unconscionably toxic. Moreover, this essay on female sexuality contains other fine remarks ("woman, with her more passive nature . . ."), and disqualifies Karen Horney, Melanie Klein and Marie Bonaparte, reputed to "deal rather cavalierly with the unconscious" even though, still according to Safouan, they have "a few intuitive breakthroughs . . ."!

To come back to the Baruya: Godelier sees them within the frameworks of liberalism while Mathieu, pointing to an ideational violence that is permanent in men as the dominant group but is only occasional in women as the dominated group, sketches a materialist or "factualist" framework that makes visible what a certain form of liberalism obscures (real violence) and allows us to grasp women's internalization of it as a product derived from an oppression inscribed in institutions, political relations, and social practices. Such a point of view could, however, lead to a crushingly mechanistic model; I think it has to be completed by a twofold project that would first analyze the institutions that administer domination and then propose counterweights or institutions capable of helping women, every woman, to resist. Every time a shelter is created where battered women can (re)discover calm, each time legal assistance is provided for them or a language articulated for recounting their experiences and self-esteem, a real tool is fashioned, making both factual and ideational resistance possible. To take up the question from another angle: describing the sacrifice of personal interests that loyalty to the group requires of the individual, Amartya Sen pauses over the sacrifices traditional family relations require of women. The survival of these traditions, he says, is often supported by the fact that a particular type of "ethics" is accepted, and in this framework, gross inequalities in standards of living may not consciously be recognized by the woman who is affected by them nor presented for her judgment and consent. The question of perception is thus central, and an ethical challenge of traditional "moralities" presupposes a debate at the cognitive level.[100] Developed with reference to Indian societies situated between tradition and modernity, Sen's point of view differs markedly from Godelier's. If we emphasize women's failure to perceive inequalities and if, rather than believing that the dominated support the ideas of the dominant (men), we present ideational violence as a closing of the mind, we may hope that knowledge will lead every woman to understand the need to protest inequalities and defend herself in her everyday existence. But the realization amounts to nothing more than false consciousness if it does not generate a vision of what must be substituted for present reality. The American women delegates at the 1840 Anti-Slavery Conference in London knew at first hand the injustice of those who, wanting to deny them the right to speak, vote, and play a role in committees, relegated them to a gallery behind a curtain, like the choir in a church. But the important thing was that, several years later two of them, Lucretia Mott and Elizabeth Cady Stanton, along with Martha C. Wright and Mary Ann McClintock, organized the first great assembly for the rights of women at Seneca Falls. They had found their vision of what had to be done to change the destiny of all women, and a language in which to articulate their plan.[101] Not only the right to speak, civil rights, the right to vote, eligibility, access to all occupations including religious ministry, to all levels of education, and so on, but also a technique that would allow them to translate these wishes into political reality: the mass movement. The first great feminist movement emerged from this assembly in an insignificant little town in New York State. That meeting shaped the world into which your mother and I were born.

10. Visions

Among philosophical or literary genres, utopian writing seems to have been the genre least cultivated by women. Before wondering why, we must ask ourselves whether in fact they have produced very little of it, or whether reference works simply fail to take note of what they have produced. We must first critique the reference works. The largest compilation I know omits the *City of Ladies,* whose right to inclusion in this genre can certainly be argued, as well as *Herland* by Charlotte Perkins Gilman, *A Woman's Utopia* by Ellen Olney Kirk, and the *Relation de l'Isle Imaginaire* by Anne Marie Louise Henriette d'Orléans, "la Grande Mademoiselle" herself.[102] In it we find the names of Thomas More's two wives, of Mme de Warens with reference to Rousseau, and that of a woman who seems to have been a utopian writer, Christina Poniatowska, just her name. Who is she, and why is she mentioned instead of others?

Georges Nivat, whose assistance I acknowledge with gratitude, provided a lead.[103] In exile after the Battle of the White Mountain (*La Montagne Blanche*), Comenius gave shelter to a young girl who had visions of the liberation of Bohemia and the downfall of the reigning tyrant.* To judge from what the historical record shows, her prophecies expressed a highly relevant political hope: what could she convey to the exiles who gathered around

---

*John Amos Comenius (1592–1670) was a Czech theorist of education. His most important work, *Didactica Magna*, explored learning styles and the pedagogical approaches suitable to them.

her that was more pressing than the hope of seeing Bohemia liberated some day? Alas, no female prophet or soothsayer can establish her authority all by herself; two men will come to argue about how to evaluate her sayings: Comenius, who is inclined to validate them and a distant relative of hers who calls in the doctors, thus acting as a precursor of the modern commentator who represents her as being "of fragile health and probably suffering from hysteria."[104] The meaning that would be attributed to Poniatowska's utterances, whether sickness or prophesy, was subject to the good will of two men closely related to her, a situation so unremarkable that it is absurd to look for an example of it in seventeenth-century Central Europe. But her story allows us to understand several things. If every nascent construction of a political hope can be read as a sympton of mental illness, why would we be surprised at the minimal female presence among the numerous writers of utopian literature? Correlatively, what is called hysteria in this context seems to be linked to control: when direct speech is forbidden, an inspired trance is like an oblique manner of speaking.[105] Moreover, all political discourse includes a projection into the future, which, by definition, cannot be verified. "I have nothing to offer but blood, toil, tears, and sweat" but we will be victorious[106]—what did Churchill know about it? If he had been wedged between an uncle who medicalized everything he said and an adoptive father who took the time to justify in Latin the possibility of his saying it, nothing would remain: nothing remains of the speaker when she or he is relegated to the margins and placed under judicial control. And anticipated disapproval becomes a self-fulfilling prophecy: knowing in advance that the significance or insignificance of one's comments will be determined by those with the authority to judge, how can one go on speaking? Every day and even in our own time, we women are confronted with a strange philosophy of our language, as though we did not have the capacity to make sense of our own words. Here, unfortunately, is an exemplary instance: following a rape, the plaintiff hears a magistrate telling her that of course she said no, but so what? Everyone knows that when a woman says no, it does not mean she is refusing.[107]

Utopia is not a crazy dream. It is a laboratory where, in the space of a page where a discourse displays its premises, ideas are reflected and test their coherence. Many ideas that were thus elaborated have passed into the realm of facts. Long before it became a reality, the idea of public schooling for all children was defended in the thought of Plato, More, and Wollstonecraft. The idea of state involvement in research was expounded by Bacon, and then, a generation later, the creators of the Royal Society believed they had brought his utopia into being. To be able to act, it is necessary to have a coherent vision of what one wants. Our foremothers at Seneca Falls constructed their vision, but not without having read Mary Wollstonecraft and Blackstone. And now that women's studies exists, should we not hope for a third-wave feminist theory whose intent would be to create knowledge about the mechanisms of inequality and to understand the ideas and plans for action of those who invented strategies for resistance? If I am critical of the second wave, which corresponds to what the liberal program naturally wants to hear about women, it is because I hope to see this third wave reclaiming the inspiration of the first wave and pushing its questions further. In a certain sense, this wave has already arrived. It is characterized by the mobilization of knowledge acquired in part in the professional world, in part in practice, and not, as in the second wave, by a rejection of knowledge. An important feature differentiates it from the first wave: Wollstonecraft knew nothing of Christine de Pisan or Gabrielle Suchon. Simone de Beauvoir wrote *The Second Sex* without knowing them or really having read Virginia Woolf. Each one seems to start from scratch and from her own present. But the third wave could see that we have a past, an international dialogue, and responsibility for the future. I do not think it is a bad thing to dedicate to it the epistemology of hope, which I will try to elicit from the study of two versions of liberalism.

11. The Liberal Experience

In chapter III of *On the Subjection of Women,* John Stuart Mill makes a plea for women's access to political rights and praises female monarchs whose reign illustrates his thesis about women's aptitude for governance. The year is 1861. Victoria has been on the throne since 1837, so Mill's idea simply confirms the possibility of something already in existence. He moves on to the question of mental capacity (women's, naturally) and here he writes with a forked pen. In effect, he announces his intention to show that "even the least contestable of the differences which now exist, are such as may very well have been produced merely by circumstances, without any difference of natural capacity."[108] He then invokes a talent for practice and intuitive perception to give substance to the expression "the least contestable of differences" evident in the observable situation. But far from demolishing the idea of a connection between women and intuition, Mill produces a concept of intuition that would be most interesting if the intent were to ensure the conditions for a mental annexation of women, and his much-vaunted project collapses. In subsequent pages he says nothing more about how this difference can be related to circumstances. A different discourse surges up on the page like a tidal wave and crashes down, naturalizing the previous discourse; as though it were too powerful to resist, the delectable idea of women's "intuitive perception" carries the day. And, sweeping away with it the philosophical project he had announced, an entirely different problematic takes its place.

Thus, instead of saying what intuition is, Mill sets out to describe it according to what it *is not,* which is already a way of utilizing the concept to establish a boundary. It is not the capacity for generalizing, nor access to principles, nor careful collecting of empirical data, nor theory, nor speculation. Later in the work, he contrasts intuition with the leisure available to philosophers who always have time to reflect, without having to produce a fully articulated system under pressure of deadlines, whereas intuition is immediacy itself. He notes that it is only by happy accident that women sometimes benefit from other people's experiences, thanks to education. However, knowledge is derived from the experiences of one's forebears. Mill concedes that there can be no good practice without principles (undoubtedly women borrow from somewhere?), and he compares women's mistakes to those of self-taught men who have acquired the prerequisite knowledge only in fragments and at random, "as women do." Then he says nothing is more precious for a theorist than the company of a truly superior woman; she prevents him from wandering off into total abstraction and "women's thoughts are ... useful in giving reality to the thoughts of thinking men ..."[109]; and when masculine speculation is complete, women know how to translate its results into practice. Thus we are relegated to the category of capable performers, a term that must be understood in both its musical and political meanings—Elizabeth I, for example, was a brilliant chief executive. It is only when he invokes a further limitation, "the greater nervous susceptibility of women is a disqualification for practice, in anything but domestic life,"[110] that he returns to his initial topic: women's nervousness results from ways of life, not to mention mere fashion. In the intervening pages, he has abandoned his thesis that observable differences can be explained by circumstances; the thesis did not address the supposedly blatant opposition between theory and intuition—since intuition undoubtedly exists in women "as they are known in experience." In a paragraph with an autobiographical ending he notes that occasionally, through natural sagacity, a person may have some happy intuition that she can propose but not prove. It acquires value only if someone takes it in hand, proves it, gives it scientific or practical form, and incorporates it into the received truths of philosophy or science. Women of intellect have hundreds of these felicitous thoughts, which for the most part are lost "for want of a husband or friend who has the other knowledge which can enable him to estimate them properly and bring them before the world."[111] Then they appear as his own, and "who can tell how many of the most original thoughts put forth by male writers, belong to a woman by suggestion, to themselves only by verifying and working out? If I may judge by my own case, a very large proportion indeed!"

Mill's "own case" was Harriet Taylor, who was to spend the last years of her life as Mrs. Mill. According to the testimony of the ostensible author, at least one chapter in the *Principles of Political Economy* was hers. Some copies intended for friends would include an additional page in which he dedicated to Mrs. John Taylor, "as the most eminently qualified of all persons known to the author either to originate or to appreciate speculations on social improvement, this attempt to explain and diffuse ideas many of which were learned from herself."[112] So Harriet Taylor is "beautiful, romantic, cultivated, intellectual and progressive,"[113] say the preface writers, who have nothing to say about John Stuart's possible physical charms. A merchant's wife, she was a member of a radical group that Mill began to frequent in 1830. We know very little about her childhood; perhaps she was born married and the mother of two children? She was twenty-two years old, he twenty-four, and he already described himself as a "thinking machine." Love, friendship, and marriage came in 1851 after the death of her first husband. She died in 1858. *The Subjection of Women,* in which Mill expresses his views on the division of intellectual labor between women and men, between himself and Harriet Taylor, was completed in 1869, long after the dialogue with her had come to an end.

12. Saint Scholastica

It would be premature to embark immediately on an interpretation. My concern is to connect sections of intellectual history with the use people make of them today; however, the debate I want to engage in has barely begun. Thus before dealing with the exemplary Mill-Taylor case, I have to show that it *is not* incorporated into received knowledge and that in invoking the figure of Taylor and *The Subjection,* I have already positioned myself outside the boundaries of traditional Mill scholarship. My female students in Geneva who, in their degree programs in law or political science had acquired some knowledge of the more circumscribed topic, "Mill and liberal thought," brought this problem to my attention. Not one of them had the slightest idea about Mill's writings on the equality of the sexes, and even the title of *The Subjection* was unknown to them. By way of excusing their ignorance, one of them, Léa Sgier, had the brilliant idea of making a collection of standard works, encyclopedias, manuals, digests, and so on: all of them volumes that give some idea of Mill's thought without breathing a word about his undoubtedly shameful interest in improving women's political and civil status. His thought is disseminated according to what men of influence in political science find appropriate. Moreover, it is standard practice in French-language philosophy to present him as the "father of liberal thought," whereas Montesquieu and Tocqueville are "fathers of democracy."

Our modern era thus puts its trust in a string of founding fathers, just as more ancient times benefited, or so they say, from the spiritual direction of the Church Fathers. If a medieval style carries over into modern political science, it would surely be incongruous to let the future scions of social life know that one of the "fathers" of contemporary politics believed (albeit with reservations I will not hesitate to underscore) that women could be freer than they were in his time. Only with extreme discretion can one allude to this aspect of Mill's writings, and the secret of Harriet Taylor's unmentionable presence in his immediate entourage must be still more closely guarded: Harriet Taylor, a philosopher and poet who was passionately interested in the emancipation of women, and who contributed to books known under Mill's name, that "were not the work of one mind, but the fusion of two," he says.[114]

In the French-speaking world, Mill himself seems to be divided into three parts, which we will number M1, M2, M3. The acceptable Mill, M1, required in certain courses, author of works listed in bibliographies (*On Liberty, Considerations of Representative Government,* and so on), is a thinker for respectable people, and people who are not always asked to read the works themselves: for this conventional readership, a summary can suffice. M2, negligible or for people of lesser taste, is the author of *The Subjection:* feminist works alone refer to it, in order to demonstrate the possibility of a "feminism in the masculine." Along with Condorcet, M2 is the chosen example of this line of thought that is still not accepted in political science teaching although it introduces the germ of an idea that not all masculine authors were intractable phallocrats. Some of them even shone as feminists, and moreover, if feminism is absolutely necessary, all the better to leave it to the men.[115] As for M3, without violating all the rules of polite society, it is out of the question to mention an author (suitable only for those who are truly beyond the pale) who wrote a book about women years after his companion had already dealt with the question and who, as I have emphasized, acknowledged her contribution to works attributed to M1. Far from being presented together, so that everyone (male or female) can choose, the three Mills are arranged according to a system of nonreciprocal concealment. M1 is constructed by concealing the existence of M2 and M3; you would never suspect their existence as you swallowed the ideas attributed to M1. For an acceptable Mill to be constituted, M2 and M3 had to be excised, for by definition, a founding father must *not* have been interested in women's liberty and must not acknowledge a debt to the woman who was "his." M2 in his turn is constituted by hiding M3, for the idea that there could be a "feminism in the masculine" no longer sits well when one notices that Mill's feminism, as I read it, is either an impoverished version of Taylor's or a mode of resistance to it.

In the anglophone world things are a little different: M2 is sometimes associated with M1, students required to read *Considerations of Representative Government* can buy a paperback edition that includes *The Subjection*. Not all editions include both works, and no one will urge you to read the whole volume. M2 is thus only halfheartedly juxtaposed with M1, even though with a little personal curiosity you can move from one to the other.[116] But the more usual anglophone tendency is either to ignore Harriet Taylor's existence or to minimize her importance. Thus M3 especially is resisted or rejected. In 1951, in a remarkably well-documented work, F. A. Hayek cites Mill: "The chapter of the Political Economy which has had a greater influence on opinion than all the rest, that on 'the Probable Future of the Labouring Classes,' is entirely due to her: in the first draft of the book that chapter did not exist. She pointed out the need of such a chapter . . . she was the cause of my writing it. . . . The purely scientific part of the Political Economy I did not learn from her. . . . What was abstract and purely scientific was generally mine; the properly human element came from her: in all that concerned the application of philosophy to the exigencies of human society and progress I was her pupil. . . ." Hayek comments: "I think it could be shown that in it Mill attributes to Mrs. Taylor's influence ideas which he demonstrably owes to the Saint-Simonians and Comte."[117] Indeed! while arrogating the scientific and abstract dimensions of the work to himself, Mill nonetheless leaves their social and humanitarian applications to Taylor. For Hayek, even that is excessive—even those aspects must come from masculine sources, and demonstrably so. In 1960, a certain H. O. Pappe, who thinks Hayek is still too kind, takes up the cudgels against the Harriet Taylor myth (*sic*), challenging the very idea that she could have had the influence on John Stuart Mill that Mill himself had maintained. According to Pappe, Mill was too generous. He had an exaggerated estimation of Taylor's talents, for she was "only a minor influence on a philosopher who continues to be a major influence in our century." My interpretation is that Pappe seems to believe his century is free of feminine interference, just as, according to certain thinkers (both female and male), every trace of femininity has been erased from the scientific mind. Besides, on several matters Pappe takes issue with Taylor. We learn from him that she had an aversion to sex, that she made herself into a *Seelenfreundin* (soul-mate) of her first husband and of John Stuart (we are to believe that Helen, her third child, was conceived by parthenogenesis). We learn that she was an extreme feminist like Mary Wollstonecraft, who saw no essential differences between masculine and feminine character, that she was masochistic, narcissistic, and domineering. The entire argument is bolstered with references to Helen Deutsch or to a certain Mrs Borchard, and it culminates with a thought from Deutsch: by identifying themselves with the socially oppressed classes, women reject their unfulfilling role. Taylor was interested in the working classes, her work is "a *cri de douleur* rather than a reasoned case."[118]

It goes from bad to worse. In 1996 the preface to an anthology of the works of women philosophers, compiled by Mary Warnock, justifies the absence of two figures in her choice of texts.[119]

> Before we turn to those who have been included, there are two more omissions to be explained. First, one of the earliest of the women philosophers who began gradually to emerge in the first half of the seventeenth century was Princess Elizabeth of Bohemia, the shrewd and energetic correspondent of Descartes. I have found it impossible to include any extracts from her letters, because it is impossible to make them free-standing. They are unintelligible without Descartes's replies. She may sometimes have been right where Descartes was wrong or confused, but the difficulty of showing her as the thinker she undoubtedly was is a presentational one, as far as this book is concerned, and cannot be overcome (an annotated edition of both sides of the correspondence would be worth undertaking). The other woman philosopher who is, sadly, not represented is absent for the excellent reason that she never wrote anything. I refer to J. S. Mill's friend and eventual wife, Harriet Taylor. We know how deeply his writing was influenced by her; during the period of their marriage he wrote the essay *Enfranchisement of Women.*[120]

What? Mary Warnock, a former principal of Girton College, Cambridge, is apparently confusing Mill's *The Subjection* with Taylor's *The Enfranchisement of Women* (even though a twentieth-century rumor persists in doubting Taylor's authorship—not only of this work, but of all her writing). Even more than M3, then, Taylor herself is stifled. In *Sexual Equality*, which brings together some of her writings and those of her daughter Helen and of J. S. Mill, Ann and John Robson include a portion of Taylor's work, but they include neither her essay on conformity nor the one on the seasons nor her book reviews, poems, and letters. Hayek publishes both essays, some letters and two poems (remember, she wrote nothing). Juggling these two volumes, you may form an idea of Taylor herself. And Somerville College, Oxford, houses some of the archives.

The *Enfranchisement* was first published in 1851 by the *Westminster Review,* where, as in all periodicals of the time, it was customary to publish texts without naming the author. After Taylor's death, Mill reprinted it in a collection of his own articles, *Dissertations and Discussions,* with a preface stating explicitly that the essay, alas!, was written by his companion—alas because Mill does not like the text very well. In 1868, it was reprinted in the form of a small book with Taylor's name appearing on the cover as "Mrs Stuart Mill."[121] I think before that it may also have circulated as an offprint from the *Westminster Review:* In the Somerville College collection I found two copies, one bound with some other pieces, the other presented as an autonomous brochure: they are "reprinted from the *Westminster Review* of July 1851," but the title section has been reset and the whole thing looks like the offprints that a periodical prints and binds for the author, sometimes after the fact. In 1872, Margaret Mylne praises "The admirable essay by Mrs. Stuart Mill" and provides a valuable bit of information: having been absent from England when the first edition appeared, Mylne did not discover it until about 1865, when she was asked to sign a petition: militants, both female and male, were probably making this text their point of reference. As early as 1854, Mill received a letter from a certain Mr. Chapman asking his permission to republish "Mrs. Mill's essay on woman"—when you have something to ask of a married woman, you naturally turn to her husband! He passed on the request, not without complaining about that person's vulgarity (Chapman had cited the title incorrectly), which may have led Taylor to refuse. Again in 1870, he wrote to Paulina Wright Davis: "What she was, I have attempted, though most inadequately, to delineate in the remarks prefaced to her essay, as reprinted with my 'Dissertations and Discussions.'"[122] The case might seem to be closed: for her contemporaries, Taylor was indisputably the author of *The Enfranchisement of Women*. Only later did the rumor start—perhaps she was not the author after all—and, moving from doubt to suspicion, we arrive at Lady Warnock's blunder. She wrote nothing (neither that, nor anything else!), and Mill wrote *The Enfranchisement*. The mistake is nonetheless astonishing, for those two were not pre-Socratics and some of their papers have come down to us. But the remark about Elizabeth of Bohemia provides the key. Her letters do not stand on their own, they are unintelligible without Descartes's replies! Quite logically, this response is sometimes difficult to understand without the letter to which it replies. But a sexist presupposition—the source of intelligibility is bound to be a man—has displaced common sense and also produced this hyperbolic gaffe with respect to Harriet Taylor.

13. A Woman and a Man in Philosophy

To take Taylor's existence seriously, we must set aside the hazy question of "influence." With the Mills, it was common practice to write for someone else. As an adolescent, John Stuart wrote rough drafts for his father, James Mill; Helen Taylor, Harriet's daughter, wrote articles for him. The household functioned as an intellectual cooperative, in the manner of a cottage industry, with a definite structure: the son wrote for the father, not the reverse, the daughter for the stepfather—the head of the family took care of the finishing touches or the proofreading; Taylor is Mill's collaborator, he says so, and their correspondence confirms it. When a second edition of the *Principles of*

Political Economy is undertaken (and we have pointed out her role in the first), Mill complains: she no longer agrees with a passage he had inserted into the original edition at her request and almost in her own words. "By thinking sufficiently I should probably come to think the same—as is almost always the case" he writes to her; but if the passage is no longer defensible, then two or three other pages are likewise incorrect and finally "there is nothing to be said against Communism at all."[123] Now there was no time to spare—should he postpone the second edition? Mill and his commentators have attributed the gap between the two editions to the revolution of 1848. Perhaps, but 1848 had its own advocate at hand: Harriet Taylor who regarded the situation of the working class as "the other great question of our time,"[124] and an explicitly feminist question, since women could find no way of earning their living except in marriage or in hard, poorly paid jobs. It is not certain that her argument prevailed; but if she asked for one of her texts to be altered or suppressed because her point of view had evolved, this was a matter of cooperation, and it is important to take literally other indications Mill provides. He states: "During the two years which immediately preceded the cessation of my official life, my wife and I were working together at the *Liberty*."[125]

This admission troubles both men and women who like to believe men are the only valid sources of philosophy, that they rely on no one else in generating their thought, or that they are the heirs of an exclusively masculine tradition. Worse still, the rare commentators who mention the couple are interested only in the points on which they seem largely to agree, and, as a result, wonder which one of them influenced the other. A couple sees eye to eye, you see![126] To disentangle the relationship between Mill and Taylor, I propose instead to adopt a method that takes their disagreements seriously, and thus to rediscover a woman author who thinks for herself. By identifying which of Mill's theses are out of step with Taylor's point of view, it should be possible to expose a debate within this couple. We must therefore compare what she wrote alone with what he wrote alone; we will then be able to understand their agreement, when it occurs, as a resolution of the debate and not the work of a *fusion* of two minds.

It is 1832. Just as people exchange wedding rings, Mill and Taylor write essays on marriage for each other, each text a gift of love designated for just one person and not for the printing press; and each including extensive discussion of divorce.[127] Taylor's essay is written in the second person (*you*), Mill's addresses itself to her as "she to whom my life is devoted," then continues without referring again to a particular addressee. She locates the recipient on the horizon of her thought: he will have to take responsibility for what she proposes in the way of unfinished business, so he will have to understand her project and find the means of carrying it out. "If I could be allowed to be Providence to the world for a time, for the express purpose of raising the condition of women, I should come to you to know the *means*—the purpose would be to remove all interference with affection. . . ."[128] Outlining an ideal state of affairs and demonstrating the unacceptable nature of the situation as it was, she presents herself as a utopian who does not know how to move from the deplorable to the desirable.[129] But she offers some clues: education for everyone, a good divorce law, equal access for men and women to rights, employment, and politics. In one draft of the text, she complains only of not knowing how to spread and promote her ideas; the role she reserves for Mill is perhaps that of a herald. A certain utopian style recurs also in her manner of deducing the implications of a radical hypothesis: "I have no doubt that when the whole community is really educated, tho' the present laws of marriage were to continue they would be perfectly disregarded, because no one would marry."[130] But Mill's essay does not look for utopia, it centers on "the best popular morality," for mankind just as it is, all popular morality, according to him, being a compromise. The year 1832 is the year of *On Genius:* just like the Hindus and the Spanish peasants, average human nature must be knowable if one wants to outline a morality suitable to it.

He looks for an initial compromise, anticipating that he will have to think of a broader synthesis when Taylor has taught him everything he has found out on his own (*sic*) and all he has not found, for "in what concerns the relations of Man with Woman, the law which is to be observed by both should surely be made by both. . . . "[131] In response to this fine idea, I want to explain my criticism. Mill was no doubt the best man of his time: if, good-hearted, a good head on his shoulders, and in love with a feminist whose thinking is coherent, he still fails to think emancipation all the way through, there must be a deep-seated cultural given blocking his way. It is useful to highlight it in case anyone (female or male) would like to get rid of it now. There is a small problem in Mill's principle that requires both men and women to contribute to formulating the law intended to govern their relationship: in his opinion, it is his prerogative to think through the synthesis of the two points of view. He is thus the producer of one point of view *and* the future agent of the synthesis. The interest in intuition he conveys in *The Subjection* is consistent with this schema: when a man produces a theory according to which women are intuitive and men are theorizers, he locates himself on the side of the determining authority *and* of half of the people who are determined by it. As the author of a dualist theory, he determines both *himself* and the otherness of his other. To this other, he can only leave what remains after he has claimed ownership of the theoretical, theory being in itself a determining factor because theory is more or less closely connected with facts.

Indeed, the description of theory in *The Subjection* presupposes a disjunction between theory and practice, and between the theoretical and the factual, facts being supposedly perceived instantaneously by a mode of understanding called intuition. Intuition is feminine just as theory is masculine. Mill, who claims to be "looking at women as they are known in experience," admits that men do not always clearly see what is really there, in the facts; rather, they see what they have learned to anticipate.[132] Does the theory thus function quite separately from any perception of facts and the thought machine run on empty without coming face to face with reality? Imagining a theoretical apparatus that operates separately and under its own power, or one that is neither a theory *of* something nor of an object accorded some reality, we leave the realm of theory to fall under the spell of a fantasy proposed in the guise of an explanation. The term has this sense in the Freudian expression "theory of infantile sexuality": as children, we concocted images of genital organs or sexual relations by making up an idea (any idea is better than none at all) of something we knew nothing about. When one makes up ideas "about"—sexuality or sexual duality—the "theorization" is not knowledge but pseudoknowledge: its function is not to produce knowledge but to generate ideas that do not admit of factual proof or invalidation. The duality Mill proposes, with disastrous consequences for women's intellectual status, is no less disastrous with respect to theory, which comes very close to a fantasy of substitution. Moreover, it serves as a principle of control over women's intellect and speech: a man in an intimate relationship with the female speaker takes it upon himself to propose, ostensibly as a theoretical proposition, exactly what she had suggested in an intuitive mode. Thus it is he who determines the meaning and import that should be accorded his wife's "happy intuitions." Mill will say that he listened to Taylor just as anyone would read an author of the past; when one of her ideas seemed good to him, he incorporated it into his system—but how? And what did he do with those he judged less worthy?

We can reconstruct an example. In 1832, Taylor declares it shocking that women are taught to earn their living by marriage; thus, they sell their person for bread and acquire habits of dependence that can contribute to mental degeneration. In a just society, they would have no reason to act this way; they would earn their bread themselves and would have children only if they knew they could feed them. Mill was never to accept such a straightforward theory; in 1832, he said that even though a woman might be *capable* of earning her living, it does not follow that she must *actually* do so; normally she *will not* do it, it is not desirable to overload the labor market by doubling the number of those competing for work, *her* job, rather, should be to adorn *his* life and to share in *his* activities—the emphasis is Mill's. He was not to change his opinion. In *The Subjection* he returns to the idea he had defended as a young man. He was never pleased with Taylor's radical critique. Because we must not double the number of competitors in the labor market? The argument does not seem particularly liberal, and it could simply be an economic pretext for the final, more emotional comment, "and to share *his* occupations."[133] We can draw a parallel between Mill's support for material dependence and his "theory" of intuition, according to which a woman's thought could not survive autonomously and would be lost if a man were not there to integrate it into *his* system. The historical context bears out the parallel: at least since the time of Mary Wollstonecraft, access to knowledge amounted to independent access to the world of work. Wollstonecraft, who wants independence, wants schools that provide a professional education to children of both sexes. In 1859, Herbert Spencer discusses the value of knowledge as it pertains to the future entry into the world of material goods. In order to master the art of building, a bit of mathematics is necessary; at least a nodding acquaintance with scientific knowledge is essential for anyone involved in production, trade, or distribution; thus, boys must receive healthy rations of physics, chemistry, and so on. Girls must learn what they need to become competent mothers, and Spencer warns against education: "Men care little for erudition in women; but very much for physical beauty, good nature and sound sense. How many conquests does the blue-stocking make through her extensive knowledge of history? . . . Where is the Edwin who was brought to Angelina's feet by her German?"; education sacrifices the body to the mind, and in a woman, it is the body that counts for men.[134] Since the man is the sole purpose of a woman's life, anything more would be superfluous, useless, ineffective for seduction, and thus harmful! Whatever the talk about women's cognitive life, and even if its relevance is to be found in access to skilled work, everything leads back to the ongoing project of keeping men at the center of women's lives. Mill never abandons this wish; in a manner that is more than honorable he will campaign for the right to vote, but even after he has become liberal, when he hears talk of conditions that would allow women to escape the life of the married couple, he stumbles, even to the point of wanting to exclude married women from the labor market.

If he sees Taylor as a garden of intuitions from which he gathers at will, she seems for a long time to have considered her status as a purveyor of ideas both acceptable and useful. In an 1848 letter to Fox she notes, "*ideas* are just that needful stock in trade in which our legislators are as lamentably deficient as our Chartists"—she is speaking about ideas concerning justice for women.[135] She thinks it is a good thing to supply some of them to the "upper classes of men," whom she credits with a wish for greater justice, and she explains why: it is impossible to hope that women will liberate themselves by their own efforts, for "each one owns a master, and this mastery which is normally passive would assert itself if they attempted it [to liberate themselves]." Fox was wrong, therefore, to maintain that anyone who wants to be free should fight for freedom her/himself, or at least express the desire to be free; according to Harriet Taylor, it falls to the progressives to initiate the process but someone has to give them the ideas they lack. The Chartists should not campaign for an alleged "universal suffrage" that excludes half the nation. A garden from which one gathers at will? Really! Rather, a female interlocutor who criticizes your ideas; and quite probably she helped Mill in just this way.

The young Mill was not a liberal when he sought a compromise suit-able for average human natures: had he not already escaped from the rut of thinking that ordinary humanity needs compromises formulated by en-lightened guides, he could not, with Taylor, have written a text such as *On Liberty* that is so incompatible with his earlier views. Now in 1832, she has moved far beyond that way of thinking; the philosophical perspective of her essay on conformity is such as to make nonsense of any project of defining a compromise, a norm, a popular morality. Praising individual character and unlimited diversity, she objects to the standard of conformity defended by the intellectual laziness of the majority, a phantom power, she says, that punishes every sign of mental independence. It is plausible to see a precursor of *On Liberty* in this line of thought only if we emphasize its discrepancy with the young Mill's point of view. In 1832, he is still dependent on a Platonist point of view; for him, it is the philosopher or the philosophical couple who must define a popular morality, whereas Taylor deplores the efforts we all (both women and men) devote to achieving a standard of the good or of duty as defined by one group or another. The remedy, she says, is to make everyone strong enough so that no one, female or male, needs support; people have to stop being led and every mind must govern itself. If in 1832 Mill is still a Platonist, she is already radically liberal, or, as the British say, libertarian. And in this essay she does not turn to him to discover how to realize her program. She thinks pleasure will bring it about: "whoever has once known the pleasure of self-dependence will be in no danger of relapsing into subserviency"[136]; there are no fixed natures, whether weak or strong, but only people who have tasted independence and those who have not yet experienced it. And freedom is immediately addictive.

For her, there is no reference to a human nature (average, masculine, lofty, feminine), no fixed characterization of human beings, indeed quite the contrary. She proposes a contrast between the sciences of nature and moral knowledge; the sciences of nature operate by discovering more and more comprehensive laws, and moral knowledge is valid only when it goes "beyond all classifications."[137] It is a bold idea at a time when philosophical anthropology was flourishing like a fictionalized botany of humanity. The moral sciences must renounce thinking in categories; each individual should count as one page in the book of human history and there should be no two pages alike. Thus, in her writing, the principle of individuation (as vast and as numerous as the forests of this world may be, one never finds two identical leaves) moves into an ethicopolitical register, and the leaf becomes a page because individuation is not a given. It is up to each person to "write" her- or himself, by making her/himself into an individual, through behavior reflecting an independently-formed opinion, for which one can take responsibility. Her disagreement with Mill is not only on the question of earning one's bread. She is opposed to the content of his opinion as well, and to the philosophical operation that through its claim to define other people's destinies for them, defines only a single destiny for woman: dependence on a man for bread. "Let each mind guide itself by the light of as much knowledge as it can acquire for itself by means of unbiased experience."[138] She was probably the first woman to be offered the role of a Platonist philosopher, and she declined it unequivocally.

14. The Admirable Essay

Harriet Taylor's text on conformity does not make a single allusion to sexual duality. The concepts it uses are valid for both sexes—people, persons, character, individuals, we, *everyone,* the universal *you,* every mind, and so on. It is I who see intimations of her subsequent rejection of the very idea of a norm based on sexual nature in her polemic against classifications. When she writes "no human being ever did or ever will comprehend the whole mind of any other human being. It would perhaps not be possible to find two minds accustomed to think for themselves whose thoughts on any identical subject should take in their expression the same form of words," she is disagreeing with Mill's views about genius, which he needs in order to define a norm appropriate to human natures.[139] Taylor carried the day: *On Liberty* affirms the value of rejecting classifications on principle. But subsequently Mill returns to the idea that a mental functioning peculiar to women can be described; so, Taylor had not really convinced him that her principle was applicable to women. Even if the couple's liberalism originates in her feminism, Mill seems not to see that connection. Besides, the logical consequences of *On Conformity* became clear to her only in 1851, when she was writing *The Enfranchisement.* By contrast, her 1848 critique of the Chartists draws on an idea of the feminine: "society requires the infusion of the new life of the feminine element. The great practical ability of women which is now wasted on worthless trifles or sunk in the stupidities called *love* would tell with most 'productive' effect on the business of life...."[140] When, in *Subjection,* Mill again takes up the idea of women's practical—and thus their political—nature, it really does not matter whether he owes it to Taylor or whether she first discovered it in their conversations; he takes it up only in 1869, whereas by 1851 she had already rejected definitions of peculiarly feminine attributes.

So what happened? Taylor stopped believing that women are incapable of initiating their own liberation. In the *New York Tribune,* she had read about the American conventions for women's rights, sparked by the Seneca Falls conference to which we have already referred. She had also become aware of a petition that the female inhabitants of Sheffield had sent to the House of Lords, in a pioneering initiative not unlike the American movement. One detail is worth noting: rather than calling *The Enfranchisement* an essay, a subtitle in both the original edition and the softcover reprint at Somerville College presents it as a review of the *New York Tribune* article. When he reissues the text in *Dissertations,* Mill suppresses this fact, as do all subsequent editions. Public response transformed the review into an essay and read it as an expression of Taylor's ideas, which indeed it also was. However, this transformation erased any sense that the essay had initially been the work of a female journalist or historian of the present reporting a current event she describes as historic, namely, that the issue of women's equal access to all rights and their enfranchisement in law and practice is no longer merely an idea, but now manifests itself in something hitherto unheard of—organized agitation. This issue has sparked public meetings and inspired political action. It is no longer a matter of advocacy by orators or male writers on women's behalf, but of "a movement not merely *for* women but *by* women."[141] Thus the text is primarily an analysis of an event in which Taylor had no direct involvement; however, she does not dissociate herself from it. Indicating both her agreement and her disagreement on at least one point, she says what she thinks of this project in which she makes common cause with the Americans. She is pleased to learn that what she had believed impossible is in fact possible, pleased that History has shown the error of her earlier belief, and that the hope that had been missing in 1848 now allows her to articulate implications already contained in her 1832 philosophy. "We deny the right of any portion of the species to decide for another portion, or any individual for another individual, what is and what is not their 'proper sphere.' The proper sphere for all human beings is the largest and highest which they are able to attain to. What this is, cannot be ascertained, without complete freedom of choice."[142] She praises American women for having refused to debate the issue of sex-related aptitudes, saying that once perfect freedom is put in place, roles and professions will be open to women and men alike, to those most capable of performing them. She notes that, on the other hand, ordaining that a certain sex or social class may not exercise its talents and faculties is not only unjust to people, nor is it merely prejudicial to society, which in this case loses what it most needs; but also, and fundamentally, it is the most effective means of guaranteeing that abilities thus thwarted cease in fact to exist. *"Those faculties shall not be exerted* [...] *the qualities* [...] *shall not exist"*: Taylor's argument presupposes that a faculty is brought into being only through use, or more precisely, that prohibiting its use ensures its non-existence. The style is reminiscent of a Biblical register, for it uses a future tense that functions as an imperative in prescribing-predicting the order of things. The norm engenders the fact, or rather its absence.[143]

In 1848, when Taylor did not yet believe women could be agents of their own liberation, she advocated presenting ideas to male legislators or militants in order to make them understand what Mill never stopped saying, namely, society could not fail to benefit from enlisting women's capabilities in its services. Both Monsieur de la Palisse[*] and I will tell you that by definition, the argument incorporates precisely the idea of capabilities regarded as feminine. In 1851, having seen real women take charge of their own liberation, she rejects the debate about aptitudes, and the social benefit of including women becomes secondary: to predetermine the aptitudes of a group in such a negative fashion is *not only* a loss for society *but also,* and fundamentally, an act of mutilation. If Harriet Taylor's thinking changes so significantly with the dawning of hopes and expectations (and she acquires hopes and expectations from learning about the action women are taking), we too can deny the existence of an identifiable feminine mode of thought, whether about specific aptitudes or not. To judge by its evolution, differentialism is a theoretical position linked to the idea that women are incapable of political initiative. In 1851, Taylor refuses to engage with "the question of the alleged differences in physical or mental qualities between the sexes" and limits herself to a note citing a Reverend Smith's claim that there is no difference that cannot be explained by the circumstances in which the two sexes grow up.[144] Can we believe her when she says that, to avoid a lengthy debate, she is limiting her discussion to a citation in a note? Nothing is less certain, for she has moved to a more radical frame of thought. Leaving it to Sydney Smith to propose his own version of a social genesis of such differences, she casts doubt on their very existence. Thus, I think, she invites her readers to move beyond the inadequacy of this merely speculative stance, which is inadequate even with respect to analysis (I call a point of view speculative that, without wondering whether the existence of a "phenomenon" is well established, tries to explain it directly). According to Smith, it is easy to "explain so simple a phenomenon" of intellectual difference, which he believes is patently obvious. Yet, for Taylor in 1851 to say that the differences between girls and boys are socially produced is, in my view, to miss the

---

[*] 1470–1525. One of the most famous military figures of his time. When he died in battle, his soldiers composed a song whose most famous line is: "A quarter-hour before his death/he was still alive (Un quart d'heure avant sa mort/ Il était encore en vie)." Such a tautological expression is known as a "lapalissade."

essential point. There is not always a difference, she suggests, but in general, there is a radical and fundamental disparity between them: one is free and the other not, one arrogates to itself the right to decide what the other is, one class can put another in chains. The concepts she introduces go well beyond the whole problematic of difference, whether its genesis is social or not, thus contributing to her analysis of connections between power and a libertarian ideal.

Moreover, the thesis attributing sexual difference to a double social construction tends, by contrast, to lead also to an imagined similarity between the sexes that could just as easily be a construct. This other possibility is clear in Sydney Smith's observation: "As long as boys and girls run about in the dirt, and trundle hoops together, they are both precisely alike."[145] A charming image, depicting the joyous freedom of movement and children's voices, the equal and complete freedom to play and express oneself, at the risk of disturbing adults who are obliged to devote themselves to mundane tasks such as laundry, having been interrupted in their meditations by the noise outside. Even today, adults' equal tolerance of disturbances created by girls and boys cannot be taken for granted, and one can but dream of having been a child under Reverend Smith's regime. But his concluding sentence falls flat; "they are both precisely alike"—what is the point of this conclusion, following such a lovely image of children at play? The ultimate effect of the ideology of difference in which we have been floundering since the eighteenth century is that even a critique of it tends to occur in the same register: substituting identity for difference, such a critique reaches the point of positing an idea that, in itself, is of no interest at all. There is nothing satisfying in the idea of having been produced—whether uniformly or differently—nor in the project of producing identical individuals, or two groups of individuals identical among themselves. The major flaw in Smith's point of view is its insistence on human malleability. In other words, by denying that differences are natural, it advances a thesis in no way more attractive than its opposite. On the fringes of a debate about the natural or social character of differences, there are, in the end, only hollow choices: do you prefer your differences natural or social? Which would you have wanted, to be produced alike, or different? If I reply that none of it matters any more to me than having an even or odd number of hairs, I will conclude that this point of view, which is already inadequate as a means of analysis, proves inoperative. It is also unstable.

In 1846, Mill refers to Smith in order to declare that the distinction between "feminine attributes" and "masculine capacities" is "untenable"[146]; when we are talking about the Greek mind, the critical principle seems to function. But in the *Subjection*, speaking of supposedly real sexes, he suspends judgment: "it cannot now be known how much of the existing mental difference between men and women is natural, and how much artificial."[147] This agnosticism allows him to adjust the differences as he sees fit and to apply the regulative principle to one question rather than another: intellectual life. And when he affirms, "the social subordination of women thus stands out as an isolated fact in modern social institutions; a solitary breach of what has become their fundamental law; a single relic,"[148] he fails to contest mental subordination. To trace differences to a social genesis is thus a fragile methodological principle, which risks reverting to the very beliefs it claimed to dispel. Taylor goes much further when she contends, "[we] deny the right of any portion of the species to...,"[149] a challenge that locates the active speaking subject within the discourse [we], thus constituting a total speech act, a declaration that pronounces itself in action and creates its own subject in so doing. For in challenging the right of anyone to claim the power to determine the norm, a subject emerges from the challenge, a kind of "we" that floats between America, Sheffield, and the Harriet Taylor holding the pen. I, not I alone, but certainly I, an I-with-others and thanks to others, in a *we* from which *I* can disconnect myself if need be. One by one, Taylor freely judges the demands of the American women, approves of many of them and objects to one, the demand for a sentimental priesthood or spiritual superiority of women, which to her is mere "verbiage". Beyond the purely speculative analysis, she finds the "we" of a speaking political action, in which every *I* maintains its vigilance and its right to dissident thought. When some women and one woman establish themselves as subjects with the capacity to make judgments about reality and rights, instead of situating themselves among the objects on which people can expound ad libitum, this is a major political-intellectual event that necessarily displaces the givens of discourse.

Me-with-the-American-women: how could that have given Mill any pleasure? In the final analysis, he himself might be the source of the rumor contesting Taylor's authorship of the text. For Mill's preface to it in the *Dissertations* confesses to some regrets, even while acknowledging her authorship and noting that this was generally known when it was first published. He would prefer that "it remained unacknowledged, than that it should be read with the idea that even the faintest image can be found in it of a heart and mind ... which were unparalleled."[150] He refers to her by this paraphrase and never names her, thus already erasing her; and, regretting that the text is not a faithful self-portrait, he paints the true portrait of Taylor. She, being the woman she was, should never have written the *Enfranchisement;* and the work does not emanate from who she really was! If her authorship had not been known in 1851, Mill would perhaps have been tempted to leave it to others to reissue the text, and without attribution. It must be said that she makes her case forcibly: every woman should have a strong mind of her own and be prepared to reject the idea of loyalty to a man, which is the basic virtue of femininity. And she asks: for a woman, what is democracy, what is liberalism, if it leaves her, as it has found her, a pariah?[151] Mill will take up the gauntlet on the question of suffrage and bypass all the rest. When one speculates on what part of Taylor's discourse does not carry over into his, it is easier to see the core of his resistance to her. Taylor briefly refers to women who have inherited a throne, and female sultans who, once they have become regents, have assumed political responsibilities overnight; but she focuses particularly on women citizens actively engaged in opening a space of action and political reflection for themselves; Mill, on the other hand, mentions only queens in his *Subjection*. Without hesitation, Taylor espouses American women's demands for access to university, and shifts the emphasis. Women must be offered a more advanced and more rigorous education; they must be educated for their own sakes, not to be made into more pleasant companions for men; people are wrong to believe that, even now, they are intellectually inferior to men. John Stuart breathes not a word either about access to universities or about a solid education. When he says women make the same mistakes as self-taught men, he does not connect this point to their exclusion from formal education, and he waxes eloquent about the happiness, for a man of intellect, of having a woman of intuition at his side. His lack of real enthusiasm for a formal education even appears in the codicil to his will, despite his ostensibly progressive stance. In the event that his nephews and nieces do not reach the age of majority, he bequeaths three thousand pounds to the first university that will grant women access to all its degrees, but he adds a clause stipulating that if, twenty years after his death, no university meets this condition, the money must be used otherwise. His good will is permeated with a conviction that the factual order of things will render it impossible.[152] Elected to the honorary office of rector of St. Andrews University, he will make an interminable speech on what a university should be; "Men are men before they are lawyers, or physicians", ... *man, he, men* all the way through it! And it includes a eulogy for the old established universities, which "formerly seemed to exist mainly for the repression of independent thought" and are at present the sites of "free and manly inquiry."[153] Some elements of *her* discourse are absent from *his*: for example, any mention of women's capacity for grassroots political initiatives, and their access to an education, whether or not it is offered by institutions of learning, enabling women to be *strong-minded,* thus no longer of *passive mind.* Two things stimulate thought, she says: intellectual interest itself and a field of practical application; but both of these are placed beyond the reach of women, who are told from infancy that thought and all its greater applications are matters for others while their task is to make themselves agreeable to those others.[154] Mill's feminism can be defined as follows: there is a mental difference, but there is complementarity, thus a fused couple of which he is the head; provided that this structure is maintained, then anything goes. The right to vote, yes, the capacity to earn her living, yes . . . , but . . . that is debatable for married women, and if marriage were reformed, not necessary at all.[155]

15. Equality, Difference, or Divergence?

Today's political scientists are interested in the appearance of a phenomenon called the gender gap. Just one generation after acquiring the right to vote, we French women began to exercise it differently from our male compatriots.[156] In the 1988 presidential elections, the distribution of female versus male votes was especially apparent on the extreme right: 10 percent of female voters, contrasted with 17 percent of male voters, voted for the National Front candidate. Since then it has been said that women are less racist and xenophobic than men or, as Janine Mossuz Lavau wrote in *Le Monde diplomatique* in May 1988, they resist neomachismo and vote against it. One must at least infer from this that there is no contradiction between equality and difference, since equal citizenship makes it possible for a difference of opinion to be clearly expressed. Such a difference has a significant formal quality: it has been orchestrated by no one. Thus those who refuse equality in the name of difference are wrong in every respect. Conceptually, to confuse equality with identity is to reason like children who are said to have trouble understanding that a kilo of feathers weighs as much as a kilo of lead. In fact, I've never seen a single child who let herself or himself be taken in by this trick. That a basket of cherries and a pillow can have the same weight does not establish any identity between them, or else there are some surprises in store for you. From a historical point of view also, judging by the electoral gender gap, it is a mistake to object to equality in the name of a difference that has to be maintained: the greater the equality, the greater the statistical difference of opinion. But the concept of difference is inadequate to assess what is at issue; and even if it appeals to the imagination, I do not think the expression "the female vote" is accurate, nor can it accurately explain a statistical difference. Rather, we should speak of a divergence that is even more pronounced when women's independence from men is greater. The important fact, in 1988, was that there certainly was a difference, but not with respect to women who stayed at home: they voted exactly as men did. There is a difference within the difference, and the discrepancy between the voting behavior of salaried women and those who stay at home has remained constant since that time, despite general fluctuations or those brought about by the vote of women applying for work. Consequently, we can propose that in couples where both members work, there can be divergence, debate, perhaps even disputes, since each one decides how to express his or her opinion, whereas evidence suggests that a woman who has no economic independence aligns herself with her man's opinion. Far from producing "similarities" or the infamous assimilation of women to men, more equality in a couple establishes a minimal condition for divergence. My weight has to be more or less equal to yours in order for me to dare occasionally to contradict you; I need independence from you in order not to accept everything you say to me.

From time to time I have led debates with young women who have had none of the privileges the social and educational system offers. Difference is the least of their concerns in their objections to thinking about equality. They sometimes show their lack of interest by saying "we don't necessarily want to be part of the elite" or "why do we always have to compare ourselves?", a sentiment I would willingly echo: if only one could! If only we did not encounter violent discrimination underscoring the double standard the social system invokes in comparing us to men! On the other hand, these young women may be trying to point out that in recent years the question of equality is posed mainly from the vantage point of affluent or dominant social groups, whereas they know life offers most people very little. And I have to admit they are right, but we must keep the debate alive if we are to rediscover equality's true center of gravity. When you show them that more equality means greater independence of opinion and opens up the possibility of contradicting the other, suddenly they catch on and rush ahead to draw further conclusions, for such reasoning bears on many matters other than voting patterns. One of the registers in which equality becomes meaningful is in freedom of expression, including in everyday life. The right to speak is a product of material conditions, economic independence, and a certain level of political equality, all of which allow the exercise of moral and mental autonomy in social life. If I can judge by the example of Taylor, the existence of a fully fledged women's protest movement can be vitally important to each and every woman's exercise of mental autonomy.

In his autobiography, Mill mentions his own commitment to "the complete equality in all legal, political, social, and domestic relations, which ought to exist between men and women. . . ." It would be futile to remark on the absence of equal *intellectual* relations here, if his incomplete list were not in a sentence rejecting the idea that he might have owed his feminist convictions to Taylor. On the contrary, he says, those convictions were among the first fruits of his own political reflections; and, he was far from being indebted to his companion for them. Moreover, he says, it was probably his ideas that first attracted Taylor to him. The two points seem to echo one another: he does not owe his egalitarian ideas to Taylor and he omits intellectual equality in enumerating the spheres in which, according to him, equality must be defended. We need not dispute his right to think of himself as the source of his own convictions, although we may find it surprising: does this really mean that Taylor's intuitions inspired everything but the idea of equality? It is partly true, we have seen, but in a negative sense. Taylor is certainly not responsible for the restrictions he imposes on the project of liberation. But is he not also claiming that it is impossible to learn from a woman what to think about the status of women?

A detail in Bertrand Russell's autobiography similarly makes me wince: "I had been a passionate advocate of equality for women ever since in adolescence I read Mill on the subject. This was some years before I became aware of the fact that my mother used to campaign in favour of women's suffrage in the sixties."[157] Orphaned at an early age, the young Russell may well have first encountered the idea of equality between the sexes in Mill's work, only then to learn that his own mother had been a suffragist. But the care he takes in setting out the order of events does not strike me as accidental: the spiritual godfather first and then, some years later, the mother. His convictions come from Mill, not from his mother. If intellectual equality really existed, it would, for example, matter little to a Bertrand Russell whether he had learned something from Mill, his mother, or Taylor. Here the idea of an intellectual inequality appears in its most pernicious and perhaps most absolute form. It is not a matter of spending one's time weighing up souls and minds one way or another, it is that a man, men, a society consider it impossible for the source of an idea (constructed, articulated) to be a woman or women. Russell emphasizes the opposition of Queen Victoria and certain groups of women to female suffrage. It is true that Victoria would have liked to take the whip (sic) to a lady who defended the rights of women, and she even wanted to enlist the distinguished minds of the time in a campaign against these rights. The problem is that Russell bypasses the women who were fighting for rights: in the end one sees only Mill, Russell himself, and far away in the background, his mother, not the mass movement of suffragettes whom he confesses he does not like. He says the cause was quickly won. Quickly? It took American and English women seventy-one years of mobilization from 1848 to 1919, but he took it up in 1907. Visible throughout this story is the power, arrogated to themselves by this group of supposedly enlightened men, to determine the validity and the exact extent of women's rights: these men have a sense of what is just, "[b]ut the determination of large numbers of women to prolong the contempt of the female sex was odd."[158] Women do not want to be free . . .

Since throughout this analysis we have been trying to emphasize a mental block that undoubtedly continues to afflict many people, let us quickly describe one of its elements. It is possible to allow women political access because they will not bring their own ideas into politics; only philosophical men have ideas about justice and the public good (and thus, occasionally, an accurate assessment of the value of women's access to the political realm). The prehistory of this schema can be traced back to Bacon. In *Of the Advancement of Learning*, he sings the praises of the public happiness that prevailed during an emperor's age of minority, when Rome was governed by women assisted by certain men of great learning.[159] Under the reign of Elizabeth, Bacon no doubt saw himself as the brains of the kingdom. When women govern, they are counselled by learned men. They put wise men's ideas into practice, and "wise men" take delight in such a schema only if women have no ideas of their own, if a deep sexual difference prevents them from constructing any such ideas, or if they are in such a state of difference that no room is left for divergence. Just as Mill insists on women's qualification to take on the *executive leadership of mankind,* to be the executive supervisors of humanity, so he regards it as an established fact that "no production in philosophy, science, or art, entitled to the first rank, has been the work of a woman". In his view, their literary works lack originality; they "have not yet produced any of those great and luminous new ideas which form an era in thought" and "their compositions are mostly grounded on the existing fund of thought."[160] His vacillation is very clear and the attempt to balance some rights which can be given to women against some capacities which women cannot attain is already evident in Condorcet: "It is said that no woman has ever made an important scientific discovery, or shown signs of genius in the arts or in literature, and so on, but we would hardly attempt to limit citizenship rights to men of genius."[161] Thus he announces complete equality between "women and all other men", but by producing a new inequality: there is a "superior class", "a small class of enlightened men", and "this small class apart", equality between the sexes is complete. The problem is that this very class might be the one in charge of the *principles* of politics.

One July afternoon in 1914 Parisian activist groups lobbying for women's suffrage decorated the statue of Condorcet with flowers, thus making him into a founding hero and father of the idea of women's right to vote. The Marguerite Durand library houses a file of press reports of this demonstration, which its female organizers, concerned primarily to distinguish themselves from the English women, represent as nonthreatening—"what would anyone fear from a woman with flowers in her arms"? Reading the reverse side of the press clippings, we learn that there are rumors of a bomb in Sarajevo, and we know those rumors were well founded. In the same library, you will find texts written by women just prior to or at the same time as the Condorcet article; a petition from women of the Third Estate to the king, dated January 1, 1789; motions addressed to the National Assembly at the end of 1789; a notebook containing the complaints of a certain Mme B: "we are asking to be educated and to have work [. . .] so that we can protect ourselves against misfortune." The poverty and lack of education of women, whose work allows them no escape from penury, are highlighted, and "we beg you to establish free schooling" so that women are no longer "the prey" of the first seducer to come along.

In the years before and after their marriage, Harriet Taylor and John Stuart Mill wrote articles together about spousal murder and domestic violence that he would describe as "joint productions."[162] Texts worth rereading today, because the problems they denounce still exist—and one can repeat, with the authors, that men believe in their right to inflict physical violence on their wives and children because they see them as their property just like their shoes. We could also reiterate their criticism of the legal system. Mill and Taylor had certain values in common that allowed them to act together as the committed intellectuals they were. One can protest against family violence, even without theoretical agreement on the status of the family. And even the object "family violence", as the target of a discourse and a condemnation, seems to me to come out of the theoretical divergence between them. For such an object is not a given, not something just waiting for the pen that will take up the cause. First of all one has to identify it, highlight it, and name it. Taylor and Mill constructed it as a problem in itself that could be isolated from other questions, a new territory beyond their disagreements. When, for example, no agreement can be reached on the possibility of all women earning their living and having a mind of their own, people can still look for other points of possible agreement. Taylor and Mill were unable to create a general theory together about what, for her, would be the bases of an art of enfranchisement, and for him the analysis of subjection as a residue of a more general social subordination. Their disagreement is perhaps already apparent in the title of their respective works. But particular objects, such as the condemnation of violence or access to the right to vote, begin to emerge against the background of disagreement. More generally, reformism emerges when a radical divergence cannot be resolved; it is like the active face of our fragmentary perceptions of a succession of social "dysfunctions". One day we allow ourselves to see domestic violence, incestuous rape, longer unemployment for women; the next day we manage to discuss the sexism of schoolbooks or language, day-care centers that are insufficient in number and unsatisfactory in quality, the situation of single mothers; on yet another day, prostitution networks, pornographic billboards, female circumcision, immigrant women's lack of autonomy, and then because all of that makes us uncomfortable, we quickly turn our backs on it, and no longer see anything. And at the very most, people see the women who are suffering, rather than the perpetrators of the problem. Two million women beaten in France must mean there are two million violent men among us. What would it cost the Republic to write into its constitution that "persons who live under the same roof must practice mutual respect"? What would it cost us to launch a movement demanding that this principle be inscribed in all legal documents about the family, cohabitation, and familial relationship?

16. Corporations

A male philosopher willing to recognize civil rights for women is still a historical rarity. But the fact that Mill does not want to recognize our capacity to think without a man is also reminiscent of a common historical practice. At the beginning of the seventeenth century the brewers' guilds forbade women to be brewers, although for a very long time this occupation had been open to them. In 1639 a poor woman named Mary Arnold was thrown into prison for subbornly persisting in earning her living as a brewer. But this is what interests me: the brewers' fraternity had nothing to say about women's right to be carpenters, printers, or doctors, and for their part, the printers' guilds, who said nothing about brewing, did everything in their power to expel women who were often the daughters or widows of its members from the trade they had occasionally practiced. And if, for a long time, the medical faculties had been waging war on those who practiced without their endorsement, and thus on female practitioners, they were silent about carpentry, printing, and brewing. At the end of the nineteenth century in France there would be strikes and petitions by male interns, refusing to recognize in women all the physical, intellectual, psychic, and moral capacities required to perform the functions of a hospital intern. At the turn of the twentieth century, strikes by male typographers together with specific measures taken by the trade unions would aim to bar women from the typesetters' trade.[163]

In all of these cases, apprenticeship in a trade is the issue. The guild or corporation exists to control the acquisition of skills specific to each domain. If in prohibiting the practice of medicine by lay people, medieval faculties of medicine were targeting members of both sexes, the same was true of the other corporations. But what disqualified a man was not knowing, whereas a woman was disqualified in spite of having learned. Daughter or wife of a brewer, carpenter, or printer, she had acquired skills only incidentally, by assisting her father or husband. The sexism of the corporations sought to distinguish sharply between the apprentice's role and skills acquired incidentally through exercising that role. Let every corporation defend its craft against women, and all will be well. The very principle of corporatism—a certification in plumbing does not qualify a person for dentistry—erects barriers around specialized occupations, each one defined by a legally established qualification (the guild controlling the skills and standards of practice of its members), and this establishes the occupation at the intersection of a skill and a jurisdiction. For example, one is a watchmaker only when one knows how to make watches in the manner duly established by a collective institution of which one becomes a member. If a corporation refuses such a status to women, thus forbidding them to earn their living by producing goods or services equivalent to those produced by its members (men), the principle has the effect of relegating women to the role of spouse-assistant, servant, nun, or prostitute, but this only if the other guilds do likewise. When we wonder why a particular trade excludes women, we can explore all the secondary rationalizations ad infinitum. But if all professional bodies act in the name of a common, implicit but deep-seated masculine social pact, then we must ask ourselves whether any man, from drapery merchant to philosopher, can escape the obligation, unconscious though it may be, to apply the same principles to his work as are operative for mathematicians or watchmakers. In any case, the main point is that from Mill's perspective, the corporation of thinking men can or must conduct itself as the other guilds do. The masculine social contract is not only about the state; it is not limited to a political body or male *Body Politick*. Whether it is a matter of representing culture and the sciences, or various occupations, a masculine body acts as the point of reference, just as the body of the king was formerly the symbol of social bonds and the body of Christ that of the religious community. If the principle of identification amounts to an obligation for each man, perhaps each man might well consider how free he really is!

Epilogue

After *Hipparchia's Choice* was published, Gilles Deleuze wrote to tell me he hoped I would at some point write about the figure of the fiancée in Kierkegaard's writings. I confess I saw no urgent reason to comment upon this personage, a young girl courted by a Pygmalion who, by abandoning her, subtly completes the process of endowing her with a mind. Or rather, I would not see the interest of it if it were not possible to connect this theme to the ending of *The Second Sex*. For Simone de Beauvoir gives the last word to Rimbaud: "man ... having let her go, she, too, will be a poet", a strange idea when one thinks of it, especially at the end of *The Second Sex*. If at school she had had to read Mary Wollstonecraft in English class, Anna Maria van Schurman in Latin, if a good history course had told her of the Anglo-American saga of women's right to vote, if in philosophy she had read Gabrielle Suchon and Harriet Taylor, if a popular edition of *The Book of the City of Ladies* had been available, would she have concluded her magnum opus as she did? Simone de Beauvoir in 1949, Kierkegaard, Rimbaud, and perhaps Deleuze seem to admit that a woman finds her way only in a state of abandonment—for which the initiative must come from the man. And what next? Can we count on the one here named "the man" to leave us to our destinies, whether by abandoning us or otherwise? The figure of the rejected fiancée suggests that we are dependent on the other sex for the freedom we may obtain, and that freedom comes through separation from them. All in all, it denies a woman's capacity to take the initiative for establishing even the ever-so-slight distance that emancipation implies. Once again, in this story man thinks he is God; he is the creator who puts the finishing touches to his creation by leaving his creation on her own.

However far we go back in the history of their relationship, Harriet Taylor never was a disciple of John Stuart Mill. Still less was she his creation. Even if there is an English edition of *La Nouvelle Héloïse* among the remains of their library housed at Somerville College, their story was not written in advance, by Rousseau or any other. This story of a real woman and a real man in philosophy is a double biography, not a novel, more interesting than the drama of two fictional people produced by a philosopher-novelist. Each stood up to the other, neither was completely under the "influence" of, or "incorporated" by, the other, but each had to defend her/himself against the other, each had a slight tendency to want too much from the other, as perhaps we all do. The commentators make another kind of fiction of it today when they reduce Harriet to having been only the friend and then the wife of John Stuart, absorbed in their relationship, and a negligible quantity in it, a silent angel in his shadow, wrongly placed by him on a pedestal from which she must be removed forthwith. Or, since we can hardly remove her, she is a shrew who quite simply never should have been part of the life of the founding father: it would be shocking, it seems, to see a man such as Mill being strongly attached to a woman.[1] The portrait of Xanthippe, wife of master Socrates, by Plato his disciple, perhaps derives from a very particular jealousy.

Just once, Harriet refers to John Stuart as destined to teach, but she does not say to teach her: "It is for *you* . . . to teach, such as may be taught, that the higher *kind* of enjoyment, the *greater* the *degree*."[2] Conflicting in many respects, their essays on marriage are not at odds on one point: both think that sexuality is wonderful; Taylor speaks lyrically of it, *sex in its true and finest meaning,* sexuality is a way of showing the highest and finest good of human nature, of perceiving the beauty of the material and spiritual world. The goal of creation is best fulfilled by infinitely refining the five senses given to us. Mill cites Robert Owen: sexuality with affection is chastity, sexuality without affection is prostitution, and he probably implies it to be so in marriage too. The rumors that their love was merely platonic seem quite implausible, but it is probably they themselves who prompted them, for an Owenist definition of chastity allows one to fool one's friends and deflect the curious without really lying. They had more than one important motive for doing so; John Taylor, the first husband, was in an awkward situation and doubt might have been cast upon Helen's legitimacy as his daughter. Not to mention the benefits, for one's tranquility, of concealing the details of one's life somewhat.

There was a time when, if ever I encountered a Mill scholar I would mention my interest in Harriet Taylor, "Oh? I was taught that she was quite insignificant!" was the immediate response, and so negligible indeed that no one took the trouble to form a personal opinion about the matter. Then, less than three minutes later: "Do you think their marriage was unconsummated?" The question pertains to the seven or eight years at the end of their life together, not to the twenty youthful years during which Mrs. John Taylor and Mr. Mill sometimes lived together in the country, went off to Paris accompanied by young Helen, or exchanged letters in which passion is mingled with great friendship. The rumor might have been reinforced by the fact that the declaration Mill insisted on writing in 1851 has now come to light:

> Being about, if I am so happy as to obtain her consent, to enter into the marriage relation with the only woman I have ever known, with whom I would have entered into that state; and the whole character of the marriage relations as

constituted by law being such as both she and I entirely and conscientiously disapprove, for this among other reasons, that it confers upon one of the parties to the contract, legal power and control over the person, property, and freedom of action of the other party, independent of her own wishes and will; I, having no means of legally divesting myself of these odious powers . . . feel it my duty to put on record a formal protest against the existing law of marriage . . . I declare it to be my will and intention, and the condition of the engagement between us, that she retains in all respects whatever the same absolute freedom of action, and freedom of disposal of herself . . . as if no such marriage had taken place; and I absolutely disclaim and repudiate all pretension to have acquired any *rights* whatever.[3]

Marriage will not give him any rights over Harriet's person; I understand this to mean they are marrying under the aegis of Owen. But numerous are our contemporaries for whom marriage is a man's acquisition of rights, and particularly sexual rights over a woman; thus, when a Victorian disavows all claims to the "odious powers", people conclude that he did not share Harriet's bed.

That was their business. We would have no reason whatsoever to discuss these rumors if they did not follow an all-too-familiar pattern in assuming there is something amiss in the sexuality of a woman of intellect, hence her ideas are worthless because they are the products of an abnormal sexuality. The end result of this blatantly circular reasoning is that a woman's idea is never worth considering. And curiously, no one seems to wonder about Mill's sexual life, in case these rumours of chastity were well founded, or about the impact either a state of virginity or an active sexuality might have had on his philosophy. In all fairness, and whether his own work was M1, M1 and M2, or only the *Logic* as he said, we should wonder whether celibacy, assuming celibacy to be an anomaly (the ultimate superstition, perhaps), inflected his theory of causality or of the laws of nature that are not causal. My own view is that the essays on marriage were written by a woman and a man who were lovers or on the point of becoming lovers, but that this question would be of no importance if their double biography did not seem to speak to us of our own life. Not everything in what she thought pleased him; he had trouble swallowing the *Enfranchisement*. And not everything in the *Subjection* would have pleased Taylor, who had criticized the self-styled arbiters of differences (*sic*). Not everything pleased her in Mill's essay on marriage, even though its conclusion was such that one would like to restate it: that is, if divorce existed, society, unjust in that as in everything, would treat the woman who had resorted to it much more harshly than it would treat a man. When Taylor or another woman undertakes an intellectual emancipation that is not a separation, society judges her initiative more severely than it does the devious strategy of Kierkegaard's fiancé, who seduces only to abandon.

The *Conformity* opens with a eulogy to tolerance. No one among us does enough to cultivate tenderness and sympathy; no one has enough kindness, no one is gentle enough, a morality in harmony with the new situations that emancipation brings into being. In a traditional couple, understanding or sympathy was unnecessary; each owed the other certain prescribed services and could assume she or he knew what to expect. Because every form of freedom won by the other makes her or him more unpredictable, and symmetrically a woman's mental emancipation brings her to discover that her man is mired in retrograde views, a wholehearted tolerance is more necessary than ever—it cushions both disagreements and surprises. The need for tolerance would also hold for a society where people were not stereotyped at all. Moreover, the formal aspect of this morality interests me. To say that no one has a good enough heart situates the whole of humanity always just a little beyond the grasp of each person. Whereas the problematics of identity are seeking an *ipseity* (I must be I), individuals here are caught up in a movement of surpassing themselves. To be "exactly alike", à la Sydney Smith, or "naturally different", is to remain always within the definite and the fixed. To those mobile people who have less predictable intersubjective relationships, a morality of understanding is necessary, but always just out of reach.

It is of our own life that these two romantics speak to us. I see John Stuarts in the rising generation—men who reveal themselves as such on the occasion of their first experience of fatherhood though not on other questions. They know, because their women partners know, that they owe the joys of fatherhood to the choice that motherhood has become, a gift of love toward them as well as a promise made to the child, thus a joy and no longer an obligation or an unhappy accident. Some men know how to acknowledge and thank the women to whom they owe their companions' freedom; what their fathers experienced as an alarming loss of power becomes for them a heightened humanity. To them, we must say that the pattern has more general implications because every freedom gained by the other opens a space for affectivity and for a dialogue that has at last become necessary. And to younger women, we must say that their life as it already is casts doubt on a very old idea, "if we had friendship, we would no longer have any need for justice, but if we had justice we would still have need of friendship." We women all have to know that this maxim is not true. Even if we had friendship or love, we would still need justice; but only when there is justice can the question of affectivity finally be posed, and differently now than during twenty-five centuries of philosophy. For that same tradition assured that the friend would see the friend as another self. That is neither what we want nor what we live and, I hope, even less what awaits us.

Notes

Introduction

1. François de Salignac de La Mothe Fénelon, *Fénelon on Education: A Translation of the "Traité de l'éducation des filles,"* trans. H. C. Barnard (Cambridge: Cambridge University Press, 1966), 48.

2. Anna Maria van Schurman, *De ingenii mulieribus ad doctrinam et meliores litteras aptitudine* (Leiden: Elzevir, 1641). English translation: Anna Maria van Schurman, *The Learned Maid* (London, 1659). See also English translation: *Whether a Christian Woman Should Be Educated and Other Writings from Her Intellectual Circle,* ed. and trans. Joyce L. Irwin (Chicago: University of Chicago Press, 1998).

3. Immanuel Kant, *Considérations sur le beau et le sublime* [1764], section III; French translation by M. David-Ménard, Paris, GF-Flammarion, 1990, p. 122. English translation: *Observations on the Feeling of the Beautiful and Sublime,* trans. John T. Goldthwait (Berkeley: University of California Press, 1960).

4. Christine de Pisan, *La Cité des dames,* ed. Thérèse Moreau and Eric Hicks (Paris: Stock/Moyen Age, 1986), 14–15. English translation: *The Book of the City of Ladies,* trans. Earl Jeffrey Richards (New York: Persea Books, 1982). Note: Christine's name can be spelled Pizan or Pisan.

5. See F. Mayeur, *L'Enseignement secondaire des jeunes filles sous la troisième République* (Paris: Presses de la Fondation nationale des sciences politiques, 1977); *L'Éducation des filles en France au XIXe siècle* (Paris: Hachette, 1979); Nicole Mosconi, *Femmes et savoir* (Paris: L'Harmattan, 1994).

6. Jacques Derrida, *Éperons: les styles de Nietzsche* (Paris: Flammarion, 1978). English translation: *Spurs: Nietzsche's Styles,* trans. Barbara Harlow (Chicago: University of Chicago Press, 1979), 65.

7. A devastating review by L. Scubla, of Sarah Kofman's *Aberrations, le devenir-femme d'Auguste Comte,* in *Le temps de la réflexion* (Paris: Gallimard, 1981), 506.

8. For instance, in Lorraine Code, *What Can She Know? Feminist Theory and the Construction of Knowledge* (Ithaca: Cornell University Press, 1991), there is a vaguely defined norm. Since "the sex of the knower is epistemologically significant," women may know differently from men. The simple result is that any intellectual woman whose work doesn't demonstrate a difference disappears. There is no mention of Marie or Irène Curie, in spite of their importance to women physicists as exemplary figures and to everyone because of their scientific achievements.

9. In 1902, a professor in Nancy thought he had discovered rays, that out of pure patriotism he named N rays; it was a mistake made in all good faith, based on mere experimental carelessness.

10. Quoted in an epigraph of Claire Michard-Marchal and Claudine Ribéry, *Sexisme et sciences humaines* (Lille: Presses universitaires de Lille, 1982).

1. Cast-offs

1. Paul Gauguin, *Avant et après.* Quoted by Pierre Leprohon, *Paul Gauguin* (Paris: Gründ, 1975), 15.

2. René Descartes, *Rules for the Direction of the Mind,* trans. Laurence J. Lafleur (Indianapolis: Bobbs Merrill, 1961), 10.

3. Book V of the *Republic* (451d, 454e, 546a ...) indicates that women and men are equally called upon to be Guardians of the polis, and thus to receive an education that culminates in philosophy. This is mentioned again in Book VII, 540c, in which Socrates says: "You mustn't think that in what I have been saying I have had men in mind any more than women— those of them born with the right natural abilities." Plato, *The Republic,* ed. G. R. F. Ferrari,

trans. Tom Griffith (Cambridge: Cambridge University Press, 2000), 250. For *noêsis*, see the *Timaeus* 28a, *Republic* VI, 511d; mathematics (and the operations of reason) produce contemplation in the soul, itself the work of a discursivity that relies on hypotheses (VI, 511 c-d); even if this form of contemplation is inferior to the intellectual activity attained in dialectical reasoning, the study of mathematics is a propaedeutic to philosophy, particularly because it "radically cleanses" the organ of the soul which is the power to know. If Platonic philosophy distinguishes between intellection and reasoning, it is nonetheless impossible within the framework it puts in place to isolate intellection by attributing it to people who possess only it, and no reasoning whatsoever.

4. Jean-Jacques Rousseau, *Émile*, trans. Barbara Foxley (London: Dent, 1993), 248.
5. G. W. F. Hegel, *Phenomenology of Spirit*, trans. A.V. Miller (Oxford: Clarendon Press, 1977), 4.
6. G.W.F. Hegel, *Hegel's Lectures on the History of Philosophy*, vol.3, trans. E.S. Haldane (London: Routledge and Kegan Paul, 1955), 550.
7. G. W. F. Hegel, *The Philosophy of Right*, trans. T. M. Knox (Oxford: Clarendon Press, 1942), 263.
8. Hegel, *Phenomenology*, 149.
9. *Hegel's Lectures*, 550.
10. Genevieve Lloyd, "The Man of Reason," in *Women, Knowledge, and Reality*, ed., Ann Garry and Marilyn Pearsall (Boston: Unwin Hyman, 1989), 124. Author's italics.
11. The term "folk epistemology" appears in an article by Miranda Fricker, "Intuition and Reason," *Philosophical Quarterly* 45, no. 179 (1995): 181.
12. See chapter 3, section 2 of the present work and my essay "L'homme et la nature dans les jardins de la science," *Revue internationale de philosophie* 4 (1986): 159.
13. I owe this example to a participant in a conference held by the association "Femmes et Mathématiques."
14. My thanks to David Colclough for *Jane Anger, Her Protection for Women, 1589*. Reprinted in S. Shepherd, *The Women's Sharp Revenge: Five Pamphlets from the Renaissance* (London: Fourth Estate, 1985), 36.
15. John Frazer, *Deuteroskopia: A Brief Discourse Concerning the Second Sight, Commonly So Called* (Edinburgh: Andrew Symson, 1702).
16. Gabrielle Suchon, *Traité de la morale et de la politique*, vol. 2 (Lyon: J. Certe, 1693), 14.
17. The term *épicène* comes from the language of the grammarians: *épicène* is a word that may refer to either sex. In French, *enfant* "child," *girafe* "giraffe," *souris* "mouse" are *épicènes*. Now it is also used to designate things that would be equally suitable for both sexes: an "epicene education" would be an education that would serve the material and moral interests of girls and boys equally. There are "unisex" hairdressers; the term *épicène* is the equivalent of this word, but in literary language.
18. Frazer, *Deuteroskopia*, 1.
19. "Popular superstition" is a historically produced category. There was a time when only kings and great men could avail themselves of the services of an astrologer. If governments today consult a clairvoyant they do not boast about it and businesses that recruit their executives according to their birth chart or numerological characteristics prefer to remain anonymous. But some decisionmakers, those for whom "the people" are bound to be someone else, were dabbling in the irrational at the end of the first millenium. See Caroline Brun, *L'Irrationel dans l'entreprise* (Paris: Balland, 1989).
20. Arthur Schopenhauer, *Le Monde comme volonté et représentation* [1818], vol. 2, 46. Quoted in André Dez, *Le Vouloir-Vivre* (Paris: PUF, 1956), 7. English translation: *The World as Will and Idea*, vol. 2, trans. R.B. Haldane and J. Kemp [1883] (London: Routledge and Kegan Paul, 1964), 53.
21. Schopenhauer, *The World as Will and Idea*, vol. 1, 65.
22. Henri Bergson, *Laughter: An Essay on the Meaning of the Comic*, trans. Cloudesley Brereton and Fred Rothwell (London: Macmillan and Co., 1911), 180.
23. Hélène Monsacré, *Les Larmes d'Achille: le héros, la femme et la souffrance dans la poésie d'Homère* (Paris: Albin Michel, 1984). For another example of a signifier that was first applied to men and then has come to be applied only to women: "they even dare to be themselves without being enslaved to the maxims of a *caillette* (magpie)" (Jean-Jacques Rousseau, *Lettre*

à d'Alembert. English translation: *Politics and the Arts: Letter to M. D'Alembert on the Theatre,* trans. Allan Bloom (Ithaca, N.Y.: Cornell University Press, 1968), 105.) *Caillette* (magpie), which here means a gossipy woman of little virtue, was used initially for men, taking its origin from a certain clownish Monsieur Caillette. In this application to the other sex, the invective takes on the supplementary meaning "little virtue," which is rarely said of men.

24. Suchon, *Traité de la morale,* vol. 1, 79, reprinted in part by S. Auffret (Paris: Éditions des femmes, 1988), 151–52.

25. Helen Deutsch, *The Psychology of Women,* vol.1 (New York: Grune and Stratton, 1944), 222.

26. Deutsch, *Psychology,* 290–91. Who is this Autonoë, the Wise One? In ancient literature there is a sea nymph of that name who was never anything but a body; a chambermaid, who goes in and out in a verse of the *Odyssey;* and a Theban woman, who participated in hacking Pentheus to pieces, which is not indicative of wisdom, intuitive or otherwise. There is some reason to think that psychoanalysis, a new form of knowledge at the time, has invented its own Greek mythology here, perhaps by virtue of an unconscious play on *autonoêtos* (which understands itself all by itself). No matter, if that puts women of intellect in the wrong! And where does Helen Deutsch locate herself in this story? However absurd it may be, her book is an example of learned research, which she claims is a masculine monopoly.

27. Deutsch, *Psychology,* 291.

28. Ibid.

29. Immanuel Kant, *The Conflict of the Faculties* [1798], trans. Mary J. Gregor (New York: Arabis Books, 1979), 31–41.

30. Ibid.

31. Kant, *Conflict,* 25.

32. Ibid., 27.

33. Aristotle, *Nichomachean Ethics,* in *The Basic Works of Aristotle,* ed. Richard McKeon, trans. W. D. Ross (New York: Random House, 1941), VI, 2, 1139b 5.

34. Kant, *Conflict,* 209.

35. Anna Maria van Schurman, *De ingenii muliebris ad doctrinam et meliores litteras aptitudine* (Leyden: Elzevir, 1641), 33. English translation:*Whether a Christian Woman Should Be Educated and Other Writings from Her Intellectual Circle,* ed. and trans. Joyce L. Irwin (Chicago: University of Chicago Press, 1998), 36.

36. François Poullain de la Barre, *De l'égalité des deux sexes* [1673] (reprint Paris: Fayard, 1984), 9. English translation:*The Equality of the Two Sexes,* trans. Daniel Frankforter and Paul J. Morman (Lewiston, N.Y.: Edwin Mellen, 1989), 4.

37. Ibid., 33 (French); 43 (English).

38. In 1675 Poullain wrote a piece called *De l'excellence de l'homme contre l'égalité des sexes,* which annuls the conclusions of *L'Égalité,* but I think that the problem is already evident in *L'Égalité.*

39. For a simple example see Bacon, *Advancement of Learning,* in vol. 3 of *The Works of Francis Bacon,* ed. J. Spedding, R. L. Ellis, and D. D. Heath, 1857–74 (reissued Stuttgart: F. F. Verlag, 1963), 480. (Hereafter Spedding.)

40. René Descartes, "Lettre à Mersenne", November 11, 1640, in *Correspondance de Descartes,* vol. 3, ed. Charles Adam and Gérard Milhaud (Paris: Alcan, 1899), 230–32. Descartes expresses his grievances against Voet or Voetius, "the most pedantic fellow in the world," who "is bursting with rage because there is a professor of medicine in their university of Utrecht who openly teaches my philosophy." He has done everything he can to have the examining magistrate bar him from teaching, but the Magistrate gave the teacher permission to teach as he wished.

41. Descartes, *Correspondance,* vol. 10, 214.

42. Francis Bacon, letter of April 20, 1622, in Spedding, vol. 14, 364.

43. Monseigneur Dupanloup, *La femme studieuse* (Paris: C. Guignol, 1869), 147.

44. Dupanloup, *La femme,* 65.

45. *Ecclesiastes,* 1:18 and following; I *Corinthians* 8:11.

46. At great risk, but supported by their readers both female and male, Mary Wollstonecraft, Simone de Beauvoir, and Kate Millett thought beyond the confines of an institutional framework; the "second wave" is the *women's studies* wave, oriented by postmodernism and the culture of difference. The periodization comes from the second wave, which regards the first

wave as obsolete and has constructed itself by relegating such Beauvoirians as Kate Millett or Ti-Grace Atkinson to the sidelines, along with the powerful questions they articulated. Since men govern the universities it would have been futile to hope that the traditional idea of what a woman may think, and how, would not infiltrate the development of women's studies that they allowed to come into being.

47. Claudine Hermann, *Les Voleuses de langue* (Paris: Éditions des femmes, 1976), 8–9. English translation: *The Tongue Snatchers*, trans. Nancy Kline (Lincoln: University of Nebraska Press, 1989), 7.

48. Joseph de Maistre, *Lettres et opuscules inédits*, vol. 1 (Paris: A. Vaton, 1851), 194.

49. "there is [. . .] a propriety in her patient, meticulous, restricted readings," "a certain [reverence and] respect [for key philosophical texts]," "an affirmation and acceptance of a masculine rationality," etc. This is from Elizabeth Grosz, *Sexual Subversions: Three French Feminists* (Winchester, Mass.: Unwin Hyman, 1989), 212. All of this echoes Meaghan Morris's challenge to *L'Imaginaire philosophique* (1980) (see Michèle Le Doeuff, *The Philosophical Imaginary*, trans. Colin Gordon [Stanford, Calif.: Stanford University Press, 1989]), which she reads as "a salvage operation to rescue philosophy from the more damaging charges of feminist critics in France." (Meaghan Morris, "Import Rhetoric: 'Semiotics in/and Australia,'" *The Foreign Bodies Papers*, series 1 [Sydney: Local Consumption, 1981–82], 77.) At a time when the idea that women should relinquish rationality (bound to be male) in favor of sentiment, or that philosophy is intrinsically to blame for phallocentrism was developing across the ocean, my first book endeavored to show that there is no pure rationality—anything that is thought in philosophy being woven into a web of images. The book may have been seen as negative intervention in a philosophical industry that was already thriving ("you are taking issue with an object that does not exist") or as an invitation to unseemly criticism of the philosophical heritage. As long as women take literally philosophy's claim to be purely rational and identify reason with masculinity and as long as they draw the conclusion that they should occupy themselves somewhere else, most of our male colleagues are not upset in the least. On the other hand, if a woman takes the philosophical project seriously, refuses to leave the territory, and maintains that no text meets philosophy's own high standards, that the a-rational determines the configuration of concepts and intellectual strategies, that there is no text that is not held together by an imaginary, something is shaken up; this bothers certain male colleagues and is a risky position to take.

50. Hermann, 165 (French); 135 (English).

51. Grosz, *Sexual Subversions*, 1.

52. Spedding, vol. 3, 327.

53. Spedding, vol. 3, 404. The expression *ad filios scientiarum* is common in Bacon's work; *filii* meaning "children of both sexes" or "son."

54. Suchon, *Traité*, vol. 2, 5. Isabelle Graesslé, a theologian, and Pierre Borgeaud, a historian of religion, kindly discussed this unusual interpretation with me. Translation of Biblical source by Ilya Parkins, following *Genesis*.

55. Suchon, *Traité*, vol. 2, 7.

56. In the seventeenth century a medieval Arab text by Ibn Tufayl, translated into Latin under the title *Philosophus autodidactus*, and later on into various modern languages, was much admired. Leibniz praised it, and the work was to inspire Daniel Defoe's *Robinson Crusoe*: the idea of autodidacticism was of interest at that time.

57. Suchon, *Traité*, vol. 2, 5 and 174.

58. "God intended this natural inclination [for knowledge] to be accompanied by necessity, usefulness, and pleasure. These three great attractions have complete power over the human spirit [. . .] their charms and enticements [. . .] Providence has given us this touch of natural curiosity." Pleasure is the end result of curiosity, the reward of all research, and there would never be any satisfaction in studying, reading, arguing . . . "without this curious attraction which contents and satisfies us" (Suchon, *Traité*, vol. 2, 238–40).

59. Suchon, *Traité*, vol. 2, 32.

60. Ibid., vol. 2, 44.

61. Ibid., vol. 2, 268.

62. Ibid., vol. 2, 23. See also Aristotle, *Rhetoric*, book 1, chapter XIII, 1373b.

63. Ibid., preface. Her comment: "Women have not yet made use of their pens in defense of their cause" would suggest that she does not know Marie de Gournay, nor Anna Maria van

Schurman, Diogenes Laertes, and/or Ménage, who would have alerted her to Hipparchia's existence. It is not certain that she acknowledges everything she has read.

64. "Great souls can find contentment only in sublime objects", *Ibid.*, vol. 2, 102 and 33.

65. Ibid., vol. 2, 206. "It appears to me that every creature has some notion—or rather relish, of the sublime. Riches, and the consequent state, are the sublime of weak minds," Mary Wollstonecraft notes in her novel, *Mary. Mary Wollstonecraft, Mary and Maria,* ed. Janet Todd (London: Pickering and Chatto, 1991), 22.

66. René Descartes, *Discourse on Method and Meditations on First Philosophy,* ed. David Weissman, trans. Elizabeth Haldane and G.R.T. Ross (New Haven, Conn.: Yale University Press, 1996), 8.

67. See Plato, *Symposium,* 201d.

68. Marie Le Jars de Gournay, *Égalité des hommes et des femmes* [1622 but augmented by the author until 1641] (Paris : Côté-Femmes, 1989), 72–73. The best edition is Geneva: Droz 1993, see 48.

69. Suchon, *Traité,* preface.

70. Suchon, *Traité,* preface.

71. Ibid., vol. 3, 11–12.

72. "Pleasant it is, when on the great sea the winds trouble the waters, to gaze from shore upon another's great tribulation: not because any man's troubles are a delectable joy, but because to perceive what ills you are free from yourself is pleasant." Lucretius, *De rerum natura,* trans. W.H.D. Rouse (Cambridge. MA: Harvard University Press & London: William Heinemann Ltd., 1982), Book 2, 1–4.

73. Sonia Bertolini has found a document that casts doubt on the episode of the papal decree that Philibert Papillon recounts in *Gabrielle Suchon: une écrivaine engagée pour une vie sans engagement* (Geneva: Faculté des Lettres, 1997).

74. Suchon, *Traité,* vol. 3, 37.

75. Ibid., foreword to vol. 3.

76. Suchon, *Traité,* vol. 3, 22.

77. Ibid., vol. 3, 36–37.

78. Ibid., vol. 3, 25 and 36.

79. "Equity is eternal, that is why it requires change in the laws," Suchon, *Traité,* vol. 3, 34.

80. Ibid., foreword.

81. Ibid., vol. 3, 32 and 136.

82. Ibid., vol. 3, 32.

83. Ibid., vol. 3, 24. And see Rousseau, "A Republic Needs Men," *Letter to d'Alembert.*

84. There is a summary of this text in my *Hipparchia's Choice,* 149.

85. Helena Kennedy, *Eve Was Framed* (London: Vintage, 1992); Odile Dhavernas, *Droits des femmes, pouvoir des hommes* (Paris: Seuil, 1978). See also the books of Catharine MacKinnon.

86. Rousseau, *Oeuvres complètes,* vol. 2 (Paris: Gallimard, 1995), 1254 (my emphasis).

87. Rousseau, "Lettre à Christophe de Beaumont" in *Oeuvres complètes,* 952.

88. Rousseau, *Émile* (Paris: Gallimard), 700–701. *Émile,* trans. Barbara Foxley (London: Dent, 1993), 391.

89. Mary Wollstonecraft, *A Vindication of the Rights of Woman* in Mary Wollstonecraft, *Political Writings* ed. Janet Todd (Toronto: University of Toronto Press, 1993), 92.

90. Wollstonecraft, *Vindication,* 76.

91. Ibid., 293.

92. Ibid., 275.

93. Ibid., 90.

94. Jean-Jacques Rousseau, *Discourse on the Sciences and Arts (First Discourse) and Polemics* in *The Collected Writings of Rousseau,* vol. 2, ed. Roger D. Masters and Christopher Kelly, trans. Judith D. Bush et al. (Hanover, N.H.: University Press of New England, 1992), 15.

95. Michèle Le Doeuff, "Problèmes d'investiture," *Nouvelles questions féministes* 6, no. 2 (1995).

96. Julia Annas, *An Introduction to Plato's Republic* (Oxford: Oxford University Press, 1981), 181 ff.

97. Annas, *Plato's Republic,* 182.

98. Ibid., 181. The same concern is evident in her contribution, "Plato's Republic and Feminism," to *Feminism and Ancient Philosophy,* ed. Julie K. Ward (London: Routledge, 1996).

99. Ibid., 183.
100. See Plato, *Republic,* III, 413–16. The myth that compares the three classes in the polis to metals—gold, silver, and iron—says that, in each class, parents will usually produce children of the same metal as themselves. There is, however, a risk that a silver child will be born into the gold class, and a chance that a golden offspring will be born into the silver class. In which case one must, "without pity," exclude the first child from the ranks of the Guardians and elevate the second child to this rank. I think the symmetry is merely apparent: the essential worry is that of seeing the Ideal City fall into the hands of the unworthy, an event that would cause it to perish, rather than to be short of future Guardians. But if there is a kind of metallic heredity, Plato perhaps judged it necessary to select the future mothers of golden children.
101. *Republic,* V, 465a.
102. Plato, *La République,* in *Oeuvres Complètes,* vol. 2, ed. and trans. Léon Robin (Paris: Gallimard, 1950).
103. Plato, *La République,* ed. and trans. Robert Baccou (Paris: Flammarion, 1966).
104. According to Claude Mossé, various Athenian documents that bear on succession and other juridical acts allow us to see that, in reality, matrimonial connections were more complex than the norm suggests. See Claude Mossé, *Politique et société en Grèce ancienne: le modèle athénien* (Paris: Aubier, 1995), 28.
105. Plato, *Theaetetus,* 174a.
106. *Republic,* X, 614ff and 620a ff. In this text there is a theory of underlying resentment with respect to misadventures attached to sexual life (Orpheus) or with respect to human life as such. But above all the myth sets out a continuity of existential interests that is stronger than sexual identity: Atalanta chose the life of a male athlete since she was incapable of resisting the appeal of sporting honors; Épéios, the builder of the Trojan horse, is drawn to "the naturalness of a skilled woman."
107. In France, in the six years following the legalization of abortion and its inclusion in Social Security coverage, the number of abortions on demand decreased by 11 percent.
108. Gilles Lipovetsky, *La Troisième femme: permanence et révolution du féminin* (Paris: Gallimard, 1997).
109. A spectacular version of the test aimed at establishing whether someone prefers the study of wisdom to the acquisition of material goods and social standing was invented by Diogenes the Cynic: "Someone wanted to study philosophy with him. Diogenes invited the man to follow him through the streets dragging a herring behind him. The man was ashamed, threw the herring away, and departed." See Diogenes Laertes, *Vies, doctrines et sentences des philosophes illustrés,* vol. 2 (Paris, GF-Flammarion, 1965), 19. If we find women in the School of the Cynics it may be because, in it, the philosophical way of life is seen as a departure from the way people ordinarily live and from concern about what others will think: it was, in effect, an uprooting for everyone, men and women, particularly with respect to standing or prestige. "It is thanks to exile that I became a philosopher," Diogenes went on to say (Ibid., 24): here, exile could well be a metaphor for all kinds of discontinuity. By contrast, those who maintain that women would not be able to do philosophy imagine that philosophy exists in continuity with their male mode of existence, along with its social advantages.
110. Gregory Vlastos, "Was Plato a Feminist?" *Times Literary Supplement,* March 17, 1989. Reprinted in Daniel W. Graham, ed., *Studies in Greek Philosophy,* vol. 2 (Princeton, N.J.: Princeton University Press, 1995).
111. Plato, *The Apology,* in *The Apology, Phaedo and Crito of Plato,* ed. Charles W. Eliot, trans. Benjamin Jowett (New York: Collier, 1909), 41a-c, 28.
112. Bonnie G. Smith shows that nineteenth-century male historians invented a new space for knowledge, the closed seminar, accessible only by invitation, and that they saturated this new place with virile values. See her "Gender and Practices of Scientific History: The Seminar and Archival Research in the Nineteenth Century," *American Historical Review* 100, no. 4 (October 1995).
113. Plato, *Phaedrus* 246 ff. Hera is named later in the text (252c). The twelve divinities are undoubtedly those, well known to every Athenian, who appeared on the altar erected by Pisistratus on the Agora, says R. Hackforth, in *Plato's Phaedrus* (Cambridge: Cambridge University Press, 1952).

114. The Heideggerians and Luce Irigaray fantasize a great deal about the figure of Hestia. See Jean-Joseph Goux, "L'oubli d'Hestia," *Langages* 85 (March 1987), who assimilates the forgetfulness of being with the loss of *Heimat* (home) and with rootlessness. It is necessary, he says, to recover a "forgotten guardianship, and this can be assured only by female virginity *[garde oubliée que seule la virginité féminine peut assurer]*." A note of Irigaray's specifies that this virginity is to be understood as fidelity of the feminine to its gender in the sacred dimension of the dwelling place. All of this does not simply amount to a return to conservative and even fascist norms, but to an injunction given to women to be traditional and at home, so that Heideggerian philosophy can come true. All things considered, I prefer Plato, for whom Hestia merely represents one feminine figure among others and not the common essence of the feminine. Every project that seeks to examine Platonic philosophy as a function of a possible representation of the *feminine* that might have been his (if Plato had a representation of something that one could name as such) should take note of the fact that Hestia is never more than a goddess among several others.

115. Annas, *Plato's Republic*, 183, commenting on *Republic* 563b.

116. *Republic*, 276.

117. *Republic*, Book 3, 414b.

118. Plato specialists say that the term "dialectic" is a floating signifier: its sense varies from one dialogue to another. Thus the fact that the future Guardians, both female and male, learn "dialectic" guarantees nothing.

119. R. H. Barrow, *Slavery in the Roman Empire* (New York: Dial Press, 1928), quoted in Hannah Arendt, *The Human Condition* (New York: Anchor Books, 1958), 129.

120. Évelyne Le Garrec, *Les Messagères* (Paris: Éditions des femmes, 1976), 40–41.

121. Plato, *Laws*, 817e-822.

122. See the *Odyssey*, IX, 114; Plato, *Laws*, vol. 1, trans. R. G. Bury (London: Heinemann, 1926), III, 680b. See also Aristotle, *Nichomachean Ethics*, X, 10, 1180a 25 and *Politics*, I, 2, 1252b 20.

123. Plato, *Laws*, VI, 783d; see also *Republic*, V, 460e and Aristotle, *Politics*, VII, 16, 1335b 18.

124. Plato, *Laws*, Bury translation, 780a-781a.

125. Ibid., 784a-e.

126. Ibid., 784b.

127. Plato, *Theaetetus* 148e and 149d.

128. I *Corinthians*, 14:34–35; I *Timothy*, 2:11–15 and 3.11; see also 4: 7.

129. *Titus*, 2:3–5.

130. Henri Estienne, *Commentaire de Diogène Laërce* (Geneva, 1570); Gilles Ménage, *Historia Mulierum Philosopharum* [1690], in *Commentaires sur Diogène Laërce*, vol. 2 (1692).

131. Eduard Zeller, *Die Philosophie der Griechen in ihrer Geschichtlichen Entwicklung* (Leipzig: Fues, 1865–75), vol. 3, 84. English translation: *A History of Greek Philsophy from the Earliest Period to the Time of the Present* (Longmans, Green and Co.: 1881). See also F. Wilhelm, "Die Oeconomica der Neupythagoreer Bryson," *Rheinisches Museum*, LXX (1915), 161–223.

132. Mario Meunier, *Femmes pythagoriciennes: fragments et lettres* (Paris: L'Artisan du Livre, 1932). Thanks to Michel Onfray for the reference.

133. Luce Irigaray, *Je, tu, nous: vers une culture de la différence* (Paris: Editions Grasset et Fasquelle, 1990). English translation: *Je, tu, nous: Toward a Culture of Difference* (New York: Routledge, 1993), 19.

134. Irigaray, *Toward a Culture*, 12.

135. Plato, *Laws* III, 689.

136. Ibid., II, 663–64.

137. Plato, *Republic*, III, 414b.

138. Plato, *Republic*, IX, 590a. Without the support of Monique Labrune and Susanne Bobzien, I am not sure that I would have dared to say all of this.

139. Hegel, *Phénoménologie de l'esprit*, vol. 2, 41. *Phenomenology of Spirit*, 287–88.

140. Jeanne Hersch, "Eve ou la naissance éternelle du temps," *Textes* (Fribourg: Le Feu de Nuict, 1985), 27.

141. Genesis 3:16.

142. Leigh Hunt, "Bluestocking Revels," *Monthly Repository* (July 1837): 33–57.

2. Renaissances

1. Anonymous, *Women Doctors* (London: Groombridge and Son, 1867).
2. Natalie Zemon Davis, review of *The Renaissance Notion of Women: A Study in the Fortunes of Scholasticism and Medical Science in European Intellectual Life,* by Ian Maclean, *The Renaissance Quarterly* 34, no. 2 (summer 1981).
3. Charles Webster, *The Great Instauration* (London: Duckworth, 1975), 255.
4. Sandra L. Chaff et al., *Women in Medicine* (Metuchen, N.J.: Scarecrow Press, 1977).
5. Aristotle, *Poetics,* trans. Stephen Halliwell (Cambridge, Mass.:Harvard University Press, 1995), 1451b and Aristotle, *Topica,* trans. E.S. Forster (London: William Heinemann, 1960), book II, chapter xi, 115b 10.
6. Using inscriptions on funeral urns, archaeologists have established the existence of *elatreiua* or *latrive* in Greece, and *medicae* in Rome; A. Chéreau (*L'Union médicale,* 31: 93 [August 7, 1866], 241–48), notes that eight female practitioners are included on a Paris tax roll in 1292. In their discussions of Jewish doctors of both sexes, both Richard Landau and Jutta Rall base their arguments on similar proof: in the fifteenth century women must have practiced medicine in Frankfurt, for some are listed on tax rolls in their capacity as medical practitioners.
7. Oliva de Sabuco des Nantes Barrera, *Nueva Filosofia* [. . .], dedicated to Philip II of Spain, and reprinted in the sixteenth, seventeeth, and eighteenth centuries. In 1707, the Inquisition compiled a list of passages to be expunged. A modern edition was published in 1981 (Madrid, Editora Nacional, Biblioteca de Visionarios, heterodox y marginalos).
8. J.-M. Guardia, a double article published in *La Revue philosophique* (1886), 42–60 and 272–92. "Are women capable of philosophy? [. . .] Conceding that women are capable of masculine conceptualizing and creative originality is based on a misunderstanding of the physiological attributes of each sex, and a willful refusal to distinguish what nature has quite clearly separated."
9. Two useful books: Barbara Ehrenreich and Deirdre English, *For Her Own Good* (New York: Anchor Press, 1978); Bonnie S. Anderson and Judith P. Zinsser, *A History of Their Own* (London, Penguin: 1988). See also Caroline Schultze-Bertillon, *Les Femmes médecins* (Paris, 1889), and Melanie Lipinska, *Les Femmes médecins* (Paris: G. Jacques, c. 1930).
10. These notes were published after her death: see Elizabeth Grey, *A Choice Manual of Rare and Select Secrets in Physicks and Chyrurhery, Collected and Practiced by the Countess of Kent late Deceased* (London, 1653). This publication was very successful: a fifteenth edition appeared eleven years after the first (Edinburgh, 1664). She invented a remedy for certain infectious diseases and melancholia, known even in the twentieth century as Grey's Powder or Kent's Powder.
11. See E. Joyce Cockram, "Tribute to Sabine," *Journal of the Medical Women's Federation* 43 (July 3, 1961): 86–89.
12. Plato notes the duality: he contrasts medicine for slaves, practiced by auxiliaries who themselves are slaves and who prescribe what is dictated by habit without any explanation of the disease, with medicine practiced for free men by practitioners who themselves are free, who have the patient explain his difficulties and who in turn explain their diagnosis to the patient. See Plato, *Laws,* vol. 1 trans. R. G. Bury (London: Heinemann, 1926), 307, 720a.
13. This division between two categories of medicine was still current in the seventeenth century: the fifteenth edition of Grey's *Choice Manual* (Edinburgh, 1664) includes *addenda* written by a professor of medicine who took Grey's remedy seriously enough to test it on patients. If we compare his experiment to her own account, we can see the categories defined by the professor. He tested the remedy on five children, two male adolescents, two women of breeding, a girl, and a young woman for the following problems: phlegm, convulsions, smallpox, abdominal or stomach pain, hysteria, and a probable case of plague. The absence of men, noble or otherwise, is noteworthy; he used the powder on patients who in his opinion could have been treated by Grey herself, although she herself also treated men. And according to the countess, her powder was a remedy for infectious diseases and melancholia. But melancholia is a noble disorder, gentlemen and men of genius suffer from it; women and children merely have stomach aches! The professor's procedure thus followed the social division of diseases and medical practitioners. It was kind of him to take the trouble to

validate a remedy invented by a woman. But since there was no record of any cases for which the remedy was ineffective, the test falls short of the demands of scientificity.

14. Boccaccio tells the story of a certain Helena. She cured a king whom the "great doctors" had been unable to cure (this story is found in Shakespeare's *All's Well That Ends Well*). In dealing with periods that have not left documents as reliable as tax rolls, funerary inscriptions, or royal authorizations, historians resort to literary sources for lack of anything better, for example, an article on female doctors in the Viking era, published in the *British Medical Journal* of January 20, 1917, cites Nordic sagas as evidence.

15. A. Chéreau, *L'Union médicale* 31, no. 93 (August 7, 1866): 241–48; Marcel Beaudoin, *Gazette médicale*, 22 (June 1, 1901); Muriel Joy Hughes, *Women Healers in Medieval Life and Literature* (New York: King's Crown Press, 1943). The trial of Jacoba Félicie is of particular interest because some of her patients who had been cured testified on her behalf; however, this is far from a unique case.

16. Virginia Woolf, *A Room of One's Own*, ed. Morag Shiach (Oxford: Oxford University Press, 1992), 34.

17. Francis Bacon, *Advancement of Learning, The Works of Francis Bacon*, vol. 3, ed. James Spedding et al., 1857–74 (reissued Stuttgart: F.F. Verlag, 1963), 373; French translation: *Du progrès et de la promotion des savoirs* (Paris: Gallimard, 1991), 147.

18. "Whereof numbers do escape with less difficulty than they did in the Roman proscriptions." Bacon relates the comment of a Jewish doctor comparing his Christian confreres to bishops: all they know how to do is pronounce the patient incurable or declare that he will survive. Ibid., 375.

19. See Woolf, *Room*, 116. Marilena de Souza Chaoui has allowed me to relate the following anecdote. A committee was about to name her the first female professor of philosophy in Brazil. Someone pointed out that she was still of childbearing age, and proposed to make her election conditional on her being sterilized.

20. Linda Nochlin, *Women, Art, and Power and Other Essays* (New York: Harper and Row, 1988).

21. Maurice Merleau-Ponty, *La Phénoménologie de la perception* (Paris: Gallimard, 1978), 182. English translation: *The Phenomenology of Perception*, trans. Colin Smith (London: Routledge and Kegan Paul, 1962), 156.

22. W. Rawley, *The Life of Francis Bacon*, in Spedding, vol. 1, 3. From Anne Cook comes a translation with a preface and dedication, *Sermons of Barnardine Ochine of Siena, Godlye, frutefull and very necessary for all true Christians, translated out of Italien into Englishe*, and another of Jewel's *An Apology or Answere in Defence of the Churche of Englande*.

23. The exaltation of the female sex is a genre developed in proximity to female monarchs. In addition to Boccaccio and Christine de Pisan, we may note Antoine Dufour's *Les Vies des femmes célèbres*, as well as Marie de Gournay, to a certain extent; Agrippa's work, dedicated to Marguerite of Burgundy, is related to this genre and to the skeptical essay. In 1530, he published *De l'incertitude et de la vanité des savoirs*. For is it not true that the most polemical manner of demonstrating the uncertainty of everything in human doctrines consists in using the most deeply rooted of these doctrines, the inferiority of women, and showing that it can be reversed? It is said that pregnant woman have a craving for charcoal, but the fact is that they digest it. This is the principle underlying an extraordinary manipulation of signs. In this instance, the excellence of women is but a pretext aimed at demonstrating the validity of skepticism: we can know nothing with certainty if we cannot even demonstrate the validity of a notion as transparent as that of masculine superiority. We have already noted that Poullain de la Barre's *De l'égalité des deux sexes* follows a similar principle.

24. Sor Juana Inès de la Cruz, *La Respuesta* [1691], cf. *The Answer/La Respuesta*, ed. and trans. Electa Arenal and Amanda Powel (New York: The Feminist Press, 1994). The translators point out that the title of "doctor of the Church" was informally given to Theresa by nuns writing as early as the sixteenth century.

25. Jakob Burckhardt, *Die Kultur der Renaissance in Italien* (Basel, 1860), section 5. English translation: *The Civilization of the Renaissance in Italy*, trans. S.G.C. Middlemore (London: Phaidon, 1995), 256.

26. According to Servius, a fifth-century commentator of Virgil, in the absence of a man, sometimes a woman is obliged to assume responsibility for his mission.

27. Paul Hoffman, *La Femme dans la pensée des Lumières* (Paris: Ophrys, 1977).

28. Anderson and Zinsser, op. cit., vol. 2, 83.

29. Bertrand Russell, *The Scientific Outlook* (London: Allen and Unwin, 1931), 17; and Bertrand Russell, *Unpopular Essays* (London: Allen and Unwin 1950; reprint, London: Routledge, 1995), 115 (page citation is to the reprint edition).

30. Russell, *The Scientific Outlook,* 16.

31. "Population: The Battle of the Bulge," *The Economist,* September 3, 1994, 23–25.

32. The expression "neutral masculine" (the masculine taken as neuter) was coined by Nicole Mosconi; an example is *and he shall be whole* (*he,* the patient, standing for both sexes). An opposite example is found in Elizabeth Grey. In a prescription specifying six drams of a particular ingredient, she indicates that this is the formula for a woman; for a man, eight drams would be needed.

33. Sir Humphrey Gilbert, *Queene Elizabethes Achademy,* [circa 1570], ed. Furnival (London: Early English Text Society, 1869).

34. My thanks to Margaret Bridges, an active participant in my Geneva seminar, for this observation.

35. In her edition (London: Croom Helm, 1981) of the Sloane manuscript (2463, British Museum), Beryl Rowland notes that "Trott" means an old woman in several European languages. I think that initially *Trotula* may have been a title formed from "troph (to feed)," since some elements of the text come from Greek medicine.

36. The theories advanced in a sixteenth-century English manuscript now in the Yale University Library are teleological and optimistic: menstruation is a good thing, as are sexual intercourse and pregnancy. When I was an adolescent, we would laugh at medical pronouncements about almost anything, that "puberty/marriage/the first child will put an end to that". Cf. *The Sekeness of Wymmen,* ed. M. R. Hallaert, *Scripta* (Brussels: Omirel, 1982), 8.

37. Jean-Paul Dumont, *Les Présocratiques* (Paris: Gallimard, 1988), xix.

38. Soranus summarizes the debate. Although he sees pregnancy and lactation as the sex-specific activities they are, he also says that women's diseases are not distinct. On the other hand, Galen does not recognize gynaecology as a specialty, although he considers that pediatrics and geriatrics are specialized fields. Cf. the *Oxford Dictionary of Classics,* article on "Gynaecology".

39. *Women's Problems in General Practice,* ed. Ann McPherson (Oxford: Oxford University Press, 1993).

40. Positive therapeutic results are obtained by treating premenstrual disorders as a function of general health or as a result of an unbalanced diet rather than an effect of destiny or excessive imagination. And if one pays serious attention to the complaints of the patient at such times, sometimes one's perspective is reversed. It is not when a woman manifests premenstrual anger at a violent alcoholic husband that she suffers from a disorder requiring treatment; rather, it is when she is excessively patient that she must be helped to question herself, and it is the husband who should be treated. Such a notion could be a paradigm: we should question our forbearance rather than those occasional moments of bad temper.

41. Mrs. [Margaret] Oliphant, *Madam* (London: Longmans, Green and Co., 1885), 6.

42. Collective publication by "L'action locale Bellevue" (Paris: Éditions du CNRS, 1986).

43. My usual modesty will not prevent me from pointing out that for a quarter of a century I have been working on the philosophical imaginary, which supposes that this imaginary is incorporated into the history of philosophy and that the "imaginary" varies according to the disciplinary fields under consideration.

44. French edition: Uta Ranke-Heinemann, *Des eunuques pour le royaume des cieux* (Paris: R. Laffont, 1990). English translation: Uta Ranke-Heinemann, *Eunuchs for Heaven: The Catholic Church and Sexuality,* trans. Peter Heinegg (London: A. Deutsch, 1990). I am indebted to this book for the exceptional erudition I am able to display here.

45. Ute Ranke-Heinemann and I have exchanged letters. She wrote this wonderful phrase: "I was excommunicated for heresy, which enables me to commune with other heretics." The interdisciplinarity defended by feminist studies could be summarized in the same way; feminist authors, considered insubordinate in their respective disciplines, see a community of insubordination.

46. *Matthew* 19:12.

47. Hannah Arendt, "Lying in Politics," in *Crises of the Republic* (New York: Harvest Books, 1972).

48. Ibn Khaldun, *The Muqaddimah,* ed. and trans. Franz Rosenthal (New York: Pantheon Books, 1958).

49. Amartya Sen, "More than 100 Million Women Are Missing," *The New York Review of Books* December 20, 1990.
50. Syndicat des avocats de France, *Entrave à l'IVG* ["Obstruction of Abortion"], April 1996. Cf. Odile Dhavernas, "Entrave à l'IVG," *Revue juridique d'Île-de-France*, no. 44–45 (February–June 1997).
51. Cf. "Les chevaux d'Edouard," my challenge to the politicians on behalf of the French Family Planning Association, at the 1991 conference on *L'Europe & Elles*, published in the conference proceedings.
52. See Dhavernas, "Entrave," op. cit.
53. Dhavernas, "Entrave," 68.
54. Document available from the Syndicat des Avocats de France, 21 *bis*, rue Victor-Massé, 75009 Paris. However, the jurisprudence does instruct us unequivocally about the relationships between the "rights of man" and the "rights of women."
55. M. Albistur and D. Armogate, *Histoire du féminisme français*, vol. 1 (Paris: Éditions des femmes, 1977), 133. The authors, our contemporaries, quote enough to show the agreement between the two Renaissance writers. Christine writes: "If little girls were customarily sent to school and taught sciences just as sons are, they would learn just as well and would understand the subtleties of the arts and sciences as well as boys," Ibid., 84. Agrippa writes: "Souls are exempt from the law of the sexes; in both women and men, there is the same mind for thinking, the same reason for understanding, and the same language for communicating thought," Ibid., 135.
56. Benedict de Spinoza, *Traité politique*, trans. Charles Apphun (Paris: GF-Flammarion, 1966), 114. English translation: Benedict de Spinoza, *Tractatus Politicus* in *The Political Works*, ed. and trans. A. G. Wernham (Oxford: Clarendon Press, 1958), 443.
57. G. W. F. Hegel, *The Philosophy of Right*, trans. T. M. Knox (Oxford: Clarendon Press, 1942).
58. The text is in Francis Peck, *Desiderata curiosa* (London, 1732), book VII, 22. Reference in the *Calendar of State Papers*, Domestic Series, vol. 1547–1580, August 9, 1561, 182. Elizabeth sent it to William Cecil, Chancellor of Cambridge, with a letter ordering that it be communicated to all the colleges and posted in prominent places.
59. Elizabeth's text circulated in manuscript form; the archives contain several copies. See Peck, VII, 42.
60. This idea was defended by Marc Bloch and Pierre Riché, and is found again in Anderson and Zinsser, vol. 1, 24. On convents, see ibid., vol. 1, 191.
61. Maria Dzielska, *Hypatia of Alexandria* (Cambridge, Mass.: Harvard University Press, 1995).
62. George Steiner, "Bad Friday," *The New Yorker*, March 2, 1992, 86–91.
63. Henri Arquillière, *L'Augustinisme politique* (Paris: Vrin, 1934).
64. Aristotle, *Politics*, vol. 9 of *The Works of Aristotle*, ed. and trans. W. D. Ross (Oxford: Clarendon Press, 1925), book 2, 9, 1270a23. See also Plato, *Laws*, 5, 742c and 6, 774b. The (relative) economic power of certain women troubles Plato. The law, and not their fathers, ought to regulate the marriage of the *epikleroi;* the Athenian principle of limits on dowries ought to be strengthened so that there is "less insolence on the part of the wives and less humiliation on the part of the husband because of money." Masculine citizenship and military functions seem to be at the heart of this concern. If *epikleroi* or girls with dowries are married to foreigners, citizens are impoverished and thus less able to pay for a horse or weapons. If inheritance by the female line renders husbands "servile", it is no longer certain that they can be good citizens. The *epikleroi* also exist as a target of criticism.
65. Aristippus asks that his children be endowed with goods that "can swim with them in a shipwreck," meaning with knowledge like that which enabled him to survive on Rhodes when a storm washed him ashore there.
66. Elizabeth Rogers, ed., *The Correspondence of Sir Thomas More* (Princeton, N.J.: Princeton University Press, 1947), 120–23. The letter is thought to date from May 1518. I base my reading on the translation by Jean-Claude Margolin, *Revue philosophique de la France et de l'étranger* (October–December 1956): 543–47.
67. Christine de Pisan, *La Cité des dames*, ed. Thérèse Moreau et Eric Hicks (Paris: Stock/Moyen-Âge, 1986), 51. English translation: *The Book of the City of Ladies*, trans. Earl Jeffrey Richards (New York: Persea Books, 1982), 19.
68. Information on the Nogarola sisters comes from the chapter "Education for What?" in Anthony Grafton and Lisa Jardine, *From Humanism to the Humanities: Education and the*

Liberal Arts in Fifteenth- and Sixteenth-Century Europe (Cambridge, Mass.: Harvard University Press, 1986).

69. My thanks to David Norbrook, for the gift of Martha Monlsworth, *My Name was Martha: A Renaissance Woman's Autobiographical Poem.* Ed., with commentary by Robert C. Evans and Barbara Weidemann (West Cornwall, CT: Locust Hill Press, 1993).

70. Christine de Pisan, *La Cité des dames* 276; *Book of the City of Ladies,* 255.

71. My generation read *Les Héritiers* by Pierre Bourdieu and Jean-Claude Passeron (schooling ensures the perpetuation of the intellectual capital of the family) without ever asking whether the situations of male and female students were distinguished adequately from one another. Better late than never!

72. *Femmes en tête.* Interviews by Françoise Barret-Ducrocq and Evelyne Pisier (Paris: Flammarion, 1997).

73. Demetrius Zambaco, "Onanisme avec troubles nerveux chez deux petites filles" [Onanism with nervous disorders in two female children], in *L'Encéphale,* 1882 (Reissued Paris: Solin, 1978), 44.

74. J. L. Vivès, *De Institutione Feminae Christianae: Liber Primus* in vol. 6 and 7 of *Selected Works of J. L. Vivès,* ed. C. Matheusen, C. Fantazzi, trans. C. Fantazzi and E. J. Brill (Leiden: New York, E. J. Brill, 1996). Vivès writes: "The climate of northern Thrace is bitterly cold but Pomponius Mela writes this of its inhabitants: 'There is no lack of spirit in the women either; their fondest wish is to be killed and buried together with their dead spouses and since many women are married to the same husband at the same time, they hotly contend for this privilege before those assigned to give judgment. The decision is based on moral conduct and it is a great cause of joy to win in these contests.' Serious writers have recorded that Indian women used to vie with one another in this same manner" (vol. 7, 201–203).

75. Petition published in *La Revue du Mauss.*

76. Cf. Hélène Meynaud, paper presented at the conference on "Pathologies du lien social et société contemporain" (Contemporary society and the pathologies of social relationships), Quebec, 1996.

77. Vivès, *Selected Works,* vol. 1, 39. (Please note that this and all subsequent citations of Vivès refer to the English edition already cited.)

78. Vivès, *Selected Works.*

79. Ibid. In the original, this is an amusing detail: according to the table of contents, the chapter title is *Qui virgini legendi auctores, qui non*—which authors she must read and which she must not read. In the book itself, the chapter title is *Qui non legendi scriptores, qui legendi,* which writers must not be read and which are necessary. He clearly does not know what to put first!

80. Vivès, *Selected Works,* vol. 1, 43.

81. Ibid., vol. 1, 50.

82. Ibid., vol. 1, 15.

83. Ibid., vol. 1, 5.

84. I am quoting *Le Télégramme de Brest et de l'Ouest* from memory.

85. *Le Télégramme,* vol. 1, 91.

86. Ibid., vol. 1, 19–21.

87. Ibid., vol. 1, 19.

88. Ibid., vol. 1, 107.

89. Nicolas Malebranche, *La Recherche de la vérité* [1675], ed. Geneviève Rodis-Lewis (Paris: Vrin, 1965), 140–41. English translation: Nicolas Malebranche, *The Search after Truth,* trans. Thomas M. Lennon and Paul J. Olcamp (Columbus: Ohio State University Press, 1980), 131–32.

90. François de Salignac de La Mothe Fénelon, *Oeuvres complètes,* vol. 5 (Geneva: Slatkine Reprints, 1971), 591–94. English translation: *Fénelon on Education: A Translation of the "Traité de l'éducation des filles,"* trans. H. C. Barnard (Cambridge: Cambridge University Press, 1966), 78.

91. Descartes, "Letter to M . . .", March 1638, *Oeuvres de Descartes,* vol. 2, ed. Charles Adam and Paul Tannery, (Paris: Vrin, 1898), 46.

92. Helen Deutsch, *Psychology of Women,* conclusion.

93. Dedicating the work to his "dear wife and companion"who already has two daughters and perhaps a third yet to be born, this anonymous translator wants to convince her to educate

herself in order to educate her daughters; in principle, "simple people, the lower classes, women," are well enough taught by preaching, but sermons "go in one ear and out the other, as if they were tales of the stork or vain and silly fables," thus it is essential to know how to read. In response to Vivès's repressive statements, he offers an optimistic vision, valid for both sexes: "Nature has endowed us with instincts and inclinations that are like sparks of the divine fire that lights our souls; but they are quickly smothered if they are not encouraged," and "nurture surpasses nature." He ascribes docility to his wife, which in this context means a facility for learning and sufficient judgment to understand what she learns.

94. Christine de Pisan, "My dear child, what ever has happened to your critical judgement?" *La Cité des Dames*, 39; *Book of the Ladies*, 6.
95. Ibid., 179 (French); 154 (English).
96. Arendt, 37–41.
97. Christine de Pisan, *La Cité des dames* 42; *Book of the City of Ladies*, 10.
98. Catherine Pozzi, *Peau d'âme* [1935] (Paris: La Différence, 1990), 28–31.

3. An Epistemology of Hope

1. Pierre Thuillier, *Les Passions du savoir: Essais sur les dimensions culturelles de la science* (Paris: Fayard, 1988), 72–77, referring to Carolyn Merchant, *The Death of Nature: Women, Ecology and the Scientific Revolution* (San Francisco: Harper and Row, 1980).
2. Robin Briggs, *Witches and Neighbours* (London: Fontana Press, 1996), 257.
3. Marina Yaguello, *Le Sexe des mots* (Paris: Belfond, 1989).
4. Octave Mannoni, *Clefs pour l'imaginaire* (Paris: Seuil, 1969).
5. Thuillier, *Les Passions*, 73.
6. Evelyn Fox Keller, "Women Scientists and Feminist Critics of Science," *Daedalus: Journal of the American Academy of Arts and Letters*, 116, no. 4 (Fall 1987): 77–91 (Hereafter "Women Scientists".) and *Reflections on Gender and Science* (New Haven, CT: Yale University Press, 1985), 33. (Hereafter *Reflections.*)
7. Keller, "Women Scientists," 79.
8. Bruno Bettelheim, "The Commitment Required of a Woman Entering a Scientific Profession in Present-Day American Society"; and Erik H. Erikson, "Concluding Remarks," in *Women and the Scientific Professions*, ed. Jacqueline A. Mattfield and Carol E. Van Aken (Cambridge, Mass.: MIT Press, 1965). Nancy Hopkins, "The High Price of Success in Science," *Radcliffe Quarterly* 10 (June 1976): 16–18.
9. Keller, "Women Scientists," 86.
10. Hopkins, "Success in Science," n.p.
11. Keller, "Women Scientists," 79.
12. Ibid., 85.
13. Ibid., 84–5.
14. Between Vitruvius's description of Archimedes' works and Bacon's version, there is a clear discrepancy with regard to "methodological preferences." Yet all three were of the same sex, just as Lamarck and Darwin were. Jean-Marc Lévy-Leblond once explained that Einstein could have approached his work in a manner quite different from the one he chose. However, Jean-Marc and Albert . . . or else one is forced to believe that relativity was invented by Mileva Maric. We see no unanimity among learned men, no common methodological preference. So what becomes of the idea of a difference drawn along gender lines, which presupposes identity within each sex or gender?
15. Keller, *Reflections*, 38.
16. Keller, *Reflections*, 35, referring to F. H. Anderson, ed., *Francis Bacon: The New Organon and Related Writings* (Indianapolis: Bobbs Merrill, 1960), 29. [Please note that the items in square brackets are in the Keller text but not in the Anderson text (trans.).]
17. Francis Bacon, *Novum Organum*, in vol. 1 of *The Works of Francis Bacon*, ed. J. Spedding et al., 1857–74. (reissued Stuttgart: F.F. Verlag, 1963), 157. Hereafter Spedding.
18. I have tried to translate as literally as possible. For a discussion of the difficulty in understanding the meaning of *minister* and *interpres*, and a comparison with Bruno, see Michèle Le Doeuff, "L'homme et la nature dans les jardins de la science," *Revue internationale de philosophie* 40 (1986): 359–77.

19. For the reference to Proteus, see Bacon, *De Augmentis Scientarium,* in Spedding, vol. 4 and Bacon, *A Description of the Intellectual Globe,* in Spedding, vol. 5, 503. For the reference to Pan, see *De Augmentis Scientarium,* 318–26.
20. Bacon, *Of the Advancement of Learning,* in Spedding, vol. 3, 387. French translation: *Du progrès et de la promotion des savoirs* (Paris: Gallimard, 1991), 164.
21. Bacon, *Partis instaurationis secondae delineatio,* in Spedding, vol. 3, 557.
22. Keller, *Reflections,* 34.
23. Keller, *Reflections,* 38, citing Farrington, "*Temporis Partis Masculus:* An Untranslated Writing of Francis Bacon," *Centaurus* 1 (1951):194. I have not been able to find this quotation in the new edition: Benjamin Farrington, *The Philosophy of Francis Bacon* (Liverpool: Liverpool University Press, 1964). Hereafter Farrington.
24. See F. Saxl, *Veritas filia temporis,* in R. Klibansky and H.J. Paton, eds., *Philosophy and History: Essays in Honour of Ernst Cassirer* (Oxford: Clarendon Press, 1936). (Reprinted Gloucester: Peter Smith, 1975.)
25. Keller, *Reflections,* 36, referring to Farrington "*Temporis Partis. . . .*" See Farrington, 72, and Spedding, vol. 3, 538–39.
26. Spedding, vol. 3, 573; Farrington, 70 (not quoted by Keller, but it may have influenced her reading).
27. Farrington, 133 , Spedding vol. 3, 585 (not quoted by Keller).
28. Spedding, vol. 3, 539. See "Voyage dans la pensée baroque," Afterword to Bacon, *La Nouvelle Atlantide* (Paris: Payot, 1983), 170–80. In English: Bacon, *The New Atlantis,* Spedding, vol. 3.
29. Bacon, *Novum Organum,* Spedding, vol. 4, 97; and see Bacon, *Redargutio,* Spedding, vol. 3, 573; and Bacon, *Filium Labyrinthi,* Spedding, vol. 3, 638.
30. Keller, *Reflections,* 36, referring to Spedding, vol. 4, 296 (English translation of *De augmentis*); in the Latin text, Spedding, vol. 1, 498.
31. Keller, *Reflections,* 36, referring to Farrington, 62. Latin text: Spedding, vol. 3, 528.
32. Bacon, *Redargutio,* Spedding, vol. 3, 582; and Bacon, *Novum Organum,* Spedding, vol. 4, 65.
33. Bacon, *De augmentis,* Spedding, vol. 1, 623.
34. Keller, *Reflections,* 36, referring to Spedding, vol. 5, 506 (translation of *Descriptio globi intellectualis*); "not merely exert a gentle guidance" is not in the Spedding text, which gives only: "to shake her to her foundations".
35. Bacon, *The New Atlantis,* Spedding, vol. 3, 138.
36. Bacon, *Descriptio Globi Intellectualis,* Spedding, vol. 3, 730.
37. See also Bacon, *Novum Organum,* Spedding, vol. 4, 47.
38. Bacon, *Of the Advancement of Learning,* Spedding, vol. 3, 395.
39. Ibid., 387.
40. Ibid., 383.
41. Bacon, *Redargutio,* Spedding, vol. 3, 573, and *Filium labyrinthi,* Spedding, vol. 3, 638.
42. See Michèle Le Doeuff, "Un rationaliste chez Augias," *Les Études philosophiques* 3 (1985).
43. Bacon, *Temporis partus masculus,* Spedding, vol. 3, 535, and *Parasceve ad historiam naturalem,* Spedding, vol. 1, 394.
44. Keller, *Reflections,* 36, citing Anderson, 25.
45. Bacon, *Descriptio globi intellectualis,* Spedding, vol. 3, 719. See also *Parasceve* Spedding, vol. 1, 395.
46. Spedding, vol. 6, 491.
47. Bacon, *Of the Interpretation of Nature,* Spedding, vol. 3, 243.
48. Bacon, *Descriptio Globi Intellectualis,* Spedding, vol. 3, 730.
49. See the preface to *La Nouvelle Atlantide* (Paris: Garnier-Flammarion, 1995).
50. Tony Tanner, introduction to Jane Austen, *Mansfield Park* [1914] (London: Penguin, 1966), 8.
51. Juliet Mitchell and Ann Oakley, eds., *The Rights and Wrongs of Women* (London: Penguin, 1976), 17.
52. Descartes, who believed that all contracts were excessive, tried to disengage himself from this framework, whence the fact that 2 and 2 might make 5; but, he did not remove himself from the arch-minimalist mode of methodological discussion. He writes, elaborates his reasons, publishes, and so on.
53. Here I refer to the distinction between "masculine" and "masculinist" that I propose in *Hipparchia's Choice: An Essay Concerning Women, Philosophy, etc.,* trans. Trista Selous (Oxford: Basil Blackwell, 1991). (*L'Étude et le rouet.* Paris: Seuil, 1989.)

54. Bacon, *Cogitationes de Scientia Humana,* Spedding, vol. 3, 185.

55. Bacon, *A Description of the Intellectual Globe,* Spedding, vol. 5, 506.

56. Bacon, *Commentarius solutus,* Spedding, vol. 11, 64–65.

57. See above.

58. Johannes Kepler, *Somnium* [1634]. English translation: *Kepler's Dream, with the Full Text and Notes of* Somnium, ed. and trans. Patricia Frueh Kirkwood (Berkeley: University of California Press, 1965), 87. French translation: *Le Songe* (Nancy: Presses Universitaires de Nancy, 1984).

59. Bacon, *Novum Organum,* Spedding, vol. 4, 114.

60. Rabelais, *Gargantua* (Paris: Gallimard, 1955), 42. English translation: In *The Complete Work of François Rabelais,* trans. Donald M. Frame (Berkeley: University of California Press, 1991), 36. Consider "the gay science" of the troubadours. Isn't feminism capable in its turn of producing a "gay science," the epistemology of a learned culture that is just as regressive as that of Gargantua?

61. Speech by François Mitterand on the occasion of the fiftieth anniversary of the CNRS [Conseil National de la Recherche Scientifique].

62. The iconography is also significant. This issue of *La Recherche* includes six portraits of male researchers, not one of a female researcher, and in the publicity section are the faces of four men, and just one woman's face: she is taking dictation from a man. *Le Journal du CNRS* shows twenty-one men's faces and a group photo of three women and five men. The November 1989 issue contains thirteen men's faces, none of a woman, but there is a profile of a monkey. In April 1990, three pages away from a special article on women, a photo shows one of them dressed in pink, after the manner of women as presented in women's magazines [e.g., *Modes et travaux*], who is at a keyboard. The heading: "software for those who are not computer experts." So that the angel of the laboratory can be more productive, without even doing a training course?

63. Joseph de Maistre, *Lettres et opuscules inédits* (Paris: A. Vaton, 1851), vol. 1, 194.

64. Here I am drawing from my "Women, Reason, etc.," *Differences: A Journal of Cultural Studies* 2, no. 3 (1990): 1–13.

65. Jean-Jacques Rousseau, *Lettre à d'Alembert.* Paris: GF-Flammarion, 1967, 59; Paris: Gallimard, 1995, 11. English translation: *Politics and the Arts: Letter to M. D'Alembert on the Theatre,* trans. Allan Bloom (Ithaca, N.Y.: Cornell University Press, 1968), 12n. Hereafter *Lettre.*

66. George Berkeley, *L'Analyste,* trans. Michel Blay. Paris: PUF, 1985. *The Analyst* in *De Motu and The Analyst,* ed. and trans. Douglas M. Jesseph (Dordrecht: Kluwer Academic Publishers, 1992).

67. Rousseau, *Lettre,* 11n.

68. Ibid.

69. Ibid., 105.

70. Ibid., 107.

71. Ibid., 103n.

72. Ibid.

73. Ibid.

74. Ibid., 35

75. Rousseau, *Émile* (Paris: Garnier, 1964), 48. English translation: Barbara Foxley (London: Dent, 1911) 349–50.

76. Jacques Derrida, *L'Écriture et la différence* (Paris: Seuil, 1967), 228. Quoted by Catherine Chalier in *Figures du féminin* (Paris: Verdier, 1982), 9. Translated into English with an introduction and additional notes by Allan Bass, *Writing and Difference.* (Chicago: University of Chicago Press, 1978), 320–21n92.

77. Chalier, *Figures du féminin,* 9.

78. Derrida, *L'Écriture,* 321n92.

79. Bridget Hill, *The Republican Virago: The Life and Times of Catharine Macaulay, Historian* (Oxford: Oxford University Press, 1992), 137 and all of chap. 6.

80. Catharine Macaulay, *The History of England from the Accession of James I to the Brunswick Line* (London; Nourse, 1763–1783), vol. 1, xvi.

81. Macaulay, *History of England,* xvii.

82. For the reception of Macaulay's *History,* see Bridget Hill, and Bridget Hill and Christopher Hill, "Catharine Macaulay's History and Her Catalogue of Tracts," *XVIIth Century* 8, no. 2,

269–285; and compare Bonnie Smith, "Gender and the Practice of Scientific History," *The American Historical Review* 100 (October 1995): 1152.

83. See Bridget Hill, "Macaulay's History," 21–23.

84. Bacon, *De sapientia*, Spedding, vol. 6, 683; and *De augmentis*, Spedding, vol. 1, 535.

85. Colette Guillaumin, *Sexe, race, et pratique du pouvoir* (Paris: Côté-femmes, 1992), 21. English translation: *Racism, Sexism, Power and Ideology* (London: Routledge, 1995); Nicole-Claude Matthieu, *L'Anatomie politique* (Paris: Côté-femmes, 1991), 170.

86. Erik Erikson, quoted in Keller, "Women Scientists," 85–86.

87. John Rawls, *A Theory of Justice* (Cambridge, Mass.: Harvard University Press, 1971), 99.

88. Jean-Jacques Rousseau, *Discours sur l'origine de l'inégalité* (Paris: Flammarion), 193. English translation: *The Discourses and Other Early Political Writings*, ed. and trans. Victor Gourevitch (Cambridge: Cambridge University Press, 1997), 217.

89. Auguste Comte, *Cours de philosophie positive* (Paris: Hermann, 1975), 50th lesson, my emphasis. English translation: *The Positive Philosophy*, trans. Harriet Martineau (New York: Calvin Blanchard, 1858).

90. John Stuart Mill, *On Genius* [1832]. In the *Complete Works of John Stuart Mill* (Toronto: University of Toronto Press, 1963–1991), vol. 1, 329.

91. Ann P. Robson and John M. Robson, eds., *Sexual Equality: Writings by John Stuart Mill, Harriet Taylor Mill and Helen Taylor* (Toronto: University of Toronto Press, 1994), 358. Hereafter Robson.

92. Maurice Godelier, *La Production des grands hommes* (Paris: Fayard, 1982). Quoted by Mathieu, 209. English translation: Maurice Godelier, *The Making of Great Men: Male Domination and Power among the New Guinea Baruya*, trans. Rupert Swyer (Cambridge: Cambridge University Press, 1986).

93. Mathieu, *L'Anatomie politique*, 209.

94. Taking a cue from John Locke's *Letter on Toleration*, one could show that liberal democracy inscribes distinctive identities into the putatively universal framework of civil law. If the law authorizes the consumption of wine, it simultaneously authorizes a religious group to make wine part of its rituals; if it prohibits walking naked in the streets and if a religious group has a ritual of doing just that, the law will prohibit it, not because it is a ritual, but because it contravenes a civil law. The formal corollary of such a point of view is that distinctive identities remain strictly within the space defined by civil law, and thus occupy no more space than the law allows. To be a woman is not a religion, but from the perspective of the principle Rawls calls the principle of difference, being a woman becomes a distinctive identity.

95. Jean-Jacques Rousseau, *Du contrat social*, 1766 (Paris: Flammarion, 1938), book 1, chapter 3. English translation: *The Social Contract and Other Later Political Writings*, ed. and trans. Victor Gourevitch (Cambridge: Cambridge Uniiversity Press, 1997), 43.

96. John Locke, *Two Treatises of Government*, ed. Peter Laslett (Cambridge: Cambridge University Press, 1967), 192.

97. See above.

98. Locke, *Two Treatises*, 339.

99. Moustapha Safouan, *La Sexualité féminine* (Paris: Seuil, 1976), 155.

100. Amartya Sen, *On Ethics and Economics* (Oxford: Blackwell, 1987), 20.

101. See volume 1 of *History of Woman Suffrage*, ed. Elizabeth Cady Stanton, Susan B. Anthony, and Matilda Joslyn Gage (New York: Fowler and Wells, 1881–1906).

102. Frank E. Manuel and Fritzie P. Manuel, *Utopian Thought in the Western World* (Oxford: Blackwell, 1979); Charlotte Perkins Gilman's *Herland*, written in 1915, published in serial form in *The Forerunner*, was rescued from oblivion by Ann J. Lane in 1979 (New York: Pantheon Books and Toronto: Random House). Ellen Olney Kirk, *A Woman's Utopia*, was published posthumously in 1931 (London: Benn).

103. Olivier Cauly, *Comenius* (Paris: Félin, 1995).

104. Cauly, *Comenius*, 117; Comenius, *De veris et falsis prophetis*.

105. Sheila Rowbotham, in *Hidden from History*, 2nd ed. (London: Pluto Press, 1974), presents figures of seventeenth-century women—prophetesses or preachers—who received "democratic visitations" from the Spirit, which were not devoid of temporal meaning. Since Quakers believe that the Spirit reveals itself directly, there was no doctrinal argument available to reduce these women to silence. Some of them took advantage of the fact to preach that fathers are

not the owners of their daughters, nor husbands of their wives: some of them were accused of madness and immodesty. Insubordination through mystic ecstasy remains ambiguous: it permits speech but still bears the traces of prohibition, since one must deny being its source. The responsibility for what is said remains with the Spirit. It is easy to compare these English women to their female compatriots who, in the seventeenth century, played a role in the Republican movement, while their husbands often spent long periods of time in prison. If the anglophone world is a step ahead of the francophone world, it is in part because some English women began to preach, present petitions, and organize demonstrations from the middle of the seventeenth century on.

106. Winston Churchill, Speech in House of Commons, May 13, 1940.
107. Jennifer Hornsby gives some examples in "Speech Acts and Pornography," in *The Problem of Pornography*, ed. Susan Dwyer (Belmont, Calif.: Wadsworth, 1995), 226–32; and "Disempowered Speech," *Philosophical Topics* 23 (fall 1995): 127–47. See also Catharine MacKinnon, *Feminism Unmodified* (Cambridge, Mass.: Harvard University Press, 1987), and Rae Langton, "Speech Acts and Unspeakable Acts," *Philosophy and Public Affairs* 22 (1993). Reprinted in Dwyer, ed., *The Problem of Pornography*.
108. Mill, *The Subjection of Women*, in Robson, 358. Here I am drawing on my Vaughan Lectures delivered at Oxford in 1997.
109. Ibid., 360.
110. Ibid., 361.
111. Ibid., 371.
112. F.A. Hayek, *John Stuart Mill and Harriet Taylor: Their Correspondence and Subsequent Marriage* (Chicago: University of Chiago Press, 1951), 122. Hereafter Hayek.
113. Robson, xiv.
114. John Stuart Mill, *Autobiography*, ed. John M. Robson (London: Penguin, 1989), 149.
115. "It is possible to define the rights of woman without women participating in the decision," says Otto Weininger in 1903. (Quoted by Claude Barbey-Morand, *La Fiancée orientale*, Geneva: Institut européen de Genève, 1997). If we really must have women's rights, let's not allow women to define them.
116. Julia Annas, in "Mill and the Subjection of Women," *Philosophy* 52 (1977), reveals the disdain of Mill scholars for *The Subjection*.
117. Mill, *Autobiography*, 186; Hayek, 117. I thank Raymond Klibansky for having recommended this work when I was beginning this book. Without him I would not have been able to disentangle the other references.
118. H.O. Pappe, *John Stuart Mill and the Harriet Taylor Myth* (Melbourne: Melbourne University Press, 1960), 29. Pappe's references to Ruth Borchard's book, *John Stuart Mill, the Man* (London: Watts, 1957) are extraordinary. She says in case her marriage to John Taylor had given her an aversion to sexuality, meeting Mill changed everything!
119. Thanks to Jennifer Hornsby who brought Mary Warnock's (ed.) *Women Philosophers* (London: Dent, 1996) to my attention and was as irritated by it as I was.
120. Warnock, *Women Philosophers*, xxxv.
121. Reprint of John Stuart Mill, *Dissertations and Discussions* (London: Trubner, 1868), attributed here to Mrs. Stuart Mill.
122. Hayek, 15.
123. Ibid., 135.
124. Ibid., 123.
125. Mill, *Autobiography*, 182.
126. From their youth on, they were viewed as interchangeable: a friend asked Harriet about an article, "is it by you or by Mill?" It was not written by either of them!
127. Texts by Mill and Harriet Taylor, in Robson, 3; Taylor's rough draft, 43.
128. Harriet Taylor, *On Marriage* in Robson, 18.
129. Certain utopias include both a critical section and a visionary section. See Michèle Le Doeuff, *The Philosophical Imaginary*, trans. Colin Gordon (Stanford, Calif.: Stanford University Press, 1989), chapter 3. The "Héloïse complex" which prompts a woman to hope that a man will offer her a truth to change her life is typical of many women's relationship to philosophy (ibid., chapter 5, and see my *Hipparchia's Choice*). Taylor's essay plays into the Héloïse complex, but by placing it beyond, thus outside, her work she takes charge of critique and vision, leaving Mill in charge of finding the means to realize the vision.

130. Taylor, *On Marriage,* in Robson, 19.
131. Mill, *On Marriage* in Robson, 3.
132. Mill, *The Subjection* in Robson, 359.
133. Robson, 11.
134. In Herbert Spencer, *Essays on Education* (London: Everyman, 1911), 15.
135. The text is in Hayek, 122.
136. Harriet Taylor, "An Early Essay" in Hayek, 276.
137. Ibid., 278.
138. Ibid., 276.
139. I will risk interpreting the chain of ideas in their youthful writings in the same way: they had conversations on the relations between men and women, and then she, because the initiative fell to her, proposed the exchange of texts on marriage. She then wrote *On Toleration* to respond in depth to the philosophy Mill presupposes in his text and in *On Genius.*
140. Harriet Taylor to W.J. Fox in Hayek, 122–23.
141. Harriet Taylor Mill, *The Enfranchisement of Women,* in Robson, 186.
142. Ibid.
143. Ibid.
144. Ibid.
145. Sydney Smith, quoted by Harriet Taylor, Ibid., 187n11.
146. Mill, 1846, in Robson, xix.
147. Mill, *Subjection of Women,* in Robson, 323.
148. Ibid., 323.
149. Taylor, *The Enfranchisement of Women,* in Robson, 186.
150. Mill, Preface to *Dissertations and Discussions,* in Robson, 178.
151. Mill, Preface to *Dissertations and Discussions,* in Robson, 178.
152. John Stuart Mill, *Complete Works,* vol. 31, 332–33.
153. Mill, 1867, in the *Complete Works,* vol. 21, 250. Taylor was well aware of the sexist risk of using a word like "men", cf. *The Enfranchisement,* in Robson, 182; Mill, in 1867, asked Parliament to substitute the word "person" for the word "man" in a text about the right to vote. Thus when he says "man" or "manly research," he knows very well what he is saying.
154. Robson, 196.
155. Ibid., 350.
156. Janine Mossuz Lavau and Mariette Sineau, in *Le Monde diplomatique,* May 5, 1988.
157. Bertrand Russell, *The Autobiography of Bertrand Russell,* vol. 1 (London: Allen and Unwin, 1967), 155.
158. Ibid.
159. Bacon, *The Advancement of Learning,* Spedding, vol. 3, 270.
160. In Robson, 369–70.
161. Condorcet, "Sur l'Admission des femmes au droit de cité," in *Le Journal de la société de 1789,* vol. 3, July 1790. English translation: "On Giving Women the Right of Citizenship," *Condorcet: Foundations of Social Choice and Political Theory,* ed. and trans. Iain MacLean and Fiona Hewitt (Aldershot, UK: Edward Elgar, 1994), 335–36.
162. The texts are in Robson.
163. For further information about female printers, carpenters and brewers, see Sheila Rowbotham, *Hidden from History;* about type-setters, see Évelyne Le Garrec, *Les Messagères* (Paris: Édition des femmes, 1976). On the subject of medical interns, I honor the memory of Marguerite Cordier.

Epilogue

1. Pappe, 27, praising Mrs. Borchard for having shown herself clearly to be shocked (although that does not seem clear to me at all) and for having had enough sense about feminine realities to see through certain of Harriet's strategies.
2. Robson, 20.
3. Ibid., 48.

Index

abortion, 100–3, 188–9. *See also* reproductive freedom
Annas, Julia, 49–50, 57, 58, 60, 61
anti-intellectualism, 27–9, 30, 31, 32; in Rousseau, 47–8
Arendt, Hannah, 59–60, 99, 136
Aristotle, 33, 51, 150–1
Austen, Jane, 156–7

Bacon, Francis, xiv–xv, 25, 32, 33, 37, 145, 153, 162, 181–2; Baconian science, 144, 147–51, 152–7, 164–7; on doctors, 229n18; on equality, 213; as male chauvinist, 144–5, 147; and prohibitions on knowledge, 30–1; on women doctors, 78–9
Beauvoir, Simone de, 65, 134, 165, 192, 217, 223n46
Bergson, Henri: and feminine intuition, 16–17
Bettelheim, Bruno, 145–6, 149
birth rate, 84–5, 188
bluestocking, ix–xi, 1–4, 30, 68, 133, 202. *See also* Blue-Stocking Parliament, 1; Bluestocking Revels, 227n142
Brouwer: on intuition in mathematics, 9
Burckhardt, Jacob, 82

Cartesian method. *See* Descartes
Chaff, Sandra, 72, 74
chastity, 40, 44, 63, 98, 115, 126, 129, 132–3; and education, 125–7, 130–1, 132
circumcision, female, 122–4
Code, Lorraine, 221n8
Comte, Auguste, 184
convents, 40, 44
Cook, Ann, 80
Curie, Marie: as an honorary man, xiii

Deleuze, Gilles, 217
de Maistre, Joseph, 26, 29, 170, 173
Democritus, 90–1
de Navarre, Marguerite, 74–5, 78–9
de Pisan, Christine, ix–xi, 81, 104, 119, 121, 135–8, 231n55; as representative of the *epikleros*, 114

deprivation of women, 38–9, 44. *See also* oppression of women
Derrida, Jacques, xi–xii, 177–8
Descartes, René, 25, 33, 37, 178, 223n40, 234n52; on intuition, 4–5, 7, 8, 23; on intuition and deduction, 7–8; and Princess Elisabeth, 25; on science as a woman. *See also* intuition
Deutsch, Helen: on the intellectual woman, 17–18, 196, 223n26; and original sin, 32
Dhavernas, Odile, 43
difference, ideology of, 9–10, 15–16, 31, 60–2, 129–30, 206–8, 213, 215, 221n8, 233n14; and equality, 210–11; and Mill, 207–8, 213–15; and Rawls, 186; and "second wave" feminism, 28, 223–4n46; Taylor on, 203–5, 206–7. *See also* sexual division of capacities
doctors, women. *See* medicine
Dumont, Jean-Paul, 90–1
Dupanloup, Monseigneur, 26

education of women, ix, xi, 22–3, 66, 116–19, 120–1, 123–30, 132, 134, 139–40, 153, 158–9, 202, 214, 231n55, 232–3n93; as a chastity belt, 126, 129, 130–1, 132; disapproval of, 30; as disciplinary, 131; and the *epicleracy*, 120–1, 125–7; and the headscarves affair, 123–5; Kant on, 11; Mill on, 209; More on, 115, 118–19; and original sin, 31–2; prohibitions on, 29–30, 31; Rousseau on, 46–8; Suchon on, 34–6, 39; Taylor on, 209–10; Vivès on, 126, 128, 130–1; Wollstonecraft on, 47, 121–2
Elisabeth, Princess of Bohemia, 25
Elizabeth I of England, 105, 106, 107, 110–12
emancipation of women, xii, 39–41, 46, 47, 53, 194–5, 200, 202, 205
epicene, 14, 227n17
epicleracy, 113–16, 120–1, 125–7, 231n64
equality and inequality of women and men, ix, x, 15, 41, 43, 47, 65, 183, 184, 192,